THE CIVIL WAR DIARY OF ANNE S. FROBEL

Wilton Hill, Fairfax County, Virginia

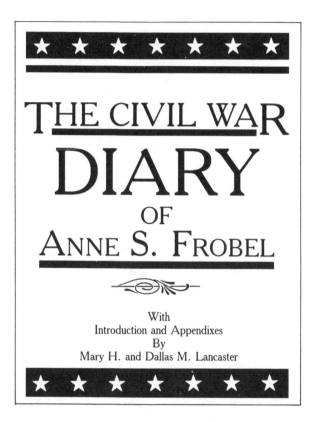

THE CIVIL WAR
DIARY
OF
ANNE S. FROBEL

With
Introduction and Appendixes
By
Mary H. and Dallas M. Lancaster

EPM
PUBLICATIONS, McLEAN, VIRGINIA

Library of Congress Cataloging-in-Publication Data

Frobel, Anne S., 1816–1907.
   The Civil War diary of Anne S. Frobel / with introduction and
appendixes by Mary H. and Dallas M. Lancaster.
       p.   cm.
   Originally published: Florence, Ala.: M.H. & D.M. Lancaster,
1986.
   Includes bibliographical references and index.
   ISBN 0-939009-69-2
   1. Frobel, Anna S., 1816–1907—Diaries. 2. United States—History—Civil
War, 1861–1865—Personal narratives. 3. Virginia—History—Civil War, 1861–
1865—Personal narratives. 4. Fairfax County (Va.)—Biography. I. Lancaster, Mary
Holland. II. Lancaster, Dallas M. III. Title.
[E601.F86   1992]
973.7'82—dc20
[B]   92-21439
                                                                                                              CIP

EPM Publications, Inc., 1003 Turkey Run Road
   McLean, VA 22101
Printed in the United States of America

Cover and book design by Ron Flemmings

CONTENTS

MT. VERNON DIST. No. 3.

Fairfax Co.

Scale 1¼ Inches to a Mile.

Note: The figures on the Roads show the Distance in Rods from junctions thereof.

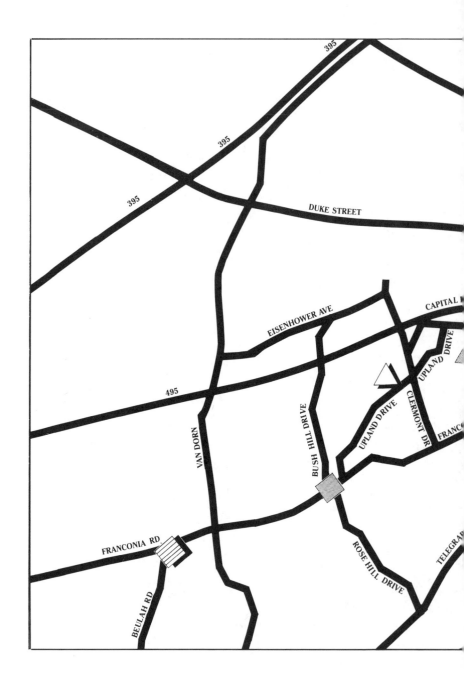

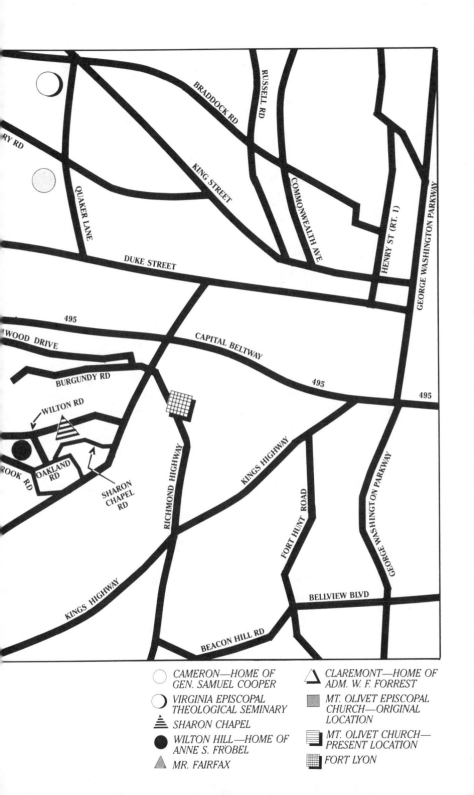

BRADDOCK RD

RUSSELL RD

KING STREET

COMMONWEALTH AVE.

HENRY ST (RT. 1)

GEORGE WASHINGTON PARKWAY

RY RD

QUAKER LANE

DUKE STREET

495

WOOD DRIVE

CAPITAL BELTWAY

495

495

BURGUNDY RD

WILTON RD

ROOK RD

OAKLAND RD

SHARON CHAPEL RD

RICHMOND HIGHWAY

KINGS HIGHWAY

FORT HUNT ROAD

GEORGE WASHINGTON PARKWAY

KINGS HIGHWAY

BELLVIEW BLVD

BEACON HILL RD

○ CAMERON—HOME OF
GEN. SAMUEL COOPER

◑ VIRGINIA EPISCOPAL
THEOLOGICAL SEMINARY

▲ SHARON CHAPEL

● WILTON HILL—HOME OF
ANNE S. FROBEL

▲ MR. FAIRFAX

△ CLAREMONT—HOME OF
ADM. W. F. FORREST

◼ MT. OLIVET EPISCOPAL
CHURCH—ORIGINAL
LOCATION

◪ MT. OLIVET CHURCH—
PRESENT LOCATION

▦ FORT LYON

FOREWORD

In 1986, Dallas and Mary Lancaster published *The Civil War Diary of Ann Frobel of Wilton Hill in Virginia*. The book was transcribed from the original diary of Ann Frobel who resided in Union occupied Alexandria during the Civil War.

After the original printing was depleted, the Lancasters generously offered to transfer their copyright to the Friends of Fort War, in order to keep in print this detailed primary source account of life in Civil War Alexandria.

The offer was readily accepted and much work has been expended on this new presentation of Ann Frobel's Diary. Modern computer technology has been used to reformat the original text into an easier-to-read print, and an index has been prepared. Period illustrations of scenes, places, and houses mentioned by Miss Frobel have also been added to enhance the narrative.

The Friends of Fort Ward would like to express their appreciation to the individuals, companies and organizations that contributed to the success of this project.

First, and foremost, to Dallas and Mary Lancaster for recognizing the value of Ann Frobel's Diary to historians; for not allowing it to become just another out-of-print tome. To the Officers and Board of Directors of the Friends of Fort Ward who worked to move this project to completion. To Betty Bolte, for the laborious task of copying the original text and creating an index to make the book more reference-friendly. To the Mount Vernon Ladies' Association of the Union, who now hold the original copy of Ann Frobel's Diary in the collection at Mount Vernon. And, to Mrs. Evelyn Metzger of EPM Publications for recognizing the importance of Ann Frobel's Diary to the history of Northern Virginia.

The illustrations were reproduced by permission from: the American Heritage Picture Collection from *the American Heritage Century collection*; from Castle Books, a Division of Book Sales, Inc., for illustrations taken from *Battles and Leaders of the Civil War*, Vols. I, II. Also, from Samuel Cooper Dawson, grandson of General Samuel S. Cooper, the Ford Ward Museum Collection, and the Cartographic Branch of the National Archives.

The Friends of Fort Ward
1992

INTRODUCTION

The diary of Anne S. Frobel provides a significant coverage of the years of war and reconstruction between 1861 and 1879 along the Potomac River, as well as a historical link connecting the eighteenth and twentieth centuries through a notable family.

Anne S. Frobel was born in 1816 at "Wilton Hill" in Fairfax County, Virginia. She lived practically her entire life at Wilton, only leaving in her last years to live with relatives in Mt. Meigs, Alabama, where she died in 1907. She was buried in Alexandria, Virginia, in the Ivy Hill Cemetery, not far from "Wilton Hill" and "Sharon," the small Episcopal Chapel which she often refers to in her diary; nearby is Christ Church in which she was a devoted communicant during her lifetime.

John Jacob Frobel, Anne's father, a native of Amsterdam, Holland, of German and French parentage, came to this country at the age of twelve or thirteen in the 1780's; her mother was Mary Scott Marshall, a Virginian. Because of her father's musical interests, Anne had the opportunity in her early years to be in the company of a number of prominent families of that day. As a young musician and piano teacher in Richmond, Virginia, her father was associated with Judge Bushrod Washington and his wife, Ann, one of his piano students. Soon after the Washingtons left Richmond and moved to Mount Vernon, which his uncle, the President, had left to him. Young Frobel was persuaded by Ann Washington to locate in the area of Mount Vernon in 1804 and to continue his career as a music teacher; among his students were a number of Ann's and Bushrod's nieces and nephews. During the period of time between 1804 and his marriage in 1809, he lived at Mount Vernon. In a number of instances in the diary, Anne relates her visits, as a young girl, to Mount Vernon and the participation of her family in various social events.

In the War of 1812, Anne's father was a member of the 60th Regiment (Minor's) of the Virginia Militia. He served on the vestry of Christ Church and was employed as church organist as early as 1814.

Anne's parents had eight children, five sons and three daughters. The five sons were John M., Bushrod Washington, Richard Scott, David, and Thomas D.; Anne S., Elizabeth Douglas, and Mary Clagett, were the daughters.

John M., the eldest son, died in 1849; Bushrod Washington lived until 1888; Richard Scott died in 1831 at the age of nine; David was still living in 1870 according to the *U.S. Census* of that year; and Thomas D. died in 1832.

Anne's brother, Bushrod, who was named after her father's very good friend, Judge Bushrod Washington, had a distinguished life. In the 1840's and 1850's, he served in both the U. S. army and navy for short periods of time, and as a railroad surveyor in the western part of the country. At the beginning of the Civil War, he volunteered for the Confederate army and served with distinction as Chief of Artillery with the rank of colonel under a number of generals, among them being Generals H. C. Whiting and John B. Hood. After the war, Bushrod continued his engineering interests by serving the State of Georgia and the U. S. Engineers. In his last years, he was very active in the building and operation of the Macon & Covington Railroad in Georgia. He died in 1888 at Monticello, Georgia.

Mary Clagett Frobel, Anne's youngest sister, was married in 1845, to an Episcopal minister, the Rev. Benjamin Franklin Mower, a native of Canada, and graduate of the Episcopal Seminary at Alexandria, Virginia. During his ministry, he served churches in Georgia, Kansas, Louisiana, Kentucky, and Alabama. Their daughter, Mary Marshall, married Thomas Cooper Raoul, a member of the historic Raoul family which settled in South Carolina and Alabama. Anne Frobel died at "Longwood," the ancestral home of the Raoul family at Mt. Meigs, Alabama, in 1907.

Anne's relationship to her sister, Elizabeth or Lizzie as she was known, was very close throughout her entire life. Being two years older than Lizzie and living together at the home place, "Wilton," for almost eighty years until Lizzie's death in 1898, and by themselves most of the time, as their father died in 1851, and their mother in 1857, they became very dependent on one another, and as Anne points out in the diary, each was always concerned about the other's welfare.

"Wilton Hill" was acquired by Anne's father in 1807, two years before her parents' marriage. It was located in the extreme eastern part of Fairfax County, near the intersection of the Telegraph and Old Fairfax Roads. On the map of Mt. Vernon District No. 3, Fairfax County, which is included in this book, the location of "Wilton Hill" is that point named Elizth Frobel. The Episcopal Chapel, "Sharon," is also shown on the map. At the time of the death of Anne's father, there were 114 acres in the estate and slaves worth in excess of six thousand dollars. Anne and Lizzie inherited the home after the death of their mother.

Part I of the diary relates to the war years between 1861 and 1865, and constitutes approximately ninety percent of the manuscript; Part II covers a six year period during reconstruction, 1873 to 1879; and Part III includes five letters which deal with Anne and Lizzie's efforts to obtain compensation from the U.S. Government for property losses suffered at "Wilton Hill" during the war years. Information in the appendixes on the

Frobel family, "Wilton Hill," Sharon Chapel, and Ivy Cemetery, will not only supplement and substantiate various developments recorded in the diary, but also provide a greater understanding of Anne's life and that of her family both prior to and following the years covered in the diary. Through Anne's writings, in the valley of darkness of the war years and reconstruction, runs a thread of nobility, courage, and hope—no misfortune could suppress the elegance of her culture, and no enemy eliminate her refined manners. Though Anne and Elizabeth were victims of the tragedies of the times, they displayed strength and wisdom in those difficult days. On the inside back cover of the diary, Anne wrote from the Book of Isaiah, chapter 60:10, "In my wrath I smote thee but in my favour have I had mercy on thee." This quote could have been Anne's biblically expressed reference of her life in those days of peril.

Anne's purpose for keeping this diary was stated in her entry of May 25, 1861:

> "This day I thought of and determined to keep a daily account of all that occurs, or that we know anything of, hoping, that if either, or both of us die before these troubles are over or if we are destined never to see any of our relatives again, this book may by some lucky chance find its way to the hands of some one who may feel an interest in our fate."

Divine Providence may very well have been the guiding hand in bringing Anne's hopes to fulfillment as it was through our research on the Rev. Benjamin Franklin Mower, a minister of Trinity Episcopal Church, Florence, Alabama, that we learned about Anne Frobel's sister, Mary Clagett Frobel, the wife of the Rev. B. F. Mower. We were privileged to establish friendship with Rose Raoul Rutland, the great granddaughter of Mary Clagett Mower, and with Mrs. Rutland's daughter, Ann Rutland Jordan, who made the diary available for publication.

In an attempt to bring back to time the spirit of that period of our history, and to preserve the personality and life of one in its midst, this manuscript is printed as originally written in so far as possible, and especially with respect to the capitalization, punctuation, and spelling.

We are especially indebted to Rose Raoul Rutland, Fitzpatrick, Alabama, and her daughter, Anne Rutland Jordan, Hueytown, Alabama, for making the diary available and providing information on the Frobel, Mower, and Raoul families. We would also like to acknowledge the assistance of the following for furnishing information on the Frobel family: Franklin M. Garrett, Atlanta Historical Society, Atlanta, Georgia; Edward Allen Myers, Jr., Oakland Cemetery, Atlanta, Georgia; Gordon E. Smith, Florence, Alabama; Edith M. Sprouse, Fairfax County Historical Commission, Fairfax Virginia; Donald A. Turner, Florence-Lauderdale Public Library, Florence, Alabama; Alexandria Library, Alexandria, Virginia; All Saints—Sharon Chapel, Alexandria, Virginia; Christ Church, Alexandria, Virginia; Fairfax County Court House, Fairfax, Virginia; Fairfax County Public Library, Fairfax, Virginia; Lloyd House, Alexandria, Virginia; Middle Georgia Archives, Washington Memorial Library, Macon, Georgia- Mount Vernon Ladies' Association of the Union, Mount Vernon, Virginia; Office of Ivy Hill Cemetery, Alexandria, Virginia; Pioneer American Society, Inc., Falls Church, Virginia; Virginia State Library, Richmond, Virginia; and Wilton Woods School, Alexandria, Virginia. To all these persons and offices, we wish to express our gratitude and appreciation.

Florence, Alabama
June 1, 1986

Mary H. Lancaster
Dallas M. Lancaster

Part I

May 1861

There has been excitement and commotion all over the country ever since Lincoln crept into Washington one night in disguise just before his inauguration as President of the U. S. on the 4th March of this year 1861-. Indeed the excitement commenced with his nomination and every day has added to its intensity, and troops have been organizing and preparations making all over the country for war. Two or three companies of Confederate soldiers have been quartered in Alex- [Alexandria] and drilling about every day, and we have gone out to the Common once or twice to see them drill. But as to its turning out to any thing serious it never for a moment entered my mind, I thought it would serve as a little amusement pastime, and then blow over and never be thought of again, as all political excitements have hereto done. But one Sunday morning in the early part of May we went into town as usual to church, services were at St. Pauls, Christ Church, our church, was closed, I do not remember why, I think perhaps the minister Dr Walker had left town with his family.

But as I entered St. Paul's I could but observe how exceedingly solemn and quiet every thing and every body looked, and before the sermon was half over the ladies were all in tears, the men looked stern and neither to the right or left—I could not understand it—I could not feel it—and as I rode home I thought how silly it was for people to put on such air but still it produced an uneasy sensation, and the next day we rode to town again, to see and hear all we could about it. When we got with in sight of the Orange depot we both exclaimed, "What on earth is the matter—what is going on," Such a dense crowd thronged the streets, carriages filled with people, wagons, carts drays, wheelbarrows all packed mountain high with baggage of every sort, men, women, and children streaming along to the cars, most of the women crying, almost every face we saw we recognized, and all looking as forlorn and wretched as if going to execution.

I believe every body from both town and country that could possibly get away left at this time, and for the first time it dawned upon me that it was something more than *pastime*, and O what a feeling of loneliness and utter despair came over us when we thought of every friend and acquaintance gone—and poor Lizzie and me being left entirely alone to battle it by ourselves. O how little we knew, or dreamed of what was going to befall

A few weeks before Bushrod had come home from Wilmington N.C.

on leave of absence, and while here had been to Richmond once or twice, and all the time seemed so restless and uneasy. It seemed as if he could not make up his mind. I think he wanted us to advise with him what to do. But we never said one word on the subject—*pro* or *con*, but were on the *qui-veve*—all the time so afraid he would go back to Wilmington, and whispering to each other. I felt so sorry for him I could hardly keep quiet. at last he made up his mind and wrote to the Secretary resigning his commission, and received in reply that he was *"Dishonorably Dismissed* from the United States service" We all laughted over it, it did seem so contemptible. He went again to Richmond and offered his services to Gov- Letcher and was appointed to one of the Potomac batteries under the command of Comd- Linch (Cock Pit Point, the battery nearest to Mt. Vernon.) Then he came home for the last time, though he did not dream it was for the last time, as he would be so near us he supposed he should see us quite often But he seemed so light-hearted was so relieved, had met with a great many old friends, of course talking with them, and their being so happy, and in such high hopes, and confident of success had a happy effect on him and when he left home again in a few days he was in "tip top" spirits, Little thinking what terrible scenes we all would have to pass through and how many weary years would pass over our heads before, "we three should meet again" O! When I look back and think of it all, it seems like a terrible nightmare as if there could not possibly be any reality in it. David had stopped at home the Sunday night before with his family on their way to the Confederacy.

Every time Bushrod came home from Richmond he brought us kind messages from Mrs Gen. Cooper urging, and entreating that we would scrape up all our effects, and all our servants and come to Richmond and live with her—But it was too late, Bushrod was gone, and David gone There was no one to help us get ready, and Lizzie and I could not do it alone and we well knew if such a thing was proposed to the negroes they would hoot at the idea and perhaps all take themselves off to *Wa* [Washington] and who was there to prevent them. Indeed we were so inexperienced as to suppose in being at home would be a protection to them and keep every thing intact. (*"a foolish galatian"*

After B. [Bushrod] left we remained at home several days perfectly quiet and undisturbed. Washington filled with yankee soldiers, and all the stables and every place with horses, and all the preparations for war going on, the Stars and Stripes flying from every place. One poor lone Confederate Stars and Bars floating to the breeze in Alex. The old war steamer Pawnee has been lying in the stream sometime, grinning, and-

On the Way to Manassas*
Allen C. Redwood, Courtesy of Castle Books, A Division of Book Sales, Inc.

showing her teeth to frighten the poor Alexandrians. There is little or no communication between the two citys if any. We had been going to Alex. whenever we pleased

May 24, 1861 Rose bright and lovely as any May morning ever dawned upon the earth, and every thing about and around us was as serene and peaceful as it could be, not a sound to brake the stillness but the songs of birds and hum of bees. The trees and plants had put on their lovliest spring attire, and the garden was resplendent with the bloom of rare and brilliant flowers, and the fields were all smiling with a bright prospect of an abundant harvest. The beautiful hedges all so evenly shorn, the little gravel paths so neat and clean, the smoothe velvet grass all glittering with dew drops. Every thing about the place was in order and shewed a high state of cultivation. I never saw "Wilton" my dear old home looking more lovely and inviting, and our little *Bays* when they came around with the carriage for us to take a ride into town, were as feisty and as playful and as fleet as the wind

---

* With the occupation of Alexandria on May 24, 1861, the military units in Alexandria boarded trains to join the Confederate Army at Manassas, Virginia. Civilians also left Alexandria for the duration of the war.

I do not think we saw a vehicle, or a single person on the road as far as "South run", there stood group of men talking and gesticulating in the most vehement manner, when they saw us they threw up their hands crying out, "stop-stop don't you go to town, Linckton's [sic] men are there, got there only this morning, and there is no telling what they will do—they'll take your horses—they certainly will take your horses." After talking with them a few moment we concluded we would risk it. Cousin Mary Foote was there, and other friend who we thought might be safer in the country, and perhaps we could persuade them to return with us. But when we reached Cameron run there stood another party of men, who came forward and urged us by all means not to attempt going into town but just to turn round and go home again, Linckton's men had come in early in the morning and were *playing the very mischief* with the people, several men had been killed already, they could not tell how many or who. Then they pointed out the railroad bridges, as far as we could see all on fire. When we saw that we concluded it was indeed best to turn and retrace our steps homeward.

The turnpike road, and all the roads as far as we could see were filled with vehicles of all sorts and description, filled with women and children, and goods of all kinds, men on horseback and on foot, a continual stream. Old Fairfax surely never knew such commotion before.

We reached home safely and after resting a while I proposed to Lizzie to walk to the road, to see if anyone was passing that we knew. Some of the servants told us they had seen early this morning a Confederate Soldier flying by on hors-back. When we got to the road nothing was to be seen for a while, then a wagon came along filled with women and children beds and blankets, and patch quilts that could be seen from afar, and all kinds of household goods, and a little distance behind them a man on foot. When he got near enough to speak to I said, "good morning I suppose you are flying out of the reach of "Linckton's men." He shook his head and said "yes." He looked very despondent and pointing to the wagon said that is my family going off. I don't know where to look for a home, mine is a hard curse I have been a hard working man all my life, an now that I have succeeded in making enough to keep my family comfortable, we have to break up and run off and leave every thing to find a new home and begin again, "Well I said you know misery loves company, and you have the comfort of knowing there are thousands in like condition, I suppose you will when you can join the Confederate army, he replied that was his intention as soon as he caught up with it, he should certainly join it. I said well when you do and get a chance at the yankees *give it to them* with all your might and main! He threw back his head and lifted both hands exclaiming in the most vehement manner, "My God I will" and dashed off as fast as he could go to overtake the wagon which had gotten considerably ahead.

and that was the last I ever saw or heard of that man. I regretted so much after that, I had not thought to ask his name, and many times since have thought over that scene, and wondered what the fate of that poor man was.

We lingered a while longer at the gate and then returned to the house and had hardly gotten seated before a knock came to the door and Mr Ballanger a neighbor living on the opposite hill came in, and with him a stranger who he introduced as Col—(I have forgotten the name) "of the Confederate army. He said his men had run off this morning when the yankees came in, and while he was engaged collecting up some harness belonging to the Confederate army and trying to secure it from their clutches, and begged we would send him in our carriage up to "Burk's Station." We both felt shocked at the request, we did not know whether it would be right or wrong, or what risk we might incur, but nevertheless, Charles, the carriage and horses were brought out, and they are started for the rail road. and in about five or six hours Mr. B-returned all safe after having deposited Mr Confed-on the cars. They told us the railroad bridges were burned by the Confederates in their retreat.

I do not think it was until the next day that we heard of the amount of enormities committed by the yankees in Alex. yesterday. The first who company of soldiers who came into town were the "Fire Zouaves" of N. Y. City. and of course, as might have been expected, they rushed to the house where the Confederate flag was flying. The Marshall House hotel and before Jackson the proprietor was out of his bed, or had any warning of their coming they had reached the second floor, when he heard the noise he imagined what it ment, and all undressed as he was he threw open the door, and found a party coming down from the attic, their leader Col. Elsworth with the flag in his hand which he had torn from its staff at the top of the house. Jackson had a double barreled shot gun in his hand which he leveled at Elsworth and down he dropped and rolled to the bottom of the stairs, quick as a flash Lieu, Brownell fired and killed Jackson. Then they all knocked and beat his body about shockingly and finally kicked it down the stairs to the front entrance where they pinned it to the floor with any number of bayonetts. The stairs and front hall flooded and streaming with blood. The Soldiers ran all through the building locked the doors and took all the keys, and such a scene of riot, and confusion, blasphemy and screams. Mrs. Jackson when she discovered what was done ran to her husband in the wildest state of frenzy uttering the most pearcing and heart rending shrieks. Cries and shrieks, and demands for the doors to be opened were coming from all the rooms, ladies threw up their windows, and begged and implored all they saw in the streets to come to their assistance, and let them out. Poor foolheardy Jackson just threw his life away. He fixed up that flag several months ago and swore the first man who put his hand on it to take it down he would kill.—and he did it—and what good did it do?

May 25, 1861—This day I thought of, and determined to keep a daily account of all that occurs, or that we know anything of, hoping, that if either, or both of us should die before these troubles are over, or if we are destined never to see any of our relatives or friends again, this book may by some lucky chance find its way to the hands of some one who may feel an interest in our fate, and for the whole four years not a day passed without my writing something on it. But unfortunately it fell into hands of a malitious person who destroyed the most of it, leaving a few leaves here and there which I have tried to fill in from memory. I do regret so much the losses many things have passed from my recollection, and many of the dates are lost.

We have many northern families settled around us, to all of whom we have been as kind and attentive as we could be, but one family especially Davis by name, have become quite intimate here, are coming and going almost every day. One evening last week several of the ladies came over to spend the evening with us. Said the gentlemen would be here later on. They sat and talked of all that was going on, but I noticed how restless and uneasy they all were, moving about, going to the doors and windows, and starting up at every sound. But as to their being unfriendly or spies, it never entered our minds for a moment—at last when the evening was about half over the two gentlemen were announced. Mr James Davis was recently from N. Y. His wife started up and received him in the most excited and effusive manner, flew into his arms and threw hers around him exclaiming "O I am so glad—So glad you have come back all safe, I was so afraid I should never ever see you again." The ladies asked a great many questions about the roads, and if they had found all quiet, and if they had met with many people, and with no difficulty, and if they had accomplished all they went for, all of which questions the gentlemen answered with "Ill tell you another time" The little girl said "Papa did you see any of the Rebels, O I am so afraid of the rebels." The Mother said "Why Mr Frobel is a rebel are you afraid of him." "No" she replied "not afraid of him," and still with all this talk going on, we poor foolish creatures that we were! never suspected any thing wrong—a long time after we learned they had been up to Fairfax

Courthouse on some secret mission, we never heard what, and these people we thought our friends, and talked so unreservedly before and told them thousands of things that we should not, a long, long time after we learned it was all published in the Northern news papers, every thing we said and did. I am so in the habit of saying things in joke, and have no idea of its being taken literally as once when visiting old Pohick Church with one of the *yankee ladies*. She stood looking at the old building on the out-side, and murmured in a sort of soliloquy "Well, can this be the old church in which Gen. Washington used to worship" O yes, I said, and turned and leaned against a right good sized oak tree near and this is the tree he used to tie his horse to every Sunday, I never thought of the circumstances again until I saw the full account in print in one of the Northern papers—the trip—the old church, and grave yard, and "the venerable tree that Gen- Washington tied his horse to every Sunday." I really thought the woman had more sense than to believe that small tree had been growing there for over a hundred summers.

From the porch here we can see now the groups of white tents dotted about the common and growing up each side of the railroad, as yet we remain unmolested although we hear of parties of the military prowling all over the country committing all manners of depredations and violence, some families they have despoiled of every thing they could lay hands on, some they have turned out of their homes to seek shelter wherever they could find it. One party went to Mr. Fairfax and rummaged the house through and through under the pretence of looking for firearms, they went into the pantry and ran their hands all through the meal and flour barrels, forced their way into poor old Mrs Dawsy's room who was sick in bed, they turned her whole room and bed upside down even searching under the mattress she was lying on. Then after visiting the pantry and opening every box and barrel and bottle and running their hands all through the meal and flower Mrs. Fairfax told the Lieutenant of the party of us and begged him not to come here as she knew it would frighten us to death, and as there were no white people on the place but two ladies they certainly would find no fire arms here—and he promised not to disturb us. But the very next day, Lizzie having gone on an erand to a neighbors I was left entirely alone sitting in the dining room at work when in walked three officers (horrible creatures), dressed up in all their trappings, pistols stuck in their belts, and swords clanking against the floor—I was frightened almost out of my wits. I never asked them in or to be seated, I never said a word. I don't believe I could speak if I had tried. I did not know what was coming I expected to be annihilated. Two of them stationed themselves on either side of the fire-place and held

up the mantel piece with their shoulders the other one strutted up to me and said we have come to search this house. He turned and walked across the room to the side-board and pulled open one of the drawers
At this time one of our neighbors came in, looked in the door perfectly agast with her mouth open and darted up stairs. Mr. *Lieu. Searcher* after opening the drawers and turning over the table cloth and napkings and things that were in it turned to me and said "this is a very disagreeable business." I stood up all the time as streight as a line, by this time I was too indignant to feel afraid of them, and replied, "I should think so and not only disagreeable but very degrading." The man let go the drawers and dropped back into a seat as if I had shot him, said "I assure you any search is only for fire-arms" I replied, ladies have very little use for fire-arms, and as my sister and myself are the only white persons living in this house you could hardly expect to find any thing of the kind here, "O" he said "You are the ladies I have heard of, if I had known it I would not have disturbed you" as they were about to start I happened to remember an old *fire lock* that had been standing in the back passage since, "long before I was born", and stopped them to run and get it. I produced it saying this is the old musket my father used at the battle of Bladensburg in 1812 and if it will be of any use to you you are welcome to it. It was an old time flint-lock, only the stock without any barrel. (*I suppose poor dear old Papa shot that away at the time of the battle*) They took it and looked at it and laughed at, of course did not take it away, left it, I suppose for our protection. They put the gun down and all *nodded* at me and marched off. I afterwards learned they had brought a number of soldiers with them and had them posted at every door and window before they would venture into the house themselves. When Lizzie got back and found the whole yard and garden filled with soldiers, she says her very heart stood still She did not know what might have happened. But she met the officer near the door with a *bold-front* and asked if they allowed persons to enter their own houses, "O yes" they said and passed on- and that was our introduction to the "Grand Army" and that was the nearest we ever came to having our house searched, though numberless were the trials that were made to do it.
The next day another party came with their bright gleaming guns and bayonets stuck on the ends, (fixed I believe they call it) and demanded something to eat, which was given to them, and the next day they came and the next,—and the next and every day, morning, noon, and night always the same tune *something to eat*, until it is enough to run one crazy and they have nearly eaten up all we have, all the roads in and about town are picketted and they will not allow us to bring any

thing from there so that with our own family and all these horrible yankee germands we are getting rather scarce of provisions.

At this time as the pickets have not been advanced as far as this and we do not know how soon they may be, and as we wished to communicate with Bushrod in regard to some of his and our own affairs, we held a *Counsel of War* and determined, as there is no other way of getting a letter to him, that one shall be written and tomorrow morning early Lizzie shall ride up to Fairfax court house and mail it there, while I remain at home to defend the *Castle*. I am to be the, "Agnes Douglas", this time.

Accordingly the letter was all ready and Charles with the carriage was ordered out at an early hour this morning, they started off with many fears and misgivings. Charles did not know where he was bound or what for when they reached the public road, as usual he turned towards town but she said, "turn the horses heads up the road Charles", and she would direct this way, or that way, as they proceeded, and not until they got within sight of the Court house did he know their destination. They did not meet or see a living creature, until about a mile this side of Fairfax they saw a few forlorn looking creatures on the road side which she supposed were Confederate pickets, all with old looking shot guns, but they never said a word or made any sign to stop her. She went to the house of the Rev Templeman Brown They were very poorly dressed, she felt so sorry for them and so sorry to see them so poorly equipped

When she reached the court house she went to the house of the Rev- Templeman Brown. Mr & Mrs Brown were old and valued friends and they were delighted to see her, such an unexpected pleasure and so glad to hear all she had to tell of the doings in these parts. There were a number of gentlemen there, and persons who had gone from Alex- both gentlemen and ladies who had gone to find a home in the Confederacy. She told them all about the anoyances we are dailey subject to, from the soldiers and gave them a minute and graphic account of the visit we had recently been honored with from three finely equiped, and elegantly caprisoned officers, with their bodyguard, who came to search the house-They laughed and clapped their hands and hazzed for me and Miss Nancy when they learned of my part in it and said they had no idea I could be so spunky. She saw and heard all there was to hear, and told all she knew to tell Mr. B- took the letter and mailed it for her and altogether it was a very satisfactory trip. Directly after dinner, she took her leave of her good friends and started on her homeward journey. She never saw a living creature after leaving the turnpike until near old Back-lick church. A man darted out of the woods so suddenly as to frighten her horses, and stopped her to inquire if she had passed any pickets on the road and if they were, "Federal or non-Federal." She answered him very curtly and passed on, and he dodged back into the woods again. He was a very coarse rough looking person, but she knew him to be a yankee from his nasal dialect as well as the questions I am sure not one of the people of that stamp in these *diggins* would have known what he meant, they never even heard the word *federal*—and *poor me* left to battle it alone with the *Federals*- But wonderful to relate—and most fortunate for me not one came to the place the whole day. But still I was kept in the greatest state of anxiety and exitement, could not eat or rest—walking—walking—all day long, not knowing what moment I would be pounced upon, upstairs, and down stairs, in the kitchen, in the garden down to the road-

By and by toward sun set, in one of my perambulations to the road I espied the carriage a long way off coming pretty briskly. I just clasped my hands and cried out loud "O! I am so thankful she's coming" and her first greeting—"back—back all safe and sound-" O I was too, too, glad to see her! and then to hear all she had to tell, and I think Charles was as much pleased with the trip as she was.

June 1st—1861 And now war fare between us and this vile refuse of the earth begins in earnest. They came day—and night—any all day long. The first thing in the morning, before I am up I hear their vile, abusive, scurilous, blasphemy, O how can we live through it to have our peaceful home thus invaded—and our ears pained and blasted by such [illegible] sounds. We kept all the lower part of the house shut up, every window and door, locked bolted and bared, and we ourselves shut up, and stationed at the upstairs windows, and with what heart sickening terror do we see their approach to the house—their guns and bayonets only showing above the top of the cedar hedge—all glittering and gleaming in the sun light- Sometimes one party will rush into the kitchen and snatch and take off whatever they find, to-day they took a dried shad hanging against the wall. Old mammy seized it and tried to wrest it from him but he very soon got the better of her- They got all the setting hens out of the coops. One party came to the front door, when they come there we think it best to confront them ourselves, one or both thinking we can better keep them out of the house than the servants can, and there they stood using all manner of vituperative language, and calling us all the vile shocking names that could be thought of. They dance, hoop and yell, and make all manner of threats, They behave and look like demons. Nothing that I could say, no words could convey, an idea of the horror of these scenes, and all without any provocation. The officers are not a whit better than the men for these marauding parties are nearly always accompanied by one or two officers. I do not know how they can attend to their military duties when such throngs of them are constantly ranging all over the country in quest of plunder. I never was spoken roughly to, or encountered rudeness from a man before. One man who was particularly insolent I remonstrated with and asked if he was not ashamed to speak to a lady in that way, he turned upon me in the most contemptous manner and said I would like to know who in the h___ made you a lady

and these are the people who we have been led to believe were so much in advance, and so much better, than *us poor ignorant* Southern people in morals, and manners, education, piety, sobriety, and every christian virtue I can only say deliver me from such.

O the horrible, horrible red legs—the fire Zouaves—here they come again with their tight blue skull caps and long cords and tassels hanging from the top-knot I think if possible they are more savage than the rest they are our perfect terror. Their red clothes can be seen from afar, They are the New York City fire Zouaves—The soldiers seem to have no particular uniform. Each company seems to be caprisoned according to their own peculiar style and fancy. They came here dressed in all manner of frippery, some in dark clothes with broad brimed hats and long black plumes, others in gray with tight caps with a long fox tail stuck streight up in front, and O the *Fox Tails* are a vile vile set! They searched Mr Reid's house recently and found a Confederate flag, and then such vile doings never anyone heard of before, they tore the whole house and place up generally. They manacled him and dragged him off to town through all the water and mud-holes they could find—and up and down through every street until he was wearied and worn almost to death, and then put him in prison where they kept him until he was forced to take the oath, (whatever that is)

Today is the first time we have ventured to leave home since the invasion. Some pickets were stationed about on the roads but they did not interfere with us, but it was dreadful to see the destruction all about, fields thrown open, fences all down, fires all burning in the fields piled up with rails, grain fields that so short a time ago were looking so beautiful and flourishing, now covered over with tents, and trampled over with horses, and wagons, and soldiers and every thing pertaining to an army. The streets were also filled with them, and so shockingly filthy that it made me shudder to walk on the pavements. And every body looking so sad and sorrowfull, and all having a tale of horror and wrong to tell.

We went to the office of the Provost and made our complaints of how the army was treating us, we gave him the full particulars, told him we were two ladies by ourselves. I was determined they should not have the opportunity of pleading ignorance of what was going on. Col. Stone is the Provost Marshall of Alex- He was very polite, and said we must have a guard. He then told us that no soldier had a right to search a house, and no officer under the rank of Colonel unless with a written order from that office, and gave us a printed paper to that affect with his signature.

On our way back home when we got near "Sharon" (our little chapel) Charles pointed with his whip and said "look dar Miss Lizzie dem dar people dun ben to our house and got de hens," and sure enough there was a perfect stream of feathers By the time we reached home I had forgotten the hens, but when we went into the kitchen, there sat old mammy crying—crying as if her heart would break, we both exclaimed, mammy what is the matter, what on earth is the matter—and then such an outburst and such a flood of tears—O I was so frightened! I thought surely somebody is dead. But after a little, when she had some what subsided we got out of her. "Dat dem dar people, ever so many of dem, had don ben here and tuck mos all de hens away. (and then another torrent of tears "I try my very bes to stop em—but shaw—da did'en min me. da run dis way an dat way, under de hedge, through an through de barn an stable, and every whitcher way, and stick em wid dem sharp things da get stuck on de end of de gun, den da all march off wid de gun up over de shoulder and dem sharp things all chuck full of hens, and da all a fluttering an hollarin—Da run de cows and milk dem, den da come to me for corn bread. I holler at dem like I holler at de dog— go off I got no corn bread, and if I had I wouldn't give you a mouf full of it to save your life" We commenced this year with a fine poultry yard, between four and five hundred, and they are thinning out rapidly. I never saw such hawks as these yankees are in all my life. I don't believe they ever ate a chicken before they came to old *Virginy*.

Lizzie is constantly sending and writing, and sometimes going herself from camp to camp begging and entreating the officers for a guard They all know how we are here alone, and how shamefully we are treated for they have all ranged round the country as far as they dare go, and acquainting themselves thoroughly with every bodys business. Some times they will allow me and her a guard, and sometimes, "no *Madam* it is Rebel property and we can not make use of our men to protect rebel property," and no protestations to the contrary, or no pictures of our distress will move their, adamantive, obstant hearts. When they do send

The Fate of The Rail Fence
Alfred R. Waud, Courtesy of American Heritage Picture Collection from The American Heritage Picture Collection

us a guard it is four or five men, and we have them all to feed, and at times we are in the greatest straits, send and withdraw them all. Some times when the Soldiers are in the greatest furore, taunting and tearing, cursing yelling, they will trifle and dally until they think all the mischief is done and then send the guard for us to feed.

More yankees here again today chasing the hens all over the place. We took out all the little negro children and made them shew-shew-shew them first on one side of the hedge, and then on the other to try and save them. but in spite of all they got some, and then went off. We congratulating ourselves on getting rid of them on such easy terms, when on looking down the fence side saw the shadow of the hens through it and found they had a whole flock driving before them. We told the children to runrun and drive them into the hedge, and off they all flew as fast as their little black feet could patter and succeeded in securing every hen. It was fine fun for them. I was almost afraid to send them and wondered the yankees did not run them through with their bayonets— if they had been white children no doubt they would.

This morning a great laughing and noise in the front-yard and mirth is such an unusual sound with *us* I got up and peeped out of the window, and there stood a squad of soldiers. They had Bob (a little negro boy who Lizzie always had made a great pet of) on the porch steps, and they are standing round, half beset with their hands resting on their knees. Bob cutting all manner of monkey shines. They would tell him to open his mouth and he's open it, and to shut his mouth and he would do it, and to shut his eyes, and lift his hands, whatever they told him he did it, and at every move he made, such yells and shouts of laughter I never did hear, just like a pack of idiots. I wondered if they had never seen a negro child before.

This evening we have observed three officers dodging in and out of the stables, going round and round taking a general survey of every thing, talking to the men at work in the fields. Late in the evening while we were sitting on the porch talking to some ladies, neighbors of ours, they all three marched in and in the most familiar manner called out "Good afternoon ladies it's a very pleasant evening" of course we had to make some slight response to their salutation but *it was very cool*. No body took any other notice of them, they were not asked in or even to take a seat. One sprawled himself at full length on the grass in front of the door, another seated himself on the steps while the third sauntered about and looked at the flowers, and joined in the conversation they all made themselves perfectly at home. We were telling these ladies of the shocking treatment we had received from the soldiers. The one on the grass who we afterwards found was a Capt. Johnson, lifted himself on his elbows, shook himself, and made grimances and muttered as if to himself "Shamefull shameful" and the others joined in chorus, and how reprehensible in the officers to allow the men to prowl all over the county with guns and bayonets to mistreat and frighten poor unoffending women and children. If they only had the power how soon all such abuses would be corrected, and all of them wished they had only been in sight when the soldiers were carrying on so here, and they would with pleasure have shot them down like dogs. Capt. Johnson belonged to Gen Franklin's division, Lieutenant Washbern is about the office of the Provost Marshal in Alex- The other was a lame man I never could learn his name. They hung about here until it was quite dark- The ladies, Mrs and Miss Davis in commenting on their very polished manners pronounced them all perfect gentlemen.

The first thing next morning there was a great outcry. The carriage horses were both gone. Of course the thieves were the officers who were here the night before. They, and the two horses were tracked through the cornfield to where they had pulled down the fence and gone into the public road.

Lizzie was so disconcerted and distressed at the loss, the horses were great pets with her, that I believe she cried about it, and said she was determined to leave no stone unturned to get them back, she would visit every camp within ten miles round but she would have them back. She sent to a neighbor and asked him to come with his carriage and his sister and take her over to Gen Franklin's encampment on Seminary hill.

Accordingly soon after breakfast they all sat-out on a tour of discovery. When they got into the camp grounds they asked for Gen Franklin, *he was not there for the Colonel—he also was away.* Then for a number of other officers but none were to be found. She says she knew as soon as she entered the grounds from all their meneuvers that they all recognized her and knew what she had come for. "Well," she said "there must be some one in command here and I am determined to see an officer before I leave these grounds. Then after a great deal of shuffling to and fro and talking together, she could see Maj Doughty She drove round to his tent and sent to inquire if he would come out and speak to her. She said she could see him sprawled out on a lounge. He seemed to be very much enraged at the request and balled out in the most insolent tone and manner, loud enough for her to hear, "As she has more business with me than I have with her she had better come to me." She felt so nettled at hearing all this that she was determined to have it out with him.

She got out of the carriage and took the two persons she had with her and they all walked into the tent together. He mumbled out something if an apology of "not knowing it was ladies." (He had been here and knew perfectly well which one to address) She said it did not make any manner of difference with her she was very haughty, but condescended to state her business, and asked to see Capt Johnson—he was not there— yes she said he was for she had seen him only a moment ago (whenever she mentioned the horses she always said one of your officers stole them out of my stable at such a time) after a great search and much delay the Capt. came forth, and the very first thing he said was "I do assure you Madam I did not steal your horses." She replied "Well it is very strange that the horses should have disappeared at the time you did, and the same night you were at my house." I do assure you I did not steal them, the horse that I was seen with was one I bought from Mr. _____ and if you don't believe me I can show you the bill of sale, and he produced a very soiled scrap of paper with name and date, and handed it to her. He did not pretend to say it was not her horse, but that it had been stolen from his tent the night before. She said to him it was all a very strange transaction altogether—the horses leaving her house when he did, and that scrap of paper which purported to be a bill of sale for her horse was made out when he was in her stable and dated two days before he was stolen. And after a great deal of useless palaver, she had to leave without her horses.

In the evening an officer rode up to the door, quite a fine looking handsome man, and told Lizzie that Capt Johnson had without doubt one of her horses, he did not know where the other was, but Johnson certainly had one for he saw him on parade the morning before riding him. She told him of her trip to Gen. Franklin's camp and how unsuccessful she had been. He said that is the very place your horse is in, and if you will write a note to Gen. Franklin and give him the names of the officers, and all the circumstances of their being on your place at such a time, and when they left the horses disappeared and send it by a trusty messenger who will place it in his hands you will certainly get them back. According to advice a note was made ready and Charles dispatched with explicit directions to put into no other hands than Gen. Franklin's. After a time he returned perfectly radiant with delight at his success (That is if a tar black face could radiate) at any rate the face smiled all over. Then he went into a most satisfactory detail of particulars.

I walk up to de tent whar Gen Franklin sot by de table a writing an I han him de note- I put it in his own hand—myself—I did—an I stan and look rite at him is he read it, his face gitin reder an reder is he go along, den he jump up an fling de note down on de table, an holler at some body like he hollerin at de dog, "go and fetch Capt Johnson here to me" When he cum Gin Franklin turn roun up on him like he gwine ter snap his head rite off, an say whar dat hos yah tuck out er Miss Frobel's stable. de man look is if he wuz fit to faint and say some body stole him outer my tent last nite.

General Franklin sticken his fis down on de table, and den struck it at him an say if dat hos aint in Miss Frobel's stable before twelve o'clock to morrow den epertets will be cut rite open your shoulders, sir- now go."

And sure enough before we had finished breakfast the next morning here came a soldier riding up with the horse.

Then we went off to town to see if we could discover the *where abouts* of the other one. First we went to Mr. Miffleton the carriage maker and asked if he would know the horse if he saw him in the street- Ah, he said, he had shod that fellow too often not to know him again, why if they would kill him and bring his skin he would know it, he had seen him several times passing by his shop since he was stolen, with an officer on his back.

The Provost Marshal had been changed since we were in town last and as Gen- Montgomery occupied the post of ruler and judge, when we entered his office he was all succority, bows, and smiles. He has quite taken the hearts of the people by his friendly manner. He was sitting by a table writing when we went in- we told him what we had come for, and asked his assistance in the recovery of the horse, he said he would do all he could for us, and then asked our name, when he heard it he looked up and bowed and smiled, said he recognized it, having heard it before and also of the loss of our carriage horses. We told him yes both of them had been stolen but Gen Franklen had one sent back. we were very anxious to get them back, they were beautiful little playful creatures and pets, indeed they were valuable in themselves as we had refused $500 for them. He said "ladies I do feel much interested in the recovery of those horses and if it is possible you shall have them again I will certainly do every thing in my power. Now if there are any friends of yours, or *any one* who could identify them I authorize that person to lay hands on him wherever he may find him. It makes no difference whether man or officer is riding him—to make him at once dismount and bring them before me and I will insure your getting him back. We told him the blacksmith who was in the habit of shoeing them knew the horses perfectly well, had seen them a number of times since they were stolen passing his shop with an officer on his back. When we arose to take our departure Gen Montgomery said "by the way have you an idea what the name of these officers are,"

O yes one is Capt Johnson of Franklin's command, and the other one who is often seen about town is Lieutenant Washbern. When that name was uttered the man actually started and changed color, Lizzie did not observe it but I did for I was looking streight at him. He never uttered another word but followed us to the street door and bowed us out, but all the smiles and sweetness was gone/ as soon as we got out of earshot, I asked Lizzie if she observed the change in Gen Montgomery's manner when Washbern's name was mentioned, but she did not, said she was not looking at him. I told her what I had seen and told her moreover as sure as you live that old pick-pocket has had a hand in the stealing of that horse, and we will never see him again if it depends on that old thief to find him and we never did see or hear of him after that. Nevertheless we determined to see Mr Miffelton again and tell him the whole story. The old man stood very patiently and listened to it all, never saying a word, when she had told all she had to tell, he threw up his head, and pushed up his spectacles, and said in the most deliberate quiet-manner "Miss Liz-e-beth Gen Montgomery may be a very clever old fellow some people say he is, but he stole my buggy. He did'en come here and take the buggy out of my yard himself, but his Lieu. did.

Lieutenant Washbern did, they took it down to Mr. Somebody and had it painted over thinking I would not know it when I saw it again. But I did the moment I set my eyes upon it I knew it, and they have got it now, and I see it every now and then. Washbern driving it and old Montgomery setting back in it, *who but him*," and now they have got your horse to drive my buggy. Ah! you will never see that horse again" and never was there a truer prophesy spoken for we never did, or the other one either Monday morning, Charles came home this morning with great news and in much excitement. A party of rebels came down last night and fired into the pickets at South run. There was a good deal of noise making and yelling and bullets whistling through the woods in every direction one Confederate was killed and two yankees. As he, Charles, came from town a little after sunrise he found the roads filled with noisy soldiers.

The whole face of the earth seemed to be alive with them. The Confederates had all retired. When he got near Cameron run he met hundreds of yankees they had the dead body of a man on a plank carrying him toward town with his legs and arms swinging, and every few steps they would fling him on the ground and kick and knock and beat him with their guns until it was sickening to look at- and such a noise, such hooping and yelling! and O-O-such curses and blasphemy we *never* did hear. When they met him they dashed the dead man right down before him—just at his very feet and screamed and yelled at him to know if he did not want to see a dead rebel. Charles seemed to be sick and disgusted with their beastly doings said he thought they may be satisfied when they have taken the man's life he was dead and that was enough. After breakfast we went out to reconnioter the premices and returned with the information, "dat dem rebels as dese people call em" had passed through this place last night and for fear of being impeded in their retreat had opened all our gates and fences, but he did not think they returned the way they went as he couldn't find any of their returning foot marks. We did not go to town for several days after the attack on the pickets and when we reached the place where the skirmish took place Charles pointed it out to us "des is one place, and dat is tother, where the soldiers wuz killed, de rebel wuz foun over yander hang in ove de fence, da kil him gis is he wuz climin over de fence. It was dreadful to see two immense stains of blood, but it was newly obliterated by travel we could only see the outlines. In town we heard the whole story pretty much as we had heard it before. Jolly was the name of the poor Southern soldier, from Georgia- after treating his body in such a savage indecent manner on the road, they got it into town, doubled it up and put it in a goods box, placed it in a wheelbarrow and carried it out to Penny Hill the pauper burying ground, scratched a hole and tumbled him in. The whole town was up in arms about such unheard of indecent doings and some of the gentlemen of the town called on the Provost Marshal and said to him they had come to ask Christian burial for a Soldier- The request seemed to be quite a startling one, but after some deliberation it was acceded to, of course they could not do otherwise. These gentlemen went straight to the undertaker and ordered what they wanted. They had the body taken up and prepared in the nicest—neatest manner, he was dressed in the very best and nicest of clothes that could be purchased, and everybody seemed to think it a privilege and honor to contribute, some one article and some another, the very best and handsomest casket the town could afford was procured- all the carriages in the town- all the ladies turned out- every body men, women and children- white and black attended poor Jolly's remains to his grave. The streets were filled with yankee soldiers looking on, and one of them said he didn't believe if Lincoln had died he could have such a funeral. Some one answered, "no not in Alexandria he could'ent" Poor Jolly! his was the largest funeral ever seen in Alex- and his first blood spilt in this part of the country in the Southern Cause

Our troubles and annoyances seemed to multiply day by day. I wonder some times how it is possible we can live through it or how we can retain one particle of reason through it all

This morning a whole troop of these horrid, vile looking savages made their appearance at the front door. I went immediately to know what they wanted, or rather I hobbled out as quickly as I could for fear of some violence, for at this time I have a very painfully sore foot. They all stood in a body in the walk and when I asked what they wanted, one, a very common, vicious, wicked looking wretch, rather elderly, steped towards me holding up his face in the most insulting manner, and demanded most authoritatively, "Where is your husband." I said I have no husband. "That's a lie," he responded very promptly, "for this man down the hill here told me there were two of you and both have husbands in the rebel army" O well, I said if *that man* down the hill knows more about me, and my business than I do myself, you had better go and get all the information from him you want and I walked into the house and shut the door.

Then they went round to the kitchen after old mammy and asked her the same questions- and they got back *lie* for *lie*, as good as they sent and when they mentioned "that man down the hill here" She squalled out "now dat's ol Smith, dat's ol Smith, I knows who dat is, an he's a liar, and he knows he is a liar, don't I know if day's got husbands or not aint I bin wid em all tha lives, I nused dem every one, I knowed dem all ever since da bin born,—yes and before da wuz born." Old Smith is an old yankee, who settled next to us, down between the hills ten or twelve years ago, and has been a perfect annoyance and nuisance to the whole country around ever since, a regular old John Brown. Mammy's testimony seemed to satisfy them and after getting as many chickens as they could, milking the cows, taking the honey, and many other *little acts* of *kindness* they all cleared out-

Lizzie was obliged to go into town this morning, and not withstanding my terribly sore foot *I was obliged* to go too. I always felt uneasy when she goes alone, and then it is some little variety in our isolated lives to get away if only a short time from the anoyance endure at home— although we know not that we will have any home to come back to whenever we do go we hear of more and fresh outrages committed on the people, although the towns people do not suffer as much as the country people do.

After going to see one or two friends, and transacting all the business we had to do we turned our faces homewards again, but after getting a short distance from town we found our road bared no egress permitted We turned back to the Provosts office to try and get a permit to go home but he would not issue one. Said "there was some little some thing, some obstruction that would pass away in a few hours, and that we could go out of town if we wished." We started off again in the direction of home, but when we got to the first-picket station they stopped us again, and told us there was a General at Cat's Tavern who would give us a pass, and he sent us to one at Shuter's hill, but nowhere would they give us one- neither would they tell us how the safety of the army depended on our being kept in town-

By this time there was the greatest commotion every where. The turnpike road filled with soldiers, and officers on horse-back dashing up and down like mad, shouting out their orders and brandishing their swords- and such a noise and suffocating dust—an immense mass of noisy disorderly soldiers came rushing down the road and up towards "Shuter's Hill"—laughing, shouting and huzzaning "the Rebel's are coming, get out of the way the Rebels are coming" and the people did get out of the way, and in the hurly burly we kept moving up, and moving up a little at a time, thinking we might possibly get without being noticed beyond the pickets- But no such good luck attended us a little this side the water works we found a number of carriages, buggys, wagons, filled with country people, our neighbors and acquaintances trying like ourselves to get by. Two of the ladies were in tears, crying, and begging and pleading to be allowed to go home to their little infants that they had been away from so long. Lizzie said to one of them that was nearest to us "O I would'nt cry, I would not gratify them by letting them see me cry. I know they delight in doing any thing to distress a poor woman who is in their power." O she replied you can take it all quietly, and talk that way because you have no little baby at home crying for you, and needing your care as I have"—another lady was Miss Roberts living at Cameron Mills just in full view of our own home, only a field between. She was sitting in the buggy with her husband, she pointed out her house, and begged and entreated to be allowed to go to her infant. I dont think she cried, I believed she was too spunky for that, but they were obstanate, would not allow her to move off the turnpike road, at last she became so exasperated she vowed she would go, and out of the buggy she jumped and over the fence, and half way the field before the wretch who was running after caught her, she pulled and pushed and tusseled with him and at last got away and off again through the field, and through the yard, up the steps and across the porch and into the front door and dashed it in his face, and O how the soldiers laughed and shouted when he had to come back without her.

And poor old Mr. Roberts sat up in his buggy all the time with his whip in his hand, looking after her, so unruffled, never moved a muscle of his face or a hand to help her. If it had have been me I certainly would have given that man a taste of that whip and braved ft. La-Fayett

Sitting so long on the glareing turnpike road in the boiling sun I turned sick, my head ached so dreadfully and my foot became so painful that at times, I felt as if I should faint away. From that day to this I never could find out what scared the yankees so that day, or what protection our remaining on the road could have been to them, for hours and hours roasting in the sun. After so long a time some body shouted out "go on" and were only too glad to avail ourselves of the permission to get home and two more jaded, faged out sick creatures never welcomed the sight of home. With Charles' assistance I managed to get into the house, and sank on the bed—so sick—so sick- And then—such a sickening, shocking, horrible tale to listen to- The servants had been attacked by the savage, beastly Zouaves- I can not recount it,- I can not think of it- it is too revolting to every feeling of human nature- O! that we could be forever rid of these detestable people! and they said they were coming back again at night.

I could not do a thing, I could not lift my head off my pillow, and poor Lizzie although so sick and broken down, had, after swallowing a cup of tea, and having the horses fed, to start off again in search of protection.

And O with what a sinking, sick feeling at heart did I see her preparing to leave me. There is such uncertainty, such a restless anxiety about our movements She went streight over to our good friend and neighbor Mr McCluer and made known our situation, and enlisted his kind offices to obtain for us a guard. He took Charles and the carriage and went from camp to camp and from place to place, and told the whole story and begged for a guard if only for the night, but all in vain, none could be allowed to protect rebel property. Then he determined to apply to the Provost in Alex who at this time is Gen Hynszleman an officer of high standing in the army Mr. Mc- again told the story of two ladies entirely alone and unprotected and of the attack upon the family in the morning and of the threat to return at night, But the answer was if he sent guards for all the rebel property in the country he would have no men to guard himself, and that it was not at all probable that after being here in the morning and committing such atrocious deeds they would come again at night. So all his representations and entreaties were without avail and he had to come back as he went

While they were gone I suffered agonies both of body and mind, and kept all the servants on the watch, and to let me know the moment a man appeared in sight, I was too sick for any thing I do believe if they had come and made an attack on the house, while I was in that condition I must have died. Lizzie and Mr. Mc concluded that it would never do for us to remain here that night by ourselves. It was getting quite late and they had to hurry up. The wagon was hitched up and a bed put in and I placed upon it and we both went over to Mr. McCluer's and staid allnight O, I never can forget that day and night- They brought me down stairs just as the sun was going down, and as I passed the dining room door I turned my head and looked in, and there was the table all so nicely set, with every thing on it, and the supper all smoking hot- But not one mouth full could any of us touch, but all went off and left it as it was, as we passed out of the front door I felt as if it was forever, I never should see my home again, and I just put my hands over my face and screamed. I cried all the way, Mr. and Mrs McCluer were very kind and put themselves to much inconvenience to accomodate us for the night. But I do not think I ever closed my eyes to sleep. I was picturing to myself all manner of evil all night long- Our dear old home in flames— the servants scattered hither and yon—The soldiers destroying and carrying off every thing we have-

But we managed to get through the night somehow, and soon after breakfast Charles came over with the carriage for us. The first thing he said was "none of dem people is bin dar yit but I don't know how soon da may come-" The servants all call the soldiers, *"dem people"*

We found the house all locked up, and every thing just as we had left it even the supper on the table, the only difference was it had cooled off. It produced a very sad lonely feeling, we are so unsafe, so unprotected, and feel at any moment we may be pounced upon- all the doors and windows are kept constantly shut, locked, barred, and bolted, and all the little negro children playing about out of doors are constantly on the watch and when they see the glitter of a gun, ever so far off they come dashing in screaming at the top of their voices "yankee dogs coming, yankee dogs coming" No doubt if the *yankee dogs* hear them, they will set it down as our teaching but indeed it is their own idea

Mr. McCluer advised us to write a note to Gen. Mansfield, who is now Commander in Chief at Washington, and to send Charles off with it as soon as possible, with explicit directions to go to his Headquarters, and to place it in no other hands but his.

The note was written accordingly. Lizzie giving as definite an account of the transaction here as she well could, particularly yesterdays, how we are over run by the soldiers, and in what constant terror we are kept, their attacks, and demands upon us, are daily I might say almost hourly how they are allowed to rove all over the country with their guns and bayonets and their ferocious treatment to the poor unprotected women and children is a perfect disgrace to the army, how a number of Zouaves came to our house yesterday in the absence of the white family and treated the servants in the most scandalous manner. And when they left said they intended returning at night- We found a gentleman friend who kindly offered us his help, and he went for us from Camp to Camp, and gave the officers a full and explicit statement of the case, and of the peril of our situation, and implored them to give us a guard, but he was refused most positively, and in most instances with contumely. Then he determined to apply to the Provost Marshal of Alex- But his request was received there with equal contempt-

All this was written to Gen Mansfield and Charles despatched with it but it was late when he started, and as his family live in Wa he did not return that night. But he came back early next morning. Said he had gone to Gen Mansfield's Head quarters as directed and put the note in his hands and stood there while he read it, after reading it he gave it to another officer and a number of them read it. Gen Mansfield asked him a great many questions and seemed very angry Then he wrote a note and gave it to him with Miss Lizzie's note and told him to take them both to Gen. Hynszelman in Alex. which he did and had to encounter another Soon after breakfast an officer came with five men. Said Gen. Hynszelman had sent him to place them here as guards. In a short time Miss Emily Davis came down and told us all about the Zouave doings here the day we were in town, she said there were a number of them hanging about their place for hours and came streight from their house here, she saw them come and would certainly know them if she saw them again

Then Mr. Frowle came with an officer who he introduced as Lt. Fairland He said he had come by Gen. Hynszelman's orders to try and investigate *that matter.* Lizzie refered him to the servants, they could tell him much more than she knew about it, Off he went to where the men were at work, and talked and walked about with them for a long time, then he came in again and said he had learned all they could tell him, and he knew where the soldiers were to be found. He told Lizzie Gen Hynszleman wished to see her at his office.

So to the office she went again the next day. I was too sick and she had to get Miss Emily Davis to go with her. And a most stormy interview they had of it. The old Hynsz was as furious and savage as any other wild animal. He walked up and down the room and gritted his teeth and raved at her, "Why didn't you send to me instead of writing to Gen Mansfield I could have done as much as Gen Mansfield." She replied you remember Gen Hynszleman, I did send to you, and you positively refused to do any thing for us, or to send us a guard. My sister and myself were entirely alone and in the utmost peril, and as you refused us protection I was determined to apply to some one who I knew would *give us* protection

She afterward learned that Gen Mansfield had repremanded him soundly for refusing her a guard- and that was what enraged him so, that she should have had the tenacity to send complaints to W*a* of him Charles said "dat ol thing wuz jist fit to bite his own head off, jis mad like he wuz tother day when I giv hin dem two notes"

The next day a number of officers came with a large number of the vile Zouaves. They said it was the whole regiment. But we knew very well it was not more than a fourth of them. Mrs Davis and Miss Emily stood on the porch to inspect, and to identify them. The officers called them up one by one and they passed before the ladies, holding up their ugly dirty faces and contorting them in the most ludicious shameless manner, some looking cross eyed, others with the mouth drawn back almost to the ear, every sort of grimace that it was possible to pucker the human face into-Of all the non-sensicle scenes- it was a perfect farce. The officers became so convulsed with laughter they had to hide themselves behind the trees. The two ladies would shake their heads as each soldier passed, not one was recognised, but they had provided themselves against that by not bringing the guilty ones.

Neither Lizzie or myself put in an appearance that day, but reconnoitered the performance through our *concealed batteries* up stairs. I would not have asked, or subjected any female belonging to this vicinity to such an ordeal, but these ladies seemed to have no objection. Indeed I think they proffered their services, and as they all belonged to the same refined decorous nation I supposed they knew what propriety was better than I did. And I really do think and believe they enjoyed it- They had quite a jolly time over it afterward

We are often in want of many things that we are obliged to do without for weeks at a time, some times it is flour, sometimes meal. at one time Charles took a bag of corn on his back to the mill, and had to hide himself and the meal in the bushes for hours before he could find an opportunity of avoiding the pickets which are placed all along the railroad. He said he knew they would take it away from him if they caught him

When that bag was exhausted he filled the wagon, with bags, and barrels, of corn, as full as it could hold and started again for the mill. We waited and watched for his return all that day. The next day it was the same thing. Charles- as night came on we felt very anxious and uneasy, and mammy comforted us by saying, "Oh! Charles is gone off to look for freedom."

But the third day early in the morning, here comes Charles with the two horses, but no wagon and no meal. He says when he got about a mile from home that morning he found the roads filled with soldiers, every thing in excitement and hurry, working as if for dear life

The officers ordered him to place his wagon across the road to unhitch the horses and tie them to the fence while he assisted in barricading the road.

They pressed every wagon and cart into service that came along, and trees and fencing and every thing they could lay hands on was piled against the wagons.

And every few minutes they were ordered to "hurry up, hurry up, the Black Horse Cavelry is coming, an you is in as great danger as I is" It was the first time we had heard of the Black Horse Cavelry. We did not know whose it, was or where it came from.

They all worked at the barricading until near sun set, then he was ordered to take his horses and go to the camp some where about the rail road. He says *he took his time* to untie them, got on one and lead the other,—he walked along very slowly, six men following, as guards to keep him from running away, presently they began to lag a little, and he to move a little faster, then to trot quite briskly, while they stopped to talk first to one, and then another he got a long distance ahead before he was noticed. They hallooed to him to halt, but he whipped up his horses and into town he clashed, found an empty stable where he stowed them away, and bought feed for them all the time they stayed there. He tried his best to get a permit for the horses and for himself to get home, but without success, at last he heard of an officer he had known before the war being on the old steamer Pawnee then lying out in the stream, he got a boat and went out to him and through his means obtained a pass.

Now here we were, a large family without a mouthful of bread for two whole weeks, fortunately we found some old potatoes of last year in the cellar and they had to answer as substitutes for bread.

At last our good friend and neighbor Mr Fairfax saw the wagon and knew it, and wanted to take the corn out, but the barricades were watched and they would not let him do it, he waited his opportunity and got it however sent to the mill, had it ground and sent it up to us. It was so kind in him to take all that trouble for us, and we did appreciate it, and both white and black enjoyed having a little bread once more. No one knows what it is to do without bread for so long a time, unless they have some experience in the matter

The searching, plundering, and destroying of houses in the neighborhood continues. The houses that have been deserted by their owners and left to the care of the servants, have had every thing they contained entirely swept off and all sent North. The camps, and all the houses are filled up with yankee women, and they certainly are adept at plundering and securing their plunder. I understand that at "Clermont"—Comd Forrest's residence they have been packing up, and packing up for weeks and sending off wagon loads, after wagon loads. Poor Mrs Forrest fled

for her life as soon as she heard the yankees had crossed the Potomac leaving every thing, excepting perhaps some few articles of her wearing apparel, and like us her breakfast steaming-hot on the table.

"Vaucluse"—A Virginia Homestead*
Edwin J. Meeker, Courtesy of Castle Books, A Division of Book Sales, Inc.

O that was such a harvest for the army of marauders. "Clermont" was a lovely paradise of a place, and so filled with every thing rare and beautiful and costly. It seemed to me such a sin to destroy it all.

---

* "Vaucluse", the home of Constance Cary Harrison, was located on Seminary Road, near the present-day Alexandria Hospital. The house was "sacrificed . . . to military necessity in 1862.

Our house has not as yet been searched although many and strenuous have been the efforts to get into it. We always confront them with Gen. Stones proclamation. Some will say, "there is no such officer in our army, and others yes that's some d- rebel!" But still they seem rather afraid to attempt any violence even though Gen Stone is a rebel.

Miss Emily Davis came down to day to tell us of the violence and robbery that has been perpetrated at "Rose Hill" within the past few days

An immense throng of officers and soldiers went over there and searched and plundered the house from garet to cellar, then they went out and hitched up the carriages, wagons, carts, everything they could find, killed the hogs, sheep, poultry, and filled every thing with it, and went off with a drove of horses, mules and cows. There were none but ladies, children, and servants on the place. Misses Betsy, and Kitty Tompson, were staying with Mrs. Mason at the time. Miss Betsy is old and infirm. The violence, noise, and oaths of these infuriated demons alarmed her so that she gave way as if in a fainting fit -and had to be put to bed, paralysis ensued, and never from that hour to the day of her death did she utter one coherent sentence.

Miss Emily Davis came down as she usually does to inform us of all the vile things that are being perpetrated on the people around, and to day "Rose Hill" was the theme of her discourse. Her brother John was her informer. When asked in astonishment, "Why was he with them", the answer was "O no he was only passing by, he could do nothing to stop them, or to help the people he only stopped a few minutes to look on. A long time afterwards we learned that he was the very man, who by his tales, and misrepresentations excited the soldiers and lead them from place to place to do all manner of evil deeds. They all seem to have the most venomous hatred to all of the Mason name I am sure I cannot tell why The Masons I feel pretty certain never did them any harm. I doubt if they even know there are such people on the face of the earth.

O these yankee settlers who have been among us for years have been and still are the bane of our Southern Country. Envy, hatred and malice seems ever rankling in their hearts- and for what? Little else for all the neighbours seem ever ready to do them a neighbourly friendship.

Sunday July 14th 1861. Sunday is always the most terrible day in the week for us. The soldiers seem to wander about, and have more liberty, go in greater squads, do more violence and robbery than any other day

While we were at breakfast this morning a number came into the back yard and commenced emptying the fatening coops of all the chickens, one of the servants called out to know what they were about. They said "the Colonel who is living down here on the road to Pullman's house wants boiled chicken for his breakfast, and sent us up here to get them, for him." We protested against it, told them we had none to spare but it was of no avail, they seized every one we had, would not leave us even one for our dinner. They hang about here a long time touting the chickens about in their hands and parlying with the negroes.

We had to go off to church and leave them here, stopped to speak to the Col. who seemed very unwilling to make his appearance, at last after several messages he slung himself out into the front yard in his shirt sleaves, his hair and beard very much dishieveled, and face evidently unfreshened by cool water that morning. When we poured forth our grievances into his unwilling ear, he made some most fearfully profane exclamation of denial and ordered some one to "go directly and arrest

every one of those men and bring them here to me" We thanked him, made our adieus, and proceeded on our way to Church. But when we got back home, about two o'clock we found the coops all wide open, and chickens all flown. After all that pretence no doubt, that deceptious creature breakfasted on boiled chickens from our coops. That is just a specimen of all their doings.

Confederate works on Munson's Hill as seen from the Union advance post at Bailey's Crossroads, Virginia, September 1861
Courtesy of Castle Books, A Division of Book Sales, Inc.

Wednesday 17. From early morning there has been a constant stream of soldiers passing up this road- They say they are going to meet the enemy, but we do not know when or where. I suppose it is "to take Bulls run." The servants never said a word to us of their passing and the first we knew of it was while at breakfast a severely shrill whistle sounded, and then the whole force in sight struck up with one accord

> Come brave boys it is most day,
> Strike your tents and march away,
> The drum shall beet and the fife shall play
> All brave soldiers march away

The morning had been so serene and beautiful, and every thing so quiet and calm that the shriek of the fife all so suddenly was a startling sound and we both started up and rushed to the gate to see what was going on, and there up and down as far as we could see the roads were filled with soldiers. There was no cavalry, no artillery, no wagons on this road, but one dense mass of infantry pouring past here all day long- all day long- and into the night they were going-going. Although it is with a feeling of relief we see these horrid wretches at last making a move, still the sight makes me sick-sick at heart, we know not what is coming.

All our Union neighbours went out to the road to greet the Grand Army and Wish them *God speed* But we did not pay them that compliment, contented ourselves with one *cursory* peep at them through the garden gate and then retired into the house, occasionally taking a look through the windows to see if they were still going in such numbers. We afterwards learned that on all the roads between here and Washington it was the same thing, one continued throng of moving men and army equipments

The soldiers did not molest us at all to-day for a wonder. I do not think there was one nearer than the road. About sun down they ceased to pass.

Thursday 18 By or before the dawn they were in motion again, just as it was yesterday- going-going-all day long. About nightfall, when it was too dark for us to see as far as the public road, there was a great hue and cry- such cursing and swearing- such a hub-bub trying to get the horses (eight in number), to haul the *Big Gun* up Frobel's Hill (as they call it)

They had to send back to town and get four or six more before it could be gotten up the hill, and it was quite late in the night before it was accomplished.

Friday 19th Very little movement on the Backlick road to-day- Late this afternoon there was heavy firing towards Fairfax Court House- But it only lasted a short time.

Saturday 20. Every thing quiet on old Backlick to day. Not a single soldier have we seen to day- O what a relief, what a relief! We seldom see a human face now excepting these inhuman yankees we know nothing that is going on in the military world. No letters- no news papers. The Post office is well watched, and every letter thoroughly inspected and looked into before it is handed out of that place, no doubt if any should by any chance get in there coming from the South, woe betide the person to whom it is addressed- Ft. Lafayette would certainly be inspection. No newspaper is published in Alex- now. The yankees tore up both offices the Gazette, and Southern Churchman and destroyed every thing in them One of their own clan told me when they first came into town and saw over the door *"Southern Churchman"* they were like a pack of infuriated demons, they cursed and yelled, and blaspheamed, and dug their claws into it, and fetched it from its place, threw it on the ground, trumpled on it, and spit on it, and did every thing they could to shew their detestation of-*South-*

July 21st 1861 This morning rose bright and beautiful, warm but not oppressive. Every thing about and around looking so sweet, and calm and peaceful Not a drum, not a single military sound to afflict painfully the senses We could not realize the tumult, and war that is raging only 20 or 30 miles away- But presently, before the breakfast was placed on the table cannon was heard roaring and thundering in the distance I was in the kitchen at the time and stopped to listen. What's that- What is that, old mammy was very deliberate, and some what reluctant about answering the question—at last she said, "why its fiton dats what it is, da is fitin up yander at dat place Bull's run I believe da calls it."

It is perfectly wonderful how readily the negroes do transmit the news from one to another. They seem to have a perfect telegraphic system of communication all over the country. No doubt she knew every thing that is going on in both armys, when they were going to fight, and where and had been listening for the sounds of battle long before it was light.

There was very little breakfast needed or consumed in this house to-day The war of cannon was incessant from early dawn till after sun set and O such a day- May I never spend such another, never-never till my dying day can I forget it- the intense misery- the wearing anxiety of that day. We did nothing from morning until night but wander- wander, from place to place, and listen- listen, so anxiously. Some times when there would be an unusually loud bust- a volley loud and long I would stop and stand still, shut my eyes, and clasp my hands- I could not prayI need no words to pray- I could not sit still for a moment- My cry all day long was-mercy-mercy-Lord have mercy-

Not a living creature did we see that day. Nothing moved on the roads, about 10 O'clock a very strong wind sprang up, and increased in intensity as the hours wore on, until about 3 it blew a perfect hurricane The atmosphere became thick and hazy, and the wind so strong and loud we could not hear the cannon, thought at times it had ceased altogether, but discovered after a while that by standing at the corner of the house where we could be sheltered from the wind we could still hear the roar. I could not keep away from the place where I could hear the sounds and I stood and stood there until I could stand no longer, and sank down upon my knees on the grass, then sat, and finally laid down prone upon the ground, rising now and again to listen- mercymercy- when will this cruel inhuman strife be over, O what we suffered- suffered to-day!

About night fall it began to rain, and we heard no more cannon The rain came down in torrents all night long, and we thought of the poor dying sufferers on the field of battle and wondered how it is with them. O how my heart ached, where are our poor boys? and how are they fareing.

Manassas was the first battle we knew any thing of, though we learned long after there were several before it, even Aquia Creek that was so much nearer to us, where we must have heard the cannonading distinctly, but we did not know a word of what was going on

Monday 22 Not a living creature did we see to-day. The rain of last night continued pouring in torrents all day. The watercourses are so flooded there is no crossing them to day, Charles went to W*a* on Saturday and did not return as he usually does on Monday- and we remained as perfectly ignorant of yesterday's transactions, or of the results as if we were on the other side of the world, and so broken down- so worn out- both in body and mind

Tuesday 23 The pouring rain ceased last night and the sun came out this morning bright and clear. Every thing around us is as quiet as quiet can be, about ten Oclock Charles came home. He looked considerably crest-fallen. But could not tell a thing, nothing about any battle on Sunday, nothing that transpired yesterday, said "it rain so hard yistiddy he never even look out-dos." But after asking him a thousand questions he said "he *seed* a great many officers and men going off the boat into the City- and the whole town of Alex- and all the roads about wuz jis chuck full of soldiers. Some were helped along by others and all seemed moving towards W*a* All appeared to be in a very dilapidated condition, one man he saw sitting on the wharf looking very miserable, first he took off one shoe and then the other and poured the blood out of them.

Lizzie said she could stand it no longer. She must have more definite information. So she ordered the carriage and off to town she started. I could not go with her, my foot was too terribly sore and painful. I begged her to make haste and gather all the information she could and hurry home with it. I had been watching for her from the time she started to town, and in a few hours here she came. I flew out to meet her and said What is it- O what is it- With both hands uplifted, and beaming face she exclaimed- O Nancy, Nancy we have had the most *glorious victory* you ever heard of. The people all say if it had been followed up, they believe the Confederates could have chased the yankees clear into Canada

Then we both had a good cry over it. Lizzie did you see or hear any thing of our poor boys? "no, no, I wonder- I wonder where they are, and how they came off that terrible day" Not one word have we heard from or of them since they went into the Confederacy.

Lizzie says she never in her life saw such a sight as the town presents, soldiers lying about in every place- in piles on the road side, on the streets, on the cellar doors, in the gutters with their heads reclining on the curb-stones, fast asleep—utterly exhausted and worn out

The first person she met in the street that she knew she stopped to ask what on earth it all meant? what was the matter? Have we been defeated?

"Defeated—defeated" he said- "no-no," *Defeated indeed*, why there never was on earth such an utter rout. The men just broke and dashed off the field pell mell, helterskelter- and down the turnpike road they tore throwing away their arms, canteens, coats, hats, shoes, every thing that impeded their flight They had not even a fife or drum left to play "Brave Boys" on, for our gratification. Indeed some had hardly any clothes on when they reached Alex- They ran, and ran for miles, until they fell down by the road side in piles utterly exhausted, and there they lay all day yesterday in the drenching rain. Many were drown in endeavoring to cross the swolen streams. The officers being on horsback could make better headway than the man and got first into Washington, and had the drawbridge opened to keep out the foot-pass, and poor Alex- and vicinity had to entertain them, all the ladies living near the roads, and all the ladies of the town had hot coffee made for them, and every thing they could collect in the way of food and carried out notwithstanding the rain and administered to them. One miserable wretch who seemed almost dead with fatigue and hunger, a lady stood by and fed him until he revived sufficiently to walk and to talk. He got up and stretched himself, and when asked how he felt made some gross disgusting reply, and with a volley of oaths and imprecations on the Southern people, said they would soon be in condition again to give them d— Rebels another good thrashing, just such another as they had given them at *"Bull's Run."*

One wild, flippant, harum-scarum girl who pretended to know nothing asked an officer where they had all been. "Why," he said "did en't you know we have been up to take Bull's run"- "O yes" she said she had heard they had taken the *Run* but were obliged to leave the Bull behind them

I suppose it is not right to exult over a fallen foe But there certainly was one wide spread note of rejoicing throughout this whole section of country when we learned that the whole regiment of N.Y. City fire Zouaves were completely exterminated, and I sent up my heart-felt thanks with the rest.

A long time after- a year, or perhaps two, I met with some Confederate scouts, Capt Kinchelow was one of them, and he told me, it had been versed through-out the Confederacy how those vile brutal Zouaves had behaved at our house, and at other places, how they had mal-treated and tyrannized over the citizens generally, and they had determined with one accord if it was ever in their power to make an end of them. Their conspicious dress made them a ready mark, and he did not believe when the battle was over there was one left to tell the tale

For a few days after the Battle of *Bull run* we remained unmolested. Then they commenced again with a renewed vigour, and O such scenes of persecution and annoyance, it is enough to turn any bodys hair I don't know how we can have one particle of reason left.

They placed pickets as soon as possible on all the roads-leading into town and every day they are extended, and extended, now they are away beyond us. There are no officers with them, but an officer visits the outposts once or twice a day. There must be Rebels up this road, or they think there might be for the officers ride as if "old Scratch" was after them. They have no mercy on horse flesh, although they are miserable uncouth riders, and if one by any unlucky chance happens to get dismounted, he has to scramble back the best way he can from the top of a fence or gate

The pickets are here annoying us, morning, noon, and night and all day long, we are just between the two roads, and are afflicted with the company of both lines. The stations are not more than two panels of fense apart, and they seem to wander about at will, all over the fields, digging up the potatoes with their bayonets, with tin cups scaring and chasing the cows, and milking them.

They take or destroy every thing they can lay their hands upon. Some times the poor cows come home dripping with blood where they have been shot, or stuck with bayonets. One cow they killed outright.

Day after day it is the same thing. Threshing down the green fruit, robbing the bee hives, tearing down the grape vines, and filling their hats with perfectly green grapes that no earthly use could be made of. Some times a whole squad will march by the windows and look in with the most insulting triumphiant air, and call out some impudence, with their guns over their shoulders and bayonets strung with fluttering chickens, and green melons.

One old Shanghai rooster who knows the *blue legs* and is as much afraid of them as we are, and is forever on the watch, when he espys them ever so far off, he makes a bee-line for the kitchen, making the greatest noise, he almost talks. He has escaped a hundred battle fields and the negroes call him "Old Secesh" "Dar, you hear of ol Secesh guine to de kichen O! you many no de soldiers ain't fur off." One night they took the roof off the hen house and made a clear sweep, "Old Secesh" and all. O I was so grieved, I felt his loss more than all the rest- Poor Old Secesh!

We had a large flock of Muscovy ducks, and kept them from year to yearwould not use them because they were raised by our dear Mother. It was a great amusement and pleasure to her in her old days to attend to and watch the little Muscoveys, and her greatest delight to have a large flock for the boys, when they came home. One morning I went into the kitchen yard and there lay scattered around all these immense ducks fluttering and bleeding, and a number of Soldiers with ducks in their hands holding up to me, "What are they what are they" I could not help crying to save my life- "I said who did that- Ma's ducks" I put my hands over my face and flew into the house as fast as I could go.

In a little while, there were the fires smoking all the way up on the road and the corn, tomatoes, beans, potatoes- every thing cooking- ducks and chickens roasting- and the "Sars" made out of green peaches stewing

We have been subjected to such incessant annoyance day after day that Charles has been constantly traveling from camp to camp and recounting in the ears of first one officer and then another the history of our wrongs and perils but to no purpose, one would not protect rebel property and another would not, and this morning to our utter amasement a Capt Edwards came with three men, I think from some Massachusetts regiment, camped at "Bush Hill" and placed them at the garden gate. He came in and introduced himself to Lizzie. He was very kind and polite indeed in his manner

Told her to make the men do any thing or every thing she wished, and if they transgressed to report to him and he certainly would have them punished

I was not visible, but was making my observations through the up stairs window-blinds. Capt. Edwards after making many kind wishes and hoping we might not again be molested by the soldiers made his adieus and departedas soon as he could get behind the house, out of her sight (but I could see and hear distinctly all he said) he called the men up and told them as soon as he was gone to go all over the place and take any and every thing they chose, and to go through and through the house, and to take and do just whatever they pleased and he would bear them harmless. Then he went off, and I flew to Lizzie and told her all I had heard him say to the men, and O I cannot tell the state of terror we were in, we looked forward to the nights coming on with perfect horror.

And all day long we were thinking, and planning, and arranging how we could best lock, bolt, bar and barracade ourselves up for the night.

We determined not to think of going to bed that night but to sit up already dressed to receive them when they came. We told all the servants what Capt-Edwards had said to the men. They seemed perfectly shocked and terrified at the story I told them. We begged them not to go to bed but to sit up and watch with us, and try to protect us all they could.

The guards walked about the garden and looked at and admired the flowers, and amused themselves in various ways, talking and laughing together, reading and singing, and to all appearance seemed to be quite respectable men

At supper time Milly (our chamber maid) was sent out with a waiter on which was fixed a very bountiful and nice supper, we made it particularly so hoping to propitiate them. But we have always fed the guards well and they have always expressed themselves as highly pleased with their fare here. Milly came back highly pleased with them, said they were civil well mannered men, spoke very politely to her and thanked her, and sent their thanks to us for sending them such a nice supper, and she did not believe they would do us any harm Nevertheless we determined not to go to bed

About 9 oclock there was a very gentle tap at the front door we both started up. O my goodness what is to be done! I clasped both hands about my throat, my heart gave such a bound I thought it would jump out.

Was it safe—who would open the door, both stood still for a mement uncertain what to do then both ventured into the hall. The man could see us through the glass in the door and no doubt saw how frightened we looked and he said in a very soft subdued tone, "Don't be frightened ladies." Then we opened the door. It was one of the guards. He said, "I hope I have not disturbed or alarmed you ladies, but I thought it best before you retired to come and say to you if you hear any noise, or firing in the night not to be scared, but just keep perfectly quiet, and we will protect you One of the men from camp has just run over to tell us there is a conspiracy among some of the officers and men to rob you of your bee hives to-night. Capt Edwards, the officer who placed us here has made an agreement with several of the men to come over here to-night and carry off all your hives. And we have determined if they do attempt it to shoot, some body may be killed, But you keep quiet and we will see that no harm happens to you, Capt Edwards is a mean, low, treacherous, deceitful wretch, and the men do despise him, and they swear if he does come here to-night they will kill him if they can. But don't you fear." Then he told us just exactly what I heard pass between Capt E- and themselves in the morning- He said he had told the servants to keep close, there might be some shooting done and they had better not put themselves in the way of it. Then with more protestations of care and guardianship over us, he bade us good night, with the hope that we might sleep quietly and undisturbed

The night passed without any alarm, but "sleep did not visit our eyes nor slumber our eyelids" that night, we were too much excited and nervous, though we could not help feeling confidence in the guards they were so well behaved and respectful. In the morning an officer came to relieve the guard and they all came round to the front-door to take leave of us and to thank us for our kindness to them. It was a rare instance of civility, and we certainly did appreciate it

Now if they would all behave to us as if we were decent civilized human beings how differently we would feel towards them if they only behaved decently to us We two poor lone creatures, and entirely in their power too.

Cap Edwards did not make his appearance next day, nor for several days One morning Milly came rushing up stairs saying "Old Daddy Beehive," (as she called him) was down stairs and wanted to see Miss Lizzie L- got up, and as she was going out the door said, "Well if I don't give him a shot before he leaves here-" I flew after her and caught her by the arm saying Lizzie don't, pray don't say any thing to him you don't know what he may do to us. She laughed and went on, and I flew back to the window, my concealed batteries, that I might at least see the last of her, when her head came off- Capt Edwards was standing in the porch all smiles, all bows, and politeness. He refused to come in as his time was limited, said he had stopped for a moment to inquire if we were both well, and how we were getting along, and if we were molested by the soldiers now. He stood and talked a few moments and when about to take his leave he remarked "By the by, have you any honey to spare."

No she said, she was sorry to say she had not, and indeed she was very near having neither honey or bees "Ah! indeed why how was that" She replied, an officer in one of the near camps had made a plot with some of the men to come at night and rob us of all our hives.-I never in all my life saw any one so utterly taken a-back or one who so completely criminated himself, If I have been entirely ignorant of the circumstances I certainly could have placed my finger on him and said *"Thou art the man."* He never said another word, just whirled himself off the porch steps, and dashed through the garden, and out of the gate and out of sight like a flash. And that was the last we ever saw or heard of Capt Edwards.- It was the most ridiculous scene- Lizzie came up stairs laughing, and we both threw our selves on the bed and laughed and laughed I felt so relieved that her head did not come off in the skirmish.

This year we had a fine field of rye, as beautiful as I ever saw, as tall or taller than the ceder hedge, with very large finely filled heads although it had been considerably injured by the soldiers continually tramping through it. We succeeded in getting it harvested, and the shocks covered the ground. One evening a very black looking thunder storm was seen approaching, we were looking out noticing the movement of the clouds when all of a sudden the whole field of shocks just lifted up simultaneously and walked off. The pickets had pulled down the fence at every station and stacked the rails so as to form little huts and thatched them thoroughly with the rye. We never saved a single grain. In a few months it all came up along the road side as thick as thick could be.

When Charles is working in the flower garden he notifies us of the approach of any marauding parties by throwing a little gravel or clod gently against our window up stairs. The first time I heard it I could not imagine what it meant, but on going to the window, there he stood and indicated by a wave of his hand the point from which we might expect an attack, he dared not say a word, they were too near. To-day a party came for pears

They had been here some time ago when the fruit was very small, and knew exactly where the trees stand and all about them- no doubt have been watching them all the time, and to-day were so sure of their prey, before they reached the garden they all broke off into a trout around the hedge singing out in different tones "Coming for pears- Coming for pears Coming for pears-" But as good luck would have it, all had been gathered several days before- O I was delighted. But no doubt they compensated themselves with something else

The Confederates have recently made several raids on the railroad cars. At one time they were fired into. At another a party of them went to the house of one of our neighbors and got coal oil and matches and burned several bridges, all this kind of mischief I can see no earthly use in. It does no good to the cause, and is visited with ten fold severity on the poor unoffending citizens. The next thing was old Gen. Scott who is commander in chief issued an order that all the wood within ten miles of the rail road track both ways should be leveled with the ground, and to-day they commenced with it, and I believe ours was the very first they laid their vile hands upon. They commenced early in the morning and although we heard the axes going had no idea what it meant until the servants told us what it was. O I thought that day I should loose my senses, for besides the distress of mind at loosing all our beautiful woods, here, were hundreds and hundreds of these horrible savages with their bright gleaming axes in their hands committing all manner of depredations, and scattered all over the place. Through and through the flower garden, all round the house, numbers at the well, where we could not help seeing them, and hearing their indecent talk, such hooping, and yelling, and vile shocking blasphemy never pained my ears before. O What a wretched, wretched day! I almost felt a blessing that our dear old parents were in their graves, spared all this trouble and annoyance, safe from harm. But from many things they said to us I sometimes think they must have had some premonition of the trials and difficulties that was to beset our pathway in this life after they were gone. My poor old father had an idea that I had no capacity whatever for business, particularly for figures or calculations, and he never troubled me with any thing of the kind. In his old days Lizzie always attended to his business and did all his writing. But a day or two before his death, the very last day that speach remained to him, he raised himself up in his bed and said to me, (there was no one else in the room but myself with him) "I have taken a great deal of pains with the wood on this place, and I want you to take care of it too, and by no means let any one persuade you to have it cut, it is fine valuable piece of young timber, and has much hickory in it; and some day perhaps may answer you in good stead to fall back upon, when you are in great straits, and have nothing else- and O I beg of you not to allow it to be cut." He was so forcible and emphatic in his injunctions that it made an indelible impression on me never to be forgotten, and, O every stroke of the axe every tree as it fell smote on my heart and brought back to mind so vividly *that* day- that scene- and that death bed. I sat by the window hour after hour watching the trees fall, with eyes so filled with tears I could scarcely see. There was a fascination in it though ever so heart rending, to see every thing passing away from us.

Our melon patches were remarkably large and fine, and hundreds of melons ripe, and ripening, delightful, sweet and luscious. The soldiers soon discovered them and in the twinkling of an eye-, every one was seized upon, some loaded them selves and dashed off into the woods, while others broke them open and stood about in the fields, half bent gulping and gulping them down. O, I just wished a cannon ball could by some miraculous means fall in their midst. Long before night there was not a vestage of either melons or vines left, they utterly demolished every thing- I could not help crying to save my life, it was such a privation to be without fruit or melons all the summer, and in the midst of this demonical demonstration an officer made his appearance at the house to say he had come to withdraw the guards. We had five men as guards for several days, and we supposed they were some little restraint on the horrid savage wood cutters.

Capt Curtes walked in and introduced himself and told his busines He was a powerfull, hard looking man, as tall as a palm tree, strong and muscular in proportion, had the most ferocious looking teeth, when his mouth was shut they all stood outside, as ugly as ugly could be, with no more feeling or compassion for us than if we were made of wood or stone.

He could not help seeing how we were beset, and we told him too we were the only white people on the place, and how distressed we were. We begged, and implored, and entreated him to let the guards remain if only while they were cutting our woods but we might just as well have importuned a statue, so stern and forbiding, never relaxed a muscel, or soften down his ugliness by the slightest ghost of a smile. "No," he said, "it was rebel property and they did'ent come here to protect Rebel property" Nothing we could say to the contrary, as to the propertys belonging to Lizzie and myself had the slightest effect, except that he put on the most contemptious air and let us know decidedly that he knew we were lying, indeed he said he knew positively the man it belonged to was in the rebel army. These people are so given to falsifying themselves that they cannot understand how, where interest is concerned, there can be any truth in human tongue, and in spite of all Capt-Curtis walked off and took five guards along with him, to our perfect horror, for we did not know what might be done left at the mercy of these savage, plundering hords.

As soon as the guards were gone the axe men came pouring in ten to one, and we kept ourselves shut up as tightly as we could, windows and doors and every place,—crying—crying all day and went to bed crying.

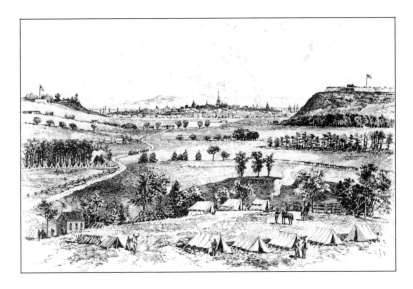

Camp of the 40th New York, from a sketch made in September, 1861*
Edwin J. Meeker, Fort Ward Museum Collection

The next day it was the same thing, and the next, and the next, and I don't know how long it continued the same way. They cut the trees and let them fall one on another they piled up so high that until the leaves withered you could not tell at a little distance the wood was cut at all.

This morning there was such a out cry- "Soldiers- Soldiers yankee dogs coming," and Milly calling out "Miss Annie better look out yankee dogs are coming" of course we rushed to the window but there was only one soldier visible, and he was working assiduously trying to mount the yard gate, he was without cap, gun belt or equipments of any kind, as soon as he managed to scramble to the top down he would tumble to the ground on the other side, and after wallowing and scuffling about in the dust and dirt for a while over the gate he would go again and down on the other side, the same manouver was gone through a number of times. I could not help laughing he was such a sight, his head and clothes all covered with dirt and sticks and straws. I never saw such a performance before and could not imagine what it ment. at last Charles came into the kitchen and they told him how the soldier was *carrying*

---

* The 40th New York established a camp near the Sharon Chapel Church on the Old Fairfax Road (present day Franconia Road) in the fall of 1861.

on "Why he said de fools' drunk dats whats de matter wid him." We told him to go down to the road and the first officer who came along to ask him please to come and take his drunken soldier away that the ladys were afraid of him In a short time two of the *braves* came dashing up one of them asked Lizzie very gruffly where the mans hat and equipments were. She told she knew nothing whatever of him until she saw him tumbling over the gate, first one side and then the other, and she wished he would take him away for we were afraid of him. They both jumped off horses then and flew at the creature and knocked him down, and cuffed and kicked him about just as if he had been a dog, then they made him stand up, they took some of the straps off their horses and tied him, and each took an end and off they started the man running between the two horses. Charles tore off after them to *see the fun* as he called it, when he came back he said the soldier would run and run until he would fall then the officers would stop a moment and whip him, off and off again as hard as they could go- O these horrid, hateful, brutal yankees! give them a little authority, and now they will Lord it over those who they know can not resist them.

September 29th 1861 Was another day never to be forgotten by us. It was bright, warm and delightful weather and every thing looked so flourishing and beautiful around us, and every thing so quiet but our quiet was soon to be disturbed in a frightful and unlooked for manner. My foot still continues very sore and painful so that I can move about little and on that account seldom encounter these savages unless violence is threatened then I fly to the *rescue* forgetting the foot and every thing else excepting, when I give it a violent knock against something in my course and leave a stream of blood behind me. This morning I was standing at an up stairs window making observations around when a party of officers came dashing up the avenue and dismounted at the garden gate. Feeling sure some thing dreadful was brewing for us I flew to my "Concealed Battery" at the top of the stair case, *to learn the worst at once*. They all marched two and two round the hedge then stopped suddenly for a moment or two and looked round and one of them re-marked, "What a pity- what a pity- that such a beautiful place as this should be camped over and destroyed." Then they continued their course their harness rattling on the gravels and echoing O so painfully on my brain.

Three or four of them came to the house while the balance sauntered about the garden and grounds, they measured the depth of the well, surveyed the house, and barn, sheds, pig-pens and took a general ob-servation of every thing. Those who came to the door asked for Miss

Frobel and when Lizzie made her appearance one of them stepped forward and said, "Madam we have come to let you know that Gen. Sedgwick with his brigade is about to occupy this place She had not heard the talk or seen the manouvers out side and the announcement came upon her so suddenly and with such a shock that without a word she put her hands over her face and screamed while the tears streamed through her fingers, when she had regained her breath sufficiently to speak she cried out "O don't, for mercy sake, for pity sake,pray don't put all those horrid soldiers on this place to destroy us. We are only two sisters living here by ourselves, with no one to protect us, and what is to become of us if the place is to be camped over" (she said she heard me scream at the same time, but I was utterly unaware of it) One of the men laughed- what wretches!- they seem to be *hardened, utterly devoid of any feeling of humanity.* He said "O it was a military necessity" that they could not help and the best thing for us to do would be to take house in town and move there, they would offer us every facility in moving we should have the government wagons to move us and Gen. Sedgwick wanted our house for Headquarters."

She said as to renting a house we have no means to do it, this was the only home we had and that here we must and would stay.

They said "*as to any losses we might sustain by the army the government would amply remunerate us for every thing of that sort*" and so they took their departure. But O what two miserable creatures they left behind them. No tongue can tell, no pen describe the wretchedness of that day, we crept about forlorn and heart-stricken and took leave of every thing about us- every thing- every *tree* and *flower* and *shrub* hallowed and endeared to us by the touch and care of our dear departed parents hands-

We knew from the apprearace of other places that have been occupied by the military what ours certainly is doomed to become what wrecks they make of every house and place, even there in town look as if inhabited by free-negroes- *wherever the yankees go they are sure to leave the free-negro mark behind them.*

These horrid people seem to select the most beautiful and highly cultivated places to fix their camps upon, and as soon as they have completely demolished it they move to another. But most of their camping grounds have been where the owners have gone off and deserted them. But even that does not seem so bad- but to come and place themselves down here where they know there are only two unprotected helpless women, it does seem too hard, to expose us to the ravages these mercyless savages. Father of mercy what is to become of us! I am so tired so wearied out, O if I could only fly away and be at rest!

Late in the afternoon they began to pour in, one regiment fixed themselves just in front of the house, and then such a din, officers flying on horses and giving their orders, wagons located with plunder thundering over the rough ground, men whooping, and yelling, hammering, and banging and making all manner of noises, axes going—hundreds cutting our wood and hauling it in to make camp fires one wagon load for each fire. I think we counted about 20 fires for the first row of tents next our house- after dark I opened the front door and such an *Inferno*- never did I behold I called Lizzie to look but one glance was enough, we turned away and shut the door in disgust

all our barn and stables and sheds filled with men and horses and our stock turned out, and O such a night lights glancing about men trampling and talking, horses kicking and neighing, all the machinery in the barn seemed to be in motion such as cornshellers, wheat fans, and every thing of the kind going-going all night long, who could sleep?

Sep 30 Very little sleep visited our eye-lids last night. The noise and confusion, and the excitement of yesterday dispelled (as I was sure it would) all calm feelings of rest and sleep. The first thing this morning was the confused sounds from the camp, the drums thundering and fifes whistling. and then the everlasting drawing of water, they seem to depend entirely on our well which is under our room window for water, and O it is such a never ceaseing nuicence, and the kitchen filled with horrid soldiers the servants, cannot attend to their business, cannot move a turn for them, and we never think of going in, there even to give an order, what is to become of us we do not know, we are just prisoners in our own house. Soon after breakfast Mr. Fowle came in, said he had been riding through the camps and visiting the officers and thought he would call in to see how we were getting along and also to inquire if we would be willing to board one of the officers and his wife. He strongly advised our doing so said it would be both a help and protection to us. He said this young officer seemed to be a very clever young man indeed, was a graduate of West Point was recently married, and one of Gen- Sedgwick staff officers, and altogether he thought it greatly to our advantage to have them in the house with us,and so it was agreed that they should come.

But O, with what a sinking of heart was the consent given. How should we behave to them, how talk to them- how have them at our table as boon companions- O my father! another sleepless night. We talked it over and over all night long.

Oct 1st 1861. To-day Lt. Beaumont called to say he was the officer who Mr. Fowle engaged board for yesterday and to make all the final arrangements. I did not see him but L. told me she was very much preposessed in his favour- was pleased with his manners and with the interview altogether. He seemed very young, so much so that she could hardly believe he was a married man

The next day or the day after the Beaumonts made their appearance pack and baggage, late in the evening when we were sitting on the porch they stepped in and introduced themselves, made their congress seated themselves with us for a few minutes and talked very pleasantly and affalby, and then were shown to their room to arrange their belongings and prepare for tea- we have dreaded *so* their advent and now that they have come I feel perfectly prostrated- I just would like to steal out of the way, and hide myself in my den for ever and ever

But the next day they rendered themselves still more agreeable, were kind and polite and we soon found they were of entirely different stamp from any of that fraternity that we had ever encountered before He told us he was at West Point with Fitz. Lee and several other Southerners that we either knew or knew who they were, and we discovered from his conversation and manners how much he admired the Southern boys for he had picked up many little sayings and doings that we knew did not belong to yankee land. He was of French parentage as might be known by his name Eugene Beauharnos Beaumont and she—Mrs. Beaumont was a perfect lady, cultivated and refined She had lived she told us several years in Virginia in the neighborhood of Charlestown W.V. both of them were from Wilkes Barre Pa- They lived with us between four and five months and in that time we never had the slightest fault with them: they treated us like older sisters so very kind and considerate and so afraid of saying or doing any thing that might- offend or wound our feelings. I believe they would have done any thing on earth to benefit or comfort us that it was possible for them to do. and I often regret being so cold and distant in my manner to them. But I could not help it- I knew what they had come down here for. They were strangers to us and we were so afraid of them. we feared treachery in every word and act. We never told them a word of our brothers, but they found out some way that we had a brother and that he was stationed at one of the Potomac batteries, I suppose the negroes informed them, But they never mentioned David I don't think they could ever have of him. They always said your brother as if they thought we had but one, and of another sister they never heard until long long after the war was over But the goodness of the Beaumonts the whole time they were with us was untiring and *we formed an at-*

*tachment and friendship for them which I hope and believe will last as
long as time endures*

Cesar one of our negro men has a wife living some three or four
miles away where he goes every Saturday evening. Four or five weeks
ago he went off and when Monday came did not put in an appearance
as was usual and as time passed on we supposed he was either sick,
or had deserted to the enemy, or which was most probable, had ranged
himself with the "Contrabands" as the yankees term all the run-away
negroes now-adays We did not disturb ourselves at all about him but a
few days ago he made his appearance among us as usual. His account
of himself is that a party of Confederates captured him at his wife's home
and took him off and he has been there ever since cooking for them.
something caused them to move away and they told him he could go
back to his mistress. How much of this story is founded on facts I do
not know, but am very much inclined to think all this time has not been
wasted on the poor *Confeds*, his friends the yanks require too much
waiting on, and his own business must have some little of the time

No doubt he found out that Gen- Sedgwick's brigade had moved
from that side of Cameron run over on this place, and concluded it was
best, more profitable, to follow, there was something to be gained by it,
and *boarding* at home would be decidedly *cheaper* than any where else.
I very much suspect "There is something rotton in the state of Denmark."

The yankees are constantly harrowing up my feelings by telling us
in what a state of destitution and starvation, "those *Rebel Devils* are"
and the first opportunity I could get I asked Cesar if he got enough to
eat while with them, he looked at one in utter amazement with his mouth
open and I had to repeat my question and explain before he seemed
fully to comprehend, then he answered "*Why Miss Annie*, they have got
every thing they need in the way of provisions, beef and bacon, and as
good as I'de wish to taste and plenty of it," then he began to enumerate,
sugar, coffee, flower etc etc It was the first *crumb* of comfort I have had
in regard to them since yankee domination here. Cesar is one of the
smartest, most really intelligent black African negroes I ever saw and
talks like a white man, smart at every thing, but *book learning*, but at
that he never succeeded, never could learn to read, though so extremely
anxious to do so. Ever since I could remember he carried Comley's
spelling book in his bosom, and manys the time when a little child have
I been stopped while at play in the garden with "please Miss Annie give
me a lesson." Then down on his knees behind a rose bush, out of sight
of the dining room windows, then out with *John Conely* and I stood by
to "*give him a lesson*," when he ought to have been at his work, He

never got beyond spelling words of two or three syllables though every member of the white family have *delved* trying to teach him from dear Mama down to the very youngest child, but without success.

Headquarters of General Sedgwick on the Leesburg Turnpike
Edwin J. Meeker, Courtesy of American Heritage Picture Collection from The American Heritage Century Collection

The tents are now ranged in regular rows through the apple orchard, with regular streets between paved with stones, and the cook houses with great fires blazing, at the roots of the trees, and the horses and mules tied to the apple trees have skinned them as far as they could reach, of course they are all destroyed. We had several hundred fine trees all in full bearing

Ah home! What a grievous sight, to see all our belongings torn from us while we look on passive, unable to lift a finger to prevent it.

The first thing after rising in the morning is to walk to the windows and look abroad to see what discoveries I can make, and the sight that met my view this morning perfectly took away my breath and made my knees tremble while I watched it- I had forgotten—totally forgotten in my own trouble Cousin Mary Foote's boxes of elegant old Canton China and beautiful cut glass that I had stowed away in our corn house weeks before for safe keeping, believing it perfectly safe there, no one would ever dream of finding such articles in such an unheard of *China closet*-and there before my sight was the corn house doors wide open—the yard full of soldiers, and Charles portioning out corn to each one in turn-O I thought what shall I do if these wretches take it into their hands to brake up all that valuable China and glass as I have heard of their doing at other placesIt will kill her- It will surely be the death of her- But to my unspeakable relief and comfort each one marched off with his corn as soon as received. They did not seem to see the boxes, or if they did determined to reserve the pleasure of searching them to some more convenient time. In the early days of the occupation of Alex- by the yankees- we Lizzie and myself rode in to see cousin Mary and found her in the most terrible state of alarm and distress I might say in a state of frenzy- She cried, and rung her hands and cried, and walked up and down the floor with her hands clasped over the top of her head. It was some time before she could command herself sufficiently to tell what was the matter. At last she gasped out, "Old Jim Lane is coming to take possession here with hundreds and thousands of his mad desperadoes from the far west, and then what is to become of us all it will be far worse they tell me than when *these people* first came (poor Lady Mary she never used vituperative language never, relieved her mind as I did by calling them yankees—and worse much worse, but always said, "*these people*" which really seemed to me to express more contempt than any thing bad I could say of them) When they dashed in the doors of stores, Hotels—and even private residences and dragged out, and took away every thing they chose. They broke open the Depots and seized all the baggage- broke open all the trunks, and clothes lady's clothes distributed all round the streets, and soldiers marched about with their underwear stretched on their bayonets, and hoisted over their shoulders. They sold handsome silk dresses to the negro women for a cake of corn bread— lace mantles for a pie—and O they would take her house away from her, and turn her into the street, and then- O what was to become of her-" Then another paroxysm of sobs and tears- O it was a pitiable sight to see such an old person in such a disturbed state of mind and I could not think how I could relieve, or help her in any way. at last I said Cousin Mary if you will trust me to do it I will pack up some of your most valuable things and take them out to our house. I do not know whether they will be any safer there than where they are, we can try it, our house has never yet been searched by these horrid creatures though we have had some hard fights to prevent it, and at any time if we find there is any fear of their safety with us, we will send them back. O just the proposal seemed to lift a weight off her mind, her tears dried up, and I took off my bonnet, and Lizzie turned her face homeward and sorrowful face it was, at the thought of leaving me behind—and then for packing- for several days I packed and packed, and carried things from one room to another until I was perfectly completely broken down, could hardly get along. Then the *silver question* arose- what was to be done with that? She had a great deal of beautiful and massive silver, and I knew if I brought it home the negroes would betray it and the yankees would be certain to take it away from us, for they had been doing that very thing all over the country diving into wells, and every sort of place and getting peoples silver where they had hidden it in most impossible places. We knew there was no safety in putting it in one of the banks. We talked it over for a long time at last she said "there is a large receptical in the cellar under this heater for the ashes that falls through it has been bricked up, but a few days ago I had quite a large opening made and the place all cleaned out, how will that do, or how would I get it bricked up again without its being known" O I replied that is the very place, and as to bricking it up again I can do that very easily if I can get a little sand and lime. She remembered there was plenty in the sheet where some men had been at work so we sent and got all the requisite material, then what was to be done with the two servant women, but she managed to find some excuse to send them on different errands that would keep them away sufficiently long to give me ample time to accomplish all I had to do. Then I went to work and in a china plate with a knife I mixed the mortar. I wrapped up every piece nicely and securely and then I started on my dark and down-ward journey with a heavy gasket of silver in one hand, and a lighted lamp in the other. Just as I had reached the cellar steps and was about to decend she said you must be careful for you have two wells to pass over. I looked back and gasped- *Wells* (for if there is any thing on earth I have a horror of it is a well—and in a deep dark cellar-) But I said they are covered? yes- they have some planks over them but they have not been attended to for a long time and I am afraid the planks may be very rotton- O I felt for a moment I would have to give it up- then no—not for my foolish fears would I disturb her mind any more- and off I dashed down the steps at the first door I stoped and peered in for a moment, I could see neither well nor planks or any thing else, then I ventured in a few steps holding the lamp as near the floor as possible,- and there was the horrible well just before me, not covered, only two or three planks thrown across the middle of it, I stoped, drew in a long inspiration feeling I suppose it would lessen the weight—and over I skipped to the other side, my feet seemed scarcely to touch the planks- and then only to think, another well- It was impossible to avoid them the sides had fallen in looking like an enormous pit, the "Black hole of Calcutta," or any other horrible place, and these awful places I had to traverse at least one dozen times, back and forth before I could collect together all the articles and material I had to work with.

Then I packed in every thing as carefully as possible I worked with a will, and covered with and stuffed in newspapers and made all secure, then with the knife I spread on the mortar and placed the bricks—and spread the morter and placed the bricks until the breach was filled up. Then I took *a little* of the mould and coal dust from the floor and spread it over the morter between the bricks to keep it from looking new, then I took the knife and smoothed it all over nicely, then I passed the lamp all over to see it was all satisfactory and marked it "O K" and O with what a thankful heart did I skip over the last swaying plank and gain in the upper air.

I think it was the very next day after seeing the soldiers at the corn house that Mrs. Foote and Miss Addams made a most unexpected appearance at the door, much to our delight for we thought there was no such thing as any of our friends reaching us, of course we told her the jeopardy her boxes are in, and promised to send them back to her the next day, which we did. She said some one had told her that tents were observed out in this direction which made her feel very uneasy about us indeed, afterwards she met a gentleman friend in the street who said he did believe our place was occupied by troops, that himself with several others had been spying, and spying from the highest points they could reach, and all they could make out was camps on this place, if not they were very near, and as soon as she could obtain a pass and conveyance she hastened out to see after us and if she could help us, or do any thing for us.

There is a guard stationed all the time at our garden gate, but she never said a word to him but pushed right through- and here she was, and we were more than glad to see them. We introduced our inmates Lt. and Mrs. Beaumont—who promised her to do every thing in their power for us and to take good care of us. They took a walk towards the barn to see what was going on outside, and were shocked to find what a thorough work of demolition had been carried on in such a short-time, all the fences and gates all gone, the fields thrown open and horses and wagons and roads through and through every place. The officers had sent us word yesterday that rifle pits were to be dug through the fields and we had better secure what we could of the crops. Our men were out trying to secure some of the potatoes and turnips to serve us through the winter, of course the soldiers were there to carry them off as soon as taken out of the ground. Mrs Foote said to one of them "I suppose you know you are taking private property." He looked at her as if he would like to kill her and answered in the most impudent surly manner "I am taking them for the Coluse," and went on with his work. I suppose this year we have not made less than three hundred bushels of potatoes, and as many of turnips, 300 bushels of rye, 200 barrels of corn, 3 or 4000 heads of cabbage, and vegetables and fruit out of number of all kinds, poultry by the hundreds I don't know how many, all kinds of fine stock— every thing in abundance needed on a farm, and now four regiments will soon sweep off and demolish every *thing* and now we thought it best to send away all our house hold goods that we could possibly do without. Several feather beds, all the carpets but the one in our own room, all the house linen, blankets, quilts—almost every thing out of the parlour leaving the poor old room looking forlorn. When Col. Staples of 3rd Maine regiment called to ask if we would let him have a room. He expects to be married shortly and wanted accomodations for his bride. Lizzie told him she would consult with her sister and let him know the next day. So we talked it all over and with many sighs and tears concluded to let them have our parlour. But she told Col. Staples he would have to find wood for his fires as they had nearly consumed our whole woods, and it was hard work for us to find enough to burn in our own room. He said he only wanted a room with a fire, their meals they would take in their tent. After a while several *ladys* and *gentlemen* came to take a look at the room, they found it bare and comfortless looking enough the old Broadwood piano on one side and a chair or two on the other no carpet, but the floor well waxed and dry rubbed looking almost as bright as a mirror. They all stood at the door and peeped in, seemed to be afraid to venture in- They exclaimed, and marveled over the wonderful looking floor asked a thousand questions, stooped and felt it, rubbed their hands over it, "They had never seen any thing like it before."

When Mrs. Staples took possession we found her a thoroughly pre- sumptious exacting yankee woman who wanted as much, and more waiting upon than if she had been used to it all her life. In the morning as soon as the Col. left, in the room a soldier comes with an arm full of wood and made up her fire, and laughs and talks with her while she commences her toilet after the fire is well under way Rose (one of our house servants, makes her appearance and the soldier departs- then Mrs. S. must have cold water, and warm water and hot water, and towel after towel, soap—every sort of thing until Roase's patience is entirely exhausted and she bounces out of the room and says, loud enough for Mrs. Staples to hear her, deese here yankee women wants more wait'en on en white people does" One morning soon after she took up her quarters here, she came dashing out into the hall in a perfect fury, and happening to meet Lizzie addressed her in the most insulting, impertinent manner, "I would like to know why my room is not attended to before this hour in the morning." Lizzie drew herself up and in a very dignified manner said, "good morning Mrs. Staples, I hope you are well this morning. I understood from Roase it was your direction to her that your room was not to be touched until after your return from camp- I am very glad you spoke to me about it I will give her directions hereafter to do it at any hour you wish it done." She was standing at the dining room door at the time and throwing it open said, "we are just going to breakfast, will you walk in and take breakfast with us." Mrs. Staples *declined.* But I never saw any one so completely taken down. Poor Mrs. Beaumont was witness to the whole scene, and after Mrs. S. had flown out of the front door, said in the most excited manner, "O I was frightened to death I thought you were going to have a regular *set-too* with that woman." "O no Mrs. Beaumont," Lizzie replied I would never demean myself by having a scene with such a person as Mrs. Staples.

a few days after this Mrs. Staples was taken violently ill, or imagined herself so, the Doctor was sent for, and one of the hospital nurses made her way in here, Mrs Sampson by name and she was another yankee upstart as impudent and audacious as these camp followers can be, she ordered this thing, and called for the other thing. and Lizzie heard her in a very loud key order Rose to go and get a carpet and put it down on Mrs Staples floor. Roase told her there was not a carpet in the house but the one Miss Lizzie had on her own room floor. Then she protested "she would search the house and drag up any carpet she could find and put it on Mrs Staples' floor. Mrs Staples should have a carpet." Roase was too indignant- she threw up her head and walked out of the room banging the door after her and saying "Well Mrs. yank- you may wait on yourself now for I won't put my foot in that room again while you are on the place." Soon after hearing of Mrs Staple's illness Lizzie presented herself at the door, to ask what was the matter and if she was better, and if she could do any thing for her, Mrs Sampson received her, very suavely, introduced herself, answered all the questions offered her a seat and entered into a very amicable conversation said she was living at Claremont and attending to the sick, said she believed it had been the residence of Com- Forrest. She talked of the beauty of the place, and how elegant every thing was when she first went there- and how the officers had appropriated and sent to the north every thing they could find, and how she had gone into Mrs. Worley's room and found every thing so nice and beautiful just as she had been taken out of it, and what a number of letters she had found from Douglas to his mother while he was at college, and such beautiful letters she had never seen before. She said she had secured a member of Mrs. Worley's dresses and other clothes and would keep them until the war was over and then would return them to Mrs Forrest. L. said she felt very doubtful of them ever being returned. indeed she knew they never would and she said to Miss Sampson, "Mrs. Forrest is a very particular and dear friend of mine, and I am sure she would much prefer my having the care of them to any one else- and I think I am the one to have them, and if you will send them to me I will take care of them and give them to her myself when she comes back." But she did not promise neither did she send them, and we never saw Mrs Sampson again, she disappeared that evening and never showed herself here again

But we took care to obtain her address from one of the Maine men who lived in the same town with her, and gave it to Mrs Forrest the first time we saw her after her return who immediately wrote to Mrs Sampson and asked that the things might be returned. and in reply she positively and emphatically denied ever having seen or heard of any such things, though she acknowledged having lived at Clermont, but when she got there the house and every place was denuded of every article of furniture or any thing else

a few evenings after Mrs Staples' illness several of the officers were here taking tea with Lt and Mrs Beaumont, and Lizzie gave an account of the illness and Mrs Sampsons professional visit, and the interview she had with her and the conversation they had together, and the request she had made of her. They looked at each other and laughed, and one of them said Mrs S- was kind indeed, had been over here to nurse him when he was sick, and was *much* scandalized that an officer should have to take his medicine out of a pewter spoon, "indeed he should have a silver spoon she would see that he had a silver spoon," and the next time she came she brought a *Silver Spoon*. another one said, "did she though- no doubt she had stolen it out of some ladys house," and they all laughed heartily, thinking it a fine joke and one that every one of them had perpetrated whenever they had the opportunity. another of the officers said, "Mrs Staples was very sick, yes they said these yankee girls— these *Down Easters* estimated their ritches by the number of achres of Cod fish their fathers can count."

Charles always gives us notice of what is going on, but for him, we would be entirely ignorant of everything, but in a very quiet way and in a subdued low of voice, sometimes with his face turned entirely away. This morning he said "Mars Bushard's guns is been a lumbearing down the river all the mornin, but we had not heard them, he exclaimed" Cors Miss Lizzie da jes thundered las night down de river and da kep it up I do believe the hole night I hears dem consantly, mose every day, away ever since, way yander in the summer- dar-dar-da goes again, you hears em now don't you." We flew up stairs and raised the windows next the river just high enough to admit the sound and down on our knees we listened and sure enough, "Mars Bushe's guns wuz a lumbering." We clapped our hands and cheered him on, hurray Bush, hurray give it to them with a will, you don't know they are persecuting your poor sisters who they have here shut up entirely in their power. The next day or the day after when Charles got home from town and saw Lizzie he looked at her very significantly and jerked his head a little to one side which is his way when he has a secret and important communication to make and as soon as he had an opportunity he said "dars a heap of vessels comin up the river, knocked all to pieces you can see dat as da goes along and da ses da are filled with dead men, dars been a fight some where, da say Mars Bushard's guns done it but I dun no." Charles has learned in some way but how he got his information I *dun no* that Bushrod is at Cock Pit Point. It is the nearest Confederate battery on the Potomac, the next one to Mt Vernon- Great preparations are makeing now for Sedgwick's brigade to winter on this place, tents are giving way to log houses, we see them springing up every day, in the four fields occupied by the four regiments Col- Ward of the 28 has quite an extensive mansion with several rooms in it. He has also helped himself largely to our wood for his own individual use, long ricks and stacks are piled up as high as his house which is just in front of ours. I looked out this morning and saw it and asked what in the world is that immense quantity of wood corded up there for, some one must surely be going into the business with such an extensive wood yard, O yes they said "Col Ward had supplied himself generously for his winter's use, and all that is Hickory, he will use no other kind of wood."

They just talked as if it was some thing to boast of. O I did feel too indignant when we are hardly allowed fire enough to keep us from perishing. I said I suppose you are aware that all that wood you are making such free use of building houses, forts, block houses, camp fires, and such extensive- wood yards belongs to Lizzie and myself- "O well," they said "if you will apply to Cap. Owen's the brigade quartermaster he will pay you for it," and we did apply to him, but never a cent did we get. His reply was, If you will have the wood cut and corded I will pay for it by the cord- That answer did make me too disdainfully angry. I felt it was such a contemptible subterfuge. He knew he was proposing an utter impossibility. How were we two ladies shut up here surrounded by camps, and soldiers, and pickets to do such a work as that- besides, had they not already used up hundreds of cords No doubt he was lawyer enough to know how to put all the money for it into his own pocket

Mrs Staples did not remaining long an inmate of ours. Only until a *spacious mansion* could be erected for her out of our logs. It was on Mr Fowle's side of the road however. She went off without saying "goodbye or nothing" But we gladly closed our doors after her on such easy terms All the camps now seem to be filled with women, roveing about and flaunting their bright dazzling Balmorals to the admiring gaze of the soldiers. They are the first I have ever seen of that style of dress

This morning Cap. Owens called to ask if we would take his mother for a week, which was agreed to, and she came and spent Christmas week here. We found her a very agreeable person indeed, ladylike, kind and motherly, she seemed to take to us at once, and she was so pretty. From New York city, was unlike any yankee woman we had ever met with before- nothing like presumption, no bitterness to the South if she felt any she never expressed it. We liked her son Fred- too very much, an Ensign in Col Ward's regiment. He was here very often while his mother staid, he was scarcely any thing more than a boy, but was pleasant and genial in his manners, and we liked him. While Mrs Owen staid, on Christmas night Mrs Beaumont had a little reception for her friends among the officers. We fixed up every thing very nicely for her, had cake jellies egg nog, and every thing that was nice and good- quite a room full of officers. Gen. Sedgwick was expected but at the eleventh hour sent his excuses, I suppose he thought it too much like fraternizing with *Secesh* for him to put in his appearance. While the officers were enjoying themselves and supping their egg nog one of them had the bad taste to remark "Those poor rebel devils! Only to think while we are here in their houses enjoying the very fat of the land, they are away off, *starving*, they that have a right to be here, afraid to show their noses at their own homes." I was so mad I just wished the egg nog would strangle him. One of them got so boozy I made him drink success to Gen. Beauregard and say God help him. Some of the others who heard him very soon hustled him out of the room and made him go home. The evenings before Mrs Owens left, she was taken very sick- violently ill we thought her. We did everything in the world we could think of for her, rubbed, poulticed and doctored her in every way until ten or eleven oclock the next day. In the afternoon she was well enough to get up and dress, and go to Gen Sedwick's headquarters to make a farewell visit. She attributed it altogether to our good nursing. "O" she said "you have been so good to me. So different from any thing I expected to find at the South, and every thing here goes on so quietly, no noise, no blustering or ordering about of the servants-everything goes on so comfortable and the servants all look so contented and happy- Poor Mrs Owens! I think she must have expected to see a poor nigger's head knocked off at every turn or move they made But "she never heard an order given while she was in this house." She was a most agreeable inmate and we took leave of her with reluctance, although she had promised to come to see us when the war was over- it was a final leave taking how ever we are never to see her again in this world. Yesterday morning L. was in town and learned there was some move among the Confederates about Fairfax Court house. The people were much excited. But they did not know for certain what was going on excepting that there had certainly been a move this way, as far down as "Mt. Hebron." She whispered all she had heard into my ear but of course we never said a word. all went on here as usual until about twelve or one oclock at night when a slight rap at the front door awoke me, I was up in a moment and at my post. Lt. B-'s room is down stairs and of course we left him to answer it. I listened with the utmost attention- but could make out nothing but the whispering and the chattering of teeth for they seemed frightened to death. Then they all rushed out in the greatest haste, and after a while they came back and shut themselves up in the dining room- and more whispering—and chattering of teeth, and from that time 'til morning they were in and out, in and out all the time

They did not beat the *long roll*, I suppose for fear of being heard by the *Rebels*. I was sorry for I wanted to hear it. But we heard the men going through the camps calling out at every ten- "Turn out- Turn out-" Every thing was done as quietly as possible. I went back to bed hopeing there would be an attack- but, if there had been, dear knows what would have become of us. As soon as it was light enough we saw the road was thronged with troops, artillery, cavelry, infantry, passing passing-passing- for about two hours- "an artillery reconnaissance," they called it

Then there was such a weeping, and wailing, and solemn leave taking between the officers and *their ladys*, and as soon as they were gone the *Fair ones* betook themselves, to bed again disolved in tears to spend the time until their return, or their mangled remains were brought back to them. I told them they were pretty soldier's wives, to brake down so at the very first tap of the drum that called their *gallants* to go forth to meet the foe

They are building an immense Theatre in Col. Ward's camp, just in front of our door, large enough they say to seat two or three thousand persons

For the past two or three weeks, they have been making desperate efforts to get it finished in time to have the first performance at Christmas but did not succeed- One of the officers for some time past has been very persistant in his invitations to me to ride on horse-back with him. I have made every excuse that my brain could invent, all of which he has found means to obviate, and at dinner to-day he said, "we have a beautiful lady's horse at headquarters which will exactly suit you to ride, I will bring him up this evening, the weather is delightful and we will have a nice long ride." I was put to my trumps what other excuse to make, and on the spur of the moment, without any meaning or design whatever I said O yes, and I will take you to Fairfax Courthouse and introduce you to Gen Beauregard—I never saw such a blank look on any ones face- He never said another word—but as soon as the dinner was over he *cleared out*, and from that day to this never mentioned *Horse-back* to me again Not for the world would I have been caught riding with one of them. Often and over they have offered us the use of their ambulances, but I should consider myself forever disgraced by getting into one of them- a long time after I saw from the news papers that several times Federal officers by their gallantries to the F.F.U. have been betrayed into the hands of the enemy But such a thought never for a moment entered my mind- indeed I would not have done it if I could. We know nothing in the world about the Confederate army where they are, or what doing, or even the names of the more prominent of the officers- We had never heard the name of Beaureguard until the yankees informed us he with his army was at Fairfax courthouse. Of Gen Lee we have never heard a word although he went from this vicinity and of our own dear boys- not a word- not a line from them- where are they- where are they doing- God keep them safe under the shadow of thy wing! although we are here shut up, two poor helpless women without the means of doing any thing for ourselves, within miles and miles of picket lines, surrounded by soldiers, and camp, and quartered up to the very doors. These yankees seem to believe we have constant communication with the Confederate army- For some time past we have observed that the guards about the house have been doubled and one is placed just at the kitchen door, where there has never been one before, we forbore asking any questions knowing we would get no satisfactory answer

This morning Lt. B. asked me "how often does your brother come home, I heard him making the greatest noise last night plodding up stairs." I looked at him in surprise. I could not imagine what he was talking about. He had to explain. It appears the negroes have reported it all among the soldiers that Bushrod comes home every night riding on a white horse- and was absurd in them to pretend to believe it, but it explains the double guards. The plodding up and down stairs is the negroes tramping up and down the kitchen stairs with their plunder

I do believe they are up all night long now making pies and traficking with the soldiers. They cook for them, and wash, bake pies, cakes, biscuits, every sort of cookery imaginable. They must be making thousands of dollars (the negroes I mean) Charles told me the two first months that Sedgwick's brigade was on this place two wagon loads of gold and silver was brought into our orchard to pay off the men, and gold was as plentiful as chips at the wood pile, little squads of men could be seen about any where pitching 20 $ gold pieces, but now it is all paper money. The first I saw of the crisp new notes, bright green on one side I said to the man who had it "O these are your *Government green backs* are they? He replied "What is *this* you call them- But I knew with the avidity he caught at it- I had named them, and the next thing the N. Y. papers said the Southerners called the new money *Government Greenbacks*, and they were Government Greenbacks from that day to this all over the country. We seldom go out of the house now the roads and woods and every part of the country is so filled with the horrible vagabond soldiers prowling and skulking about that we are afraid to go, but this evening we made bold to venture it and got as far as Mr. Fairfax's, we found them all well and delighted to see us, and worlds to talk about and tell us that we had never heard before, of the vile enormities committed on the people around by the beastly yankees. Just as we were comeing away Mrs. Dawsy, a very old lady Mrs. Fairfax's mother who is very fanciful about her eating, as all old people are said, "have you any salt fish, last year's fish, do pray if you have send me some." we told her we had plenty of nice shad and would be only too glad to send her some. "O" she said "I am so hungry for fish and I can't eat what they bring from market, I know they have been so many months fattening on the dead yankees in the river. I repeated "dead yankees in the river," how did they get there. "Why," she said have you never heard of the battle of Ball's Bluff fought as far back as last May, where our boys drove the yankees into the Potomac by hundreds and thousands and nearly drowned the whole army, and the tide has been throwing them up on the banks and they have been fishing out the dead men ever since, almost as far down as the mouth of the river.- And this was the first we had heard of the battle of Ball's Bluff- Then she told us of how the pickets on either side Federal and Confederate meeting along the lines and making friends with each other, playing cards together, and trading rations, tobacco for coffee and sugar

Two sets hollowed to each other across a stream near Fredericksburg

"Hollow *Reb* can you play bluff, yes yank I can play Ball's Bluff." She seemed to think that was too funny, and so delighted she had so much to tell us.

Gen- Sedgwick was so kind as to send us word if we wished a pass to go to Fredricksburg and visit our brother he would give us one. *We appreciated the kindness*, we had long ago been apprized of his eager desire to have this house for his head quarters, we were too wary to be caught in that trap, they had tried too many crafty plans to get us away, at one time a fort was to be made and then we would certainly have to vacate to them, indeed a fort was well under way when I found it out and wrote to Gen McClellan then commander in Chief, and told him how we were situated and begged him by every feeling of pity and humanity to stop the making of a fort here, and sure enough, contrary to my most sanguine expectations he did and turned the works they had commenced into what they called a Redoubt. One of the officers spoke very sternly to me one day, as if I had been doing something very reprehensible, "have you been writing to Gen McClellan" I gave him a very decided inclination of the head and said, "Yes I have and I got what I wrote for. I know it was a great disappointment to them for they had not only planned to turn us out of house and home, but had already named the fort, but they never mentioned fort to me afterwards. Gen McClellan and staff with a long retinue of attendants rode through this place and viewed it- for every point, they halted in one place and another, and talked and gesticulated seemed to be consulting about something. We were told in the neighborhood that after that ride he condemn the fort and stopped the work

Soon after the Staples left Dr. McCruer the brigade surgeon and his wife came to board with us. Mrs McCruer boarded at Burgundy (Mr Fowle's, at the same time. She was a very beautiful girl and a great toast with the headquarters' officers, and forever mounted on a horse and tearing all over the country with them. The yankee women now seem perfectly frantic about horse back riding and any evening we see them with their whole trains bouncing up and down, up and down on their saddlers like trapballs- Mrs. McCruer with her whole bevy of admirers visits her mother very often. and hot whisky punch seems *all the go* and a very favorite beverage it is with both gentlemen and ladys. They dash up here at all hours and call for it, and the old lady seemes ever prepared with the kettle of hot water on the *hot*, and at a moments notice it is prepared and handed steaming hot, while the whole party sit on their horses around the porch and sip it with seeming gusto.

Dr. McCruer seems to be a very clever old man, a scotchman he says, he talks but little but does not seem at all inimical to us. Mrs McCruer too is nice and friendly, but the veriest yankee in both sentiment and dialect, although she has never said one word offensive to us

She is as neat about every thing as a *new pin*, and dresses so handsomely and tastefully, and so becomingly for an old lady, and wears such pretty caps- One day she said ladys I am going to advise you something about your own affairs, I hope you will not take it unless, it is only because I feel a deep interest in you and would like to hear of your welfare. I want you to do as some of your neighbors have done, one to espouse the northern cause and the other to retain your Southern sentiments, then which ever way the war terminates you can claim your own. I know your losses have been very great and should be so pleased to to know the government had restored all to you and that you were in comfortable circumstances again. We thanked her most friendly for her good wishes and advice and told her we would take it into serious consideration- In the evening, after tea, a young Lieutenant came in to make a visit, he was a perfect stranger I had never seen him before. I don't know whose regiment he was of but am sure he does not belong to the Sedgwick's brigade. He was fine looking, and handsomely dressed, and we gathered from the conversation that he was a West Point graduate, but from his nasal accent his nationality could not be mistaken. He talked a great deal of his exploits about in the County (as far as they dared go) He has recently been in the neighborhood of "Pohick Church" no doubt with a whole hoste of his rable comrads, and such deeds of violence and robbery as they practice on the poor defenceless women and children, for he said expressly there were no men to be seen, and they could not make the women tell where they were or any thing about the Rebel army, and they were determined to make them tell, or punish them well if they did not. at one poor miserable old log house when they found one woman and a house full of poor starved looking little children, they tried to make her tell where her husband was, but could get nothing out of her. They drove her cow off and then looked round to see what eatables they could find, but there was nothing on earth to be found, but a small patch of turnips in the garden, the soldiers flew into that and tore them all out of the ground and all they could not eat or carry off, they threw away. Then he imitated the poor woman's ignorant talk and her crying, and her begging and imploring that her turnips and her cow might be left to her as they were her only means of feeding her children. They all laughed very much at this witty recital. But my very blood boiled! I don't know how I kept my tongue- But I have been so often reproved for my impudence in giving them back as good as they send, even Charles tells me "you've got your head in de lion's *mouf* and you had better keep still," that I have learned in a great measure to choak down my righteous indignation.

The last words of leave taking to the poor woman was to ask if she had any Confederate scrip- They all laughed again as if that was *too* witty- It was the first I had heard of Confederate scrip and I asked what it was if he ment Confederate money, and he replied, "*Yes, paper money* I said of course does it answer their purpose, will it buy what they need. "O yes" he said "certainly", well I said I would like to know what makes your *Government Greenbacks* any better than Confederate scrip, a piece of paper is a piece of paper.- I could'ent help it- But the Lt never opened his lips after until he arose to take his leave then he mumbled out some sort of an apology- but that was more than I expected of him- we never saw him more

Lt and Mrs. Beaumont, both have considerable musical taste, he plays on the guitar and they sing together. Nearly every evening when the weather is fine she pays a visit with him to headquarters, and returning between nine and ten oclock they stop a few minutes under our window and give us a serenade of a song or two. It seems so sweet in them, these two young people, and the sweet sounds come up very soothingly sometimes to my ear when I have been greatly disquieted.

We have been invited many times to accompany them on their visits but did not avail ourselves of it until one evening recently we thought we would go just to see what we could see, and to hear what we could hear. The old General received us with great politeness and suavity, but he seemes not possessed of any great colloqual powers. I don't think we added much to our knowledge or gained much information in regard to army movements down there- They regaled us with the usual beverage hot whisky punch, but I did not enjoy it *much*. I thought it was made with musty lemons. But when I came to understand it was the finest old Scotch whiskey. I suppose my taste is entirely too plebeian to relish the Peat smoke flavour of old Scotch whiskey- There were a number of tents quite close together almost joining. The one we were in I observed the floor was covered with a handsome Brussels carpet and remarked it to Mrs. B- after we left "O yes" she said "there were two, one over the other." I said only to think of two elegant costly Brussels carpets spread down there on the dirt floor, no doubt they were stolen out of some poor lady's house. Yes she said they were gotten out of some house when they camped in the neighborhood of the seminary.

Another reconnaissance made to day, an immence body of men went up this road this morning, but we knew nothing of it until evening when they were returning. One of the ladies borrowed Lizzie's riding dress, but we never imagined for a moment she was going off to look after the *Rebels*, after several hours she returned and in a very hurried excited manner went through the house and into her own room, then sent for a needle and thread, her horse had shied and torn her dress in the bushes. Presently an officer came in, he seemed in high spirits, full of fun and pleasantry and said, "You ought just to go out and see the crowds of soldiers coming down the road, why, we have captured the whole Confederate enemy." From the glee he was in I never thought he was perpetrating a joke, but O it went to my heart, I thought I should faint, but I used my uttmost efforts not to shew it I did not move or say a single word until he had passed out. Then I got up very leisurely and got my bonnet and gloves feeling all the time as if I should drop and walked out into the front field. Lizzie was there before me, all the servants were there—and many soldiers standing about looking on

The roads were packed and packed with soldiers, so huddled and jamed to-gether that I could hardly tell what they were, seeming in the utmost confusion- I did not know what to do I was afraid to go too near the road- What, if our poor boys were among them would they recognise us and brake away and come to us- "Lord help us as thou art ever kind!"

Presently Charles came along, I did not know he was there until he said "I believe I will go down to the road and see who's there" I turned and said to him Charles do go and see if there is any one among them that you know, off he went and in a very short time he was behind us again and said, "You need'ent believe de word of what-da tells, da ain't got one single prisoner, some thin up de rodd skeered dem, I spose a rebel jumped at dem out of the bushes, an da turn and run back down de road, pell mell, helter skelter, head over heels, fit to brake de necks, every man you see out dar in de road is da own men."

O what a relief his tidings brought! No one, who has had no experience, in these matters, and times, can form the slightest idea of what we have to go through, no words can express what we endure.

Wood has been growing scarce with us for some weeks past and Charles has been ordered out of the woods a number of times while getting it for home use, and told not to get another stick from there, every time he tells us what they said to him, and adds, "I'm not-a guine to mine dat if de Lord pleases to spare me, da aint aguine to stop me as long as there's a log left I'm aguine after it." This morning he came rushing into the kitchen and sent for Lizzie. He seemed as mad as *he* could get. "Miss Lizzie da dun burnt up an stroyed every stick of our wood, seplin dem few trees standin on top of de hill nigh where de fence wuz, and now da is cuttin dem down- you had better write to Gen Sedgwick and get him to stop it. Lizzie did write and begged and implored that the few remaining trees might be left for our use, she had no means, or any way of getting any more after all our own wood was gone. She also asked Gen Sedgwick to give her a certificate for the wood of ours used by his brigade that at some future time perhaps she might get the pay for it. But the wily old Fox never answered her note, excepting a verbal message. "He would see about the cutting of the wood, and as to a certificate her name would be sent up with the others."

I can not imagine what he meant, or how or where her name, is to be sent up, unless it be in his prayers, and I am afraid his own name, or his voice either seldom travel far on that journey

Charles had hardly gotten back with the message when about a dozen wagons came thundering through the back yard and out to the wood cutting and before night there was not a tree, or the vestage of a tree left- Now in the depth of winter here we are without fuel and no earthly way of getting any.

This evening old Recker came about our cows going into his place, and I had to go down to see him, he is our perfect horror and detestation and it was greatly against my inclination that I had to encounter him.

I said to him Mr. Recker we cannot possibly help it, you see how we are situated, all our fenses gone, the sheds, and stables, and every place filled with army horses, and our own horses and stock torned out. I think our neighbours might have more consideration for us, two ladies here alone surrounded by the army, and can not help ourselves in any way. He turned upon me in the most violent fury, shook his fist at me and said, "You shall keep them away, and if you don't I'll have them driven down to Accotink and I'll sell every one of them," He danced all over the kitchen in a perfect frenzy of rage, and cursed, and swore, and threatened and blustered. It was entirely unexpected, for I had said nothing in the world to enrage him so I looked at him in utter amazement and said *Look here Mister*, you certainly have taken leave of your sences- you forget who you are talking to- I waved my hand and said, "just walk out of that door sir and as long as you live never put your foot on this place again-" He went off cursing and swearing, and that evening no cows came home as they hither to have done and the next morning there was no milk for Col Ward's breakfast. we sent him word by his servant who came for it what was the matter, and asked if he would send some of the soldiers over to Reckers and bring the cows back Very soon a corporal's guard appeared, and took Charles to pilot them and identify the cows, and presently here came all the cows galloping home Charles said, "da went over dar an knock down de fence den de cows out an *my gentleman* never said a word, he knowed too well which side his bread was buttered, Not a dog wagged his tongue at dem" This horrid creature is one of the yankee settlers in this neighborhood from one of the New England states. He has been settled here a number of years and a perfect nuicence and abhorrence to all his neighbours, has been accused of many crimes, but has always managed to elude the law, the climax was reached when he was accused of complicety with a woman in poisoning her old husband, and then marying the widow, and taking possession of all his effects. The lady was exhumed and examined, he was imprisoned a long time but finally the proofs were not sufficient to convict, "and he got off *Scott* free-" Such is the history of this despicable creature as I got it from one of his neighbours nearest

Some time in February 1862 Gen- Sedgwick left this brigade and went over to Poolsville Md. He took Lt. Beaumont with him, and at the same time Mrs. Beaumont left for her old home in Wilks Barre Pa It was like braking up our house-hold, we took leave of them sorrowing, ever since they have been with us they have been like dear kind relations to us, and we shall ever hold them in affectionate remembrance. Dr and Mrs McCruer have also gone. And Gen. Burney has taken the place here of Gen- Sedgwick.

There has been much talk of enlisting negroes into the army, and the news papers are constantly full of it, but the officers here deny it most emphatically and indignantly. The most of them say if that thing is done they will throw up their commissions. They have no idea of being put-down on a level with the *negroes-* Our servants have all behaved remarkably well excepting Cesar and Rose. Rose has been insufferably insolent on several occasions, and we have observed signs of her going off- Bob and Henry her two little boys will let fall something now and then, (such as), "When Mammy goes to town to live" Cesar *has* taken himself off, much to our relief. He has been very troublesome and forever drunk since his *return* from the *Confederacy*. We have always favoured him because our dear Mother did. She was attached to him simply because he waited on and was the play-mate and companion of her two oldest boys who both died in early manhood.

Every now and then we hear of one and another of our negroes going off with the yankee army, but we never trouble ourselves in the least about it.

One cold blustering night in the dead of winter we were awakened by a bright glare of light in our room, and the whooping and yelling of men. We both sprung out of bed and flew to the windows, to find the ceder hedges all in flames. It was some time before we could make out what it was, the whole earth and air seemed with fire, the dry ceder burned like powder sparkling and crackling, long lines of fire would run along the hedges and then burst up in great pyramids filling the earth and sky with sparks. The winter's winds had blown from the woods great mountains of leaves and lodged them all along the hedge sides- I never saw such a world of fire, we stood at the windows and watched it all night long, expecting every moment the house would catch, we knew every thing was so dry and the wind so high if it did it would burn like wild-fire, there would be no possibility of putting it. Towards morning we were thankful to see it had nearly exhausted itself, and we went to bed again. But O it was a wretched-wretched night.

This winter there have been a number of distinguished titled foreigners in this country, going the rounds and visiting the army every where- Today it is announced that the *Prince de Joinville* [son of Louis Philippe] and suit will be in camp guests of Col- Ward- will dine with him, and his cook has been popping in and out of our kitchen all the morning borrowing first one thing and then another, and each separate article demands a separate visit- and each request is prefaced with, "The Prince de Joinville is going to dine with Col- Ward to-day-" Pie-plates, dinner plates, cups and saucers, table cloths, napkins, everything and such a set as it all way, cracked, and chipped and of various kinds, and shapes, and colors, for we had sent away and hid away all our best things at last he came for knives, forks, and spoons. We had secreted all our silver only keeping out a few spoons and forks. But I saw those few go with the utmost trepidation for I knew what *spoon Hawks* these yankees are. Nevertheless they all came back safe and as *sound* as they *went* after so long a time.

The Theatre with all its appointments is now completed, will seat they tell us 3000 people, lighted with gass, fine scenery, every thing complete It will compare (they say, very favourably with any city theatre. a company of actors have been *imported* from New York. Miss Julia and Lolla Hudson the stars, Hand-bills have been struck off with great black letters at the top, "Sedgwicks Brigade" Lyceum! and stuck about every where. One was sent to us, but we did not avail ourselves of the privilege

The officers came to know if we would board the whole company of actors but we declined, the excuse, our house not being large enough to accomodate them all. The day after the first performance an officer called and in talking and telling of the entertainment of the night before said, as if incidentally and a thing of no consequence "by the way I did not see either of you there." Lizzie said, "no but our family was largely represented there, I believe every servant on the place availed themselves of that pleasure" I know they were greatly disappointed that we did not go. We asked Charles how he enjoyed the performance- He says, "he enjoyed it so much dat he want guine dar no mo, he put on his best Sunday clothes and went thinkin he was guine among spectible people, an de fus thing he know'd dar wuz the soldiers dirty muddy feet piled up on toper his back and shoulders, an squirtin dar backer juice all round him and over his feet, Oh! you don't catch him at no sick place agin."

Just before the next performance several of the officers called again to let us know all about it, and to use all their powers of persuasion to induce us to attend. The officers would come and escort us, and find us pleasant seats- no, we could not go- Then they would send to town and hire a carriage and take us- but that had no better effect- Then they proposed cutting a way through the cedar hedge, and making a plank walk all the way from our door to the theatre building- But no- no- no nothing would induce us to go. How could I go there?- How could I enjoy any such entertainment when I know, as I do know how our whole country is torn, and bleeding, and suffering, our own people- our dear ones away far away, we know not where, and perhaps at this very moment in peril of their lives- I could not- No I could not- I feel it almost a sin to laugh!

and I know very well too, it is from no particular desire to please or gratify us that they are so persistant in our going, But they think, it will make a fine appearance- a paragraph in the northern news-papers- a little sketch of "The Sedgwick brigade," in their winter quarters and what a fine soldierly appearance they make on parade, and how well drilled. Then their theatre, such an immense magnificiant affair, and at every performance thronged and packed with the *elite* of the enemy, and the F.F.L. ladies, and how much enjoyment it afforded them-

We see now any quantity of news-papers, all the camps are flooded with them, from all parts and places in yankee land, where a paper could be published. The first thing in the morning, before my eyes are fairly open, I hear the little news boys crying them in their own peculiar ringing tone of voice. "Here we are with the New York Herald- Great Union Victory- greatest battle of the war- 25000 rebels killed and *not* a Union man hurt." Some one standing near the gate one morning said "Little boy where was that battle fought?" -"deed I don't know man I don't reckon there ever was any such battle." I am told these little news boys, are the veriest little Seceshes to be found. Whenever a paper comes with extra extravigantly black figures, as large as the end of ones little finger an officer will drop in under some pretext or other with the paper in his hand as if he had that moment bought it, and after he is gone we find it lying on the table. O it does seem so strange to me that men will lower themselves by such efforts to torture and wring the hearts of two poor forlorn creatures as we are. What possible pleasure can it be to them to distress those who have never harmed them- and although we do not believe the half of what we see in the papers, yet these constant, constant reports will have a distressing, depressing, affect—when we hardly know how it is ourselves, "and leaves an aching void-"

March 1862 There has been rumours for some time past that the whole army is to make a great move shortly, and preparations have been going on in this brigade for the past week that looks very much like it. The soldiers have been stacking up barrels and barrels on top of barrels,- and great piles of blankets and clothing as high as the trees, all in regular rows from the green house down to the public road. Then they lug out barrels on barrels of grease and pour over the piles and set them on fire- and such glazes as mount up in the air I am afraid they will kill the few trees about the house that the axe has spared. The whole surrounding air is tainted and suffocating with the odor of smoke, grease, old woolen blankets and every other kinds of hand garbage they could collect together

On the morning of *17th March 1862*- St. Patrick's day they broke camp here and marched off to Alex- there to take ship for the Peninsula- and O with what thankful hearts did we watch their departure, hopeing and believing it was our final leave taking of the military, "as they are going streight to Richmond the Rebel strong-hold" and they have so often assured us that it was a matter a few months would decide, one way or the other, and we hoped, and trusted, and prayed, and believed that we never should see the face of one of them again. But O how grievously we were deceiving ourselves, time will show

The evening before the brigade moved, a very common looking illbred man, wearing the *straps*, came into the kitchen and accosted Lizzie with the news, "I suppose you have heard how the Rebels are giving our boys h- down the river, at Hampton Roads. They sunk on the 8th of this month one of our ironclads and captured another, and killed a great many of our men, and played h- all round, She did not know who he was, never saw him before or since-. It was the first time too we had ever heard of the Rebel IronClads-Merrimac and Monitor, or the "Union ships of war" Cumberland and Congress—Sedgwick's brigade of 4-regiments marched off and left every thing they had on the ground all their tents, and camp equipage, Commissary stores, hospital store, houses filled with clothes, boots, and shoes and every thing that could be named and all the plunder they had collected all around the country, all manner of house hold and kitchen furniture- Elegant carpets, mirrors, marble top furniture, every thing pertaining to house-keeping that could be named.

Each man carried his canteen, and knapsack on his back and that was every thing they took away with them. Col- Ward came in to take leave of us the evening before the regiment moved, "and also to say to us that there were a great many things in his house that would be useful to us—quantity of beds, and bedding, stoves, two cooking stoves and other stoves, and a great many other things and as they were all his own private property he felt at liberty to give them to whom he pleased, and everything was ours if we chose to send for it. He wished very much he could have had every thing hauled here before he left, but unfortunately all the wagons had been sent away several days before, The officers also wished to have given us the theatre building, but as it was built by a company it would have to be sold and the money returned to them" I thought it very kind in Col- Ward to think of us and we appreciated it sincerely. But unfortunately for us Charles had not returned from Washington, and we had no means of sending for them. And before the regiments were fairly off the grounds the people- citizens and camp followers from all quarters, for mlles and miles around came rushing in with their wagons and horses and carts, and wheel barrows and loaded off every thing they could seize upon and we never got a single article. Before Charles got back Col Ward's houses were thoroughly stripped. We never pretended to get any thing but what was in his house- Then some of our near neighbors sent their wagons in and hauled off great quantities of commissary stores, pulled down the huts and hauled off the logs, plank, bricks, dug up the flues of the hospital tents and took all the bricks from there. They knew full well at the time that all the logs, that all the soldiers houses built in this brigade came out of our woods, and many on their own places were built of the same and at that very time we were suffering for wood to make us a fire- O we have been hardly- hardly dealt by- "O save me from my *friends*."

A few days after the brigade moved off we went into town- and found the *whole world* moving toward Richmond The Potomac river from W*a* city to the fort—as far as we could see was one solid mass of white canvass- You could only get a glimps of the water here and there so thickly were the vessels-boats-, steamers, little and big, of all sizes and shapes- crowded-crowded-packed together- I never saw, or could have imagined such a sight. Under other circumstances I should have thought it a sight beautiful to look upon. But O what a sinking heart-sickness to remember the errand they are upon- and such an immence, immence army- how can our little band stand before it- leave little band- God help them! We found our old brigade squatted on the *bare cold ground*, in one of the fields near town, without covering or protection of any kind, awaiting transportation. They say they wish sincerely they were back at their comfortable quarters at Wilton. But I certainly can not say amen to that wish- "yankee- yankee I hope I shall never see thy face again." -We had hardly reached home when I found how futile was the wish, for one of our yankee *friends of former days* put in an appearance soon after, pack and baggage, no doubt from appearances with the intent of making a long sojourn, and in a few days her uncle also came with all his belongings, to stay I suppose as long as suits their convenience. I could not give them a hearty welcome, for beside their being yankees, we are getting very scarce of provisions, and the restrictions in getting to town, or getting any thing from there makes it very difficult at times to find enough to feed our own family. I don't know what we shall do

A large body of cavalry went up this road on another reconnaissance and ended as disastrously as all former ones have done. The Lincoln cavalry with Cap. Tod for its leader went dashing up this road away outside their picket lines. But in a few hours they came rushing back faster then they went a confused disordered mass. While engaged in plundering some poor-citizen away up in the forest (as they call the wooded country some twelve or fifteen miles beyond here) a party of Confederates, only a few in number came suddenly upon them and frightened them out of their wits. They seized Capt. Tod and tied him to a tree in the woods while they went back and secured a number of others and sent the whole pack thundering back but not without their booty, they had secured and held on to that. The second time they passed here they were loaded with every thing conceivable. Beds, bedding, pillows, looking glasses, and even rocking chairs, and side saddles, strapped on their horses, behind them- A few days after I met a neighbor of ours Mr. F- who told a great deal about the army doing. He says the Sedgwick brigade that was camped so long on us, were the most-notorious gang of horse thieves. Col. Berry of the 4th Maine, whose camp was the nearest one to him, near enough to occupy all his stables and barns with their stolen horses, and as he could go among them he could see and know more of their proceedings than most people. Col. Berry made horse stealing a regular business. The soldiers were given the countersign at night (which he says is contrary to all military rule) and great gangs of them would go off away outside the picket lines, and plunder and maltreat the citizens all over the country, and steal every thing they have, partic- ularly horses, and secret them in his stables until a sufficient number is collected together when vessels and means of transportation are always ready to ship them off north.

Some times Mr. F- says he recognises the horses and knows where they came from. One night Mrs Fitzhughs carriage horses came in, and were in his stable for weeks. He does not know whether after there was a *hue-and cry* about them they were given up to her, or sent north.

We were so sure that we are now rid of the army, for good and all That we want to work as usual at raising fowls, prepared a large field and planted quite a crop of corn. Made a large garden and planted it with all kinds of vegitables and melons. When that was finished all hands went to work putting up fencing, when a long line was made, nearly half of one side of the farm and all were busily at work on it, here came an immense body of cavelry dashing up the road, stopped and ordered it all to be taken down again, which was accomplished in a much shorter time than it took to put it up. Then they all pranced in to drill. It was a field that had not been camped on, neither had it been cultivated for a year or two, and was pretty much overgrown with bushes- and briars and brambles. These gallants rode around, and twisted and turned and maneuvered about until the Col-'s horses feet got well entangled and tied in the running briars, and down he came sprawling on the ground, and away went the Col- ever so far over his head into the midst of an immense patch of briers. As soon as he could gather himself up and extricate both himself and horse from their aggravating incumberances and expend a little of his extra breath and fury in oaths, and imprecations on the horse, the briars, the place and all connected with it, he mounted again and off they all tore. and that was the last we ever saw or heard of them that we know of. Soon after they were gone Charles came in, tickeled to death, he could hardly describe the ludicious scene for merriment- as soon as he could catch his breath he said, "I wish to de Lord dat horse had ev flung him an er broken his fetched neck before he had all dat fence pulled down- Now Miss Lizzie its no use having dat fence put up no more, fur if dis set don't come back no *more* another will, fur its going to be, coming an goin, comin an goin now all the time." and so it proved- O I am so tired- so wearied out with it all- I wish I could go away some where and be at rest!

another day, and now our troubles are beginning again with redoubled violence I supposed when I saw such an immense army moving off that we, in this vicinity were going to have a little peace and rest But it seems enough of these terrible vagabonds have been left to defend W*a* in case of need, and to be a nuisance and terror to all the poor defenceless women and children in the whole county around. They always go armed, their bright gleaming guns with fixed bayonets over their shoulders, rove all over the country searching and tearing up people's houses, turning them topsyturvy from garret to cellar, and carrying off any and every thing they think propper. They come here now almost every day, some times two or three gangs a day. But we resist them to the death. A large force came from the camps about Clermont and Bush Hill. They came storming into the porch and gave a violent rap at the front door, I went and asked what they wanted one straightened himself and said, "We have come to search this house" Well I said you have come to do what we do not intend to let you do, you have no authority, it is against the law and we are determined you shall do no such thing. O they raved and ranted, and blustered- I just shut and locked the door and went away. Then they all rushed round to the kitchen door, we followed and met them there, and there was another storm of oaths and curses, they swore they would brake down the door, they would come in and they would search this house, We were afraid to let old mammy go to the door knowing they would quickly over power her, but we opned the door ourselves and both stood in it. Now we said, you are a party of strong thoroughly armed men and can easily brake down the doors if you choose to do so. But if you do come into this house by force it will be at your peril. We have Gen- Wadsworth's *Safe Guard* who has government authority for issuing these papers. We also have Col- Stone's printed orders, he is Provost marshal of Alexandria. We let them see both papers. Then they swore there were no such officers in their army. They never had heard the name, they were both rebels, they know they were. I said to them you are petty soldiers of the *Grand Army*, living here too in full view of the city of Washington and do not know even the names of two of your most prominent and distinguished officers. (I did not know what they were distinguished for, and poor Col- Stone's prominence and career too was cut short by a sojourn in Ft. Lafayette after the battle of Balls Bluff, but I took good care not to remind them of that, I said to them you know to violate Gen. Wadsworth Safe Guard would be to run a great risk, I do not know but the penalty is death. They stood back for a few moments and consulted together. I soon found they had changed their tactics, they began by begging and imploring just to be allowed to walk through the house, they would not disturb or touch a single thing, then Col- had sent them out to look for some of his men who had deserted. What- I said you don't suppose we have any of your men secreted about our house, we are not so fond of you, I can tell you, and if your Col- sent you where are your orders, and where is your officer. O they said they could soon produce both, But they did not, and here they stayed and stayed and stayed and repeated over and over the same petitions, and the same assurances, until I felt as if I should drop, I was so tired and faint from standing so long. I am sure they were here at least four hours. At last old mammy poked her head out of the window and called out "officers comin." It was like magic, they were all gone in a trice, and O such a relief, I thought we were happily rid of them for the time at last but after they had reconnoitered and found it a false alarm, they came back and congregated around the well to hold a council of war and I reconnoitered them through the venetian blinds, and there they had another lengthy stay talking, and talking, recounting their exploits at other places, how the *"devilish"* woman would hide their things away, and how craftily they would find them. one woman particularly who had a gold watch how adriotly she passed it from pocket to pocket, and from sleave to sleave and from place to place, while they dragged her around in a vain attempt to get it from her. But she succeeded in keeping it in spite of their craft. "Yes" one of them said and we'll go into this house whether they will or not, another said, "I'll be the officer, I'll be the officer, and you all go in and search every nook and corner don't let a rat hole escape you and take every thing you can lay your hands upon" O I was perfectly terror stricken listening to this shocking, disgusting indecent talk. I flew from place to place and fastened up all the doors and windows as well as I could. But fortunately- most fortunately at this juncture two or three officers did ride up and they all disappeared in a moment, no one could tell where or how, they seemed to dissolve into thin air.

Our servants are now gradually deserting to the enemy, we hear of them two or three at a time. Rose went off and took her two children, soon after Sedgwick's brigade moved. Lizzie misses them very much, the two little boys Bob and Henry, she made pets of them, and they were forever taging after her or seated on the floor in our room jabbering to her. poor little creatures!

We hear cannon now roaring- roaring day and night, sometimes-away- away off so distant as scarcely to be heard, then seemingly very near.

One evening we walked up to Mr Reid's, and in coming back we heard volley after volley of musketry seemingly so near that we kept looking back expecting every moment the whole army to come in view. But they must have taken some other route. They did not come this way.

We sent most of our best things away for safe keeping, particularly our silver, keeping here only such things as were indispensable for table use while the officers and their wives were in the house. Since they left we have been hiding it here and there all about the house, sometimes up the chimney, each one carries a spoon or two and a fork in our pockets. Then we thought it best to put it outside, a hole was dug and it was covered up in the ground, then it was feared that was not a good place, or a soldier was seen walking in that direction and as soon as opportunity served it was resurected and buried some where else. Then it was taken up again and hid in the "green house" stove. There it remained for two or three week when we got uneasy about it again and moved it into the house until we could decide where to place it next. That very night there came up a tremendous thunder storm, the rain came down in torrents, and all the pickets from the road came flying up here and into the "green house" Milly came in to let us know the "Green House" was filled with soldiers and they had made up a tremendous fire in the stove. "You ought just to see how the smoke is pouring out of there it looks as if the whole place was on fire." We did not let her know, but after she had gone out we both lifted our hands and exclaimed, "What an escape- what an escape- it seems providential." All this moving to-and fro was always done under cover of darkness, we were afraid of the negroes treachery. We never know how far to trust them

There is a New Jersey regiment now camped at Clearmont which seems to be composed of mean boys. a number of them will come here some time and squander all over the place, pick up the chickens, grab up every thing they come across and off again in a trice. This morning a number came again, they were all over the garden tearing down the green fruit, and committing all manner of depredations. at last Lizzie and I thought we would walk out and see what we could do to stop it

They all took to their heels and made off but one, he stood his grounds. He was quite a handsome genteel looking youth, but the most impertinent, insulting scapt-gallows I ever had the misfortune to come across, and was the most shameless and indecent in his language. I looked at the boy in utter amusement, so young and so depraved, and asked him if he was not ashamed of himself to talk before ladies in such an outrageous way. "Ladies, ladies" he vociferated in the most insolent provoking manner. I said if you have a mother or sisters how would you like to think of them as being subjected to such language and such conduct as you have thought proper to use to us today. He bridled up, and streightened himself and stood in the most *commanding* posture and ordered me not to dare say one word against his mother or sisters. I told him I had said nothing what ever against either his mother or sisters, that I knew nothing about them and could only judge of them by his conduct. Milly came out and standing right close to Lizzie whispered, "Miss Lizzie if you will box that foist ears I'll get behind him and seige him by the elbows and hold him as tight as wax while you box him O please- please Miss Lizzie- do, do box him, it would do me so much good to see that boy taken down- the impudent puppy- the idea of his talking to you ladies as he has done." Lizzie could not help laughing at Milly, she said she would be delighted to know that upstart had a good thorough thrashing, but she did not think it would be the thing, or at all in keeping with her dignity to get into a fist cuff with a yankee soldier

Lizzie had a beautiful little lemon tree, the very apple of her eye. She had it placed very near the porch thinking to be able to protect it there, She had been watching the fruit, and sending two or three lemons at a time, as opportunity offered, to a poor sick lady, who was confined to her bed with a broken and severely wounded arm. She had been shot by a soldier while walking quietly through the streets of Alex- from her own home to that of her brother's. Her arm was terribly shattered. It is supposed the shot was intended for the husband as the soldier had been heard to say in the morning he intended killing a rebel before night- The tree was a beauty filled with bright yellow fruit. Soon after the New Jersey boy had gone Lizzie looked out the window and saw a soldier in the very act of snatching off the lemons, she jumped up and flew out in such a hurry she could hardly talk- "You-you man- you soldier let that tree alone." He turned and made a dash at her with his bayonet saying he would run her through. She stopped short and looked at him and said, "run me through if you dare I never was afraid of a coward, and none but a coward would attack a lady in that way. Instead of executing his threat he flew at the tree tore off every lemon and made off with them as fast as he could run, I was in another part of the house and had no idea there was a soldier on the place until I heard the out cry, then I flew to the rescue only in time to see his exit.

We had never ventured to walk through the old camping grounds until the snatching and grabbing was pretty rightly gotten through with. Guards had been placed there in the first instance but I never could imagine what their duty there was, for every body gentle and simple rushed in there and seized and carried whatever they pleased to take. They even swept and scraped the (streets as they called them) and hauled away the soil- From all I could see, and all I heard about it there must have been thousands and thousands of dollars worth of property left on this place by Sedgwick's brigade, but never a cent's worth came to us, ours was altogether losses

Now every thing is stripped off and gone but the refuse, even the guards all gone, nothing but the tents remaining flapping in the wind. There was one tent that stood a little apart from the others, and in full view of our room window. I have often observed and called the attention of others to that tent for never a man or officer passed without stopping to peer in, and sometimes they would stand there until we would tire of watching them, we would often sit and laugh at their different attitudes some half bent with their heads poked in, some holding back the canvass gazing perfectly fascinated. We would wonder and wonder what they could possibly have in that place that was so attractive. as I came near the tent I thought I would look in to see what it was and found the whole inside perfectly covered with nude vulgar pictures, outlined in red chalk and char-coal. There was nothing pretty, nothing artistic only these disgusting outlines I turned away wondering how any human being could take pleasure in either making or looking at such things- On the other side of the field was I suppose the cook houses from the remains we found there, in one place a barrel of light dough had out risen its bounds, and looked like a barrel overflowing with snow, all over the ground. There were barrels and barrels of pork, beans, rice, biscuit, the most of them lying on their sides, the contents, half on the ground, camp-kettles filled with food already cooked such pork-and beans, and rice. At the hospital tents we found any quantity of medicine fixed up in all manner of styles. The people did not seem to appreciate medicine at all but left it where they found it But they had not left a single wadded wrapped-bed-gown, bed or bedding or any thing of the kind. I don't suppose the officers left much of the "Good old Scotch whisky." I have heard them boast their hospitals were so well supplied with- at least we did not find any. But we found plenty of Bibles, Testaments, Hymn books, Prayer books, Tracts, books and papers of all sorts torn up and scattered all over the ground almost a foot thick mixed up with letters to the men from the vile yankee women. O the horrid-horrid people.

Then we turned our steps towards "Sharon," our poor little chapel, and found it a complete wreck, not a window or a seat, not a lamp— Chancel rail, chancel furniture, bibles, prayer books, Sunday school liturgs—all every thing gone-gone. The only vestige remaining were the torn up books and papers scattered about, and flying with the wind all over the graveyard. But what touched me most was to see my dear old parents lying there amidst the veryest scurf and offscouring of the earth, and to think of their filling up our grave-yard with such. The first time I went to town I told a friend and relative of it. I could not help screaming and crying while I talked to her about it.

Poor old lady! I know she felt it herself keenly, but she said every thing to console and comfort me. She put her poor old trembling feeble hand on my shoulder and said "never mind dear the day may come when you can rectify it and if not- remember The dead in Christ will rise first."

All that is left of Sharon is scribbled over with names and drawing interspersed with blasphemous oaths and all manners of horrid writings I took out my pencil and wrote in one place, "He who defileth the temple of God, him will God destroy-" Some time after I went there again and found my text scribbled all round the room and more horrid pictures drawn- and a few days after this Charles came in to let us know that a whole gang of Contrabands had taken possession of Sharon and were there now unloading their wagons and we had better see about it. We took him with us and hurried off down there. We found men women and children. We told them that building was a church, it was on our land and they could not and should not stay there. They were very impudent and insulting, said it was government property and they had more right there than we had, and they went on perfectly regardless of what we said unloading and *toating* in their plunder Charles said there was a picket station near and we had better see what they would do, but they would not interfere. Then we went to the next station, fortunately the officer of the day was there and we made known to him our grievance, he walked back to Sharon with us and told them they could not stay there, a place was provided for all Contrabands at Ft Lyon and they must go there. He gave them a note and we staid and saw them well off the place before coming home.

We were at Mr. Fairfax's this morning and told them all that we knew and all that had befallen us since we saw them last. Of course they had a great deal more to tell us, having a much better opportunity of hearing, seeing, and knowing what is going on than we have- They tell us there is fighting going all around, at Fredricksburg and all down that way towards Richmond, through Fauquier, Manassas, and all over the country, and that accounts for our hearing cannon so often. They say too the yankees tell them, there is much distress and sickness in the Confederate army, and that they are in want of every thing particularly medicine, quinine more especially, there is so much fever among them. And now the yankees have redoubled their vigilance the roads are thorough and strictly guarded to prevent their getting any from this way, and every body male and female are watched and thoroughly searched as they pass through the pickets. I said, why, surely they do not search ladies on the road- "Indeed they do- indeed they do. They have a room at the distillery, and a woman there all the time, and ladies as well as the market women are all marched up there from the road, and she stripps them all and searches them thoroughly. And poor old Mrs. Dawsey said, "And what do think of that woman they have gotten there to do their searching for them, is one born and bred in this neighborhood, and, (shaking her finger) up yonder on that very turnpike road, Ah! honey if I was the woman I once was I'de get me a good hickory, and I'de go down to that distillery, and I'de give that woman such a whipping, she would forget to search the next lady that came along. we all laughed- Poor Mrs. Dawsy she is old but, she is a firm staunch Southerner, and she does hate most cordially "these yankee rubbages" as she calls them.

When we retired last night every thing around and about was as calm and quiet as quiet could be. I went round as usual to every window and looked out and listened, not a sound broke the stillness I could scarcely believe there was strife or war in the land. Not a drum- not a fife- not a military sound- and we went to bed and slept- and slept the sleep of the just. Not a sound disturbed our slumbers- our sleep was unbroken the whole night. But the first thing this morning when I opened my eyes I heard sounds that made me start up and fly to the windows, and to call Lizziewake up- wake up- what does all this mean. And there they were, the fields piled and stacked with soldiers, The ground literally covered with hundreds of them. They seemed worn out, exhausted dead with sleep- on the bare ground, no covering or shelter whatever, and the dirtiest, filthiest, wretches, the effluvia was so over powering we had to keep all the windows closed, and the most violently hot weather in August I thought I should die from suffocation. We could not with all our efforts keep out the odour, and that with the intense heat- O, O how we did suffer!

The whole place is now covered, as thick as they can stand with officers and men, horses, mules, broken down wagons, and all sorts of rubbish I don't know what. Then I went to the windows on the other side of the house and looked out. The same scenes presented themselves, with the addition of cannon, Batteries I believe they call them with their ammunition carriages on the Burgundy side of the road they were packed together one dense mass as far as I could see. When I came down stairs there stood Charles at the front door, I said to him what does all this mean? Where did all these people come from? He replied, "del lans Miss Annie did'ent you hear 'em comin las nite" No indeed I never heard a word of them until long after sun-rise this morning. "Da come in some where about mid-night, an sich a racket as da did make I never did hear, horses a trompin, wagon a rumlin, and all dat artilery you see out yander in Mr. Fowle's field- why when do come a runnin in da famly shack de grown, An den when de officers come dashin into de garden an all round de house a hollerin an a hoopin an a given da orders I never heard sich a racket I spected you an Miss Lizzie would be sceared to death. Da been drivin from some place, de Lord knows where. da don't say so, da ain't guine to own it, but da bin druv is as sure as the world, you can tell it frum da looks and every thing about em." They certainly were a forlorn looking set.

Some of the officers came to the house and got their meals here. But we never knew their names or where they came from. They were very silent and surly and we were afraid to ask them any questions only as to how long they purposed staying, They were obliged to remain here they said until the regiments were reorganized and consolidated. They said many of the companies that went out to the front full, a hundred strong now had not ten men left in them

They staid here some where about two weeks, but O such a weary dreadful time as we had of it, these dirty filthy wretches lying all about the yard and under the windows, close up to the house, day and night grunting and fussing, and talking all kinds of vulgar disgusting talk. We could not help hearing every move they made, and the weather so intensely hot. Their arms were all stacked up in the walk from one side of the garden to the other We could not speak a word without their hearing, and whenever a door or a window was opened they would stretch themselves in and grab and run away with whatever they could reach. They stole all our clothes that was hung out to dry, at last we had to give up having any washing done while they remained. We never went outside the doors, or even looked out excepting from the up stairs windows. But at last- after so long a time they all disappeared no one could tell where or when, But we were too truely thankful to get rid of them if only for a few days to make any inquiries about them.

When a regiment is camped here the Col- will give the servants passes and then we can send to market for what we want, and that is the only time we have no trouble about this miserable pass business. But it takes nearly every cent they pay us for board to supply the table while they are here, the little that is over is all we have to live on, and a precious little it is.

Our two yankee *friends* who came in March remained with us until about the middle of August, and a deadly burden they have been to us. I could not tell for the life of me, when I think of it, it really seems a mystery to me, where we found means to feed them all- Five in our own family and these two added. And from three to five guards, always to feed. And these yankees are so dainty and so hard to please, and as hungry as hounds always- "Some thing to eat- some thing to eat-" is always the cry. And such chicken eaters- so fond of chicken I feel perfectly sure they never tasted chicken until they came to "Ole Virginny"

Our *lady* friend seemed when she came to have her trunk filled with pieces of new goods. And piece after piece of new garments she made up and piece after piece of fine embroidery she was engaged upon, and finally she pieced up a large patch work quilt. O we were too too thankful to say farewell to that old *party-* and would gladly, and thankfully say farewell to the whole yankee nation—if I could. O will the time ever come! Gen Lee, Gen Lee, Why do your chariot wheels so long delay!

One day soon after these people all left, we were sitting at the dinner table and heard the *war hoop*, and knew the savages were coming. No more dinner was eaten that day. We flew to the doors and windows and fastened them up as securily and quickly as possible, and then went to the up stairs windows to make observations. Such tramping and rushing and hooping and yelling, no band of wild savage indians could have made more frightful noises, we could hear the limbs on the few apple trees that remained in the orchard cracking and crashing and the green apples pouring in showers on the hard ground. They made openings in the cedar hedge round the flower garden, (the only piece of hedging we have left) and whooping and yelling, through and through, the flower beds just like a pack of hounds in full cry, Then they flew at the fruit trees and tore off the green fruit, dragged the grape vines down and filled their hats with the perfectly green grapes. They they came rushing to the house some to the front door and some to the kitchen. They wanted something to eat, they would have some thing to eat- they would tear the house down, they would set fire to it and burn every body in itthey would shoot every body- they would kill every d- rebel in it. I am sure there were at least five hundred men here venting this mad fury- We had passed through many scenes of wild tumult and horror, but never had encountered any thing quite so terrific as this. We told them we had nothing to give them, we had not enough to feed ourselves, "You must go and get what you want from your government supplies, you don't suppose we could have enough to feed a whole army." O that was like putting spark to powder. They jumped up and threw their arms in the air, and raved, and blasphemed, they were like a pack of infuriated demons such volleys of oaths, such language, O may I never witness such another scene! May I never have to encounter such people again, wild savage indians are civilized to them. They swore they would tear the house down- they would set fire to it and burn it over our headsthey would kill us, they would shoot us- they would run us through with their bayonets at one time they made as if they were going to the barn for straw to set fire to the house. O I felt as if my brain would turn, as if I should go crazy I did not think there were such inhuman wretches upon the face of the earth particularly in "civilized America." I could not feel as if they were human beings. At last Charles came in and said these men belonged to a new regiment, "20 Michigan" that had just come in, and squatted themselves down here at *Old Smith's* just below the hill, *and he was the one* who incited them to come here, and rob and annoy us. They had no tents, no wagons, no provisions of any kind, just squatted down on the naked ground to forage on the people. Lizzie said she could not stand this she was going to the camp to see if she could not find an officer who would give us protection and Charles must go with her, and off they started, and in less time than I thought it would take her to get there I looked out the window and saw them coming back. Lizzie looked so broken down, she actually staggered, I was so alarmed I flew out to meet her. She threw herself into my arms, and screamed and screamed- O I never can forget that night I did not know what had befallen her. What insult she had met with We stood there in the walk locked in each others arms and screamed and screamed. At last she said, "they would do nothing for us, treated all I could say, all my appeals, and supplications, to be protected from these men with utter contempt, and at last told me flatly and plainly they would do nothing for me. I turned to Charles and said, go home and get the carriage ready I will go to Washington and see if I can't get protection there. I spoke in as loud a tone as I could so that they might all hear, then I turned and raced off as fast as I could go." By this time it was nearly dark entirely too late for her to attempt to go to W*a* We turned to go into the house and there stood a *creature* with straps on his shoulders who followed her from the camp. We said everything to induce him to send the crowd away, he never said a word but stood like a stock- after a while he dragged himself to where they were and seemed to hold a parley with them and after so long a time they all disappeared, but not until it was dark night. Then the officer came back to us and offered his services to stay all night and protect us, which we very gladly accepted. But I verily do believe he only staid to get his supper and a bed, for long before light he was up and away. We had written a note and sent Charles, too, very early to Mrs. Foote, and she sent him and the note both to Washington to Lt Beaumont- who was at this time Aid to Gen Halleck. Lizzie and I never pretended to go to bed that night. We sat up dressed the live-long night. And as soon as our *protecting officer* reached camp the next morning the whole crowd came rushing back here, like a pack of ravening wolves, and the same scenes were enacted that we had the evening before. We were both wearied out with the nights watching, and when breakfast was put on the table we could not touch it. And in that condition I determined I would make my way to Ft Lyon and see if I could not obtain protection from there. Lizzie tried to dissuade me from my purpose she was so terrified at the thought of my going alone. But I found there was no other course to pursue, so I got my gloves and my sun bonnet as that would best shield my face, but it was with shrinking and many misgivings that I made a start I was really afraid- afraid- to put my head outside the door. Most of the bandit were on the kitchen side of the house, and I stepped out of the front door- I thought I was unobserved until I had almost reached the garden gate when one man called out, "Where are you going." I pulled my bonnet over my face but made no reply, he ran after me and called several times, "Where are you going, because if you are going to our camp for protection you may as well save yourself the trouble for you will not get it." I never answered a word, but kept on my course as fast as I could walk. When I got below the hill I found Milly had followed me. I was mighty glad to have her, but would have preferred her remaining with Lizzie. I thought she might be some protection to her, as a negro's word and opinion has more weight with the yankee than the whites have. We proceeded on our journey with all speed- and when we reached the foot of the hill on which Ft Lyon stands we met a soldier, and as he looked very dirty and forlorn, as if he had been through the wars, or as they term it to the front, I thought I might venture to speak to him, I stopped and asked, can you tell me whose army that is on the top of the hill. He said Gen Hoocker [sic]. I asked if he thought I could get a guard from there, that the soldiers (pointing to the camp in the valley) are behaving shamefully at our house and I must have a guard. O yes he said no doubt they would give me a guard, That is a new regiment 20th Michigan, they have not seen any service yet, and they don't know how to behave themselves- but never mind they will be sent to The Front in a few days, and there they will learn some sense." I think the man knew me- he was very respectful, but I had no time to waste on him, so I thanked him- bade him good morning and sped on.

O I was in mortal terror at the thought of going on. It seemed such a degradation to me to have to encounter all that rabble. All the way going along I used my utmost efforts to nerve myself to the encounter-

But when I looked back to home and wondered how they were fareing there it seemed to add wings to my speed, and we dashed up the hill- and *such* a *hill*- it was like climbing a wall. I had never walked up it before I would have now and again, to stop a moment to catch my breath and then on again with my mouth wide open- gasping- when we reached the top I had to stop in wonder and amazement, such a sight I never behald. I had not the slightest idea I was going to encounter such a multitude- such a vagabond host. I expected to see only a few officers and men who maned the fort. But there they were all over the hills and valleys just as far as I could see, piles, and heaps, and stacks, on the naked ground, as thick as one pile could stand by another, looking more like broken up furniture, and wagons, and men all mixed up together and women too seemed to be mixed up with the other *debris*. It came upon me like a flash, and so unexpectedly too. Mules, horses, old broken wagons, all a broken down mashed up set, They must have come in late in the night for most of the piles were still fast asleep. I had to thread my way very cautiously for fear of stumbling over them, stopping now and again to inquire of some *early riser*, where I could find Gen Hoocker's tent. Every few minutes Milly would seize me by the arm "not that way Miss Annie, horses- mules will kick you- too many men that way." Never mind Milly if I can only find Gen Hancock I don't care if the mules do kick me, Stopping every moment to inqure where is Gen- Hoocker's tent- which is Gen Hoocker's tent. At last an old patchwork quilt was pointed out to me stuck upon four sticks "That's Gen Hoocker's tent." I walked up to it and found a sentinel pacing up and down before the quilt with his gun on his shoulders. I looked down and saw a number of legs all booted and spured sticking from under the quilt. I asked the sentry if that was Gen. Hoocker's Head quarters, and if I could see him, He seemed some what reluctant to say it was- and then lifted the corner of the quilt and slipped under. He slipped in and out several times before he came to let me know, keeping me on thorns the while, imagin all kinds of terrible things that might be happening at home, knowing that Lizzie and old mammy were the only two in the house, to face that horrible pack of blood-hounds by which they are surrounded and menaced. At last to my infinite satisfaction an officer stepped out from under the quilt, look-ing very forlorn and unkempt. He gave me a nod, I asked if it was Gen Hoocker, (but felt convinced at the time he was not, he seemed too young a person) He mumbled out something, I thought was "Adjutant, but he could act in Gen Hoocker's place of if I would tell him what I wished." I commenced- I tried to tell him but by this time I had become so utterly exhausted and overcome that I felt as if I should drop. I tried so hard to suppress my feelings. I knew what a heardhearted [sic] people I had to deal with, in all probability he would laugh and Jeer at me- But I could not help it- I broke down and put my hands over my face and screamed aloud, the tears just rained through my fingers. But he neither laughed or jeered, seemed to have some little pity for he said, "O don't cry" That seemed to recall me a little to myself, I thought how foolish I am to be loosing so much time. I choked down the feelings and as soon as I could speak, I told him as well as I could how we were beset. In my recital I forgot all my fears, I just through up my hands and said if you can do any thing for us, for mercy sake- for pity sake do it, as quickly as possible, for I do not know what enormity may be committed before I can get back home, only my sister and one old servant woman there. He called up some body, I don't know who and said to him "jump on your horse and ride with whip and spur, and clear the grounds, if you have to use both saber and pistoles. I tried to point out to the man our place, but they both seemed to know who I was and where I came from. He never stopped to listen, but mounted- and away he flew, and in a twinking we saw him rising the hill at our house. It was a great relief I thanked the officer most heartily for his prompt attention to my request And with Milly pursued my way home home again. The thought of home and what was going on there made us move with great celerity for a while, But what with the heat, and all I had undergone- nothing to eat since the day before- it was too much for me I had to slacken my pace. When I reached the road at the bottom of the hill, I met Nancy Lyles-she said they had seen and recognized me after I had passed their house, and wondered what on earth was the matter that should take me to Ft Lyon at that early hour, or indeed should take me (of all people) there at all- as we walked along I told her all about it, The soldiers were all about on the roads, and scattered every where, with some of them she seemed to be on quite familiar terms, She walked very near to me and said in a very quiet undertone that they might not hear- "Gen Lee's in Maryland it was his guns you hear." It was the first I had heard of it although we had heard the guns for some time At that moment a soldier stepped up and touching his hat asked how I was, and if I knew Gen Lee was in Maryland. I said I did not know it "O Yes" he said, "You hear firing the other side of Washington? They are Gen Lee's guns" O I thought it too good news to be true, though I did not dare to say so to him. He was a guard for us at one time and was always very respectful and well-behaved. I hardly stoped a moment to say good bye to Nancy at her gate.

When I got to the top of our hill I heard a great- a fearful noise behind me and turned to find another confused, irregular mass of soldiers, cavalry, artillery, wagons, horses, cannon, an immense host all rushing this way and in a moment they all whirled into our fields, and all over them. This sight caused me to hurry up again, and as I entered the garden on one side a hundred men with their bright guns and fixed bayonets marched two and two in at the other side and reported them-

selves as having been sent here to guard us. The order came from Wa
I was shocked how all these men are sent here for us to feed, and how
on earth are we to do it. I did not say a word to them but came streight
into the house to look for Lizzie and *make my report*- O Lizzie-Lizzie-
how did you manage- how did you get along with these horrible, horrible
savages, I have been in such a state of anxiety, dread, and terror I don't
know how I retained my senses, when I thought of your situation it almost
maddened me

She said when she found I had gone she was almost beside herself
with terror at the thought of being alone, but she stood her grounds
bravely, she never left the door for a moment. and for a time they carried
on in the same violent strain as when I left. Then a whole body of them
made a sudden rush towards the door and she really thought the *Citadel*
was taken, But she was determined to let them see she was not frightened
She deliberately made a step or two towards them and bowed, and they
all halted as suddenly as they had made the rush. She said I am the only
white person in this house, I am a lady entirely alone, while you are a
body of strong, armed men, you can easily brake the doors and force
your way in if you choose. I have not the means of preventing you, or
of protecting myself, neither have I the means of furnishing what you
demand, you have treated me very, very badly, and If there is one among
you that deserves to be called a *man*—I call on that man; that *soldier*
to protect me.- When she had finished her harangue, one of the men
stepped out from among the crowd and said, "indeed madam you have
been shamefully treated, and I for one will protect you," With that two
or three more followed his example, and said the first man who attempted
to pass that thresh-hold they would shoot dead on the spot. After that I
do not know how they managed, but in the confusion with the newly
arrived coming in they all disappeared, I always suspected the man from
Ft Lyon made himself seen by them, *and gave a signal, it was time to
retire from the scene of action.* Lizzie says she never saw, or heard a
word of him until I told her. And much to our satisfaction Charles came
in and reported, the hundred men sent here as guards from the 20th
Michigan regiment have been dismissed by the regiments now comeing
in. They say no other guards will be needed while they remain on the
place-

O I was very very tired- In that intense state of excitement I had
walked three miles in the boiling hot sun. And while I rested I had time
to recur to the scenes I have passed through at Ft Lyon, and to review
with my mind's eye the immense army I saw there, and to remember
who commanded it and it brought to my memory what old Mr Miffleton

said to us the last time we were in town. We had occasion to go to his carriage factory to have something done to our carriage- and as usual, knowing his proclivities, Lizzie asked "What news from the army" and in his deliberate concise manner slowly moving his head from side to side he commenced,-Miss Liz-a-beth there never wuz a wust whopped man than old Joe Hooker -Old fighten Joe as they call him. Down here at Fredericksburg, I had a grudge against him- and I've been watching his movements all this time, and I tell you there never wuz a wost whoped man." Poor old Mr. Miffleton! He did not tell what his grudge was. But no doubt old fighting Joe had taken a fancy to another of the old man's buggys—and surreptiously possessed himself of it- I do not think any of the officers troubled us with their presence that evening, but the next morning a number applied to have their meals at the house, among them we learned the name of a dirty old Col- named Dikeman. Filthy, looked as if he had been rolled in the ashes, had no clean *under gearing* since he has been in old Virginny. But notwith-standing the adhesion of "the sacred soil," he seemed to be a right clever good natured old fogy. He never said a bitter or disagreeable thing while he was here, He was Col- of infantry. Then there were two cavalry officers Cap. Wilson and Lt. Freeman. They were just the opposite to old Dirtman (as we used to call him when by ourselves) in dress and appearance. They were the very quintessence of neatness and elegance. I think they must have had a fresh suit for every meal. Their cloth clothes looked as if just from under the taylor's hands. Capt Wilson always wore white vests and pants not a speck—not a blemish—not a crease—immaculately white and glistening. The very pink of perfection They were both very gentlemanly, and as polite and respectful always to us as possible. But Lizzie and Wilson would have a little spat in an amicable way every day before they left the dinner table. Much to the old Col-'s amusement, he never entered into it, or said a word but would laugh most immoderately at every thing they said. Capt Wilson commenced it one day be saying, after he had pushed his chair back preparatory to leaving the table, "Well I will *under write*, that in less than a month we wil be into *Richmond*." She replied without looking up from her plate, in a very quiet undisturbed manner, "You have my very best wishes to be there in a much shorter time than a month." It seemed a most startling and unexpected remark to him for a moment he seemed not to know how to take it, Then he said, but I don t mean to be there in the way you would like us to go, we are going to give those fellows such a thrashing as they won't forget." She replied, "Let not him that buckleth on his harness boast himself as he that taketh it off." As he got up and passed out of the room, he said "Well, you'll see." Old Col- Dikeman almost expired, he threw himself back in his chair and laughed, and laughed, but he never said a word, never made a remark. after that every day as soon as he had swallowed down his meals he would streighten himself back in his chair and wait for what he expected would come next. Lizzie, after the first time would usually make the attack by saying, "Well Captain where are those *vile rebels* to-day." Then they would have it up and down, We could see that he was very irritable, but he never said any thing rude. And old Col Dikeman had his laugh. I do not know how it was, but none of the others ever ventured a remark, although there were several other officers at the table. But they all belonged to the *Ash-pile Company* and I think, Cap- Wilson and Lt Freeman were as much disgusted when they saw them there, as we were to sit there with them. They never spoke to or noticed them in the slightest manner. We supposed that the well dressed, well fed and *fat kine* were perhaps West Point men, while the others were *only volunteers*, and no fit associates. We were also under the impression that the *well* fed had as yet seen no active service—had not as yet been to *The Front*, their clothes were too *clean*. After they had been on the place a week or ten days, we went to town one morning and heard so much, O so muchfighting- fighting somewhere, no one seems to know where- but O, it sinks with terror to my soul! Who knows what may come next.

The wounded have been coming up the river by the boat loads, and all the large buildings and private houses have been seized upon to accomodate them and all the large houses in the country around, Theological Seminary and High school—all the Professors houses, Malvern, Bp house, Clearmont, every place filled with them. At one time a boat load of wounded Confederate prisoners came, as soon as it was known every body in the town packed up every thing to eat they could find and off they went, the streets were lined with, men, women, and children all with baskets on their arms, but at the wharf they were repulsed, insulted and driven off. But while they were fighting with one party another would find means of unloading their baskets, and when they found the poor creatures got some little of what was brought for them in spite of all they could do to prevent it they shoved the vessel out into the stream, and there it lay for twenty four hours, these poor sick wounded men in the boiling sun nothing to nourish them, not even a drink of water to cool their burning fever until all the yankee wounded was accommodated, and then some lothsome hole was found to put them in. Some ladies went to the hospital and asked to be admitted that they might minister to the sick Confederate Soldiers. It was to the surgeon they made application. He answered them very roughly and rudely indeed, "No-What did they want to go in there for, to see a house full of naked men." Sometimes cars came in loaded in the same way and the ladies fly out to the depots- and round and round and in spite of opposition find means, through a door or window to throw in meat, bread or any thing they may have, to keep life in these poor famished creatures. It does seem too inhuman in these hardened ruffians to deny to the poor sick and wounded soldiers, so entirely in their power, a piece of bread, or a drink of water We feel it the more because Lizzie and I have been for months gratuitously feeding and attending to their sick, whenever we have the opportunity It is the yankees I'm talking about, we never saw a Confed the whole time of the war

In coming home that day we found the whole face of the earth filled up again with old broken down dilapidated soldiers- all Cameron valley and all down the railroad they came a compacked body, all bristling with bayonets, their bright guns flashing and glittering in the sun light. All over the hills—and away away towards the Seminary and Washington one dense mass I said Lizzie look- look did you ever see such thousands, and millions of men- O how can our dear little Confederate band stand before such countless numbers. "Ah well! she said "you can pretty well judge from present appearances- how they have already stood before them. We have only to hope on hope ever." And then to think this immense, immense concourse of thieves and maurauders are all settled down among us to be, "consociated-reconstructed-reorganized." And how long will it take to do all that- and O what is to become of us in the mean-time. It makes my heart-sick-sick to think of it.

This seems always the objective point, whenever the yankees get a thorough whipping and are demoralized to the utmost they rush in here for refuge, and as soon as they can draw one full breath Heaven help the poor citizens, They wreak all their deadliest vengance on us, we who have always been in their power, never for a moment outside their lines. But joyful to relate when we reached home we found our birds had flown- But where he had gone or how he fares nobody knows and no body cares.

It was a long long time before we found out who these smashed up hosts belong to But after so long a time we found out it was Pope's army, gloriously retreating after second Bull Run. The Confederates had driven them from a way beyond the Bull run mountains- and to think Bushrod was after them too, followed them in sight of Washington, almost in sight of home. Dear Bushrod! I am glad we did not know it, at the time he was so near us. I wish the Rebs had taken the yanks by way of Balls

Bluff and saved them in the Potomac there. The dear knows they needed it badly. It was done once before.

And now comes in the old diary. The first date of the part recovered is *Wednesday 17th [September] 1862* The very distant sound of cannon has been heard all day. We have just heard of the recapture by the Confederates of Harpers ferry, with 12000 yankees, and immense quantities of ordnance, ammunition, commissary stores and a large number of Contrabands, which in yankee parlance means negro, This is their own account, if they acknowledge such a great loss what must the reality be. They say the Confederates lost in a recent battle in Maryland 15,000 while the other side only 3000, They always have the *good manners* to give the confederates the credit of loosing three men to their one, sometimes five. This was the day, we learned long after, that the great battle of Antietam was fought, and it was the guns of that battle we heard. Lizzie was at Mr McCluer's, he was just from town, says nothing is to be heard but vague rumorus, nothing reliable, The soldiers are again at work cutting Mr Fairfax's wood. I am afraid before spring there will not be a tree left standing in the whole neighborhood. But it is opening a beautiful and extensive prospect for us Thursday 18 Our guard went over to his camp this morning, he was hardly out of sight before the wood cutters from Mr. Fairfax's, came pouring in and in the least time our yard was filled with them, all with their bright gleaming axes, prepared for any emergency. The sight of these savages thus armed is enough to strike terror to any poor womans heart But the guard soon returned and cleared them all out. He is much more viligent since Gen- Grover's reprimand last Sunday. He is very fond of talking and telling me all about his officers and regiment, says GenGrover was a tobacconist and Col- Carr was a dancing master. I think he feels quite a contempt for their former calling since he, himself has been *so elevated by his position* or rather I should say guarding Secesh in the "Grand Army." The whole regiment is from Troy N.Y.

Friday 19 The wood cutters are at work on Burgundy woods today They think there will be an attack soon, and the rebels are coming down Cameron valley and the trees on that side obstructs their view of the rail road from Ft Lion- They are all of that notorious, vile, Sickles brigade They will not let our servants go outside the yard without hooping and running after them, The guard will not let them come inside even for water

Saturday 20 Work in the woods is going on vigorously again this morning and although we have no more to loose, it grieves me to the heart to see and hear, the fall and crash of the fine old trees, it produces a boiling up of feelings- not at all akin to love, when I reflect it is the invader's hand that is thus despoiling us, when they have us too, so entirely in their power, and we cannot lift a finger to prevent it. Yet there is a fascination in sitting by the window and watching it, each tree as it comed down adds to our view of Washington, Georgetown and the surrounding county, we have little glimpses too of the bright placid Potomac, with little white sails here and there, and long lines of white fleecy looking smoak left by the steamers which are constantly plying up and down the river. It certainly has given us an extended and beautiful prospect

Sunday 21 I went to Alex- this morning to attend church, The town seemed entirely cleared of soldiers I have not seen it so quiet since the war, it seemes the military governer has banished them all, those that were in barracks there, to the common on the outskirts of the town. The fine large houses they have been occupying are left perfect wrecks, all the inside torn out and gone, and so disgustingly filthy as to be perfect nuisances to all living near. They look just exactly like places that have been occupied by free negroes. Before the advent of the yankees- I never could have imagined it would enter into the heads of white people to commit such acts of wanton destruction. Alex- is now the city of refuge for all *Contrabands*, hundreds and thousands are packed in there now, in the most utter state of destitution and starvation, and disease is now sweeping them off in great numbers-For some days nothing has been heard of the army that is reliable. Four pickets stationed at the Stone bridge demanded a pas. But as such a thing had not been required since the army left for the Pennsula of course I had none, and they were about to turn us back. But fortunately Charles produced his for Washington and said he should return that way in a short time they let us pass, But I am sure he was the one they were afraid of escaping- as I had heard that very day a great many negroes are most anxious to return to their homes, and would do so gladly if they were permitted. One day last week thirty started in a body for their homes in Middleburg and did every thing in their power to get through the lines but were all driven back. I can not imagine what on earth they can want with so many negroes cooped up in Alex- for unless they wish to breed an epidemic. As I neared home I found the wood cutters have been at work all the morning. Sunday though it is, and all the proclamations to the contrary notwithstanding-It was intensely hot, and the men and axes were thickly strewed along the road side, and in the ravines, wherever a bush or bank could be found to shield them from the burning sun, resting after their Sunday's colours. The pickets up this road were driven in this evening. We can see the gards on Ft Lion pacing back and forth all the time from our window and to-day they were doubled, They all seem to be on the *Qui vive*. They say Gen- Beauregard was in Fredricksburg on Friday and they are in momentary expectation of an attack here. Milly brings us all this news, she is very *intimate* at Ft Lyon-

Monday 22 Our guard drew his pay on Saturday and has been drunk ever since and useless to us. He went off this morning under the pretence of mailing a letter and staid away all day, and we have been tormented with soldiersA good friend of ours knowing how destitute we were and how much we were suffering for the want [of] fuel, went a few months ago to Cap Furgerson, a quartermaster, and represented our case to him and begged him to help us by sending wagons here and hauling some of the logs from the soldiers old quarters up to the house for us to burn, and he was kind enough to do so, and hauled quantities, and quantities of logs, and plank, and old broken lumber of all sorts, and piled it all about the house. It was all ours (as he told Fergerson, but we were afraid of touching it ourselves. This morning a number of wagons marked 3rd N.Y. from Gen Singer's brigade came lumbering into the yard. We looked out and saw the men filling them with the wood Furgerson had hauled for us. We flew out into the yard and remonstrated with them, told them who had hauled it to us, for our own use, shewed them Gen- Wadsworth's safe guard- They stopped taking it from the yard but went off into the fields and tore down the huts and hauled it off as fast as they could carry it all day long. I do not believe they will cease to torment, and plunder us as long as there is a yankee south of the Mason's and Dixon's line

Tuesday 23 Charles who has been in the habit for years of going to Wa Saturday evening and returning Monday morning- did not get home until this morning, says no one was allowed to pass between the two cities yesterday but the military. The guard was gone, and not a man on the place last night- as soon as Charles got back Lizzie sent him with a note to Gen Grover informing of our guard's having absented himself for the passed two days, and also of the depredations committed here in his absence, and asking that another might be sent in his place, In about two hours another guard. This evening three red faced, horrid inflated looking creatures, with scarcely the semblance of humanity about them but with shoulder straps were prowling about here, pointing and jabbering in some unknown foreign jargon. I feel very certain they were planning to rob us of something, wood I expect as that seems getting scarce, and greatly in demand.

Wednesday 24 Just as I expected. The same creatures that were here yesterday came again this morning with about fifty soldiers, and ten or twelve wagons. They came thundering into the yard, and commenced dashing axe on the wood. Lizzie who has always Wadsworth at hand, seized it up and out she darted, and I after The officers were all mounted on horsback, and with their straps and immense spurs sticking away out from their heels more ludicrous figures of fun I never did see- I have not an idea to what nation they belonged But when Lizzie handed them the safeguard, and they all commenced chattering and jabbering like a parcel of monkeys, it was too much for me I had to pull my bonnet over my face and retire from the scene I was afraid of mortifying them by laughing But L. stood her grounds, she did not understand a word they said, but them seemed to understand her, and with the guards' assistance they got them off without taking a single log

Thursday 25 Only a few soldiers have been here to-day, with their annoyances it seems impossible for us to live without a guard. Only five or six camps now can be seen from here, and they keep up an incessant drilling, drumming and blowing of horns. The soldiers tell us, music has gone out of fashion in the army, they don't have any more bands, it is too expensive, the government cannot afford it.

Friday 26. A great number of soldiers have been here to-day, insisting they will take the plank and things out of the yard, that we are *Secesh* and they have a right to it, our guard as pertinaciously insisting that we are good Union people and he intends to protect us, one of them looked at him in the most sneering manner "said much you know about it, pretty Union people they to be owning slaves." There was quite a prolonged yell in the camps to-day. The guard said it was cheering a new regiment that had just come in. And a band played a long time I suppose they brought their music along with them It is the first we have heard in several months.

Saturday 27 We were at Mr. Fairfax's this evening and learned that Lincoln's recent proclamation has caused great dissatisfaction in the army They think he intends superceeding Gen McClelland by Freemont, and that does not accord at all with the wishes of the army. The soldiers say it will put a speedy termination to the war. But they talk a great deal of what they know nothing about. The works of defence in this neighborhood have been greatly strengthened in the last few weeks- They are constantly digging more rifle-forts, here and there and every where. This week a long barricade was made across Mr Fairfax's meadow of sharp sticks. I don't know what they call it, but the like I never saw before.

Sunday 28 We both ventured to leave home this morning to attend church in Alex- Our guard seems a very quiet, watchful sort of a person. He is a poor sickly miserable looking creature, almost dead with consumption, and at times can scarcely drag one foot after the other. We have been nursing and doctoring and feeding him with every thing nourishing we can get, and today he says he feels much better. In town we heard there was some hope of the yankees giving up Christ Church. They think it useless longer to preach to empty benches. Christ Church, and the Catholic Church, were the only churches that were not made hospitals of, or used for other than church purposes. Some lady found out the yankees were going to take possession of Christ Church, and put one of their army Chaplains there in place of our own minister, and knowing the yankee proclivity of possessing themselves of other men's goods, she slipped in there and unscrewed and carried off for safe keeping the silver plate that was on the Washington pew With the Washington name inscribed upon it. When they found out the plate was gone O such a hue and cry as they did make, the whole town was turned upside down to find it. But the ladies baffled them, they never got it. When they wanted to make a hospital of the Catholic church there was a regiment of Irish Catholics who marched down to the church and stacked their arms before it, and swore that the first man, other than the ones to whom it belonged, attempted to take possession of that church they would kill them on the spot- And they let the Catholic Church alone.

Monday 29 Lizzie and I walked up to Mr Reids this evening and on the road met Col. Dulaney. He told us that GenSigal was at Fairfax court house with 10,000 men and GenBeauregard at Manassas, but that every thing is quiet as far as he knows. He seems to know as little about what is doing in the army as we *poor creatures* who hold no rank among them. He is a Virginian, as all his fore-fathers were, since the time they came over from England. He still holds the title of Col- among the yankees, but never seems to take any part with the army, or have any thing to do whatever. He is very kind and polite to all the people around, and is ever ready to do them any kindness in his power. He is always full of jokes, and has some thing pleasant to say to every one he meets At one time when there was a great commotion an attack momenterely expected, as he rode along he saw a little girl standing in the door, about four or five years old, he stopped to have a little pleasantry with her as usual, and asked her when the rebels get here what is to become of- "and as quick as thought she replied, "O you will have to call on the rocks, and the hill to cover you." The yankees tell us we are fighting for our negroes- or to perpetuate slavery, and it does seem so strange to me when I think of it that the poorest people in our community that never owned a slave or never expected to own one, and even the youngest children will not fraternize, but hate and despise the yankee- and are always so pleased to tell of any success they hear of among the Confederates, and are so over joyed when they see the yankees driven in here pell-mell-helter-skelter breaking their necks to get out of the way of the rebels, although it is always to their detrement, for we always get the worst of every battle, we poor insiders.

Tuesday 30th September 1862 It is just one year this day since the officers of the Sedgwick brigade came to let us know they were just about moving to occupy this place, and O what a day of consternation and terror it was to us, I shall never never forget! Then we had every thing in abundance. The farm in beautiful order, luxuriant crops growing- every thing that heart could wish And now what a contrast, our beautiful home laidwaste and destroyed, every thing swept off and gone, all the out houses, barn cattle sheds, fences, hedges, all our beautiful, valuable timber, every tree gone, all our orchards, every thing- only desolation remains- and we almost in a state of starvation and beggary. Nothing remains to us but the old house we live in, and that they constantly threaten to burn over our heads- and to knock down with the cannon at Ft Lyon. And where are the hands now that entered just in this wholesale destruction (Sedgwick's brigade I mean) Of one regiment of a thousand men only ninety four remained when they came out of the last Bull Run-fight, and another lost nineteen officers at the battle of Chantilly-and so on -

Wednesday 1st October 1862 We walked over to Mr McCluer's this evening and find the yankees are still fortifying and entrenching them-selves. They have lately made another fort on Edsol's Hill, and are now hauling cannon up there Mr Mc says they purpose finishing the fort on our place, and making winter quarters on poor old desolate "Wilton" again. But I have become so heardened that these reports and threats do not affect me so grievously as they used to do We had hardly gotten back inside our yard when an officer of 34-Massachusetts regiment, with two soldiers came to borrow a wheelbarrow. Said they had found a dead man in the road near here, or one who was *playing* dead and he wanted the wheelbarrow to take him to the camp. They talked of the dead man with as much indifference as if it was a dead dog they were hauling out of the road

Thursday 2 As provender, as well as every thing else, is getting very low and scarce with us, we have at last made up our minds to reduce our number of cows and with great reluctance saw two of them driven off to day. The sale of milk, to the soldiers (when they don't come and take it away from us) has been our only means of supplying ourselves with food this summer. I do not know how we can get along without them, but we have no earthly means of getting food for them. When Mr.

Benter the butcher came for them Lizzie told him why she was obliged to part with them, and her price- "O" she said, I think I can do better for you than that, they are worth more than that" and he actually gave her five dollars more than she asked. He seemed to feel sorry for us. He certainly is one man in a thousand- The officer who borrowed the wheelbarrow yesterday sent it back this morning, with many thanks for the use of it. The man who brought it sat in the kitchen a long time, while our dinner was being cooked, and I suppose the savory odor from the highly seasoned viands whetted his appetite, for he wished most ardently he had money enough to buy himself a good dinner. He said he had never received a cent of pay since he had been in Virginia. Milly seemed to have her sympathies deeply touched and she came in and told what he had said and how hungry he appeared to be, and as he had behaved himself very respectfully and polite to us, we sent him out as much as he could possibly eat, for which he sent us his most grateful thanks. The servants said he did seem to enjoy it, and said it was the only good dinner he had eaten since he left home. To a poor old man in the neighborhood, one of our own people, who we knew needed it we sent another part of our dinner, for which he returned many many thanks, and said, "he prayed God to bless us, and that we might live forever."

Friday 3rd We were obliged this evening to go to GenSickles' headquarters for a pass to town. He has fixed himself in Mr. Witmer's new house, on the hill above the turnpike road. And such a looking place as they have made of it. The yard, and all the top of the hill, and the beautiful, fine old oak grove filled with tents and soldiers, knee deep in dust. They have trampled off every spire of grass, and broken down, and scattered about all the beautiful, ornamental lattice work in the yard. We did not go into the house, the pass was given us from a tent in the yard. I saw a woman's face in an upstairs window and wondered if it was that of the famous, or rather in famous *Madam* Sickles. In town we saw a great number of paroled Secesh Soldiers marching toward the wharf but no one seemed to know any thing about them or their place of destination.

Saturday 4th The weather is as hot now as it has been any time during the summer. And to-day the scorching wind is thick with dust. There is a great deal of sickness in the camps around, and scarcely a family without two or three of its members under the doctors care. To-day five or six officers with their attendants came dashing through the fields, looking no doubt for camping grounds

Sunday 5th This morning before I was up a Col- or General or some great military official came up to the kitchen and took Charles off to shew him the old camping grounds, Springs etc etc Said another camp was to be made here immediately. Lizzie and I both expected to have gone to church this morning, but after this news, concluded it best for me to remain at home. She had not been gone more than half an hour, when here they came rushing and pouring in, Long files of men, and trains of wagons and O what a day I had of it, what a sabbath day! "O where can rest be found rest for the weary soul." From early morning until long, long after dark there was nothing but noise, confusion, and dust. Men racing in and out in every direction, seizing up and carrying off whatever they could lay hands on Then the building of shanties, putting up of tents, knocking and hammering cursing and swearing, and every kind of noise, and sounds was mingled together to swell the tumult. In less than two hours after L- had gone, they had carried off at least half the plank out of the yard, taken down and carried off the large double doors of the barn, dug all our winter potatoes, and in short done every kind of mischief that could be thought of. It proved to be Gen- Patterson's brigade of six regiments. Four camped on us, and the other two on the Burgundy side of the road. They only came from Ballenger's hill and why they could not have remained where they were, or why they should have chosen Sunday to move I can not find out. They commenced fixing their tents as near to the house as they could possibly get them, one just at the kitchen door I walked out into the porch where about a dozen officers had collected, and used every remonstrance, and entreaty with them. I said if any of them had families of their own, they certainly must under stand the inconvenience and exposure they were subjecting us to. That I really did think the officers might show a little more consideration for two ladies who were entirely at their mercy But all I said fell on deaf ears, I might as well have talked to sticks and stones. After I left the door I heard one, sickly, sallow faced, lank jawed looking thing with two swords, one in each hand say he had to hide his face, and bite his lips to keep from laughing in my face- I could not see the joke- But certainly these yankees are the most insensible, inhuman, of all created beings. Soon after dinner Mr Beck our old acquaintance, the Frenchman who was making ovens for Sedgwick's brigade, called to pay his respects. Says his wife and family are in Alex. He told us he had a great many grape vines growing- but is afraid he will not be able to plant them here this fall. I think he would like to possess old Wilton Says he has examined these hills and believes them rich in all kinds of minerals- The Rev Mr Moore Chaplain of 6th New Jersey introduced himself and begged we would allow an old lady, mother to one of the soldiers to stay all night, and soon after he brought in a Mrs Kelly

Monday 6th We are again hemmed in on all sides, tents up to the garden on one side, and to the kitchen door on the other, Gen. Patterson has his head-quarters just at the corner of the garden, and the tents arranged all along the hedge side, entirely shutting us in from the view of the town or any thing outside. The front field is literally filled with wagons and horses, all standing thickly together in rows, with streets between. There seems to be more wagons and horses than soldiers, and more officers than men, and as many run away negroes as both, and women innumerable. In one regiment alone, the 6th New Jersey of 150 men, there are twenty seven women. The tents are spread all over the fields and around the house, and although there is such a display of tents, the whole brigade has not as many men in it as Col- Wards regiment had in it last winter, when it was camped on the same grounds. Gen-Patterson is a very lame man, walks with two crutches, and then with great difficulty, always has two attendants (negro men) to assist him in mounting and dismounting. I do not know where he came from, or what he has been doing. But from appearances they must have come inside the lines in a hurry, and where they have scraped up all this throng of women is the mystery I don't suppose they could have grabbed them up as they passed through *Secesh lands* They all seem to think they are fixed down here for the winter, and say they chose this situation because it is less exposed to the wind. No one who has had no experience in these matters can comprehend, or have the slightest conception of the feeling of utter hopelessness, and sinking of heart that comes over one at the thought of being surrounded, and imprisoned and exposed to all the insults and annoyances for months of these detestable abominable people.

Tuesday 7th- We heard considerable, distant cannonading yesterday, and Chaplain Moor told us there was a skermish at Manassas- O I feel so depressed this morning—so heartbroken—The desolate heartsickness is indescribable I feel I have no home- No place is sacred to ourselves but our own little room, we lock that and keep them out of there. These horrid people are coming in and going out, through and through the house, and in the kitchen from morning till night. There is neither peace or comfort for us. All day and all night, all manner of confused, discordant and distasteful sounds reach us from the camp, The rumbleing of heavy wagons, galloping of horses, and the never ceasing-tramp-tramp-tramp of men to the well and all round the house- until I am completely worn out, "O when will this cruel war be over!" Mrs Kelly did not leave us until to-day. She is the mother of one of the drummer boys on the 7th New Jersey She is a coarse uneducated person, but seems to be honest, and expressed more honourable sentiments than any yankee I have yet met with. Perhaps her opinion of the war, army-officers, and every thing connected with it so exactly coincides with my own, that I am prejudiced in her favour. She thinks the frauds perpetrated on the soldiers by the officers is intolerable, and she says the amount of property stolen by this army and sent North is incalculable. One woman in the town she lives in, displays, silks and satins, and all manner of elegant ladies paraphernalia and boasts that they are trophys from Bull Run Another woman has splended costly china from *Malvern Hill-* She has seen boxes upon boxes filled with all manner of beautiful, elegant, costly things, and knows a man who has now any number of boxes hid away some where down South waiting for an opportunity to send them home. -What pirats! It all sounds like the exploits of some old times sea robbers, or the *Araban Knites* The water in our well has been very low ever since *Berry's brigade* gave it such a thorough draining, and this morning it became very thick and bad and Lizzie wrote a note to Gen Patterson telling him how it was, and asking him to put a stop to so many getting water here period. He sent a guard with positive orders to let no one have water from the well but the officers

The guard stood by it all day and the water carriers came and went as before until it became so thick we could not use it and had to sent to a neighbours for all we used, and this evening when Gen Pattersons servant came for some he could barely succeed in getting about a quart of mud He was about to throw it out of the pitcher, but Lizzie said, "no-take it to the Gen- and let him see how it is, and what I have to use," and aside to herself, "if it is good enough for me, it is good enough for him." I was delighted

In less than five minutes, guards were placed at every entrance with strict orders to allow no Soldier to come inside of the garden, and if the officers wanted water they must come with their cups and drink at the well. Our cattle are not allowed to come outside the barn yard even for water fortunately Charles had the fore-thought to water them very early in the morning and also the flowers- before the water carriers turned out- But for the green house plants and the cattle I would be glad for the well to dry up

Wednesday 8th The soldiers say I do not know what warrant they have for saying so, that they expect to remain here and fix up quarters for the winter There was a grand brigade review this evening, and between three and four hundred of the dirty ragamuffins turned out, I could but observe the officers all booted, and spurred, and mounted on splendid, highly mettled charges, flying from field to field- or as they stood in front of the ranks giving orders, their steeds curveting and chomping their bits in their impatience to be off. Then dashing up to head quarters, where grooms stood ready for the rains, which were rudely thrown into their hands as the gallants dismounted and strutted into their tents feeling O so grand. O what a charge for the *con* boys! I wonder if any premonition of their glorious future ever for a moment flitted athwart, their mental vision as morning and evening they were wont to wend their way to the cow pen milking stool and pail in hand, assisting in "doing up Chowers." and O how they do luxuriate in being waited upon, they take it with perfect *sang froid*, as they had been accustomed from their youth up- and O what a contempt I do feel for them, for I know all those beautiful creatures they bestride are not captured on the field of battle but stolen ignominiously from some poor citizens stables. When Gen. Patterson reached his quarters two sable sons of Africa stood ready to attend him, one received the rains and the other held his crutches and assisted him to dismount

He was wounded they say in one of the recent battles. This evening the report is, that an order has come, that three days rations be prepared for a speedy march to reenforce Gen McClellan. Wherever he may be- I don't know. But there was enthusiasm manifested, no shout to welcome the tidings and when we retired about ten o'clock the whole encampment was apparently in a profound state of repose, "All was quiet along the front" I am afraid it is entirely too good news to be true-

Thursday 9th Lizzie went to town this morning, and about ten o'clock Gen- Patterson sent his aid Lt. Fisher to say he intended having the only little piece of fencing that is left taken down to enlarge his drilling grounds. I remonstrated and plead that it might not be done, But like all my other pleadings it went for naught. I sent Gen P- word, as Gen Sedgwick had found room to drill at least four times in number of men on the opposite side of the road I hoped he would not find it necessary to take down that little piece of fencing all we had saved of Charles summers work. That I really did expect more from gallant military men than to fix themselves down here and persecute two poor defenceless ladies as they had done us, But I might as well have saved my breath for in a very short time a train of wagons, and men with spades and shovels was seen moving up the road and in less than two hours it was all swept off and gone. After dinner there was a great parade and drill, and in stumbling over the old corn hills Patterson fell off his horse and hurt himself very much- *But no lady cried*. I have not a doubt he was drunk, and think he had better chosen the fields that were smoothe with tramping over.

The Col of 2nd New Jersey has been trying to make the guard Gen- Grover sent go back to his regiment, but he swears he will not go. To-day he sent the Col- word he is not able to do duty, and at none of the hospitals would he get such food as he could eat, that here he is well treated and attended to here, and here he was going to stay

No guard that we ever have had is willing to leave.

Friday 10th There is still much talk among the soldiers of a move. But the putting up of tents, hauling lumber, wood, hay and commissary stores are indications of a much longer stay than is altogether agreeable. These regiments seem to have gone into the negro stealing business extensively. Every officer has one or two to wait on him, and the dirty, ragged, discontented looking creatures are constantly hanging about our kitchen and yard, with their hands in their pockets and segars stuck in their mouths. Ive heard one of the guards at the well ask one of them if he had ever gotten any pay yet. He said, "no, but he speck if every thing go right he git some after de war's over." He said he had come from some where near York Town, had seen this one and that one of the rebel General's "Jeff. Davis, and Beauregard, he was well acquainted with" "Well" said Mr. yank "and how does Jeff. look," "O," he replied "he's a fat chunky sort O'man." *This is reliable* information *from* an *intelligent contrabant*

Saturday 11*th* About 12 o'clock to day Lt. Merriam 6th N.J. who had engaged a room here several days ago, arrived with his bride, They were married on Thursday last After dinner Dr Vandavier of the 5th N.J. and his wife came. The soldiers of the 5th N.J. are making loud complaints of Col Starr, they say he is the severest disciplinarian, and the most cruel man in the army. He has punished several of them so severely as to disable them for doing duty. One mode is to tie them hand and foot for twenty four hours, and make them work all the time, another is to suspend them by the thumbs. As I told one of the officers, I have not the slightest objection to any manner or degree of torture they chose to put them to, only I suggested the neck instead of the thumbs, as decidedly the most convenient and effictious mode of hanging them up

Sunday 12*th* I was too sick this morning to ride in to town to Church Lizzie had to go alone, she brought out Mrs Neal and Chapman. As I sat at my room window after breakfast I could distinctly hear the chaplain preaching and praying away off in the direction of the fort, and the men chiming in with all manner of vile, wicked blasphemy, in exactly the Methodist tone he was praying in, no doubt the reverend gentleman thought them devout and pious responses to his prayers.

Monday 13*th* It has rained nearly the whole day, but notwithstanding the rain I believe every officer in the brigade has been in the house, to call on the bride. Dr. Vandavier has in his employ a negro man captured at Fredricksburg, and our kitchen seems to be the most homelike place he can find, and he spends much of his time there, and whenever he finds Lizzie there he has something to tell her about his own home, and his adventures with the yankees. He says he belonged to the Temple family in Fredricksburg, one morning as he was going to the pump a soldier seized him and carried him off and shut him up with a number of other *colored* folks they had captured, he was only kept there a short time and then they were all sent to Wa He really seemed deeply grieved to think the family at home would think him so unfaithful as to run away from them, that none of them knew where he was or anything about him. "But O" he said "if these people ever carried him any where near home they would have to kill him to catch him again." He says as soon as the yankees got possession of Fredricksburg they placed guards over the town, and the moment a negro shewed his face he was seized and carried off

Tuesday 14*th* This morning the first news that greated me on coming down stairs was that Patterson's brigade was certainly ordered off to Wa But as the day wore on and there was no move of course it was a false alarm, and every day we hear the same thing- "to-day, or tomorrow"— There seems to be a restless uneasy feeling. I don't know why. To night a Mrs Angel came to spend a few days with her two sons who are officers in the 5th N.J. and one of them is very ill, not expected to live. To night they tell us another order came for the regiment to be in readiness to march towards Manassas. Some of the officers say they may start off in the night. Notwithstanding their hope and expectation of wintering here I think there is too much excitement about a move for them to remain much longer, at least I hope and flatter myself so.

Wednesday 15*th* Milly came into our room early this morning with the most startling intelligence. We all were within a ace of being captured by the rebels last night, and even now they are drawn up in line of battle ten thousand strong between this and Springfield station- a great number of troops and quantities of artillery went past here in the night, and there you can see some of the artillery now in Mr. Fowle's field. She could not understand how it was possible we should have slept all the time, when there was such alarm and commotion, in the camps, and the men were under arms the whole night. She is so full of news, and so anxious for an excitement, and to tell something marvelous, that I pay very little heed to what she tells. But the officers who came in after breakfast confirmed all her reports, and some of the artillery we could see was still in Mr. Fowle's field. O was so sick all night, I fear I should have given my captors a very poor reception had they made their appearance. Dr. French had to be sent for. He says there has been fighting for several days up towards Fairfax—courthouse.

Thursday 16 There is still great excitement on account of the proximity of the rebels. The rifle pits are kept manned, and the whole brigade rest on their arms night after night. And every body they find on the roads they arrest. Dr. Vandavier told us that yesterday they took a very suspicious looking man near Occoquan with a fiddle. Lizzie said to him "Well I really do think the *Grand Army* ought to be ashamed of themjselves to be afraid of a man and a fiddle I dare say if you had allowed him, he could have rehearsed a lay to their shame, more thrilling than that of The Last Minstrel." Lizzie and Mrs Neal rode into town this morning, but did not hear any thing new- Mrs. N. and Chapman seem to enjoy the variety of camp life, and C- is quite a tost with the camp ladies, they call on him whenever they want an escort, or any thing, and he is all politeness and suavity, and they are delighted with him. About one o clock Col Berling of the 6th N.J. arrived with his bride. He engaged a room here several days ago

As soon as winter quarters are talked of the brides begin to pour in. The idea of ladies coming to such a place as this, where an attack is momentarily expected and they all seem to be in such a state of uncertainty. They have been sending away the sick for several days, there seems to be a great many sick in praportion to the size of the brigade. There was another grand turn out this evening. Maj. Gen- Sickles was over to review the troops. I had some curiosity to see the old assassin, but was not apprised of his being here until after he had gone, or I might have seen him from the window. Dr. French came to see me again to-day. He thinks my symptoms decidedly Typhoid

Friday 17*th* Last night the soldiers slept on their arms again. Now it is a cavelry raid they are expecting, as a large body is said to be near. Each morning the reports vary as to what they are fearing. This evening we were surprised and delighted by a little visit of two dear friends Mrs Foote and Miss Adams. O these visits are so cheering it is so delightful to see the *human face divine*, after being for so long shut up and surrounded by these inhuman creatures. Cousin Mary told us she has recently seen her nephew Judge W*m* Carter from Easton, who told her much of what he had witnessed of the violent and inhuman atrocitys committed by the Union army out west, nearly the whole state of Missouri is laid waste—a perfect desolation. He has often seen the Union soldiers ride up to house, after house call out the men and shoot them down like dogs, and then call to the wife and daughters to come and put this d- rebel under the ground- O mercy, mercy-where is it all to end. How long- O Lord how long!

The officers are very fond of talking at the table, recounting and expatiating on their wonderful exploits on the Peninsula. Lt Merriam was giving a long detailed account this evening of the manner in which he would conceal himself behind the trees, and the marvelous success he had in shooting down the enemy. He talked of it as the grandest sport. Said he had rather kill a rebel than to eat a good meal. Dr. Vandavier in speaking of the scarcity of water on the Peninsula said he had often to give his patients bloody water to drink, and that during the battles when he was constantly engaged in performing surgical operations he was obliged to work days and days without washing his hands, until they would become perfectly stiff with blood

Saturday 18 The ladies have all equiped themselves today for a grand horse-back ride, they are going to visit the outside pickets. They have been to us to borrow saddles, bridles, riding dresses, whips etc etc. I sent my best wishes after them, that they might meet with warm reception from the outsiders—Stewarts Cavelry—or the renowned Black Horse cavelry- or even two or three rebels would jump at them out of the bushes, and send them all scampering back here, even if it was to the detriment of Lizzie's riding dress. I would be delighted. The ladies have also been planning, for some time an excursion to Mt. Vernon But I believe their *gallants* are afraid to trust the fair young ladies in such close proximity to rebeldome. One of them said what a terrible thing it would be for all these ladies to go to Mt Vernon and have them all captured. O, I said, I did not think there would be much harm done even if they captured, I was sure the Southerners would be very willing to exchange them.

Mrs. Neal told Lizzie, that once when we were out of the room, these ladies were talking of us, and what we had endured. They said it was a matter of astonishment to them all how she could be so polite and kind to every one of them, when we had received such shameful treatment from the army.

Sunday 19*th* Lizzie went into town to church this morning and took Mrs. N- and Chapman back home. about an hour after they left, two of the ladies came in and rang the bell, and inquired of Milly if dinner could not be an hour earlier than usual, as they expected to start for Mt Vernon at one oclock. She answered as promptly and decidedly as if she was entire mistress of ceremonies. "No, Miss Lizzie had gone to church and she did not get back until about one." They said no more but returned to the camp and got their dinner there. This evening Milly staid so long at the cowpen that L- got impatient waiting and went out to see what kept her, and there found Lt Fisher, aid to Gen- Patterson, and another officer hanging over the fence holding her in very familiar chat Lt Fisher is a lowbred creature from Lancingburg N.Y. and exceedingly addicted to negro society, and the fair Milly is particularly attractive to him, and the kitchen and cow pen his place of trist

Monday 20*th* This morning Dr and Mrs Vandavier took their leave. Mrs V. expressed herself as highly pleased with her visit, and says she will certainly come again if the regiment winters here. They are certainly the most genteel we have seen among this set. Every morning there is some thing new in the way of reports. This morning it is a requisition on Patterson's brigade for two hundred of his best men for the regular service, and such a commotion as it has produced, men and officers all protesting against it, and most of them swearing they will resign. Then again it is that they are to be sent again to Peninsula, then such raving and swearing, and with united voice they declare if any such order comes they will throw down their arms and proceed in a body to their homes. That there is scarcely an effective man left in the regiment, five to a company, is the largest number that are able to drill. They are only fit to be disbanded and sent home.

Tuesday 21*st* Every thing is going on to day pretty much as usual. But there is some anxiety and fears that we do not understand, I believe it is the fear of a mutiny the men are so discontended and hate their officers with a deadly hatred. Col- Burlin told his wife last night she must not be alarmed if he is called off in the night.

Wednesday 22*nd* We went to town this morning and I remained for a few days by L. persuasions hopeing it may benefit my health. I have been sick ever since those horrible Michigan men made that fearful attack on us. The Rev Mr. Smith came in this evening. He always speaks so cheeringly and hopefully that it is a pleasure to meet him He told us that the Rev- Mr Stringfellow has lately visited the battle fields in Maryland and says the yankees had any thing but a success, as they are so anxious to make us believe, they lost at least three men to our one I do sincerely hope the 20 Michigan were there and got their due reward

Thursday 23. I saw a number of friends to day and all were cheered with recent news from their absent one. And why is it no letters come to us-no cheering accounts from our poor boys, we don't even know that they are in the land of the living. All those frightful battles from the Rapidan to Fairfax court house, and all through Maryland have taken place- and not one word yet from them-

Friday 24*th* They tell me the street guards are largely increased this morning Many gentlemen not knowing the fact went out on the street

and were not permitted to return to their homes until they were arraigned before the Provost Marshal and I suppose obliged to take the oath before a permit would be granted them as that is the way such matters are managed. The yanks don't seem to have learned the old proverb, that says, "He that's convinced against his will Is of the same opinion still"

It is reported there was a very severe battle at, or near Brentsville in Price Wm county on Saturday, in which the yankees were much worsted. A family who have just returned from a visit to Niagra falls in telling about their trip to a friend, said, while there, they met with a wealthy lady from New Orleans They asked her, how it was that she was so fortunate as to make her escape from that oppressed doomed city. "O," she replied "nothing is easier to those who can find the means of paying their way out. Gen Butler finds the sale of passports a very lucrative business, and is amassing an immense fortune by that means and various others equally as *honest*."

Saturday 25*th* Charles called on his way to W*a* to let me know how they are getting on at home, but the news he brought was not at all satisfactory- He said in a very dissatisfied tone, Dem dar people is burnin up all our wood, da is done made way wid all our hay, and dis morning five hogs wuz dead in de pen-

Sunday 26*th* I expected to have returned home this morning after church but L did not come in, the rain has poured, so as to prevent most people from turning out to church

Monday 27*th* It rained all the morning, and ceased about twelve. In the afternoon we walked on the street and very soon met an immense funeral procession, filling up the entire street for two squares. First came a carriage with one or two men in it, who I supposed were Chaplains, then a number of other carriages filled with officers, all dressed off in they gayest, most showy military trapping, then two hearses, one directly after the other, with the two coffins looking so long and narrow, both draped entirely in the U.S. flag, with the arms and equipments on the top of each coffin. Then the band playing a solemn funeral dirge, the drums all muffled in black, and last an immense body of men with arms unraised, not marching two and two, but the whole street filled up with them. No one had ever seen a hearse in one of their funeral processions before, ambulances are always used for such purposes. It being so entirely out of the common I thought some great personage had died, or met with some untimely fate and stopped and asked a soldier what it meant, what had occured, "O he replied it was nothing only the funeral of two young men belonging to Sickle's division, who had been shot for mutiny by the Provost Marshal." I am sure he did not tell the truth. They certainly would never make such a parade for two criminals. We inquired of several other persons but no one knew. at last we spoke to a gentleman of our acquaintance, who was standing in his store door looking on, Very pleasant and smiling, and bowing and rubbing his hands together he replied, "Indeed madam I can not tell you, I do not know, and not wishing to give you a short answer, I do not care," and is the common feeling- "The more the merrier"

I saw to-day a long letter from Mrs Sully who is at Williamsburg Va giving an account of the yankee doings in that locality. She speaks of a raid of Confederate cavalry into the town about the middle of August last, in which they captured Col Campbel of 5th Pa and a quantity of commissary store, and wagons loaded with ammunition, several officers, 100 men 20 negroes, and then made off. It was all news to us, nothing of the sort was ever published- But, O, O the punishment, the cruelties, the atrocitys, showered down upon the poor defenseless women and children is beyond credence- windows and doors forced in, elegantly furnished apartments dashed into by savage ruffians, dismantled and every thing torn and broken to pieces

The wild and frantic shrieks of ladies and little children as they would be pursued through the streets by soldiers on horseback, who would dash after them and through and through their houses, raving and swearing like infuriated deamons- She says the terror of the scenes she could not do justice to, they begger description. As she ran to the house of a sick friend a soldier in the street fired at her but fortunately he was too drunk to take steady aim, and when he found he had missed such volleys of blasphemous oaths and imprecations never before fell upon her ears. She applied to an officer hopeing he would exert himself to arrest such mad violence, But his reply was "every one has his own path and must walk in it," and to interfere was not his business." But in short she says her pen could not depict the scenes, she could not do justice to them.

The old time honoured College of William and Mary has been burn-ed - utterly demolished with all its valuable books and apparatus.

Tuesday 28*th* I was really sick last night. I am afraid my sojourn of a few days in town is destined not to be of much benefit. The two long coffins wrapped in the gay stripes haunted me, I could not sleep but depicted to myself the mangled and bleeding bodies, and the feelings of the friends to whom they were sent, and O, I prayed God that such a return might never be ours- Lizzie came for me this morning- she seemed perfectly broken down, and disgusted, with the degraded creatures we are now surrounded by. Our house is constantly thronged with them, and we have to submit, or be exposed to all manner of insults and annoyances. Col Berling, a few evenings after he came, walked into the dining room with a number of other officers, they deliberately lifted the leaves of the table, without saying with your leave, or by your leave, and without ceremony dealt out the cards, they all seated themselves around, and there they played all the evening perfectly ignoring her presence. She very soon arose and left the room, not to return again that night. Since then they all betake themselves nightly to the bed room—the room that was formerly our parlour—and then such bursts and shouts of uproarous laughter and loud screams, and all sorts of riotous sounds never did she expect to hear issuing from our peaceful habitation. At times it seemed as if they were knocking over and breaking up the furniture, and rioting and romping in the rudest most boisterous manner, she does believe they played cards all day Sunday. There were a number of officers in the room with them, and afterwards the ladies told that they were highly entertained by the funny comic parodies the officers made on different hymns and sang for their entertainment

Wednesday 29*th* Lt Col- Franseen of the 7th N.J.- Brought two women here on Monday, one is said to be the woman he is to marry and the other his sister. We had no room unoccupied excepting a little back room, very poorly furnished no carpet on the floor, and a straw bed. The Col. who inspected first was perfectly satisfied with it, But when the ladies came to take a view of it, they both came rushing back into the dining room declaring they could not live in such a place, they would freez there. Lizzie replied, very loftily, I have no doubt you would be much more comfortable in the camp, and I advise you to return there. Not another word was said in disparagement of their apartment, they went off and took possession immediately. They have a lap-dog which sleeps in the bed with them, eats at the same table, and is carried about in their arms all day, at the table the very best of every thing on it is selected and carefully prepared for it. This morning, not knowing the company I was to breakfast with I was startled when I looked round for my coffee to find this ugly little snarling wretch seated in the next chair and deliberately drinking out of my cup. I gave him one slap, and dis-counted him and shoved the chair away, They never said a word to me. But as Milly passes round, waiting on the table she keeps him in a perfect fury all the time, growling and barking, and snapping at her, no body ever sees what she does—but she does it- and first one, and then the other of the *ladies* will snap at her just as furiously as the dog. "Let my *darg* alone,- why don't you let my *darg* alone," and her answer was just as gruff as possible- "I ain't a tetchin your old dog-" I told L- after they were gone out, I hoped hereafter she would be particular, and admit no more dogs to our table. I thought it degradation enough to sit down with yankees. But I never did imagine I would come to eat with dogs- This evening there were several officers present, and as usual, when either of us is in the room, they were boasting of their great exploits in the army, and what they had accomplished, and what they were going to do, and one of them sighed very deeply, and ejaculated most fervently.- "O if we only had a Jackson," and all the others conceded "They had no Jackson" I was utterly amazed at the acknowledgement

Thursday 30*th* This evening we, for the first time since the war ventured to go as far as "Rose Hill." We heard by some means that little James Mason is very sick We found him very very sick indeed with Typhoid fever, too much so to admit any into his room but his nurses. We found the place, like our own, filled with soldiers committing all manner of thefts and depredations, Five or six ladies shut up there subjected to all manner of privations, insults and annoyances, one of them told us that a short time since a party of them were surprised in the very act of disinterring three little negro children who died last winter with Diptheria, They fled, but left a board with the following inscription on it, "Here lies three Rebels killed by Elsworth Zouaves." The wonder is why they thus disturb the dead. We all know too well their lazy propensitys to believe they would take all that trouble without some object of gain But what it can be is the mystery- We were introduced while at "Rose Hill" to a Col- Revere of 7th N.J. He seemed to be there on a visit to Col. Dulaney. He talked of his being last winter in Maryland said at one time his regiment guarded Budd's ferry- I remembered that Bushrod was just opposite at "Cockpit Point" But of course I did not say so. He spoke very contemptuously of the ignorance of the M*d* farmers, their lack of scientific skill, talked most learnedly of the nature and propertys of the soil and its susceptibility of improvement under proper cultivation. Then he enlarged on the immense Marl Beds, their value, and so on. Said he had sent a specimen north to be analized, and finds it to be worth at least 50 *cts* per bushel- O poor Maryland! When they have finished stealing every thing on top of the ground, they will turn their attention to the exportation of the soil- or perhaps he has an eye on some fine farm that he expects to "*confisticate*" to his own use after the war, as they very often threaten us. Ft Lafayett for ourselves, and *confistication* for all we have, we tell them, very well, you will have to feed us, and that is what we find it a hard matter to do, for ourselves. Col Dulaney was so kind, and thoughtful, as to speak to Col Revere about us, of our lonely unprotected situation, and tried to enlist his sympathy, and care for us. He said he would do any thing in his power for us, he had never met with the ladies before but had often heard us spoken of by the officers in the highest terms, for our kind politeness to themselves and wives, and our lady like deportment generally. Col. Dulaney's thoughtful kindness in mentioning us, and asking his care and protection, was most thankfully and greatfully appreciated

When we reached home we found the ladies in the porch with a Capt- Ewin, they were laughing and giggling and trying to conceal something, we soon found they had been in the *green house* and stripped off every flower that was in bloom, and he was arranging them into a bouquet. L told them they had entered on forbidden grounds, she tried to tolerate their taking them out of the garden, but she never allowed her most intimate friends to touch her green house plants.

For about an hour this evening there was a vigorious cannonading, seemingly in the direction of the court house, and we thought quite as near, One of Col Franceen's *ladies* said a messenger had been sent out to inquire into it, but when she left the camp he had not returned.

Mrs. Burling with Mrs. Merriam and several officers were shut up in her room this evening, and such a riot as they made, and such shrieks I never did hear. I really was ashamed that the servants and guards about the well should hear such sounds proceeding from our house. The *ladies* told us afterwards as very funny, and a good joke that the *gentlemen* had them tied hand and foot until they promised to be obedient wives.

Friday 31st Three of the camp *ladies* left to-day much to our satisfaction. They all took French leave, but we do not feel at all inclined to quarrel with them on that account, particularly the two with the dog. Col Franseen never introduced these *ladies*, neither would he be induced to tell their names though asked several times. At Mr. McCluer's this evening one of the guards said the N.J. regiments on this place were in a state of perfect revolt, swearing vengance against the officers, and that last week the 7th N J were in such a state of uproarious mutiny that the officers went to bed every night in fear and trembling, not knowing but they might be killed before morning. This accounts for Col- Berling telling his wife he might be called up in the night and she must not be alarmed. And for the excitement of the officers, and their running in and out of the house here all hours in the night We lock ourselves up stairs in our own little room and they have free access to all the other parts of the house.

Saturday November 1st 1862- There was great commotion in the camps last night And the officers with their heavy boots were tramp, tramp-tramp all night long, coming and going through, and through, the

house. Drums thundering long before light, and the first thing we heard
was that orders had come in the night and they are all to be off to day
And their lamentation, weeping and great mourning, the *poor ladies*
could not be comforted, they were about to be parted, perhaps *forever*
from their hearts dearest treasures, O *it was pitiable!* Long before I was
up, they were both dressed and standing in the porch receiving the
sympathy and condolances of the officers which they manifested by
singing comic songs, whistling, shuffling, dancing, and performing various grotesque and amusing buffoonerys to divert the thoughts of the
poor grief stricken mourners from their troubles, I stood at the window
and laughed, the whole performance was so ludicrous, and so exactly
like their *colored friends*, that I called Lizzie to the window to look if she
ever saw anything more thoroughly African. At this early hour the cannon
were thundering away in the direction of Bull Run. As soon as breakfast
was over the note of preparation sounded, and all was in motion. The
moving about of horses and wagons, taking down of tents, and packing
up occupied the whole morning Chaplain Moore came in with a large
rocking chair, and asked L- to keep it for him, said he had brought it
from the Peninsula, and if he never called for it she was to consider it
her portion of the plunder. Just before dinner Adjutant Hill, one of Patterson's staff officers, came in with his wife, told his name, and who he
is and without any other preliminary announced the fact that, she, with
Mrs Merriam and Mrs Burling, are to remain here until their husband's
secure accomodations for them in the county to which they are going,
I inquired of one of the soldiers who he was. He said he was an Eng-
lishman, and before his elevation to the army, a stove black. One of the
ladies informed us that bets ran high this morning among the [officers]
and a great deal of money was staked that they would be in Richmond
in less than a week. A good many of the soldiers were in and about our
kitchen, who seemed perfectly furious at having to go when they had
made all their calculations to winter here. They swear they will never
fire another gun, and if forced into battle will insure success to the South
by killing their own officers. One of them said to me, in an under tone,
that the men hated their officers, and were so enraged against them that
he feared there would be a revolt before they got off the grounds here.
They had received no pay for over four months. Lizzie went to town this
morning and says it is next to an impossibility for any one to get a pass
to-day particularly negroes She went to the office of the *Provost* Marshal,
but he told her he had been positively ordered not to issue any. She said
to him it was absolutely necessary that she should get home. She had
come in to market- had her house filled with officers and their wives

who would get no dinner until she got back. He immediately turned wrote the pass and gave it to her. When she got home she found Patterson still here she told the officers it was high time they were off, the Southerners were giving it to them right and left at Centerville. They have been running in and out here all day just as if they were in a tavern, Lt Fisher was one, I have not seen him since he had the fence all taken down. He stalked in without making the slightest acknowledgement of my presence, although one of the officers introduced him, only said I've seen her before. About 3 O'clock the brigade moved off, all but those who remained to look after the baggage- And O what a relief to get them away, they have kept us in such a continued state of anxiety and fear that something tragical might take place all the time they were here- The *ladies*, with Sutler for an escort, accompanied them several miles on their journey, and did not get back until long after dark.

Sunday 2nd The ladies with Mr. Sutler Patterson were off again this morning before it was light to overtake the army, which bivouaced at Anandale last night. They intend traveling with them to-day. I do sincerely hope they may everyone be captured it would be such a grand conclusion to their Sabbath day frolic. The roar of cannon has been heard nearly all day in one direction they are traveling. Lizzie went in to town this morning to church. I remained at home thinking it unsafe for us both to leave the place, as there are so many straggling soldiers about threatening us with all kinds of violence to burn the barn and the house over our heads. The whole place, today, and every road leading to it, is thronged with soldiers, negroes and citizens, men women and children carrying off every thing they can find on the camp grounds.

Monday 3rd Neither Sutler Patterson or the *ladies* returned last night, but reached here about 2 oclock to-day, after having, as they say, a most enjoyable trip, went five miles beyond Centerville and slept in ambulances and under ambulances on the road side. About an hour after they got back a fine open carriage dashed up to the door with two women in it, and two negro men on the box- The women wished to know if Capt Johnson "stopped" here, and when told he did not, one of them said she would come in and see Mrs Hill, one of the men opened the carriage door and handed her out, then he got into the carriage and took his seat by the other womans side, and there he sat and they talked together in the most familiar manner the whole time they remained here.

Mrs Hill said she did not know them, but she held quite a lengthy whispered conversation at the door with the one who came in, and when she took leave, she said she would be here again about the same hour to-morrow. All their movements seem singular, I do not know what to make of it, and feel uneasy and uncomfortable at having these women left here, and I understand every house in the neighborhood is filled in the same way, and as it is with us, not a cent of board has been paid.

An officer and five or six men, from each regiment have been left here to sell off all the stolen goods they could not carry away, all the plank taken out of our yard has been turned over to Old Recker in paymen for board of some of their women. Lizzie saw and ordered him off the place yesterday. But he paid not the slightest attention to what she said, went on loading up his wagon with every thing he came across. A number of officers and soldiers, with eight wagons from Singer's brigade came this morning and filled them all with logs and timber, and plank. L. sent the guard to try and prevent their taking it, and he got an officer of 5th N.J. to go with him, and to let them know it was all taken from our yard. But they said it did not matter where it came from, they wanted it to build hospitals with, and must and would have it

Tuesday 4 Lt and Mrs. Beaumont came from Washington this morning and spent the day with us. We were delighted to see them again, and also their dear little baby daughter, she was a stranger to us. It was the first time we had seen, kind good Mrs. B- since she had left the shelter of our roof nearly a year ago. We had seen him once before but only for a moment. He is now on Gen Hallec's staff and stationed in W*a*

We had a long confidential talk with them before dinner- told him something of our troubles and anoyances and how inhumanly we had been treated. He looked so sorrowful and shook his head and said, "and I am so powerless to help you." He got up and walked the floor muttering imprecations on the heads of the wretches that perpetuate such wrongs He took down Singer's name and said he would try to stop his depredations, and make him pay for what he had already taken from here. We also told him of the homes all over the neighborhood filled with these horrid women that have been left there without paying any board, and their husbands gone off with the army, and these in our own house who have been left in the same way, we not knowing what to do, or how to get rid of them- "Well," he said, "You repeat all this to me before these ladies (you need not mention them)" And so she did at dinner table where they were all present, and could not help hearing it, she gave him quite a history of our wrongs. "Well," he said "after I get back to Washington you write me a letter telling me all these things, write me such a letter as I can lay before Gen Hallee, and I will see what can be done for you"

We all had hardly left the table, when the pens, inks and papers were hauled out, and such a scribbling to the *husbands*, and next day by times the Chaplain was dispatched with the letters. They never said a word to us about it, But we had a way of finding out. Mr. Beaumont asked if Col Close was camped any where near or if we had ever heard of him and his regiment, if they were not we might be thankful for a viler set of wretches never escaped the gallows. A regular officer had to be sent from Wa to drill and discipline them, and a number deserted and went off to Baltimore and sold themselves for substitutes. And to think these vile wretches having the impudance to call themselves the 16th V*a* Regiment. Mrs Balim's father, a Mr Reckless from Phi*la* came here to see her to-day. He was a very common looking old *codger*, an army contractor, and we did hope he had come to take her away- but he would rather not. Mrs Hill went off directly after breakfast, no doubt to escape from her visitor. To Mrs Berlin she deputed that honour, who went out and received her at the Sutlers tent, which is just at our garden gate. The women came according to appointment. She told Mrs B- she has just discovered Ajt Gen Hill was a married man she had been engaged to him for three years, and produced his miniture and love letters, requesting they might be handed to Mrs Hill. Mrs Berlin said she felt sorry for the poor girl she seemed so distressed.

Wednesday 5*th* Mrs Hill did not come in last night until quite late, then she and Mrs Berlin were closited a long time, and there the matter ends as far as I know. I do not believe the *Madam* is any better than the Ajt General. They are all a vile set of infidels We see very little of them, excepting at meals. There one or other is almost certain to bring forward some thing about religion. Today it was the Bible one said it was disgusting, another dry trash, she could not bear it, and never read it. They just seem to echo each other we never take the slightest notice of such remarks let them pass as if we did not hear them Sutler Patterson continues his friendly visits, seems on the most intimate and familiar terms with them all, O I shall be too too glad to get them out of our house. I do think Singer has hauled at least a hundred loads of logs and lumber from here today over to Ft Lion

Thursday 6*th* This morning before I was up I was startled by a thundering rap on the *ladies* bed room door down stairs, and a loud voice inquiring, "Why in the world don't you all get up," and learned it was the sutler. He did not gain admittance at first, they laughed, and screamed, and talked to him through the door, then he went in and staid until breakfast was ready. The theme of discourse to-day was the South Southern people, and what murderous things ought to be done to them, to stop the war They think as the army advances that every family they have in their power should be stripped of every earthly thing they possess, turned out of their homes and driven out side the lines, and the Girillas, ought to be exterminated, no torture could be severe enough for them. We never said a word, never made a remark. But I listened to their vile talk until my very blood boiled- O these vile yankee women have done most of the mischief, their whole composition seems formed of envy, hatred and malice Mrs Hill's conversation last night seemed to turn mostly on her own affairs. among other horrible things she told was the death of her only child, a little infant, she said she was glad it was dead, she did not want the trouble of it, she had no feeling, or care or love for it whatever, to be sure when she saw it in its death struggle it lifted its little arm and seemed to be in such agony she did feel a little sorry for it, but she was glad it was dead, and all her trouble with it was over, then she laught. I listened to the women's talk until I was sick and disgusted, and I got up and left room. Col- Berlin left us one of his soldiers as a guard when he left, and to-day sent for him to join his regiment, but he refused to go. Said he was lame and could not march, here he was and here he was going to stay. This evening Chaplain Moor came in he had just arrived in hot haste from Patterson's division, he asked for the ladies bills, paid off all arrears to the end of the week and promised they should be sent for. (Thanks to Lt Beaumont)

Friday 7th It has snowed all day and at night it is several inches deep. Insco, our guard says, "old Recker" and the officers boarding with him, are all very much incensed by our objections to his hauling every thing from this place, and they have incited the soldiers to burn our barn. He has taken up his quarters there and swears he will blow out the brains of the first man who attempts it.

Saturday 8th The soldiers in numbers are prowling about. They still packing up and hauling off tents and other things. Officers are every day joined between us and the army and we hear the news, the latest is that Patterson's brigade has been driven back from Bristo station to five miles this side of Manassas. Col Berlin wrote his wife to be in readiness to spend the winter in Richmond. He expects to be there very soon and has taken rooms in the "Spotswood House." She told it with as great an air of self-importance, and triumph as if she was a queen going to mount her throne.

Sunday 9th Quarter-master Case took breakfast with us this morning. He was from Manasses yesterday, says there is no doubt of Pattersons having to fall back, his whole concern had to lay out Friday night in the cold and snow without a thing to shelter them or nothing to eat. They are in as great a state of destitution as at any time on the Peninsula. Sutler Patterson made his appearance with his stories, they surrounded the wagons seized and devoured every thing he had. All who came down represent Prince William County as a perfectly desolated waste, without food in it for man or beast, and the few houses that are left standing as without occupants, O it makes me so sad to hear it, Poor old Prince William! how well I remember it, how often have I traveled through it on hors-back with my two dear brothers, and so many nice beautiful places, and so many rich people, and so much genuine, kind hospitality as was dispenced there- a man named Gibbs and another old yankee from Wilmington Del- came this morning for Mrs Berlin and Hill. Mrs Merriam left on Friday for her home. The ladies declined leaving until we had dinner for them, and thus another day was added, not only of their company, but that also of their attendants- But O the happy release when we knew they were all gone, and we the sole possers of our home again

Monday 10*th* The news this morning is that Gen McClellan has been suspended by Burnside. Charles says the news boys were crying it all about the streets of Washington and Mr Fairfax told us they were screaming it through the camps. They have been very strict for some time about passes, and every thing as the road is searched even our carriage coming from church yesterday was searched, with no one in it but me.

Tuesday 11*th* The news of Patterson's brigade is very discouraging this morning, he has been falling back, and falling back, and now they say is under arrest for refusing to fight, and his whole command is to be sent home to N.J. to recruit

Wednesday 12th Cannons are again roaring in the direction of Centerville and Manassas, and so it has been for the last two or three weeks. But that is all we know about it. Some how we heard to-day that twenty thousand men laid down their arms on account of McClellan's removal. I do not know how much truth there is in its report, but of one thing I am certain, means will very soon be resorted to that will make them glad to resume them again

Thursday 13th Eighteen months to-day since Bushrod left these parts to join the Confederate army, and no letters, not a line from either of them, yet and so many bloody battles since- and from Mary, dear, dear, sister- no word—no line, no tidings whatever- I wonder if they all are in the land of the living, and if these vile inhuman people have penetrated as far into the country as where they are, if they have, God help her and her poor little children. The only news we have ever had from the boys was through Mr John Catts who found his way by some means inside the yankee lines, in the early summer. I had occasion to go to town, and having no other means of getting there, walked in with a friend, and in returning when opposite Mr. Cats' house some one beckoned me. I walked across the road, and to my astonishment and infinite satisfaction was greeted by Mr John Catts. I was greatly pleased to see him again. He lives in Prince William county, and had not, I knew been to his father's house since the war broke out- I sat there for an hour or more while, he talked and I questioned. He told of this one, and that one, who had gone from here, and all that was going on outside the lines, and all his news was so bright and cheering. But more than all, and best of all, he could tell me some thing of our own dear boys. He had not seen either of them, but heard of them, constantly. Bushrod he says is getting on finely, is very popular, and has distinguished himself greatly, since he joined the army, has been promoted once or twice and been breveted several times for galland conduct on the field- and David- poor David has does [sic] wonders. Was for a long time in S.W. Virginia organizing troops and was so successful- and did such important, and efficient services as to receive the commendation and thanks of the Confederate congress.- O, O, I came home on tip toe- I felt as if I was walking in the air- God bless our boys!- I hurried-hurried-hurried home to convey the glad tidings to Lizzie I knew it would do to her heart, as it had done to mine- God bless our boys! God bless and prosper our cause!-

Friday 14 Every thing about us is quiet to day a number of soldiers straggling about, But they have taken nearly every thing we had to take, and only an occasional *foray* is made upon the house now. Ever since Berry's brigade was camped here we have been devoured by flys, and now, although we have had many heavy frosts and one or two falls of snow, the place is alive with them. The outside walls are black with them, and when a light is brought in at night they buzz like bees in bee hive, and we have to fight them off even in the dark- I wish they would be content to follow *Pharoah* and his filthy hosts

Saturday 15*th* Numbers of new regiments are coming in daily, O what an immense immense army, and all moving towards Richmond- how is it possible our little handful of men can hold out much longer. O it makes me sick to see them going-going-going- day after day

Sunday 16*th* Lizzie went to church this morning, and brought me the "Baltimore Republican" paper some one had given her. In it is a letter from a clergyman who has lately been much with the Confederate army. He gives glowing, cheering, account of our own brave soldiers, and of a deep religious awakening that has prevailed through the whole army recently. O how my heart swells with joy and thankfulness when I see these accounts, and I wonder how a Republican paper is allowed to publish such accounts

Monday 17*th* Ten or twelve wagons and a number of soldiers from the 34th Massa- [Massachusset] regiment, came this morning and hauled away the four remaining log houses. We never pretended to say a word to them, or even to send the guard to try and prevent it But Lizzie wrote Col Wells the following note "To Col. Wells- Sir Several wagons and a number of men from your regiment came to my place this morning and hauled off log houses that were my property- I sent our guard to state the case to them but they would not listen to him. I am sorry to be obliged to make these complaints, But this is not the first time we have suffered like depredations from your men. And believing from the representations of some of my neighbours that you will not allow such injustice practiced by your men, on two ladies who have already suffered so much, I determined to apply to you. I was about to sell the houses as the logs were originally taken from our woods, and they are all we have left. What they have taken this morning is worth about $12- You will much oblige if you will see that payment is made. I send Gen Wadsworths safe guard for you to look at

Respectfully E.D. Frobel

The *great* General did not deign to write a reply, only said to the guard (Insco) if the wood was cut by the government, we had no longer any right to it, and as he wanted the logs to build him a stable, he should send and take every one of them And he made good his word for his wagons continued to haul from here all day- O these wearying, continual, contests, wear the life out of me. To night I feel as if I could just lay down and die. By what right has any government on earth to wrest from private individuals, particularly two unprotected females their property and use it for government purposes, and never to allow them one cents remuneration can not under stand it, and to call such a government a just one

Tuesday 18*th* This morning by sun-rise Well's wagons were here again L. wrote a note to Mr Beaumont- after breakfast we rode into town and sent Charles to Wa with it. But he returned saying he did not see Mr B he was too much engaged to see him, but sent word he would attend to it.

The town and all the country round is thronged with soldiers, more officers there than I have ever seen before. There is no reliable news from the army, the report is that Burnside has been whipped at Manassas and driven towards Fredericksburg. There has been unceasing cannonading for the past two or three weeks, and three cars loaded with wounded were sent to W*a* and Charles says he saw nine wagons loaded with them this morning as he came from W*a*

About a thousand horses were taken down the Telegraph road today, and as we came home we saw the fields and roads filled with wagons all moving toward Fredericksburg

Wednesday 19*th* A drizzling rain has been falling all the morning, but a constant rumbling of wagons on the Telegraph road induced us to wrap ourselves up warmly and walk round the redout, to find out what in the world is going on. The mist prevented us from seeing very far But when we got to the top of the fort, and looked down the almost perpendicular descent to the road, winding along the base of the hill, a scene beautifully picturesque presented itself. We could almost imagine our selves as looking down on an oriental scene- an eastern caravan, with its long train of wagons all covered with white canvass, and each drawn by four mules, with the drivers trudging along by their sides. Then a company of about two hundred horsemen all splendidly mounted, and caparisoned wound their way along. Three officers riding abrest lead the train. We were two maids of the mist standing on the top of the mountain. They did not seem to observe us at first, but after passing some distance from under the hill, they looked round and descried us through the mist and the rain. Then they made some slight sound to attract our attention and when we turned round they snatched off their hats and described circles in the air, and waved their handkerchiefs and huzzaed, and the whole train sent up such a shout that my first impulse was to snatch off my old *sun bonnet* and return the salutation, but happily the recollection of who they were recurred to me In time to stay my hand, and we both turned and ran down the embankment on the other side, I am sure they thought we had gone out there purposely to bid them God-speed and were some rusticks who knew no better than to run away or more likely they sent their curses after us as rebels

Thursday 20*th* It has rained in torrents all day, but the *tidal*-wave towards Richmond continues to rush on, wagons, horses, mules, going-going-going-day and night down the telegraph road. Burnside is so positive he will be there before Christmas that the officers are betting high upon it- He says he will persevere by inches if he only advances a mile a day- Our guard has again been ordered to join his regiment, but has again refused to go- He seemes to think he belongs here, and here he is going to stay- He is not at all anxious to join in another move towards R- and gives the most sickening account of the manner the people were treated by the army on the Peninsula, he says the soldiers would break into their houses at night turn whole families out of doors, take whatever they pleased and then set fire to every thing- one of the yankee teamsters got shot, no one knew how or by whom immediately ten or twelve families were seized upon, three men were hung on the spot, and the balance were sent off to prison, but he does not know what became of them, but every thing on earth they had was destroyed. And he highly approves of all such doings says if at the first breaking out of the war they had murdered men, women and children the rebellion would have been crushed out long ago, and this is the doctrine that most of the yankees preach, men women, and children, at least to us.

Friday 21 It has rained all the early part of the day- still the army moves on. This evening received a note from Miss McCluer. She says "Mrs Rice is going in a short time to Richmond you had better loose no time in seeing her." Mrs- R- had kindly offered to take letters for us. Lizzie wrote again to Bushrod, although the last two or three never found their way out-side the lines- Soon after dark I was standing by the window and was startled to see a bright light reflected every where. The first thought was the barn was on fire. But soon discovered the light was from an immense fire built of logs just at the corner of our kitchen with two forked sticks driven in the ground, a pole across and the teakettle hanging over the fire, and various other cooking utensils ranged about the fire, men walking about talking and warming themselves, perfectly at their ease, and at home. We sent out to inquire into it, what it all ment, and learned that the man Patterson one of Gen Pattersons sutlers had sent up all his belongings here and taken quiet possession, three wagons nine men, six horses and mules, and filled our barn, and here they are to remain until he thinks proper to remove them. I think I never did hear of a cooler piece of impudence They never asked any leave or any questions about it But just drove into our yard fixed up their tents, took our wood, made themselves a fire- Put all their horses and mules in our stables, walk in and out of our kitchen, cook whatever they please in it themselves, and the five or six run away negroes they have with them Just have taken complete possession, and we are obliged to submit, or perhaps have our barn burnt, or the house over our heads.

Saturday 22nd We went to town to day with all the letters we had written to our boys hoping to see Mrs Rice, but found she had gone to Wa. The report to-day is that Burnside demanded the surrender of Fredricksburg, and on its being refused, allowed sixteen hours for the removal of women, children, and sick soldiers before shelling the place. The town Alex is filled with the military, and the soldiers are straggling all over the country in every direction, the most of them with guns and dogs hunting rabbits. Our guard tells us there are about fourteen thousand patients in the convalescent camps, which are spread out all over the Seminary hill and "Shuters Hill," and that they are in the most deplorable state of destitution. The little that is allowed the miserable wretches to eat, they have to cook for themselves, and to find their own wood. Many of them come over here looking like death itself, walking three miles here, and three miles back, and carry off two or three little sticks of wood in their arms. Ever since Patterson's brigade left they have been coming to our kitchen every day about meal time begging for something to eat. It seems hard for us to feed the very wretches who have destroyed us, and too when we have so little to feed ourselves with- But when they come sick and hungry- and looking so miserable and wishful it is impossible for us to refuse them something to eat The yankee people about here will not give them a mouthful.

Sunday 23 We went into town again this morning, and beside going to church had to look for Mrs Rice. We found her, but she had yesterday bad news from her husband, he was captured with a vessell that was trying to run the blockade and she thinks it probable she may not go South. But kindly promised if she did to make every effort to see our boys- and to write to us if possible. The impression to-day is that Charleston will certainly fall into the hands of the yankees. That the strength of her defences cannot possibly withstand the power of the gunboats, every body looks glum, and troubled about it The sutler's men got into quarrel to day with our guard, and some went off threatening to have him sent back to his regiment, But this evening they came back so full of news that they forgot to *dismiss* Insco. The regiment they say is camped about fourteen miles from here on Wolf run and that Gen Patterson committed suicide at Fairfax Court house a night or two ago. The cause of his committing the act was distress and mortification at being superseded by Col. Revere a great many wagons have been coming up the telegraph road to-day.

Monday 24 The quartermaster of 34 Mass- regiment with his attendant rode up to the kitchen this evening and asked for Lizzie, and when she made her appearance told her he was willing to pay for the wood taken from here by that regiment. But positively denied taking but one log house, and after a great deal of parleying and haggling, concluded that two cords would be a fair equivalent He certainly is engaged in a lucrative business if he makes many such one sided bargains as this. Two cords of wood for four log houses, and at least fifty wagon loads of logs. And even the two cords he went off without paying for, and that is the last we will ever hear of it. These quartermasters are certainly filling their pockets, they are making the government pay them for all they are stealing from the citizens

A party of skirmishers made their appearance this morning skipping all over hill and dale, and were soon out of sight. I could not imagine what it ment- and had to go to Insco for information. He said they were skirmishers out in pursuit of a party of Southerners who have been seen in this neighborhood-

Tuesday 25th There has been continuous heavy cannonading to the north of us all day. Our guard has again received peremptory orders to return to his regiment, so emphatic that he is afraid to disobey longer, and this morning took a sorrowful reluctant leave of us all. For a long time he tried to put on a cheerful face, but at last the tears would come It does seem strange with all the ill treatment these horrible yankees mete out to us, not one of them that ever gets a footing in our house is willing to leave it. This evening Insco made a very unexpected appearance again. Says he rencontred to Col- Belknap at Ft Elsworth, but to his unspeakable satisfaction, they could not find a way to go for him

Wednesday 26th—The band played until eleven oclock last night at Ft Lion I have never heard it at such a late hour before. Col. Dulaney called to day. He let the sutlers know they could now obtain passes, and that it was high time for them to leave here. I was much obliged to him for the information he brought them. He says there was a battle at, or near Leesburg yesterday but with what results he does not know, as there are ten thousand rumours afloat, excepting that there were a great number of sutlers and all their stores captured by the Confederates on Saturday last.

Thursday 27 They are constantly making additions and improvements to the forts on the opposite hills- Six heavy pieces of ordnance were taken up there today- A sergeant of the 34th Mass- was here. I asked him why his regiment, that was so well drilled, and had not seen any service yet, were not sent to the front. He said they were in no condition to go, that nearly all the men are sick, and a funeral takes place from there at least every other day, and from three to five die daily in the convalescent camp. They all think this a very sickly part of the country. They very often tell me this one, and the other one of the officers who have expressed their determination to appropriate this place to themselves when the "confistication" time comes round. I say many, many have made the same resolution who are now occupying their six feet of the "Sacred soil" and will never want any more.

Friday 28th The Fredricksburg road now is daily thronged with troops going south. Yesterday evening late a large body of cavalary moving in that direction stopped and *bivouacked* in "Happy Valley" They were so near us, we could hear the men talking, and see the reflection of their bright watch fires playing on the wall of our chamber all night long

Saturday 29*th* The sutlers are here still. Charles informed us they have two large stoves in their tent- and make liberal use of our wood ever since they came, as well as of our hay, have nothing else to feed their horses and mules upon. Lizzie sent the gard to say to them, she thought it about time for them to leave. The reply came back coupled with oaths, That they had as much right to stay here as she had and that they were going to stay as long as they pleased, and go when they thought proper. Frank Patterson the head of the firm is not here, but two of his partners, Chamberline and West are

We ordered the carriage and went off to town and laid our grievances before Capt Furgerson, who took down the names as far as we knew them. He was very polite and prompt, said he would see to it that the sutlers were sent away from here, said he was aware of the great losses we had sustained, and the ill treatment we had received from the army, and was particularly anxious to serve us, and would do any thing in his power to help us, and also that he intended making Col Wells pay for the loss and wood he has taken from here. We took leave, very much prepossessed with Capt Furgeson-

The first piece of good-news that greeted us on reaching cousin M-'s house was that Miss Annie K- arrived in town yesterday, direct from the heart of the Confederacy We did not see her- she had gone out before we got there. But she says Bushrod dined at her father's house at Culpepper on Wednesday 19th. He was looking remarkably well and happy, has never had a wound, or a days sickness since he left home, Has lately been promoted to Major of artillery, and is attached to Gen- Longstreet's command O how happy this good news made us- I thought of a text I had read and copied only a few days ago- "O what great troubles and adversities hast thou shown me! and yet didst thou turn and refresh me" O with what thankful happy hearts did we turn our faces homeward, Found the sutlers all gone pack and baggage, took every thing away with them, but one poor sick run away, thickly broken out with small pox- and what are we to do with him—our servants say he has been sick for several days- They have kept him shut up in a hot tent with two stoves in it To-day the white men burned up his bed, and every thing of his excepting the clothes he has on, they took him out of the hot tent into the pearcing cold air, made him walk to our barn where they left him with nothing on earth to lie upon, nothing to eat or to drink, and but two little old blankets to cover with. We did not know a word of his being there until about sun-set. We sent the poor creature some soup tea and any little thing that we thought he might eat. Lizzie wrote West a note saying she had never heard of such inhuman treatment in her life as they had given that poor sick negro. And if he did not come or send and take the poor creature to some place where he could be cared for, and made comfortable she would complain to the authorities.

Sunday 30th This morning we found the sick man in the kitchen, where no doubt he has been all night- He was sitting over the fire with his head in his hands, said he was almost frozen- his face is one solid blister- After breakfast we had the carriage and went to town again to try and find some yankee with humanity enough to take charge of this one poor negro. The first place we stopped at was Gov- Slow's office- We told him of the negro, and how the sutlers had left him on our hands and asked what was to be done with him. He said he could only refur us to the Provost-marshal. of course we had to turn our steps in that direction- we found the street and steps and anti-room filled with soldiers, and negroes, in every variety and stage of rags and filth- one of the *grand* officials opened a way for us to pass through this motly assemblage, and we found the *Grand* Mogul seated on his throne in a back room surrounded by a bevy of his *colored* sisters, who had all to be served before we were even seen. He is a most uncouth creature named Wyman, sat all the time he talked with us, with his hat stuck on one side of his head and a cigar in his mouth. Said he did not know it was his business to take care of all the small pox patients in the country. L- replied it certainly was not hers, and as she had been sent to him as the proper person to attend to such matters, by Gov- Slow she expected some thing to be done. He then inquired if the man was a Contraband, She replied of course as there are no other negroes in the army but runaways. Then he said he was getting "Clermont House" ready for a Contraband hospital, and thought it might be ready for the reception of patients about Tuesday. Then I took it up, I said that man cannot remain in our house until Tuesday he must be taken away at once it was risking the lives of our whole family. I thought the inhumanity of these sutler men to him was beyond any thing I had ever heard of. Then he straightened up and puffed himself out, and replied in the most pompous self-important manner "Nothing develops the selfishness of man so much as W-A-R." After this *great man* had relieved his mind by this grand speach, he wrote an order to the man who drives the small-pox ambulance to come out for the man, and sent us with it to a horrid place where a number of poor, half clothed, half starved, wretched looking negroes were waiting with open mouths to receive their rations- And after all their promises and all the disagreeables we had encountered—just as I expected the ambulance never came. We waited until late in the evening, until all hope was gone Then L- made Charles and Insco take him in our wagon down to the sutler's camp some where near Hunting Creek bridge.

I stayed in town, and had the pleasure of Miss Annie's company. She told me many things that was mostly gratifying to hear of our friends, and of our army, and many that were sad and painful, particularly the death of many old friends. And also scenes of violence, robberies, cruelties, and inhuman wrongs that are now rife in our land. Pope's and Sigle's armies who went through these upper counties just slayed as they went, hogs, beeves, sheep, all kinds of stock, not to feed themselves upon, but merely to gratify their fiendish feelings of envy hatred and revenge, for they were all left to rot on the ground. Miss A. father had a remarkably fine flock of sheep. Three hundred I think she said. They were all driven into the yard to be a nuicence to the family, and these slayed fore and aft, and left in piles to decay and taint the air. Her fathers house was set on fire after one of the battles and burned with all the furniture and every thing in it. His mill was filled with the dead, and then stuffed with straw and burned. O I could not recount the enormities

Monday Dec 1st 1862 It is reported to-day that six thousand Federal troops were captured on Friday near Falmoth- The army is still moving in that direction

Tuesday 2nd Six ambulances were at work to day taking the small-pox patients from a house on King street to the Clermont hospital- It was high time to move them the place was filled with negroes and all sorts, and made by them a complete wreck, and the filthiest hole that could be imagined. It is said, eight hundred cases of small pox are now in the town. The Typhoid fever is also said to be very prevalent. There was an outcry this morning about eight oclock that one of the Monitors was passing the town, being towed to the Wa Navy yard, in a very disabled condition

Wednesday 3rd An immense number of wagons and fifteen regiments passed through Alex- to-day on their way to Richmond. A great number of soldiers were also taken up the rail road. Lizzie came in for me this morning, and together we made up a little package to send to Bushrod of useful articles, such as they tell us are not easily obtained in Secesh-land. Miss A could only take a very small package in her trunk, as she expects to take back her *bridal trousseau*. We would be glad if we could send a trunk full. Lizzie had to go to Wyman's office again, this time to ask for a pass for Charles to go to W*a* She found the place as before filled with negroes, mostly women who had all to be served before her turn came, and although he has a clerk to write the passes for him, he took particular pains to speak to every negro woman in the room first, then he turned very abruptly and rudely and asked what she wanted, She said a pass for her servant man to go Wa He asked if she was a loyal subject, otherwise the pass might be made an improper use of. She asked what he ment by a loyal subject, she was a lady, had no vote, and did not meddle with politics. But when she had, she should certainly vote for the government that protected her in her rights. He said she was evading the question, and then asked if she had taken the oath, or if she would, she said, no, she had not taken it, and she did not intend to take it, that the U S government had wrested from her all her property deprived her of all her rights, she certainly would not take an oath of allegiance to any such government. Then he wanted to know if she sympathized with the South. She said she had never violated any laws of the United States But that all her friends and relations were Southerners and they certainly had her sympathy. Then he said she could get no pass from there, if her feelings were with the South that was assisting the rebel government He too had friends and relations at the South, but did not sympathize with them. Well Sir she replied that shows the difference of opinion between you and me. My servant in going to Wa is on no business of mine, he has a wife and family there, and I have always been pleased to gratify him in the wish to visit them whenever he chooses to go. But if you think proper to refuse him a pass I have nothing more to say. "Good morning Sir." She made her congees, and turned, and walked out of the place. She says the negro women looked after her and bowed and smiled, particularly one old yellow one, who sat rocking herself against the wall, you could not mistake the inward satisfaction as she swayed and simpered! Dat we colored folks is got more influence wid de heads of Department den de white folks is- As we rode home we saw the miserable contrabands straggling about the fields, and in and out the camp, some with a few chips—others with a handful of sticks or seder bush, one poor criple, haggard and emaciated, on his hands and knees scratching up the end of a telegraph pole which had been cut off near the ground

L.- says she was at Clermont on Tuesday, and saw numbers of ambulances taking the small-pox patients there. I can think of nothing to be done with that house but to burn it down The family certainly can never live in it again- after its being occupied so long by such filthy pestilential wretches, and such a wreck and desolation as they have made of it, and what a lovely enchanting place it was when Mrs Forrest left it.

Thursday 4th The cars were going all night, and for days, and days, and weeks all the roads have been thronged with troops, going to swell Burnsides numbers. O what an immense army they will have to attack Richmond this time I wonder where they can find standing room. O it makes me tremble to think of it, and I feel I know, that such vastly superior numbers must eventually succeed. We went this evening to see old Mrs Welch who is very sick, and to carry her something. While we were out we took the opportunity of visiting several others of our poor neighbours, and learned that two trains of cars filled with troops came down the Orange and Alex- road this evening, and all marched off towards the Seminary, and every body sais what does it mean, But no one can answer. We had only been at home a few minutes when a soldier with a woman came trudging through the fields loaded with carpet-bags and bundles and applied here for board. When they found we would not take them as boarders they asked to stay all night- But we knew if they got into the house there might be no such thing as getting rid of them, so we recommended old Smith's, their fellow countryman, a good place, and started them

Friday 5th The distant sound of bugle, and the roll of the drum once or twice are the only military sounds we have heard to-day. Only two soldiers here and they from the convalecent camp, looking for something to eat, They all know where they will not be sent empty away

Saturday 6th Two Soldiers came into the kitchen very late this evening. Insco said their movements were very suspitious. I don't know what the suspected excepting that they might be rebels. They could give no account of themselves, only said they were from Ft Lyon and wanted to warm their hands. Milly, with her usual pertiness, wanted to know if they came all the way from the fort over here at that late hour of the night only to warm their hands. No doubt they were roving about after plunder, but finding we had a guard they went off very much enraged at the questions, and cursing the negroes furiously. We received a letter to-day from Com- Forrest making inquiries about his friends- property etc. Says he has met both Bushrod and David in Richmond lately both well and doing well. Mrs F- and Douglas are also well. It really was a great pleasure to hear from them, if it only was a flag of truce letter-

Date Rich- Nov 28-62

Sunday 7th We both went to church this morning. The weather is intensely cold a number of the poor wretches in the convalescent camp, and several in the 34 Massregiment froze to death last night. In going to town we met a wagon with four immense coffins in it, one piled on the top of another, going out for the Massachusetts men. We found Miss

Annie K. all fixed up, pack and baggage, ready for a start homeward tomorrow morning. Pass and all- said she had no difficulty in obtaining it. But she was very much excited, and gave me a full account of an interview she had with Mrs. S- whose tenants they were when they left town. They went away with the expectation of returning in a few weeks, but the yankees came in and prevented their return They left the house just as they had used it all their house hold and kitchen furniture, China, glass, house linen, every thing even a quantity of their wearing apparel, and jewelry Mrs S- acknoledges she had the house broken open soon after the yankees came in and rented it to a Federal officer furniture and all. But declares she will not be responsible for any losses, and would not allow Miss A- to take one article out of the house, not even a new piano and guitar belonging to her sister. Happily her declarations do not make her the less responsible in the eyes of the law. It certainly was a deed worthy of herself, and her yankee friends and allies. There is much sickness in the town. The citizens are dropping off dayly, and almost every Sunday we have one or two funeral invitations read out in church. While we were at church three soldiers from a Vermont regiment presented themselves at the kitchen door and demanded their dinners. Old mammy told them she had some cold meat and bread, and some milk, they could have that if they wanted it. They were highly incensed. They cursed and swore at her, and told her they would have a hot dinner and she would cook it for them, They wanted fried chicken and eggs, and various other dainties, and they would have it. They became so loud and vehement in their threats and demands that the guard had to be called in. as soon as they found a guard was about, they took their leave without either a hot dinner or a cold- It does seem as if we are never to be rid of these annoyances

Monday 8th The weather to-day is bitterly cold and the river is frozen across Charles did not get home until late in the day. He says the government has seized all the fuel in the town for army use.

Tuesday 9th We went to Mr. Fairfax's this morning to ask if he could tell us any thing about Clermont, or the man who the Commodore left in charge. He says the man sold all the crops, cattle, and stock and every thing of the kind and then cleared out, he does not know where But that Capt Cunningham of 4th Main regiment told him while he was camped on the place, that he, Capt Cunningham was formerly in the U S. Navy and knew the Com- well. And when he got to Clermont, and found how every thing was left there, he went to work, and with his own hands helped to pack up all the household goods and valuables, and sent them to a neighbours for safe-keeping

He told this as if his personal regard for the Com. prompted him to try and secure some of the property. But I do not believe a word of it- neither did Mr. Fairfax We heard too much from their own *Clan* of the quantities and quantities of goods sent from there north to believe any thing of that kind, they even took the marble mantles and hearths and sent them north. There was a woman at Mr. Fairfax's yesterday from Fairfax Courthouse. She too had her tale of woe to tell, of the violence and brutal wrongs committed up there by Burnside's savage hostsmore than a volume would contain. I could never recount it all- She also told of Patterson's killing himself, says he was boarding with a family and when they heard the report of the pistole they rushed into his room and found him barely alive, the only words he spoke in a faint voice were "Keep it a secret- Keep it a secret," and then died- Poor man! could not help feeling a respect and pity for him. I believe his conscience told him he was doing wrong.

Wednesday 10*th* Lizzie went to town this morning, hopeing to find an opportunity of sending a letter in reply to Com- Forrest's- She left it with the post master But he could give her very little information as to whether it would be sent or not. She found to her utter amazement that Miss A. K- is still in town. She said she started homeward on Tuesday according to previous arrangement, and as far as Fairfax Court house, there they were stopped and permitted to go no further. That vile old savage Heintzelman after giving them the pass and starting them off, telegraphed to the court house to have the whole party arrested as soon as they arrived there, but instead of arresting and putting them in prison, they were questioned very closely and then allowed to return to Alex.- One of the officers said to Miss Annie, he knew she was the greatest rebel of the whole party. She only laught at him and passed on

Thursday 11*th* We can see from here, that all the camps around Gen- Coopers place and also those about the Seminary have been re- moved within the past few days The straglers and convalescent camps are very extensive. Every family who asks now for a guard has to put up with a convalescent or two, then two or three will obtrude themselves I suppose for company, and the family have either to feed them all or stand the consequences a barn burned, or a cow killed, or some thing of the sort. They certainly are the lazzest wretches in the world- they lounge about the house and yard all day long, and do nothing but eat and sleep. I believe they would freeze rather than cut a stick of wood to make a fire

Friday 12*th* Cannon in the direction of Fredricksburg have been thundering all day long. And this evening the guard brings the news from Ft Lion, That the place is laid in ashes.

Saturday 13*th* Very distant firing has been heard all day long, from early morning until late at night, but so distant we should not have observed it if we had not known fighting was in progress. The Baltimore sun states that forty or fifty of the best houses and churches were burned in Fredricksburg yesterday. We do nothing but wander from door to window and listen-listen to the unceasing *roar roar* Heart rending though it be- O I wonder- will it never- never cease!

Sunday 14*th* Lizzie went to church this morning and brought Miss A. K. home with her. I can not express the pleasure it gives us to see and talk with her, and every body is so delighted to see her. And her narration of facts, so gratifying and so different from the news paper accounts, and so many grand success as our army had had that we never dreamed of. But O the deeds of horror—of savage violence committed on the poor defenceless people when the army falls back and leaves a place in the hands of the pitiless dasterdly foe. I wonder if the half will ever be If it is, what a catalogue of blood and crime for the perusal of future generations. My first thought this morning, as it always is was about our army, and I hoped and prayed God to take care of them, and that they might not be compelled to fight this blessed Sabbath day, so clear, and bright, and quiet as it has been to us. I trust they may have enjoyed its rest. A few days after the clergyman's letter published in the Baltimore Republican appeared of which I have named before, President Lincoln issued a proclamation prohibiting work, or any kind of military exercises, to be carried on, on Sunday- nevertheless there has been more drilling, and blowing of horns, and other military sounds going on to day than usual "A military neccessity," I suppose

Monday 15*th* A very strong wind all day from the South, almost a hurricane. Vague reports have reached us all day of a severe battle on Saturday and as usual a great Union victory "Twenty five thousand rebels killed and not a Union man hurt." Charles did not get home until very late this evening, says there was no boats running to day between W*a* and Alex- All had been sent down to Acquia Creek to bring up the wounded He had at last to come down in a *Tug*- He says they are talking of Saturdays battle as the severest of the war. He saw an immense body of Cavelry, many squares long and the few troops left for the defence of W*a* on the way to reenforce Burnside.

Tuesday 16*th* The weather last night was wildly tempestuous, the winds raged and howled and the rain came down in torrents, I have observed it, throughout the war whenever there is a severe battle, the

General Samuel S. Cooper
Courtesy of Castle Books, A Division of Book Sales, Inc.

wind rises, and then the rain pours- I opened my eyes this morning on, I think, the dreariest scene, I ever before looked upon- The wind in fitful gusts dashed the heavy drops of rain against the window panes, and the fields around, so waste, and bare, looked still more sad and gloomy as the wind and rain swept over them, in the gray light of this drear and dark December morn- When I laid my head down last night on my warm, soft, comfortable bed, I thought of our poor dear soldiers until my heart ached, and my pillow was wet with tears. No doubt many of the poor fellows lying wounded, and dying on the battle field, exposed to all the mad fury of the elements- Thank God it was not bitterly cold, and I could only pray "Him who tempers his winds to the shorn lambs," to take care of and comfort them. It cleared off before twelve, and from that until dark the distant roar of cannons was distinctly heard. Miss Annie laid down and slept, and slept as quietly and comfortable as possible- But for L- and me there was neither rest or sleep we wandered from window to window, and door to door- up stairs and down stairs and listened- listened- I said to Miss A- O how can you sleep when you know a battle is in progress- and you can hear the roar of the cannon. She lifted herself up on her elbows and rubbed her eyes and smiling said "O I know our boys have the best of it, and I can tell you for your comfort that all that roaring of cannon amounts to very little. Musketry is what does the effective work." It was a comfort to hear her talk so, even though I feared she was mistaken,

Wednesday 17 Insco came back from camp this morning with the news that Burnside has met with most signal success- has defeated the rebels at every point, and among other absurdities says, that although obligated to retreat to this side of the Rappahannock he has out flanked the enemy, and more over intends pursuing his onward march to Richmond if he only gains a mile in twenty four hours- I have heard this boastful threat before today. Miss Annie left us this morning- she hopes to leave town on Friday by flag of truce boat to Richmond. She promises to see Bushrod and Com- and Mrs. Forrest if possible- L- went to town with her, and brought back the glorious news that Burnside has indeed, and in truth been thoroughly defeated and driven across the Rappahannock river with immense los- Confederate los comparatively small

Thursday 18*th* The passes are filled today with Burnside's "disastrous defeat"- Gen Freemont is in W*a* and the papers state will soon take command of the "Grand Army of the Potomac" all our people about here are in ecstasys at the late war news. We saw an immense body of cavelry going down the telegraph road to-day, at least two miles long. We sent our best wishes along with them, that they very soon might be gobled up, thought it likely that Gen Lee might like to have the horses. We went after dinner to Mr. Fairfax's and saw a regiment of cavelry, and a long train of wagons going in the same direction- yesterdays papers state that most of the rebel casualties were in Gen Longstreet's division, and that is the one Miss A- told us Bushrod belongs to- For more than a week they have been hauling cannon up to Ft. Lion-

Friday 19*th* After every great battle the commander in chief has to give place to a new one, to-day it is said McClellan is coming to the front again. a soldier came to the kitchen this evening and asked to see one of us, L- went and found him a total stranger, he said he had an important communication to make and wished to see her alone, She had to shew him into the dining room which she did with great reluctance, as a yankee soldier had never been in any part of our house before excepting in the kitchen Lizzie says a number of thoughts passed through her mind as he followered her in. She could not imagine what he possibly could have to tell- What, if he intended to kill her, perhaps he had been sent to Ft. Lafayett- What could it be- He took his seat, and then looked round very suspiciously as if he too was afraid of assasination, then he commenced his string of falsehoods. In a low mysterious kind of whisper, he said that in the fight on Saturday at Fredricksburg he fell into the hands of a Confederate Colonel- Some sharp words passed between them at first, But after a while became better friends, and when the Col- discovered from his conversation that he had been camped about Alex- he was much interested and asked a great many questions about this family, and the other family and particularly about us- and made him promise, should he return this way to visit us, and let us know he had seen such a person, and to say from him that all our friends were well. She asked if this officer did not reveal his name, he said no, we must be satisfied to know all are well. L- knew from his talk he wanted her to believe he had seen Bushrod He described him as a thick-set man with dark complexion and dark hair, and said he belonged to one of the Alex- regiments. She asked him if he thought he had seen our brother, and he replied, he did, He said they sat on the side of a ditch and talked and presently a party of Federals came along and took the Col. prisoner But he was exchanged in about half an hour and that was the last he saw of him. But for his thinking the man was our brother he would not have bought the one pass he believed it an infringement of military rule. I just know the whole story is a fabrication- This man has some object in getting into our house, calls himself McCluer says he belongs to the Mozart regiment, and has been guard at one of the neighbours since last summer Says he came up yesterday with eight hundred of their wounded, and that the yankees certainly had the worst of it, his regiment which has recently consolidated for the forth time came out of the Fredricksburg fight with only one hundred and fifty men, and when the pay-master came round there were only seventy five to pay. He says there was only gun fired by them on Sunday as a challenge, but the Southerners took no notice of it. "He is tired of the war- did not come down here to fight for niggers."

Saturday 20*th* Cannon is still being hauled up to Fort Lyon. Miss McClure came to see us for a little while this evening. She says every one is highly elated at the recent Confederate successes. The papers are filled with Burnside's defeat, they do not pretend to deny, or gloss it over us hitherto- Our guard who is as bitter and vindictive as he is ignorant and unlettered, came back from the quite crest fallen, after telling me of the immense loss, and terrible slaughter of their men, said to my utter amazement that he did believe the South was in the right, and that Almighty God smiled on them and favoured their cause. I said nothing I knew well if I agreed with him he would make use of anything I might say to serve his own purpose. He is like all the rest of his Countrymen not to be trusted, There is neither honour, honesty or truth in any of the nation.

Sunday 21*st* I was not well enough to go to church this morning and L- had to go alone- She says every body looks bright and happy, and all are congratulating each other at the results of the recent battles They say Gen Lee is this side the Rappahannoc-at Falmoth- Large bodys of soldiers have been passing up and down this road all day. They move so quietly that I was not aware of it until a large body of them passed in front of the dining room windows, then I got up to look and found the road full of them, quiet movements is so unusual I do not understand it.

Monday 22*nd* Charles came home this morning with the pleasing intelligence that three companies of the cavalry we saw passing here on Thursday last were captured on Saturday near Occoquan by Gen-Stewart-, Stiles was leading them, a yankee who has been living in that neighbourhood for a great many years. Those who escape of them ran back this way, and we saw their fires in the night- This morning they have taken the road towards Fairfax Court house. Insco heard at the convalescent camp, that Sutler Patterson has lost all his wagons, horses, mules, men every thing, all *"gobbled* up by Stewarts Cavelry," O I was too delighted, I hope he will have meeted out to him a little of the measure he gave us

Tuesday 23 We were awakened about midnight by a bright light shining in our room, and starting up found all out doors illuminated, and a big fire blazing in the [sic] We aroused up the guard, and Charles and sent them out to see what it ment. They found five or six soldiers had taken possession of a log house they call Gravit's house and were making them comfortable. The guard would not let them stay, But drove them off, and to accelerate their movements fired his gun after them- Deserters no doubt

Wednesday 24th Drilling and drumming, cannon firing from the forts, heavy volly of musketry, rumbling of wagons and cars, the whistle of the locomotive, and the sound of the bugle, has made it seem a busy day with the yankees. Preparing I suppose for the festivities of Christmas. The Convalescent camp has been removed several miles further from us, and nearer to W*a* for which I am thankful, as it will relieve us in a measure of the burden of feeding so many of the miserable wretches. It has been no slight tax

Thursday 25th Another Christmas day finds us still in the hands, and under the domination of the hateful yankees- It is well the future is hidden from us, the thought of these two years of captivity would have been unendurable to us. We both went to Church this morning and find Miss Annie still in town, and seeming with no prospect of getting away. She gave us some most amusing accounts of her visits to the different Provost-Marshals and her efforts to obtain a pass. Finding she was so unsuccessful in Alex she determined to try in W*a* But the man there was very curt and gruff and answered her in a loud emphatic tone. "No you can *not* have a pass, it is not safe." She gave him one of her most bewitching smiles, shook her beautiful sunny curls- and said in her sweet low voice "Now you know that is not so." She perfectly disarmed his wrath, he laughed, but he never gave her the pass. Then she went back to Alex and found a rather elderly man in the office who asked her a thousand questions, that had no bearing on the case whatever, such as her fathers and mothers names, occupation, age- how *old her great grandmother was* when *she died, and her name before she was married-* and a great many nonsensical questions about herself- how old she was- "O" she said "You know ladies have an objection to telling their age. I don't mind telling *you*" (She had several persons with her) But I don't want all these to know, I'll whisper it into your ear," She put her hand on his shoulders leaned over and whispered it in his ear- She said he never smiled, sat as sober as a Judge. She said she did not mind putting her hand on his shoulder as he was a right clean looking old man A flag of truce boat has been promised, and at least six hundred applicants to go in it. But no one knows when or any thing about it, and it keeps the people in a great state of anxiety, and running from one high *official* to another, and they fear the large number that wish to go will deter them from sending it at all. We found a soldier here when we got home with soap and sugar for sale. Says "he is employed by the officers to sell all the rations that they have cheated the poor soldiers of."

Friday 26*th* Our guard is getting very much disatisfied, and extremely disagreeable I shall hail with joy the day when we are forever rid of the whole of them, if the time ever comes. He says his shoes are worn and his clothes threadbare- He has not had a cent of pay for six months- and to-day is looking for work. I think the idea is that it is our business not only to supply him with board, but clothes also. We were at Mr. Reid's this evening- They told us that a Mr. Hunter living near Fairfax Court house has been arrested and will be kept in prison until Stiles is returned. Stiles was taken while leading a body of cavelry Mr. Hunter was taken out of his house without having committed any offense whatever.

Saturday 27th To-day is dark and lowering, and every indication of a storm The heavy sound of Cannon comes booming up from towards Fredricksburg. The guard came from camp with the information that the firing we hear is a skirmish near Dumfries He says four men dressed in Citizens clothes are going around searching houses in this neighbour-hood, and he is determined if they come here to give them a warm reception

Sunday 28*th* We were at church this morning and find much to our surprise that Miss Annie is gone- very sorry not to see her again, but hope this time she will reach home in safety. She went in a buggy with Rev. Mr S- As we drove down King street observed a great number of persons going in and coming out of Mr Wheatly's undertaking establish-ment, and learned after, they were collected there to view the remains of CapLawton- a confederate officer who died in the hospital yesterday he was wounded and taken prisoner at the battle of Fredricksburg. The authorities have given up the remains to the gentlemen of the town, to care for. Our guard came from the camp in a great state of excitement says the rebels are within eight miles of the town. Four yankee cavalrymen came dashing up the telegraph road about two hours ago with the news. They were so hotly pursued they lost their hats, and came dashing up the road like mad bareheaded

Monday 29*th* The whole town and country is in the most intense state of excitement and alarm- Last night Stewart's cavalry (the great yankee bug-bare of the present time) is said to have been within six miles of Ft Lyon, all the ordnance and commissary stores in the town that could possibly be removed were loaded on vessels lying at the wharves and shoved out into the stream, those that could not be removed were fixed so as to be blown up at a moments notice. Quartermaster Fergerson had all his goods and chattels packed up and ready for a start, and all our poor African chattels stood shivering in the cold all night, with hats, and bonnets, and cloaks, all one. And all their poor old rags bundled up ready for a dash towards W*a* But all for naught, the rebs did not come. The remains of Capt Lawton were carried to the grave to-day from the residence of Mr Douglass Course, every mark of respect and attention was shown by the citizens, about six hundred followed in the funeral train, and as they passed through the streets a great many yankee soldiers stood looking on, and one threw up his hat and huzza for Jefferson Davis, and another said he did not believe Burnside could have had such a funeral. The guard returned from camp as usual with his budget of news, more accounts of the cutting up of yankee troops, and the capture of nearly two whole regiments of cavalry last night at Oc-coquan. Every man about here slept on his arms- and every car at the Depot stood ready with steam up to take off the negroes in case of an attack, and all the wagons in town stood in the streets all night with horses hitched to them ready for a start

Tuesday 30 The first thing this morning I was aroused from my sleep by the blowing of a cavelry bugle and started up expecting to see Gen. Stewart *just* at the *door wanting* his *breakfast*. But-O-so disappointed-there was no Gen- Stewart there- I think if I could see the Confederate army coming in here I should almost loose my senses with delight- Nearly two years now have we been shut up here, exposed to all the tyranny and insults of these vile people without one days cessation or relief- There has been an incessant drumming, and rumbling of wagon all day- Lizzie was at Mr Fairfax's this evening and learned that the troops are still under arms expecting an attack every moment The news papers are filled with the "gobbling up" of cavelry, sutlers stores in and about Dumfries and Occoquan by "Stewart's gurillas."—Stewart is now the *darling* of the *yankee heard*. He seems to have supplanted the Black Horse Cavalry in their affections.

Wednesday 31 This day closes the year of -62 And the catalogue of blood and crime, this year registered against the nation is frightful to think upon, What a record to hand down to future generations- and O when God shall make inquisition for blood, and the earth shall no more cover, her slain, what scenes of horror will be brought to light. The troops about here are kept in a constant state of alarm, and the chasing in of pickets, and the capturing of pickets is of almost daily occurence. This evening about eight oclock we were startled by the rapid firing of guns, seemingly in the neighbourhood of the seminary. It continued without intermition for more than an hour

Thursday January 1st 1863 We learned to day that the firing of guns we heard last night was a skirmish near the Chain bridge But it seemed much nearer than that We walked out to the fort this evening and I picked up a hand full of minie balls They were all covered with tallow. I asked the guard what it was done for, he replied the tallow was to keep the guns clean, But I had better be careful how I handled them as it was mixed with the most deadly posion, and the man who was shot with one must either die or loose a limb- I could not believe it- a yankee even could not be so savage

Friday 2nd Mr and Mrs McCluer came to see us this evening he says Alex never knew such a panic as last Saturday night when the hatless horsemen dashed in. So certain were they all of an immediate attack that the greatest consternation prevailed, and that books, papers, every thing of consequence that could be scrambled up, were borne off in the greatest hurry and confusion. He says that soldier named McCluer who came last week with such a pretence of secrecy and mystery, with communications purporting to come from Bushrod, we need not place the slightest credence in- for he has known him some time, and knows to be a villian, and not one word of truth in his tongue.

Sunday 4th We were in town yesterday, and again this morning L-went in to church. I was obliged to remain at home as the guard went off and did not return, it was a great disappointment, as it is about the only pleasure we have attend church together- Lizzie says she saw seven locomotives all steamed up and standing about the depot as she passed. Soldiers in numbers have been wandering all over the fields and hills all day. Four men, I could tell whether officers or soldiers came dashing through the yard this evening. First they rode round and seemed to be viewing the fort, and then up and down the riflepits. I very much fear looking for camping grounds

Monday 5th All is quiet along the Potomac to-day! at least as far as we know any thing about it. We heard a report yesterday that the Southerners have captured the IronClad vessel "Monitor." To-day they say she sprang a leak off Cape Hatteras with sixty men on board, and went to the bottom, (The next best thing she could do)

Tuesday 6th It has rained nearly all day, about twelve oclock there was such a rolling and rumbling of wagons, that we both started out to the fort, regardless of the weather, expecting to see Burnside and all his army performing the grand movement *de retrograde*. But we were fated to disappointment again, as it proved only a long train of wagons hauling wood from Mr Mason's. They are slaying the "Rose Hill" wood now in vast quantities. Twenty five empty government wagons passed here going towards town, no one could tell where they came from.

Thursday 8 We saw from the fort, an immense body of cavalry, and ten wagons going up the "Little River" turnpike. The Southerners made a rade upon Fairfax C. H last night and captured sixteen men- a dispatch was sent to W*a* and three regiments and some artillery was sent up.

Friday 9*th* Found the ground this morning covered with a slight coating of snow this far it has been the mildest, and dryest winter I have ever known. About fifty cavelry, and two wagons loaded with tents passed up this road to day.

Sunday 11th We could not go to church to day as we had no one to drive the carriage Charles went to W*a* on Sunday last with the promis of returning on Friday- Since then we have heard nothing of him. Whether he thinks himself free since Lincoln's recent proclamation- or has been crippled again by his soldiers we have no means of finding out- But I can hardly think, that after being so faithful to us, ever since the invasion he would have gone off so, without at least giving us some intimation of his intention of so doing Our guard went off yesterday and stayed a long time and then came back drunk and has been quarreling and fighting with Milly ever since. He has gotten very intimate with old Smith lately and we can see the pernitious influence more and more every day when he comes from there. I expect we will have to find some means of getting rid of him

Monday 12*th* Stragling parties from the picket stations, and soldiers on horse back have been passing to and fro all day- A few cannon from the forts around have been fired to-day- a sound we have not heard for many a-day. They afraid I suppose of the echos awaking the "*Southern Lion*" (Stewart) Who, from all accounts of him must possess the power of ubiquity, and is ever on the alert to *gobble* up all the yankee stores, and all the sutler's wagons, and every thing else, it matters not how much cavalry is around for their protection- Thursday or Friday of last week two women came begging, and while the tears streamed down their faces in torrents, they told of the sickness and suffering from cold, starvation and nakedness endured by their poor husbands at the convalescent camp. A soldier who happened to be in the yard and heard all their tales of woe, stepped up and said, "every word they were telling was lies, He was just from the convalescent camp, and no such persons as they described were there, and neither did they belong there." This plain talking soon dried up their tears, and aroused their ire, and they gave him back any amount of impudence until I was afraid they would into a fisticuff with him, But they very soon went off

I should have forgotten the circumstance altogether, had not Insco's conduct lately been so annoying. Last night in a drunken fit he revealed the whole plan of the womens visit here, and himself as the instigator, his object he declared being to discover whether we were secessionists or not, If he can only find out that we are he declares his intention of going to the camp and making it known, and getting a party of soldiers to help him, and coming back and tearing down the house and destroying every thing every thing. These threats he is constantly making, not only when he is drunk but at all times. He grumbles that he has not a room in the house, and is not allowed to sit at the table with us. The women were from Robert Smith's house, just below the mill, about half a mile from here. It is filled with vile women from the north, and such riots, and carousals, as they have nightly with the soldiers is a disgrace to the country. They are depredating and a constant annoyance to all the people living around Milly got so furiously mad at Insco's talk that she came right into the house and told us all- and O what can we do! When I think of our isolated and helpless condition, and what we are surrounded by, and every moment exposed to a feeling of unutterable despair comes over me. If we send away this vile ungreatful wretch in all probability they will not allow any guard at all. Charles came home to day much to our relief, as we could hear nothing of him. Illness prevented his return- He is still very far from well, and very deaf. No doubt it all proceeds from a severe beating the soldiers gave him last summer in the streets of Washington.

Tuesday 13 We were in town this morning, and the agreeable news met us that Gen. Magruder had recaptured Galveston Texas, and with it the War Steamer Harriet Lane. I was particularly delighted as that steamer was the last vessel Bushrod went to sea in, and he always seemed so much attached to her. The very last time he was at home while he was assisting in building the Potomac batteries he said, he did not know how he could ever fire into the Harriet Lane if it should be his misfortune to encounter her- O we are all so thankful and so hopeful! good news is now coming in thick and fast. And the yankees too are at *loggerheads* among them-selves- Republicans and Democrats are having it up and down- and we have the good old proverb on our side- "When thieves fall out honest men get their dues."

Wednesday 14 Every day now passes pretty much alike. We seldom have a visitor The quiet reminds us of the old Pennsula days of last summer. We read, and work, talk over the terrible, frightful scenes through which we have passed, and some times indulge in hopeful dreams of bright and happy days to come. And then after long and weary watching and hopeing and waiting- a letter—or a word, assuring us of the well-being of far off loved ones, comes to sustain, and what a comfort and hope they inspire, only they who feel it know. A very heavy south wind has prevailed for several hours almost a tornado, it has torn and injured the shrubbery greatly, particularly the old Arbavita trees Any number of soldiers, both on foot and on horses have passed through here to-day but they seem greatly subdued- The people coming up from Pohick and Hay field neighbourhood say the woods about there are filled with hundreds and hundreds of deserters

Saturday 17 Several of our old neighbours are sick- very *sick*, and scarcely a house where there is not sickness in. Mostly children and I have not been well enough to go with Lizzie to see them. This evening she took Milly and went to see old Mr Taylor who she found extremely ill. The doctor says he can not possibly recover.

Sunday 18 Miss McCluer came over to see us yesterday and stayed all night and went this morning to town to church with Lizzie. Directly after they were gone I sent to inquire after old Mrs Dawsy. Mrs Fairfax's mother who has been sick for several days- and the answer came back "She is dying." I looked out and could see from our room window men at "Sharon" digging a grave for Mr Taylor, poor old man he died this morning about four oclock. He has been sick for several weeks and L. had been unwearied in her attendance upon him, Sitting by him, and reading and talking to him, and making and carrying to him all kinds of little daintys to tempt his apetite Some times she would trudge up there two or three times a day. And not until after his death, when they were preparing him for burial did they have the least idea he died with small-pox. Then the marks came all over the body. O it was the greatest shock when we heard of it. Lizzie came home with a letter from Miss Annie dated 7th Jan and written to Mrs. Course. She reached home safely after being on the road three days. Sent us word she has written to Bushrod, and says, "What a succession of glorious victories we have had lately, peace must surely follow soon" But if there are any other than Galveston and Fredricksburg we have not heard of them. As soon as dinner was over Lizzie and I ran off to see poor Mrs. Dawsy. We were very much afraid she would have passed away before we got there. But she had breath in her, and that was all, could not speak, though I think she was conscious of our presence- It was a sad, sad sight so old, and worn to a shadow, and labouring, labouring for breath and each came with intense agony- She was our warmly attached friend, and the last thing she said, before being deprived of speach was, "Why don't they come." A number of officers and soldiers were in the yard as we passed through firing at a mark, and every report would make her start and shiver I went out on the porch and beconed to an officer when he came near I said Mrs Fairfax's mother is extremely ill. I believe dying, and these guns disturb her dreadfully. Won't you be so good as to induce the men to go away from the house with them. "O Yes" he said, "certainly." I came on home, but could hear the guns going off all the way as I came up the road. I do not believe they moved a peg

Monday 19*th* Our good old friend Mrs. Dawsy closed her eyes in death about four O'clock. I was sick and could not go. But Lizzie has been there all day helping and making arrangements for the funeral. I feel (that though humble) we have been this week called upon to part with two sincere friends. I was truly sorry I did hope these two old people would live to see this war happily terminated They were both so much interested, and anxious for the success of the Southern cause and had both suffered so much. But he who governs all things knows best The smallpox still rages, numbers both of soldiers and citizens die *daley* with it. Saw a long train of wagons taking the patience to the Clermont hospital, all houses about the town that are suspected of having the disease in them are searched and whenever found are taken off to the horrid hospitals, where they are packed in, men women and children, black and white indiscriminately, where there is little, or no care taken of them, and the most of them die. Col. Dulaney called, and wished to know if we would take the responsibility of having a guard placed over the Davis property. The Taylors are going to move away from there and just leave it to the mercy of the soldiers. L- told him we had nothing to do with it, she had written once to the family on the subject at old Mr Taylor's request and they had taken no notice of her letter and any further interfering would seem an intrusion. Col Dulaney seems to know very little more about the army movements than we do. He says however a great number of troops have been sent within the past two days up the Orange and Alex- rail road- and Col. Tate who has command of all the forces in and around Alex- has orders to be in readiness to march in twelve hours- and that Burnside's left wing has again crossed the Rappahannock

Tuesday 20*th* Our guard went off this morning to W*a* and prevented my going to the funeral, which I wished very much to have done- Excepting for the name of the thing we might as well be without one, for every day almost he is off, and then comes back drunk Two soldiers came late this evening, and searched round in every place excepting the house they did not come into the house where we were- Milly had just

finished milking the cows- They said they wanted the milk, and would have it. But she seized it up and being more fleet of foot than they succeeded in getting to the house with it. They loitered, and hung about a long time, at last the guard put in an appearance and they made off- I suppose they thought he was in the house, was the reason they did not attack the *Citadel*

"Claremont," the home of Captain French Forrest, C.S.N.,—from a sketch made in September, 1861*
Courtesy of Castle Books, A Division of Book Sales, Inc.

Wednesday 21*st* Last night was one of storm, the wind blew furiously and dashed the rain through every crack and crany, and rocked our old fabric to the very foundation The rain has continued all day, but notwithstanding the guard went off as usual and did not return until dark, then he came with great news, "peace is to be declared immediately." He could not give no other reason as a foundation for the report, than that all work on Ft Lion has been stopped, all the tools taken from there, not a pick or shovel is left, and another piece of information was that a

---

* A captain in the U.S. Navy, Forrest resigned his commission in June, 1861, and was appointed to the same rank in the Confederate States Navy. Captain Forrest supervised the rebuilding of the C.S.S. *Merrimac,* renamed the C.S.S. *Virginia,* the south's first ironclad. In 1863, he was appointed Flag Officer of the James River Squadron. "Claremont," was located on the site of the present-day Claremont Elementary School on Claremont Drive, North of Franconia Road, Springfield, Virginia. The property was used as a picket post for the 40th New York Infantry, and the house was used as a Union Army hospital.

number of persons living about four miles from the fort, were robbed last night of all their beehives and poultry, one man went to the fort to make complaint. They arrested him and kept him there all day, and then let him loose without any reason, or redress whatever

Friday 23rd The rain which has been coming down down for several days ceased this morning and the sun came out bright and warm as a May day, and although the ground is soaked with water until it is like walking on a well spring. We put on our India rubbers and walked all over the place. It was perfectly delightful to be out in the free air again, not a soldier did we see. The atmosphere was clear and lovely, and the view from the fort was magnificent, "The *cities of the plain*" came out splendidly. The old Capital too loomed up into the sky in all its grandure, looking like a thing of the clouds, so white and soft and fleecy, that you feel every moment it must disolve into thin air or assuming some more fantastic shape float away into the clouds. The river this evening was covered with white sails. We could see them from away down almost to Ft Washington, all along up to the city of W*a* and wondered what it means The papers still represent Burnside as the other side of the Rappahannoc, and some say a deadly combat is in progress some where not far from Fredricksburg. But we have not heard the sound of cannon in that direction and feel inclined to doubt the report.

Sunday 25th We were both at church this morning- "Every thing is quiet on the lower Potomac." That is as far as we know any thing about it. The soldiers now are at war with the negroes- whenever they get out of camp they do nothing but fight and quarrel with them. Say they have recently discovered that is what the war is about, and they are compelled to stay here and fight for them against their will, and they are determined to kill every one they come across- But I find soldiers say a great many things besides their prayers- A great number of locomotives are always standing at the depot steaming away, *ready for action*. The yankees are now engaged improving the Orange depot building- They have raised the center past a story, and covered it with a conical roof and finished it off with a cupola. as we rode past this morning on our way to church we saw the roof covered with men as hard at work as if it was Monday and as we came back their hats and coats and tools were scattered about up there as if they had gone to dinner, and expected to continue their work in the afternoon. At the West End camp there was a miserable wretched looking soldier chained to a tree with his hands crossed in the fork above his head, fastned [sic] together with hand cuffs He was there in the morning when we went in, and there hours after, when we returned he was there in the same position still, O these yankees know how to inflict punishment. The poor negroes may congratulate themselves that they are not *their* slaves but their "ecols"

Monday 26*th* We were at Mr Fairfax's this evening and learned how narrowly she escaped being killed on Thursday last, she had just finished dressing and had left her room, when a ball came tearing through the walls and into her room, shivering the looking glass frame and splintering her bed stead and then dropped near the fireplace where two or three of her little children were standing. She says if she had been in bed she would have been killed. Mr F- went out and searched all about, and through the bushes but could see no one- We counted from there seventeen ambulances on the turnpike road going to the Seminary where they deposited their load, and then went down the telegraph road. Every one thinks fighting has been going on somewhere to-day. Cannon was heard in the direction of Manassas. There was a prolongued cheering at Ft Lion this evening. The guard said it was a welcome to the paymaster, as nothing else now can arrouse [sic] any thing like enthusiasm.

Wednesday 28*th* We have had quite a succession of rainy days- this morning the ground was covered with a slight coating of snow, but it continued to fall all day The guard went off yesterday and did not return until this evening. as usual he brings great news. "Old fighting Joe" has again come to the front, and takes command of the army in place of Burnside, and is to carry every thing before him, and soon finish up the war- There is nothing like it change and change about.

Thursday 29th This morning the sun came out cheeringly bright and warm. Col- Dulaney was so kind as to call and inquire how we are getting on, and to bring us some newspapers. The Baltimore Sun is filled with good news nothing but disatisfaction and discord, the army, Congress, and all the yankee people are at war with each other. Since the battle of Fredricksburg three Maj Generals have *retired* either at their own request, or that of some one else Burnside, Sumner and Franklin are the three who the wheel of fortune has this time depressed. No officer now dares speak in disparagement of Lincoln or his policy in regard to the negro, and no officer dares offer his resignation. At first the punishment in either case was dishonerable dismissal, but a more recent order is that the shoulder straps are to be shorn off, and the culprit reduced to the ranks, where he is condemned to remain during the war

Saturday 31st The firing of cannon has been heard at intervals throughout the day seemingly as near as the Court house. A regiment of cavalry passed down the telegraph road soon after dinner, a wagon train followed some hours after. We saw the smoke from their fires about nine o'clock. Charles says five hundred negroes had their names enrolled for the army in Alex today. One of the officers asked him to have his name put down But he said, no, he did not want to raise a gun against any body. He said to us "No, he had no notion of guine wid dat army, to be made bres works of for dem yankees."

Sunday, February 1st 1863 We were both at church this morning. The roads are getting very bad, and but few of the military moving about, very few epaulets to be seen on the streets at this time, orders are very stringent that officers shall be kept at their posts. We were very much distressed when we got home to find old mammy very complaining, she seems to have a presetiment that she is not to remain much longer with us now. She follows us about as if she could not dear [sic] to have us out of her sight. She has been a great comfort to us during these troubles, and O if we are called upon to part with her at this time, what a terrible, terrible affliction it will be. I pray our kind heavenly father may see fit to spare her to us a little longer. Poor dear old mammy! She says she would like to live to see her young masters come out of this war, and I know it would distress them both to come home and find their old mammie gone forever.

Monday 2nd. Today three soldiers came for milk, they did not take it by main force as they are in the habit of doing, but asked to buy it. They were dutchmen and "fights mit Sigel." They say the yankees are getting whipped every where. I expressed great astonishment and asked if they really thought so- "O yes they said they did not "dint it they knowed it" But it was altogather their own fault, if they had put Sigel at the "head of affairs it would all have been right, he was the best General next to McClellan- Troops are constantly coming and being sent up the rail road. To day the negro bill passed, and before the time of "the two years men", is out. One hundred and fifty thousand negro soldiers are to supply their place, and Simon Cameron offers his services to lead them into the heart of the Confederacy

Tuesday 3rd Two soldiers came into the kitchin today and proclaimed themselves deserters in want of citizen clothes. They offered ten dollars for an old coat, but the negroes were too sharp for them Charles says they were 34 Mass-men, and wanted to catch some body and he refused to let them have any thing. We learned to day that the small pox- has broken out in Mr Reids family, and one of old Taylor's daughters, and a grand child have died with it, we feel quite uneasy about it, as Lizzie and Milly both were with the old man every day while he was sick. The whole neighborhood is greatly alarmed- "Clermont", is so near us, and filled with small pox patients. Charles came in to let us know that every tree in "Sharon" yard had been cut and carried off, we hurried down there to find it was a fact. Henry Hasper a free negro and a yankee soldier living with him in one of the old houses below the hill, cut and carried them off during the last snow storm

Thursday 5th Lizzie went to town this morning. I charged her when she started to bring me back some good news, and she did sure enough, and good enough "to make the mountains skip like rams, and the little hills like young sheep" Gen Beauregard with only two vessels has captured burned, sunk, and dispursed the whole yankee blockading fleet, of thirteen iron clad steamers off Charleston S.C. The papers to day are filled with cheering news from all quarters. But our poor old town is gloomy and desolate enough, disease and death reign there- There is no estimating the numbers down with small-pox Typhoid and other fevers. Two of Sharon's little Sunday School children are lying dead to day in one house

Friday 6th It has rained hard all day, and we have seen or heard nothing but now and then a few straggling soldiers and pickets, and an occasional squad of negroes going towards town I suppose with the object of joining the army. Understand that all ours who have run off are in and about W*a* with no intention of being soldiers

Saturday 7th We learned to day that a part of Hookers army has returned to W*a* and a most dilapidated forlorn looking set they are. The news paper report is that the whole of the "Grand Army of the Potomac" are to be transferred to the West.

Sunday 8th We were both at church this morning. As we passed through West End we saw St. Mary's chapel, the windows all torn, out, the door standing open a complete wreck. It has been used all the time as a hospital, But the patience [sic] and soldiers all gone, and the building empty. O how can a God fearing people take *his* house and use it in that manner, I wonder they are not afraid that wrath will overtake and consume them

Monday 9th The streets of W*a* and Alex are again thronged with soldiers, every one thinks that Hooker has abandoned the idea of getting into Richmond this winter at least by way of Fredricksburg. Vast numbers of soldiers are scattered around us, all over hill and valley. They have no tents, but sleep on the naked ground, we can see the smoke of their fires ascending day and night. They while away their leisure hours by occasional little fights and skirmishes with the negroes, Just to keep themselves in practice. Parties of both colors will meet in the streets and fight until the Police authorities have to interfere to stop them. This morning about five hundred negroes were sent up the O & A rail road, No one seems to know the object but the negroes seem highly elated at it—they think "da is all gone to jine the army" But they had neither uniforms or arms, and I am inclined to believe they are destined to be again, "hewers of wood and drawers of water." Heavy firing again to the northwest

Tuesday 10th Today is bright and warm as a May-day—Scarcity of provender has obliged us to part with one of our plow horses, and today we saw with sorrow poor old Bob- trotted off by his new master. Thus, from day to day we see receding from all our comforts and possessions. Nothing is left to us now but poverty in the old home. I received a letter post marked Crawfordsville, Indianna. From my dear old aunt Betsy Scott It is filled, as usual with loyalty and Unionism.

Thursday 12th Our guard Insco received his pay yesterday and also his discharge and to-day he leaves for his home in Philadelphia. Although he has been here four months, we parted with him without the slightest feeling of regret, we think him so unprincipaled. But he says he is coming back soon to peddle in the camps. Charles escorted him to town, and as he walked along the road would shout to every soldier and picket he passed, "he was no longer a soldier but a free man once more, and would crawl on his hand, and knees, and beg from door to door before he would enlist again"

Saturday 14th Lizzie was in town this morning, and heard a great many wounded soldiers were brought in yesterday and among them some few Confederate prisoners. Heavy skirmishing all along the lines the whole of this, and last week. We hear heavy firing every day. The Pensylvania Reserves are the troop from Burnside's army that came up last week and camped on Watkins' and Richard's farms. They are said to have gone down to Fredricksburg nineteen thousand strong and now only number between four and five thousand. I am more than sorry they have fixed themselves so near us, as I have heard it said by their own people that for ferocious brutality the Pensylvania troops will take the palm. I have heard the officers laugh and tell of their atrocities as some thing very amusing and meritorious. L- received a letter to day the envelope nearly covered with the Union flag, and mottos on to Richmond, and victory emblazoned in glowing colours. We could not imagine where it came from or from whome [sic] But it proved from our old guard Insco announcing his safe arrival home, and expressing great solicitude for our safety and welfare, and offering his services to come and guard us again

Monday 16 Every thing is as quiet as possible to-day, but at least as far as we are concerned, and although thousands of soldiers are camped around we have remained unmolested, not even a picket stops for water.

The change is unaccountable to us Charles says a great many vessells loaded with troops went down the river this morning. L- saw a Mr Fairfax this evening, who had just arrived from the neighbourhood of Centerville. He reports a fight near Brentsville, and also one near Fredricksburg in both of which the yankees got considerably worsted. But no reports of the kind in the papers

Thursday 19th It has been snowing and raining incessantly for a week past. Today there was a short cessation and we sent Charles into town for the papers. A party of Confederates last Saturday night made a dash into Annandale and killed some fifteen of the 5th Michigan, and wounded and captured a great many more. C- also brought a letter from Bushrod, written to Miss A. K. date Wilmington N C Jan 18th All it contained was most cheering and satisfactory, although not written to ourselves. He says he is Chief of Artillery on Gen Whiting's staff, and as well and pleasantly situated as possible. David is Capt of a battery of heavy artillery in Richmond is well and doing well. He had a letter from Mary recently. Mr. Mower and some of the children had been sick, but were all well when she wrote, they had plenty of every thing and as yet have suffered no inconvenience from the war

Saturday 21st Almost every day brings accounts of skirmishes along the lines, or a sudden dash of Confederates among the yankees, and the *gobling* up of every thing they can find. Charles came home from town with more accounts of skirmishes. He says the yankees are bringing down from "Ravensworth" the most immense quantities of wood car loads, upon, car loads, there seems to be no end to the quantities. We have been anxiously expecting a visit from the son of Mr Windser of "Hayfield" who is a paroled prisoner and has been at home for some time. He sent us word he had seen a good deal of our brothers in and about Richmond last summer, and wanted very much to call and tell us all about them. But his father has been very ill, and whenever he could leave him business called him to Wa- and now that he is exchanged, will be obliged to leave on Monday or Tuesday, he is very sorry but will not be able to see us. There has been quite a stir again about the closing of stores and making every body take the oath. Two soldiers came and hung about the garden for about an hour, they seemed to be taking minute observations, I think they have an eye to the only two remaining beehives and told C- to have his gun in readiness

Sunday 22nd No church for us to-day. On awaking this morning, we found the ground covered with snow, and the weather very cold. The storm has raged all day, about 11 o'clock a squad of soldiers with an officer came stragling through the fields towards the house, they seemed perfectly benummed with the cold, and blinded with the wind and snow. We stood at the window and laughed to see them stumbling and staggering and falling into the holes, and their guns flying over their heads. Did not feel the slightest, sympathy or compassion for them. They had dug the holes, and we felt it all right that they should fall into the pits that they had made for others. We were much afraid of their coming to take up their quarters in the barn. But the officer stopped at the kitchin to inquire the way to Fairfax court house, and then proceeded on their way, making numberless circuits through and through the fields. I don't know in that way of marching and counter marching when they will find their way to the Court house.

Monday 23rd The snow lays on the ground fully a foot thick, the heaviest we have had this winter. We have not seen a single living creature moving about to-day. Lizzie and myself- old mammy and Milly are the only occupants of the house all day Charles did not return from W*a* and as night began to draw on, we felt quite lonely. But to our satisfaction before bed time John Allen came, he is mammie's nephew, and has been very good ever since the war, he comes Saturday and Sunday to protect us while Charles is away.

Tuesday 24th Charles got home this morning, was not allowed a pass yesterday. He says they are very particular again about giving passes. There has been a constant drumming, and booming of cannon from the different forts, but the mud is too deep for drilling much-

Thursday 26th I have been sick for more than a week passed, and this morning while lying on the sofa, listening to the pouring rain was starled by a loud, hollow,—I forgot the sickness- and started up and bounded to the window to find the front field filled with cavalry all strung out in lines,- We were alarmed thinking they were down upon us again. But one of the officers rode up to the kitchin and asked to be allowed to put three horses in the stable for a short time. He said they had started from W*a* at two o'clock this morning, were on their way up the country and had only stopped here to eat their dinner. He charged Charles to lock the stable door, and to allow no other horses to be put into it, he then dashed off and shouted to the others, that they would all go down into the valley and eat their dinner there. They never put any horses in the stable, and that was the last we ever saw or heard of them. Charles tracked them down the hill, and says they came from Ft Lion. I really have my curiosity excited to know what the object of that manover was.

Saturday 28th We have been shut up here with bad sounds, and bad weather, so long that we sent C. to town for the papers, hoping to hear some thing to interest us- and we did- news to gladden the heart, and revive the spirits in our solitude. Twenty Confederate calvary near Romney captured Milro's wagon train, a mile long, all the officers with it and eighty men. They have also made captures of cavalry in the neighbourhood of Chantilley, and here and there and every where. They have taken in the West, one of the finest Iron clad steamers on the western waters., "Queen of the West." This evening three officers all handsomely mounted, and decked off in their best military trappings, and tinsel, with immense white gauntlets up to their elbows, dashed through the orchard and fields up to the fort, where they all stopped a short time, and then rode leisurely round surveying the works. One who seemed to be the Col- pointed here and there, showing I suppose the most adventehous positions to place the guns in, or perhaps to show of his own importance, and his *beautiful* white gauntlets. Charles says it was Col- Wells and staff of the 34th Massachusetts regiment, who helped himself so largely to our wood and log houses last fall, and then he and his quartermaster made such a pretence of paying for them- Though never a cent did we ever get from any of them, no doubt they are looking out again to see what they can find to steal

March 1st 1863 It rained all the early part of the day preventing us from going to church But the afternoon was clear, and Lizzie and Milly went to Miss McClures Sunday school

Monday 2nd To-day has been bright and clear- C- came home after dinner and brought me two letters from the post office, a rare occurance in this house. it has been many and many a day since I received two letters by one mail. Cannons have been firing at intervals throughout the day from every fourt in this vicinity, and this afternoon there has been a continous roar, both towards Fairfax C. H. and Occoquan, and the cars on the O. A. railroad, are going, going, going filled, with troops. We don't know where they are going or what doing. Three or four soldiers came this evening to get some plank, and seeing the Green House asked to be allowed to go in and look at it, as they had never seen lemons and oranges growing before, and as they all seemed well behaved and respectful L- opened the door and let them go in, and gave each a leaf off the old Mt Vernon tree to send home. I could not help thinking how different our feelings would have been towards the North if the army had treated those in their power with the least degree of civility, or as if we were human beings. We have never been outside their lines

March 3rd More good new for us to-day, The papers contain the official report of Admiral Porter to the Sec. of the Navy announcing the capture of another of his *Iron Clads*, "by the Rebels" on the Mississippi, the ram Indianola. It is said to be the very best *gun boat* on the western waters. If the poor rebels go on in this way, and can secure all they capture, the "Moscheto Fleet" will soon be turned into quite a navy Last night there was a continous thundering of drums until about 11 o clock, but so distant, I could not tell where the sound came from, and the capital at Washington was a blaze of light, I could see the whole building distinctly from top to bottom, it looked as if made of glass- This morning the air was keen and cold and the sky lowering, about one o'clock the most terrific cloud arose in the west and spread all over the heavens, in a little while the rain came down in torrents, the lighting blazed and the thunder pealed as if it were mid summer, in about half an hour the rain seemed to turn to snow and it came down thicker and faster than I ever saw it before, and all the time the thunder continued, and the most vivid lightning, producing the most singular effect. Then it cleared off bright and warm, and at sunset not a vestage of snow was to be seen

Friday 6th Three or four soldiers came to the *Green House* this morning. Charles was in the garden and saw them, and fearing they ment mischief, and having no other means of communicating with us up stairs, he picked up a little clod of earth and threw it against the window- I immediately went and looked out, and there he stood, he made the very slightest inclination of his head towards them, but I understood, I could not help feeling amused at his ingenuity. No doubt these pantomimes the negroes have practiced all their lives in communicating with each other. In the evening another party came with revolvers, shooting at the cats, fortunately the hens were all shut up.

Saturday 7th We walked out to the fort this evening to observe the movement on the telegraph road. A regiment of cavalary, and twenty eight wagons passed down while we stood there. The roads are in the most terrible condition, and how they can get through them I cannot imagine. I felt sorry for the poor horses, some of them were fine looking animals, but had given out and were tied behind the wagons, some with gear on them, and some with saddles. Poor things- many of them bleeding from nose and mouth, and showing other marks of having been severely beaten.

Monday 9th Charles came home this morning with the news of a raid on Fairfax C. H. last night by Cap. Moseby's *Partisan Rangers*, among a great many other captures they secured Gen Stoughton and staff. The man at whose house the Gen was quarted came down this morning with the news. Col Dulaney also came from that neighbourhood and confirmed the news. He says, but for his horses getting lame which obliged him to stay at Gooden's all night, he would have been among the missing this morning. Hooker's army they tell us is returning and being sent up the rail road. We see from here several large vesels lying at the Alex- wharf.

Tuesday 10th Lizzie was in town this morning, and heard some most amusing accounts of the gallant, and daring exploits of Cap Moseby and his men, how they dashed in at the C. H. and surprised the yankee *gentlemen* after they had retired for the night, and were so comfortable, and thought themselves so secure, surrounded by their mighty hosts. But in a few moments they were all scattered to the winds scampering to the woods and fields in their night attire. The Provost marshal spent the night under a corn-crib, in a *very* light dress for this cold season- But now the poor citizens have to pay the penalty, they are being arrested and imprisoned for miles and miles around, L- saw as she came home two ambulances filled with them-

Wednesday 11th The papers are filled with accounts of rebel raids all over the country, and to-day the accounts are varied by the yankee raids on the negroes in every town and village in the north. Their intense love for the race seems to have cooled off some-what. In Detroit they have had a terrible time, beating and killing and ill-treating them in every way, about two hundred families have been burned out of house and home, and obliged to fly to the woods for shelter.

Sunday 15th Lizzie went to church this morning, the first time in five weeks I was too sick—have been sick most of the winter, with that most miserable of diseases, the jaundice- It is said there was fighting up the country last Tuesday, no one seems to know where, only an immense number of ambulances were seen going up the little River turnpike- Refugees they say are coming in daily from the south mostly foreigners- Two ladies I head of But none of them brought us any letters-

Monday 16th Not having heard of Mr and Mrs Beaumont for a long time, sent C- this morning to inquire their whereabouts, He returned with many kind messages and that she will write in a few days- I am always so much afraid of their leaving W*a* Like to keep them in view, that we may have some one to call upon in times of dire necessity. He has always been so kind and good to us- both have.

Wednesday 18 Sent Milly to Mr McCluers with an accordean, am always glad of an excuse to send to any of the neighbours, hoping to hear some thing, But she came back without news. There has been an incessant running of cars and I believe every cannon in every fort has given forth his voice today. I suppose it is rejoicing over "the brilliant and successful dash of yankee cavalry on Gens Lee and Stewart forces on the Rappanhannock completly routing and dispersing them, with the use only of sabers"

Friday 20th The ground is again covered with snow this morning. Discovered this morning that the struglers camp is gone. We have now scarcely any means of going or communicating with town, our only remaining old horse is sick. I fear unto death I get so weary and restless, a news paper would be a relief. But for day we do not see one

Saturday 21st Charles went to town this morning, and on his way back the pickets took his pass from him, told him very stringent orders from the State Department have been published, no pass is to last more than twenty four hours, none to be issued to families, each one is to apply personally, and are required to take the oath before one will be given them. Hearing all this he determined, to apply to Maj Spaulding for one to go to Wa tomorrow (Maj Spaulding with a retinue of other officers have taken up their quarters in Bp John's house.) When he got home L- asked him what the oath was like that they made him take, his reply was, "he could not tell, goodness knows what it was for he didn't, da red a whole passel of foolishness to him and den give him a pen an told him to make his mark, he tuck da pen but he wuz so ckeered an trimbled so he had to steady one hand wid tother- den da all se up sick a laf and said look how we is skeered him."

Sunday 22nd No church for us to-day. We have no horse, Mr Fairfax has been very good in letting us have one all the winter whenever we wanted one But now he is so busy with his horses trying to secure the little wood the yankees have left him, hauling it to market before they seiz upon it again. That we could not in conscience ask for two. I believe he would let us have them if we asked, but we feel it would be an imposition

Monday 23rd We have heard heavy firing all the morning, Charles came home with the news that there was fighting going on some where but he could not tell where, he saw a great number of vessels loaded with troops going down the river both yesterday and to-day. Mrs Fairfax was here in the evening, she says immence numbers of troops are constantly, every day being sent up the rail road, and signal flags are flying from all the forts around for several days past. Late this evening there was a shout from the camps about "Spring Bank," a sound we have not heard for months All the news papers, and all the soldiers report captures by the rebels here and there and every where. Even as far down this road as "Olivet" they come and take off the pickets

Tuesday 24th This morning the air has been filled with sounds. Drums thundering locomotives screaming, cars flying up and down every

moment, and confused noises coming up from all the camps. While we sat at breakfast a long line of men appeared on the opposite hills. We soon learned it was the 37 Maine regiment moving to the front. Knowing their unwillingness to move in that direction, last night when the orders came the officers determined to deceive them into the belief that they were ordered to guard Washington City, and that was the cause of the shout we heard, They knew no better until on reaching the toll gate they were ordered to turn to the left, which they did with marked reluctance, but they knew resistance was vain

Mt. Olivet Church On the Old Fairfax Road—picket post of the 40th New York Volunteers, September, 1861*
Courtesy of Castle Books, A Division of Book Sales, Inc.

* Mt. Olivet Church was originally located on the Old Fairfax Road (present-day Rose Hill Drive and Franconia Road). The building was later moved to its present location at Franconia and Beulah Roads, Springfield, Virginia.

Wednesday 25th Very few persons are on the road to day, there is so much difficulty about passes, none given without first taking the oath. A young man who has been detained in Alex for five days, and at last found himself reduced to the necessity of submitting to their terms, came out of town to-day with Mr Reid. He says the oath they obliged him to take, not only binds him to the allegiance to the U.S. now and forever but to hold himself in readiness to take up arms in her defence at any moment he may be called upon to do so. The movement of the army now is all towards Centerville, where they say their mud works of defence are of immense strength.

Friday 27th Every thing about us is very quiet to-day, not a soldier roving about, not even a picket passed through since Saturday. We heard that a number of persons, both from Wa and Alex were last week sent through the Federal lines, and that all are to be sent who refuse to take the oath. Charles went again to Malvern to get a pass but found the place deserted Maj Spaulding and all his crew were gone- Col Dulaney and Mr Reid who were just from town, say there is something going on in the army but every thing is done with such secrecy they could not find out what, but both are impressed with the belief of its not being very favourable to the yankee cause. Troops are still moving toward Centerville. Col. D- says he will try tomorrow to get us a pass but has not the slightest expectation of obtaining one, as very stringent orders have been this week issued from the War Department that none were to have them excepting those who apply in person, and concent [sic] to take the oath. There is no trouble about getting into town, but the oath of allegiance is to be taken before any one is permitted to leave there

Saturday 28th We were sitting in our room last evening tryied to beguile the tedious hours by a game of Backgammon, when about ten o clock we were startled by the report of several guns, in quick succession, seemingly very near, Lizzie flew to the windows, and exclaimed in perfect consternation "Mercyful Father!" I do believe they are burning down "Spring Bank," house. Mr George Mason's house." I also rushed to the window and threw it up, but soon discovered it was not the dwelling but supposed it to be the barracks which has recently been vacated by 37 Maine regiment. The fire was the other side and I could distinctly see the dwelling house and also the soldiers running between me and the fire looking like wild Indians and whooping and yelling like a pack of demons. O the sight went to my very heart. I could do nothing, but sit and watch the fire and wonder how that poor doomed family are fareing, for their sufferings, and the persecution, they have endured from the vile yankees, no tongue can tell no pen describe And all so frail, and delicate.

The only wonder is how they have existed through it all, and no excuse for it, they have taken no part in the war whatever, quiet unoffending citizens, have remained at their home, and like ourselves, have never been outside the Federal lines

Sunday 29th Last night the clouds passed away, and the moon shown out for a little while, and then became obscured by a dense smoke, which smelt strongly of burning tar. We could only wonder what poor families were being burned out to night The thick smoke filled the whole country around, we could see nothing but heard several guns fired. The weather was too inclement yesterday for Col Dulaney to turn out and so got no pass. The yankees have at last succeeded in keeping us from going to church. It seems to have been their most earnest wish for the past two years, they have stolen our horses, torn our carriage to pieces, taken away the passes- driven our minister and people from church to church and from house to house But some how or other we have always found means of getting to a place of worship on Sundays, when one has been open that we could go to until now When I think of it, how wonderfully the unseen hand has lead us along hitherto, and I doubt not a way will be opened for us again

Monday 30th We were at Mr Fairfax's this evening and learned it was not the barracks that was burned last Friday night. But Mr Mason's barn, and carriage house with two carriage and a great quantity of farming utensils, harness, gears, and things of that sort that were burned by the straglers from the 37 Maine regiment. The horrid soldiers raised and circulate ten thousand reports about the people, without the slightest shadow of truth in any of them, and then act accordingly, and now the old story is revived of the sending up of signal lights to the Southern army. They pretend to say Mr Mason sends them up nightly. And Mrs M-receives dispatches daily from the South- Poor Mr M-! who is so feeble and broken down and scarcely ever able to lift his head off his pillow. They are making loud threats of fasting the whole family up in the house, and setting fire to it

While we were at dinner to day, two soldiers came through the hedge and prowled all around and poked their noses into every hole and corner, and three times came up to the windows and looked in while we were at the table. And soon after dinner two others came, one in citizens clothes, the other in officers garb. They wished to know where Gen Burney's headquarters were, and if Mrs Burney had not left a side saddle here. We told them a room here had been engaged for them, but they never came to occupy it. Gen. Burney took possession of Gen Sedgwick's old quarters, and his wife did not come to the neighbourhood at all. But he insisted that she did and he had loaned her a saddle, and had come for it. No doubt if there had been one about that he could lay his hands upon he would have borne it off- after loitering around they went off seemingly in a great state of satisfaction. The yankee women are perfectly wild about side-saddles and riding on horse-back

Tuesday 31st The air is thick this morning with the descending snow, ground covered, and a more gloomy wintery day I never saw in January. A soldier of 34th came into the kitchin directly after breakfast and spent the whole morning there, conversing with and retailing to the negroes all the news, both civil and military that is afloat He says the fire at "Spring Bank" was thought at all the forts to be a signal that the rebels were approaching, and his regiment immediately got under arms and was on the spot in less than fifteen minutes, and so it was at all the forts, they made every preparation for an attack and remained under arms all night. The soldiers surrounded Mr Masons house in a state of wild bois-terous fury- hooping and yelling to each other to drag him out of the house and throw him into the fire, as he had made it as a signal to the rebels, and to drag her out and burn her too, for they knew she had received that morning dispatches from the South. Then they yelled, and yelled, and made the most demonicle tumult and ran off to the stacks and got straw and piled it against the doors saying they were going to set fire to prevent any escape, and burn the whole family- I learned afterwards from other sources, that all this really did occur- and that the little son who is a frail sickly little boy became so alarmed it threw him into convulsions, and he lay all night long more dead than alive, perfectly insensible. And the poor parents, both too sick and feeble to carry him down stairs, while they listened to the tumult oaths threats and blasphemy out side, determined that if the house was fired, they would make no effort to escape but all remain and persist togather in the flames. And why they did not burn the dwelling I never could discover. The soldiers say there was a riot in Alex- last Saturday night, the 34th was ordered out, but it was quelled before they got there.

Wednesday April 1st 1863 All our provender is now entirely ex-hausted, not an ear of corn, or a grain of any kind on the place, and none to be had in the neighbourhood that we know of. The supply at the mills is very scant, and prices enormous. Later in the day good Mr Reid brought us a small loud of hay. Fearing we were in sore need he hunted it some where. He always looks on the bright side of things, and always brings us cheering news. His family seven in number are just recovering from the small pox. He would not come near the house, but called out all he had to say bout half way between the house and the barn, We sent Charles to town this morning on some business and he did not return until very late, the pass is always the excuse, He says the Provost's office, and the street as thronged with applicants, and they kept him waiting four hours, at two o clock one of the grand officers made his appearance in the anti-room and announced the hour to the anxious crowd, and ordered them all, peremptoraly to "clear, out clear, out no more passes will be given until tomorrow, so clear, out, clear, out every one of you clear out" a great many of the wood haulers had to remain all night with their wagons and horses, a great many now go prepared, with food for themselves and their animals, a guard stands at the Stone Bridge and receives the passes- and the same thing is be gone through with every day.

Thursday 2nd To-day has been cold and stormy It rained all the early part of it, and the wind has blown a perfect hurricane. about twelve the cannon commenced roaring-roaring towards Centerville and continued until sun set. Shenk, the military governor of *Baltimore* and Provost Fry are doing a lucrative business in the way of robbing the trunks of travelers and sending the inhabitants of the city out side the lines stripped of all they possessed Threats are made and I expect it will not be long before the same scenes will be enacted here, and it will be our fate to be driven forth homeless, to seek a shelter whenever we can find one, but we have been so persecuted and tormented for the past two years that I almost cease to care whether they do so or not, but rather think it would be a relief, destitute though we may be, we could not be much more so than we are now, they have taken every thing from us, and to find enough to feed us all, is as much as we can do-

Friday 3rd The O and A depot was so brightly illuminated last night that its light was thrown into our room and waked me several times. Heard to day that one hundred and fifty wounded were brought in during the night But every thing is done so secretly.

We went about to day among the neighbours trying to get some one to put us in a field of oats on shares- But no one is willing to risk it. They say the army will all be here again and we will lose it again as we did last year. O it is pitiable! but we have to resort to all manner of means, that we can think of to feed ourselves, and all those who are dependent on us for food, I do not know how we are to feed the little stock we have left. But I suppose a way will be made for us, "Sufficient unto the day is the evil thereof." The people around, say the families in the neighbourhood have supplied themselves bountifully, with furniture, clothes, beds, bedding, any thing, and every thing they want, from the deserted houses and places around. They do not steal it themselves, but they bribe the soldiers. If they know of any particular thing in a house they want, they will say to a soldier, "go and bring it to me and I will give you a pone of corn bread or a pie, or a bottle of whisky," and it is certain to come. One man they named who has nineteen feather beds in his house, another is wearing clothes with Dr Mason's name marked on them.

Sunday 5th The ground is covered several inches thick with snow It is Easter morn—and it brings to mind our dear old church, "Christ Church" and the beautiful Easter anthems—and the organ, as it swelled forth in deep reverential tones the music appropriate for the day, so delightful to listen to- Shall I ever hear them again- and I thought of the many seats vacated, that will never again be filled with the former occupants, -and the bell- The dear old Christ Church bell.'I can hear it to-day as I stand in the porch. It sinks into my heart like a funeral knell.

Tuesday 7th The weather continues cold and cloudy, and every thing looks dull and dreary. There is no news, excepting the yankees say they have burned Pensacola, Fl. and that they gave Capt Moseby a fearful saber cut across the forehead last Wednesday in a skirmish near Drains-ville. But Mr Reid, who brought us out a barrel of fish says they are as cross as cross can be to day, will not let any one pass the pickets, or bring the smallest thing out of town with out signing the obligation. There is not a school in town, or any where in the neighbourhood, and where there are children, the parents are so anxious to have them taught, that Lizzie determined to collect all together that live within a convenient distance and teach them every day. And to-day she opned [sic] her school for the first time. The people around have been so kind to us, and done so many things, kind and considerate, and it was the only way she had of showing her gratitude

Thursday 9th Mr Fairfax took me into town this morning in his little wagon It is the first time I have been there for two months- I had no pass, and in return expected fully to be hailed and perhaps turned back. But Mr F- had one for himself which he shewed, they said nothing to me, nor I to them, T-day's papers contain telegraphic despatches of the re-taking of Charleston, and the evacuation of Richmond, and the burning by the yankees of the beautiful town of Jacksonville, Fla. also the burning of Palmyra Missouri. This is the third town within the week they have burned

Sunday 12th It has been so long since we had any pleasant weather, and as to day is bright, and warm I thought I would like to walk into town to church. It is a privilege I have not enjoyed in many months, and as Charles has defered his trip to W*a* until this morning I took advantage of his protection that far. He says he heard about a dozen cannons fired this morning, away to the south of us. I had a pleasant surprise at church in meeting Dr and Mrs P.- Had not heard of them being there- Did not know of their being inside the yankee lines.

Monday 13th All the news this morning is most favourable and pleasing to us all In the first place the expedition against Charlston [sic] S C, which has been two years in preparation, and cost the government one hundred and fifty millions has proved a total failure after an engagement of only four hours. The "Keokuck," one of the Iron clads was completely torn to pieces, and sunk, One of the very *wonderful* recent inventions which the yankees denominate the "Devil" became detached from the vessel it was and floated over to the rebels. The yankees and their whole fleet finshed up their attack on Charlston in rather a dilapidated condition All their fortifications and guns on the Tar river the rebels have taken, and Gen. Foster with his whole force at W*a* N.C. were surrounded and obliged to surrender. But all this is yankee news. I cannot vouch for the truth of it. I do not understand it, for only a few days ago it was published that they had captured Charlston, and Richmond had been evacuated by the rebels. But all these reverses to the yankees bears heavily upon us poor captives that we are in their power We feel it although we are rejoicing in it. I heard while in town another little piece of news that I think worthy of a place in these annals. A Mr K- a lawyer of Alex- was on a visit in Philadelphia last winter- and while at a *lady's* house there, a large handsome volume was handed round to quite a room full of company, shown as a trophy of war The lady said it was confiscated property, taken by Gen. Birney and sent to her for safe keeping. It proved to be a large valuable bible with Bishop John's name in it, presented to him by the students of William and Mary, while he was President of that Institution Mr K- told the *lady*, as her husband was a lawyer, she ought to know there was no such thing as confiscating property without a regular process of law, and that Gen Birney ought when the opportunity came to send it back to the owner- Mr K thought the husband was somewhat abashed. But for myself I doubt it. I know too well what the yankees are, lying, and stealing, with them are considered meritorious acts to be applauded, and to be laughed and joked about as some thing very smart and witty I was sorry I did not learn the name of the people. But I know Gen Birney had his headquarters in Bp Johns' house be fore he came over to this neighbourhood. This story was told me as a great secret I must by no means repeat it, as she had heard it talked about incidentally in the family. She did not bind me over to secracy before telling it and I made no promises whatever, for I had determined within my own mind if ever I saw one member of the Bishop's family to tell them every word I knew about it.

Charles was detained at the office waiting for a pass until after one o clock. I did not apply for one, but determined to run the chance of getting through with out one. I had made up all my plans before reaching the stone bridge, and when the guard held out his hand and asked for the pass, I turned my head to Charles who was walking behind me and with a motion of the hand indicated that he had it I then walked on very leisurely over the bridge while they questioned him, and over hauled his luggage, As soon as I had crossed the bridge I quickened my pace as much as possible determined not to hear should they call, and to give them a little exercise if they attempted to overtake me But the officer in charge contented himself with asking questions—who I was, and where I lived, why I did not get a pass- with numberless others Said he could turn me back if he chose- But he did not do it- and thus have I twice within a week, with a little strategy successfully run the blockade. Charles tole me that while he was in the office this morning a Mrs Harper came in for a pass. The officer asked her if she was willing to sign the obligation. She replied "she expected to do so," but he said, very emphatically, "are you willing to do it" She replied rather evasively she had made up her mind, before making the application to sign it. "Well," he said that would not do, he discovered by her answers, she was not doing it willingly, and therefore she might content herself to remain in town as no pass would be given her from that office. As the lady passed out, another officer stepped up and said, "that's right Lieutenant, that's right I like to see you down on these people." Two or three soldiers were hanging about here all day Sunday. One of them told S. they came from a camp on the other side of the turnpike, not far from "Clouds Mill" and a family living over there were accused of sending up signal lights to the rebels- information was sent to Wa, the Provost guards came down and broke open the doors- and broke every lock on the place, and rummaged every place, but found nothing

Tuesday 14 There were about twenty officers and men here this morning racing all over the place with their signals, directing the target firing. They stopped all the wood wagons and turned them back. They ordered Charles to put up all his *live stock*, and sent all the family into the house where we were kept two hours and in that time they fired four times. Mr Burgen, an old Irishman came to rent one of our town houses. L. asked him how he managed to keep so much of Mr Rice's fencing, when every body had lost all they had. Ah! he said he kept a little whisky, and to some of the officers he gave a drink, and to others he gave a quart and to a Capt- he had to give a gallon, but he soon made a part of the fence that had walked off, come back again to its place!

Wednesday 15th Today has been one of ceaseless storm. For many nights passed the signal lights have been dancing up and down on the forts, and last night there was an unusual number. The depot was a blaze of light, and the cars flying up and down the road, and they kept it up all day. I understand a party of *ladies* unattended by the *gentlemen* of the army, But all mounted on splendid high spirited animals dashed through and through the camps, all with cigars in their mouth, I did wonder if Mrs Breiney was one of the party, and why her *gallant* knight was not in attendance, or if he is still foraging around looking for side saddles

Saturday 18th All the morning a great number of officers and soldiers have been racing from place to place and from field to field fixing up targets, and for two hours there was a constant whistling of balls and shells through the air, over the house and over the garden. The first one I heard, I happened to be walking in the garden—had forgotten it was practice day. O, I was so frightened, it perfectly took my senses away. It sounded like the wagons and horses coming through the air Such a screaming sound. I put my hands over my ears, and shut my eyes and poked about half bent, then I slipped down on the ground behind a tree, and there I sat the whole time with my hands over my ears, and my head buried in my lap afraid to get up and go into the house. I believe it was the most dangerous place I could have chosen, if a ball had cut the tree off it might have fallen upon me, and with all this firing not a single target was touched. In the evening we saw Singer's Dutchmen busy on the opposite hills digging up the balls, They had been trying some thing new, the steal pointed projectiles, and find they are too costly to be left in the ground- They tell one, that every cannon that is fired, cost the government ten dollars

Sunday 19th A warm, bright, glorious morning, the first of the season, and but for the distant sound of drums, and the shriek of the steam whistles, I might say a Sabbath stillness pervades every thing. But not even the delightful day can induce me to try another such walk to church as I had last week, it made me sick, The risk of passing the pickets, and being stopped and insulted is rather too exciting to be attempted too often. Lizzie went to Sunday School this afternoon, and met with the celebrated Mrs Hollins. She is a British subject, and lived before the war some where in the neighbourhood of Occoquan, has been robbed of every thing she possessed, insulted, and maltreated in every way, and driven from her home by the Union army, has been arrested and imprisoned in the "Old Capital," and passed through all the horrors we all have been subjected to an account of which she has graphically described in a letter recently transmitted to England. About four this evening a squad of cavelrymen, ten- or twelve passed down the road

Monday 20 The weather this spring has been very capricious, yesterday warm and pleasant like summer, To-day wintery again, cold and cloudy. There is now a perfect dearth of news as the papers state, "all quiet along the lower Potomac." They have reduced the failure on Charlston now to a reconnaissance, all failures now are made light of as a reconnaissance

Tuesday 21st Charles did not get home until to day, He with a great many others had to remain in town all night could not get passes. To day another target was fixed up this time on Old Smith's place, just below our hill and fired at from Ft Elsworth, it is as good a nuicence to us as the others, the shells seem to whiz right over our garden some times bursting frightfully near.

Wednesday 22nd about sunset we counted twelve cannon fired seemingly in the direction of Centerville. As we sat at the window, about eight o clock and watched the light red and blue signal lights swaying up and down in the dark, and thought how pretty they looked, we counted five trains of cars dash in one after the other, I think Moseby must have been after them

Friday 24th To day and yesterday have been dark and gloomy, and the rain coming down in torrents, the water courses all swimming. I suppose this weather will still further retard the movement of "Old fighting Joe" In his last visit to Washington he said, the mud was the only barrier between his army and Richmond for three or four months past Old Mr Burgen came again today. He brought a piece of paper with the oath printed on it, and a message from Gilbert Miner, the lawyer saying if L- would put her name to it, he would have all the tenants who did not come up to the mark turned out before tomorrow night. The old man was very urgent for her to do it Said Lord Lyons told him to sign it twice a day if it was required of him. It was nothing, he did not regard it any more than a puff of wind. But she said "no" she had conscientious scruples about the matter and she could not sign it. She would lease him one house, and he must do the best he could with the others-

Saturday 25th This morning after the rain ceased the soldiers were scattered all over the fields fixing up the targets. The excitement of having the soldiers all around and the firing from the forts, and the shells bursting so frightfully near invariably makes one so deadly sick I have to go to bed, and to day I have been dreading it and trying to prepare my ears for the sounds, But for some cause unknown to us not a single cannon has been fired, much to my relief.

Sunday 26th Another bright beautiful Sunday morning, but rather cool for the season. The soldiers about here were paid off, they tell us, last week, and to-day they are scattered all over the face of the earth, I suppose to show off their new clothes. They say there was a fight in Culpepper last week, and their men got considerably worsten L- was at Sunday School, and heard that Mrs Hollins has again been arrested but on what plea she did not learn. We saw Mr F.... with two officers walking all over our fields, and through the woods, they seemed to be attentively surveying every thing- mischief I fear is in contemplation.

Tuesday 28th The place has been filled again with soldiers, and a great number of shells fired- shrieking through the air in every direction, and frighting the people almost to death. Mrs McCluer took all her children and ran over here for safety, I could not help laughing, for she certainly got out of the frying-pan into the fire, Targets are stuck up here all over the place, and fired at from least three forts, Old Smith brought all his family up here and stood on the fort among the soldiers A number of soldiers were placed on the road to stop the wagons that were coming this way, they took the horses from them and mounted, and such racing and hooping and yelling, just like mad men, I think they must all have been drunk.

Thursday 30 To-day has been set apart by a proclamation of Pres. Lincoln's as a day of fasting, humiliation and prayer, all business is suspended under a penalty. Services in all the churches, prayers and supplications to be made for him and his success. The soldiers tell us that Lincoln has sent commissioners to offer terms of peace to the South- But that Pres. Davis will accept none, but a full and complete recognition of the Confederacy, and an adequate resitution and compensation for all loses

Friday May 1st 1863. We have heard distant cannonaiding all the morning For several days a party of surveyors have been out on the different roads, and to day they have been running off and staking this, the "Old Backlick" road.

Saturday 2nd We again heard cannon this morning, seemingly about Fredricksburg. A wagon with three horses to it, and fitted with negroes, mostly women with their chattles, and all talking in a very loud disagreeable tone passed this morning No doubt runaways, with their masters property. Charles was sent to market this morning for some provisions, but he did not return until long after dinner We never send him now that he does not spend the whole day, and the getting of passes is a ready excuse. And this time he only remained at home long enough to beg money he says, to bury his father who died to day. We learned afterwards the whole morning was spent begging about the streets for that purpose— and no doubt every one was lead to believe "Old Curtis" belonged to us. He was a negro who had been free all his life and had one of our women for a wife. I did feel too truly provoked when I hear it But could say nothing, had only to submit. I know that Charles has more ready money than any one he begged from- he has been making for himself all his life, and since the war has made hundreds, and thousands by trading in the camps. Wells the present military governor of Alex- has today published a more stringent edict in regard to passes than ever, no white person can obtain one now, without having some Union man well known at the office to prove his loyalty. The news papers also are prohibited from publishing any army news.

Sunday 3rd To day is bright and clear- Cannonaiding has been heard most of the day, to the southwest of us. The 34th Mass. regiment was marched off at twelve o'clock last night to take charge of the defences at "Upton's Hill." L- was at Sunday School, and had a little conversation with Mr Mc- who has just returned from quite an extended tour through some of the Northern States. He describes the country in parts beautifully picturesque and highly cultivated, and some of the people he met he was rather pleased with. But he happened to be in N. Y. City on Sunday, and after all he had heard of the morals and piety of the people, and their strict observance of the Sabbath day, he was utterly astonished at all he heard and saw. In strolling about in the evening he dropped into first one church and then another. At one, he was asked by the guard at the door for his ticket. He said he had none, he did not know it was necessary in going to church to carry a ticket. The man informed him that Bishop's concert was helled in that church and if he wished to attend he must pay a dollar He declined to do that, and walked on. In the next, he stepped into, he found a Sunday School celebration going on, conducted very much like a country fair. While the speaker was haranging, the congregation was amusing themselves in the way that pleased them best. Ladies and gentlemen, laughing, and chatting, and promenading the isles, paying not the slightest attention to what was said, and children amusing themselves and exhibiting their gifts. All of which, we poor savages, would consider a desecration of both church and day

Monday 4th Cannon a long distance off have been thundering all day from early morning until after dark. It makes us feel so anxious, watching and waiting This evening just before dark we heard Mr Reid's wagon coming, and we flew down the road to meet him- He says all the accounts have been favourable to us until to day. The "Republican" came out with a long account of the capture and occupation of Fredricksburg by the Federal forces, and the terrible slaughter and total defeat of Gen Lee's whole army. Four hundred Confederate prisoners were brought up the river to day, and among them a number of citizens. He says they did not seem at all subdued or intimidated by the yankees—but on reaching the Alex- wharf took off their hats and hurrayed lustily for Jefferson Davis- "O" they said a few hundreds of them made prisoners was nothing, the South had plenty of yankees to exchange for them, they had seen eleven thousand marched into their camp before they left

While we were talking to Mr Reid Col Dulaney rode up- Said he has seen an official dispatch, and there is no doubt Hooker has possession of Fredricksburg and all the defences in the neighbourhood and has captured an immense numbers of guns and ordnance stores, has flanked, and thoroughly whipped Lee's army at Chancellersville, and is now between him and Richmond. Although we did not believe the half of this, we went home and to bed with heavy hearts

Tuesday 5th The distant roar of cannon still continues and O the restless, weary anxious wandering from place to place continues too- We can see nothing- but the constant harrowing sounds. Every kind of employment is tried in vain, all fail to interrest. The evening closed with a very heavy thunder storm followed by a night of pitchy darkness. Lizzie and myself, Milly and mammy have been the sole occupants of the house since Saturday last when C- went to W*a*. Happily for no soldiers have been here for several days

Thursday 7 It has rained—rained—and as cold as winter I have noticed that invariably after a day of heavy cannonadeing the next it rains heavily. Charles came home to-day says it has been an utter impossibility to get a pass- The yankees are now draughting negroes into the army, in W*a* And although they pretend to say none are taken but those who volunteer, all the avenues to the city are closed to prevent their escaping until their names are enrolled in the army list, and he was promised a pass at least twenty times, as soon as he would have his name put down. "But he had no notion of making bress work of his self for dem dar yankees," at last he went to look for Mr Beaumont but found he had left the city, Gen Sedgwick had telegraphed him and he had gone to Fredricksburg- The papers now are filled with Hooker's signal success- Gen. Ward crossed the river and entered the city triumphantly at mid-night. Last Saturdays and Sundays fights are said to have been the most terrific and sanguinary of the war, and a few more such would leave none to fight on either side, and from persons directly from the army, although they are sworn not to reveal any thing they have seen or heard, it is begining to leak out that Hooker's success is not as great as he at first thought. The wagon mastor of 34th Mass. who was in town today and was interview. He says there never was under the sun a more thoroughly whipped army than Hooker's- His regiment 34- are under orders to march to the front, but they go in fear and trembling. They know well their doom is to be slaughterered! While camped in this neighbourhood they had the reputation of being the greatest pack of cowards in the service. Charles says while he was in Wa he saw a long line of Confederate prisoners marched up to the Provost office about three squares long, I asked him how they looked, if they were dirty and ragged, and bear-footed, and starved, and looked very much cast-down. He said they were dusty and dirty, but were all fine, hearty looking men, he did not see a starved looking one among them, he saw no straps, and only one or two with corporal's stripes, and as to being down-cast, they all walked along as boldly as if they were marching in their regiment.

Saturday 9th To day saw the "Baltimore Gazette." And Hooker's victory at Fredricksburg turns out as inglorious a defeat, rout, and disaster as Burnside met with last Dec- at the same place- I wonder how he feels after all his vain glorious boasting, and self important harangues to his men. I recollect at one time he told them he had gotten Gen Lee in such a position as rendered his defeat, and the destruction a certainty- And now the "Telegram," says Richmond and Petersburg both have surren-dered

Monday 11th Saw a letter from Swan Point Ma to-day Mrs- C- asks if there is no way of communicating with Richmond through Alex- All down there are more than anxious about our dear ones in the army. Troops are stationed at all points along the river to prevent crossing. Mr C. barns, tobacco houses and every place is filled with them. And all who live within ten mlles of the Potomac are tormented and persecuted with them, almost as we are She says every thing like provisions and groceries in that neighbourhood are scarce and high, indeed almost impossible to obtain at all, many families have to do without Sugar or Coffee, and all are in want of flour

Tuesday 12th The weather has suddenly become excessively warm. Yesterday and today are the first that we have been able to do without fire. and we feel it a great great blessing, for this winter we have had hardly enough fuel to keep us from freezing The report still continues rife among the military that the Old stars and stripes are now flouting triumphantly over Richmond, but no one believes it. If such was the case there would be more demonstrations of rejoicing than we have ever seen yet I am quite sure. Last night there was a wild alarm that the rebels were moving circulated all through the camps, within seven miles of town, and great commotion it produced- and many companies of soldiers were marched into fort Lyon, and lay there all night in the trenches

Wednesday 13th For a day or two, the papers have given vague reports of the death of our Gen. T. J. Jackson- But he has been killed so often in yankee imagination that very little credence is given to the report. They state also that Gens- Van Dorn and Paxton two other Confederates were also killed. But Gen Berry, the old horse thief of this neighbourhood, certainly was killed, for his body was sent to Alex to be embalmed, to be sent to Kennebunt or some such place in Maine. All the poor people about here who have suffered from his persecutions, openly declared their satisfaction when they heard he was killed, only they conceived it too much honour for him to have died as the battle field. They would much have prefered the gibbet for him.

Thursday May 14th Mr Reid brought us the paper to day, and the first thing my eye rested upon, and that sent a deep pang of sorrow and despair to my heart was the announcement of Gen Jacksons death, in such a form I was obliged to believe it The news came through "Head-quarters Army of the Potomac" and purports to have been taken from a Richmond paper, in the form of an address by Gen Lee to his army, in which after complimenting and congratulating them on their recent signal successes, he tells them with feelings of the deepest emotion sorrow and regret, he tells them of the death of one of their brave leaders Gen. T. J. Jackson, which took place on the 10th instant- (Last Sunday) at 15 minutes past three oclock P.M. The W*a* Chronicle speaks of him as, "a great General, a brave soldier, a noble Christian, and a perfect man."

Friday 15th For several day past there has been an unusual excitement and alarm among the military. They say the rebels are certainly approaching, and the officers are making every exertion to keep the soldiers in place. a number of them have been around warning the people not to let the soldiers have any thing to eat, not to sell them any thing. They do not want them to have any thing that will entice them to leave their post.

They fear the enemy will come and find them unprepared. They say an attack on W*a* and George Town is so confidently expected, that both places are in such a state of excitement and alarm, that they have torn the planks up on the chain bridge over on the long bridge, and all the bridges and places about the cities are mined.

Saturday 16th Sent Charles to town this morning, and he brings back great news great doings are expected in Alex- this evening- a *Colored*

regiment is expected from W*a* to visit, and parade the streets. We were much gratified and delighted this evening by a visit from our friends of "Rose Hill." There is a feeling of pleasure I can not describe in seeing and welcoming a familiar and loved face, after weeks and months of *solitary* confinement, especially so when their feelings, and sentiments are in unison with our own, and too when you can talk unreservedly. Fortunately for us the spy Milly was out of the way. We talked over our trials, and difficulties, privations, and persecutions, and find we can all understand and sympathize, and are all in one accord in disgust and hatred of the yankees. All the afternoon, while they were here cannon were thundering in the distance, seemingly as near as Fairfax Courthouse Our friends call it music. Some one belonging to the blockading squadron off Charlston reports the flags in the city and on the forts at half mast, the bells tolling and every demonstration of mourning at the news of Gen Jackson's death.

Sunday 17 From early morning until after twelve, there was an incessant thundering of drums, after that a Sabbath stillness prevailed. I have not seen a soldier to day- save the sentinels pacing their weary rounds on the ramparts of fort Lyon, and O it is an unspeakable relief to be rid of such intolerable nuisances if only for a few hours. Last Sunday all the flages were at half mast and remained so until night Monday they floated to the hugest full hight, but only a short time, then they were lowered to the half way mark and have remained so until to day. The soldiers tell us it was for the Gen. officers killed at Chancellersville. I wonder why they let a week pass before it was done

Monday 18th Heard to day that the Southerners have possession of Fairfax Courthouse A guard from one of the neighbours 34 Mass-man has been prowling about all the evening. He walked into our kitchin unceremoniously and seated himself, and then commenced questioning the servants about us and our belongings—whose this farm was and what was on it, how many cows, and how many horses, and what use we made of the farm, and what we employed our selves at, and what we expected to do, and ten thousand other yankee questions. Then he got up and moved himself off into the garden and seeing Lizzie in there, of course he had to stop, and show himself off a little to her He spoke of the desolate waste appearance of the country. So different *to* what he had been lead to expect. Then he went into a long account of the manner that recruiting is carried on at the *North*. He says three or four recruiting officers will station themselves at every corner in the cities, and stop every Loafer that comes along, and tell him fine tales about army life, and tell them that the whole Southern Country with all its wealth is before them, to go in and help themselves to just whatever they please Then they will take him into a dram shop, and after two or three deep potations they are sure of his name- But now he said we are heartily sick and tired of the war, and would gladly get out of it as we got in. Every now and then we hear of some body being sent outside the lines, to day it was Tom Jarvis, a poor man with a large family and sick wife who depend on his labour for their daily bread-, No reason assigned, no fault

Wednesday 20th It is generally believed now to be a melancholy fact, that Gen Jackson is nor more, with solomn reverence his name is spoken by all friend and foe That so great and holy a man, and one who seemed so indispensable, to our case should have fallen is a subject of deep regret and sorrow to us all- But he who gave us General Stonewall Jackson is able to raise up another in his place. All the yankees papers seem to vie with each other in eulogizing him, and in using vast swelling words to express the importance of his military knowledge and genius to the success of the Confederate cause There are no railing accusations no bitterness of speech, as in other cases. I can not fathom the reason, unless it is that knowing the tenor of his name, which in itself a tower strength, they wish to impress on their soldiers mind the idea that without him the Southern cause is dead—hopeless—and they have nothing more to fear. Charles did not return from W*a* until late yesterday evening- The ever ready excuse the passes, and then such crowds to witness a review of negro troops in W*a*.

Thursday 21st I was awakened last night about 11 o'clock by a bright light shining in my face I started up and the first thought was that Alex- which the soldiers are constantly threatening to burn, was on fire. But soon found it was some thing burning in side the intrenchments at Ft Lyon. I waked Lizzie and we lay and watched it a long time expecting every moment to see it go up like, "Sweet Miss Dina," but every thing remained as quiet as possible. did not even hear a soldiers voice, and after watching it a long time dropped off to sleep again, forgetting for a while there was a fort Lyon or a soldier in the world After breakfast one of the soldiers came over from the fort and told us it was the Bom proof that was burned, It was used as a prison, and they supposed one of the men confined in it set it on fire. This man is a Dane named Friez I have seen him several times before, and seems quite a respectable, and intelligent person. He won my good opinion from the first, by expressing so freely, what he thinks of the service he is in, and telling so openly what the officers are doing. He says he entered the army ignorantly, mostly for the pay, But now would give up all claims on the government country and all only to get out of it, His father, who is in Europe knows much more of what is going on in this country than he does, and is constantly writing to him what a disgrace it is, and on no account, when he gets back home to let it be known he was ever a soldier in the Union Army, as he would be looked upon as a thief- every body knows robbery is their chief employment. The officers, he says are carrying a perfect system of theft not only on the government but also on the soldiers, they cheat them out of pay, rations every thing, and all they can steal from the people around the government pays them for He knows Singer took a great many log houses, and any quantity of wood from here and then went to W*a* and drew so much money for fire wood furnished to his regiment, which he pretended had been bought from the farmers around- after dinner we were honored by a visit from a Mr. McF. He is a yankee who lived in this neighbourhood several years, and then gone back to the north a year or two just before the war. We felt his visit boded us no good, yet as he came in a friendly way we were obliged to treat him polightly. He is a horrible *Black Republican* of the deepest die, and a bitter enemy to the South, which he took no pains to conceal even while he lived here. He sat and talked with the unblushing impudence, and presumption of the yankee, of the success of the Union arms every where (but in V*a* in a much lower key) He could not with any face stay in Va though he tried to come as near it as he could- He said even in Va the rebels had no decided victories, a success to be complete must be followed up. The loss of a few hundred men to the Federals was nothing- The Union army was not, he thought half large enough The President ought to call out a million men more at least, and push at once into the very heart of the rebellion, and break up the facilities the rebels have of massing their men and by that means crush out the rebellion, and finish up the war at once. We had very little to say, only to sit patiently and listen to this tirade, we know the yankee treachery, and we believe them all to be spies, and ready at any moment to have us arrested and sent beyond the lines- But the little we did say was not at all complimentary to his nation

Friday 22nd We are now completely cut off from all intercourse with our friends, and only see a neighbour occasionally. The flowers now are our only resource and pleasure, to watch them and see them bloom. We have used our utmost exertions to have them a little attended to, and cultivated, but all in vaine. The few servants we have left, are so entirely their own masters, it is a trial to have them about us. Charles who did so well at first, now spends more than half of his time in W*a*- has bought himself a house and lot there, and takes up nearly all his time. Last year he planted a little lot of oats and one of corn, but this we only asked of him to attend a little to the flowers, and try and save the shrubbery But he has told us several times that it would not get worked this year. But indeed the little he made last year he sold to the soldiers on his own account- he is seldom at home more than three days in the week, and then attends to nothing but what he can pick up about the camps for himself. It is utterly impossible to hire any one to attend to the flowers for us, even if we had the means. The whole community, both white, and black, are so frenzied now about making, baking, and peddling pies and things of that kind to the soldiers that it would be an utter impossibility to hire one for ordinary purposes But O it grieves us sorely to see our dear beautiful flowers running to waste, flowers and shrubs collected and planted under our dear parents supervision, and such a source of pleasure to them, and the dear boys too, both loved flowers dearly, I cannot bear to think of their coming back and finding the old home looking so bare and desolute after fighting for us to so many years- O for magical power to make it bloom like an Eden when they come!

Sunday 24th I was walking in the garden, among the flowers, this morning when the well remembered sound of our dear old church bell fell upon my senses like music and reminded me that this is Sunday, and the anniversary of the invasion, and for two long years have we, her people been excluded from that sacred place. And for two long years have the feel of the assayers, and robber, pressed her courts and poluted her sanctuary with their unhallowed rites

Monday 25th The whole country is now filled with spies, and any one who chooses to go to the yankee authorities and make an accusation against another, whether true or false, he is seized up and sent outside the lines, only allowed a few clothes, and a small amount of money in notes, nothing valuable is allowed to be taken, Some times one or two in a family, some times the whole, sometimes a small boy, sometimes a young lady by herself taken away outside the lines, the denser the forest, or the wilder or more desolate, and uninhabited the country the better they like it to turn her loose to find herself a home, or shelter the best way she can. The Provost of W*a* has the names of a hundred families, who are now under constant espionage, and the slightest pretext will send them all the other side the lines, Indeed we hear constant threats of sending all Southerners out side. Before sunrise this morning we were aroused by the firing of several volleys of musketry at Ft Lyon. And the news that greeted our waking ears was that the rebels were down as far as Ft Elsworth last night. The poor rebels! they seem to move by slow stages, according to the yankee account it must take them about a week to go from one fort to another. We waited at the road as usual, for Mr

Reid's news, and he came freighted. He says the *yanks* about here have had a *Big Big scare*, Saturday night the rebels captured two trains of cars, some where about the courthouse, which frightened them so terribly that they went to work and tore up about seven miles of the O. A. railroad, and ever since all the soldiers about here have been under arms night and day. Yesterday and to day they are on the watch for negroes, and every one, little or (big who shows his nose is seized upon and impressed into service, and they are now tearing up the ground all around Ft Elsworth with another range of intrenchments. He saw a number of steam vessels loaded with soldiers coming up the river, supposed to be some of Hoocker's army. There are not enough men about here now to picket the road to any extent, excepting the telegraph road, on that they are as thick as black birds, and that must be they [sic] way they think the rebels are coming. News came from W*a* to day that Vicksburg has certainly fallen after a most terrific battle. Just about dark two officers came dashing furiously towards the house, and round and round the garden, and through the yard calling loudly to know if any cavalry had been seen about here to day, and to know the way to Burgundy, and away they dashed off in that direction, as if the whole army and all Moseby's garrillas were at their heels

Tuesday 26th The burrowing up of the ground is now carried on vigourously fresh intrenchments made here and there and every where, And the poor negroes are dodging away out of the sight of their *friends* in every hole alley, There are ten thousand wild and improbable reports afloat among the soldiers. But the yankees are certainly on the Qui-vive-expecting something, they will not tell us what. The soldiers say Gen. Stewart's army, two hundred thousand strong are only a few miles above here, a mounted soldier came dashing into Ft Lyon on Saturday night breathless with haste to give the alarm, He had seen them himself, only a short distance off, breaking through the woods and bushes, all with lights in their hands. I cannot imagine what they expect to accomplish with lights, unless they purpose practicing the Gideon maneuver remembering that in olden time- "With a pitcher and a lamp Gideon over threw the camp," and now I think of it. I remember to have seen the first firefly on Saturday night and remarking to Lizzie, I should not be surprised if these cowardly yankees magnify them into signal lights, sent up for the Southerners. Pickets were extended as far as Cameron this evening, and about nine oclock two cannons were fired from gun boats in the river

Wednesday 27th Mrs Fairfax was here this evening. She says Mr F-'s brother was there, from the Courthouse yesterday, and says the Southerners were certainly in at the courthouse on Saturday night and got some of the yankee horses, but does not think they were any nearer us than that. Milly came from the fort in a high glee, with the news that all the white soldiers are to be sent away from the forts, and all maned with negro troops. Lizzie's school flourishes- a small addition of three to-day

. *Thursday* 28th Seventeen hundred of Government cattle were brought into Alex- on Saturday, and driven about to graze, first on one farm and then on another, and we have been on thornes ever since we heard it, listening, and every noise we hear, there comes the *seventeen hundred-* They are certainly coming, if not to-day, then to-morrow Uncle Sam is certain to get his *nip* out of us- for when he puts his hands down on *us* there is no bounds to his spoilation. We observe to day the yellow earth thrown up all round Gen. Cooper's house at Cameron, and find they are making a fort there.

Friday 29th The papers now from day, to day, are filled with the surrender of and downfall of Vicksburg. Today Grant, and Sherman, with the cooperation of the Gun Boat fleet have achieved wonders. Gen. Pemberton's whole army have surrendered, Banks report the occupation of Alex- on the Read river, and in a very few days the whole of Louisiana will be open to the ravages of the inhuman savage yankees. These reports keep us anxious- O so anxious! and our feelings harrowed up day after day. Alex- is only twenty five miles from Cheanyville, Mr Mower's parish. Poor sister Mary and her little children! God shield! them from the grievous calamities, and horrors, we have had to encounter

Saturday 30 For many many, days the yanks have been kept in a perfect state of ferment they seem to be at their wits-ends to know what to do next. They have rooted and burrowed up the ground all over the country in every direction, and now they are tearing up Fairfax Street Alex- to protect their commissary stores—an immense gulf dug entirely across the street, and great high barricades, almost as high as the houses. They do nothing but dig,- dig dig whenever there is a fresh alarm, there is another ditch dug. Gen. Stewart is now said to be hovering near with fifty thousand men. He has reduced his forces since Saturday last

Sunday 31st The yankees all lay in the trenches last night. The wind commenced to blow yesterday, and increased until to day it is a furious hurricane. The earth looks dry and parched, and the young green foilage is thrashed, and torn, until it hangs in strings until it is melancholy to look upon, and makes us feel more forlorne and sad than ever.

Monday June 1st 1863 Every day now seemes to bring some fresh cause of alarm, more negroes seized upon to dig in the trenches, more ditches dug in the country, and more ditches dug in the town. To day all the roads have again been barricaded, and the orders about passes more stringent, neither ingress or egress to the town without one.

Tuesday 2nd More targets have been fixed up to day, and practiced upon from the forts and with the usual success. Mr Reid came to day bringing a long long letter from Bushrod to gladden our hearts. It was the first letter direct from him that has reached us, we had seen several from him to other persons. It is dated March 31st 63, and had the Liverpool, and also Boston postmark. And as it is such a beautiful letter I am going to write it out *verbatim*

Wilmington N. C.
March 31st 1863

My Dear Lizzie It has been a long time since I have had an opportunity of writing to you, But as a chance offers now I will avail myself of it, more especially as I can write to you without the reserve which it is necessary to use, if the letter was going by flag of truce or was likely to fall into the hands of the enemy, as some of my previous letters have done. I have written to you a great many times, and in all sorts of ways, But I fear you have not received my letters. Miss Annie K- wrote, telling me she had been with you, and I cannot tell you how glad I was to receive her letter. I wrote to her immediately begging her to forward a letter to you, but have not heard from her yet. I heard a few days that she was married recently and that may account for her not writing to me. I have felt very anxious about you. Last summer immediately after the battle of Manassas I was two days at Chantilley and so anxious to go into the neighbourhood of Alex- but the Gen. would not permit it, he was fearful I might fall into the hands of the enemy- and now let me tell you in the first place about ourselves

From Mary I hear but not very often, her last letter was dated six months ago They were all well and getting along as comfortably as possible. She writes me they have not suffered at all from the war, and only felt it in the high prices asked for clothing. They were all very anxious about us, and you particularly as they have not heard from you so long. How I wish you both were there, that you had gone when the war first broke out and taken all the servants with you. Ned she writes is well, hires this year for 15$ a month. This hire for last year is at interest, and only awaits an opportunity to send it to you. I wish you had it. D- is doing well, is in the army and stationed at Richmond. He behaved well at the battles of Mechanicsville, and is highly spoken of by his superior officers. Is 1st Lt of Artillery, and has been recommended for Captain I expect he will get it. I had a letter from him day before yesterday.

When I was in Richmond last he was keeping house, and quite comfortably fixed, You would scarcely know him, he has changed so much for the better. His horse was killed at the battle of Mechanicsville, but he was not wounded himself, nor has he been since the war. I expect to go to Richmond in a few days, and will stay with him As for myself- I first went into the navy, and served with Com- Lynch on the Potomac, was at the battle of Aquia Creek—and on the 7th Oct. was brevetted Captain for my services- on the 8th was made Capt of Artillery in the regular army and gave up my navy appointment. I reported to GenWhiting, was placed in command of the batteries at Cockpit Point, at the mouth of the Occoquan river, and remained there all the winter. I have no doubt you often heard my guns, as I used to pitch into the yankees nearly every day. From a hill back of the batteries I could see with a good glass "Rose Hill" distinctly- Oh! how often I used to go up there and look, and wonder what you all were doing, and long to get to you, and then when I went back, woe betide the yankee who happened to be in sight. I understand they thought me very spiteful. Do you wonder at it? When ever I fired a gun I prayed that the shot might kill a hundred, and when I could see them knocked over I felt better satisfied. When spring came, we were moved to Fredricksburg. I was then appointed aid de Camp to Gen. Whiting. In April, a year ago we were sent to York-town, and staid there about a month, when we were ordered to return towards Richmond. The enemy pressed us very close, and at Williamsburg we turned on them and gave them a good thrashing. They then attempted to pass to our rear by landing at West Point- Gen. Whiting was ordered forward to meet them. They were twenty thousand strong, but we drove them back to their *gun boats* with a loss of twelve hundred killed and wounded. The battle lasted five hours, But they would not fight again, though we offered them battle for several days. We then fell back to the Chicahominy. On the 31st of May the battle of Seven Pines was fought. Our Division was engaged all the afternoon. We captured the yankee camp, and quantities of arms, cannon, ammunition, provisions and all kinds of stores. After the battle we were sent to Lynchburg, and from there valley to join Gen Jackson, we joined him in June. Shortly after we marched across the mountains, and before the enemy knew of our movements we pounced upon his rear at Mechanicsville and drove him back on "Gain's Mill." The next day we attacked him and drove his army like a flock of sheep across the Chicahominy. Gen Whiting's men fought like devils, and their tracks across the field was marked by the piles of dead they left. They have the credit of having won the day, and well they deserved it. Friday the battle of "Savage Station" was fought, and Monday, "Frazier's Farm," and "White Oak Bridge." And on Tuesday that terrible battle of "Malvern

Hill" took place. The enemy had made their last stand and fought with the desperation of despair. From early in the morning, until eleven o'clock at night the battle raged, when they broke and fled from the field in utter confusion their route was complete. Gen. Whiting had his horse killed under him. I was riding by his side at the time. For 30 miles the whole country was strewen with dead men and horses, and all conceiviable kinds of property. The enemy lost their guns, cannons, store wagons, and thousands of men. You can form no idea of it. Do not believe one word you see in the papers for they never tell the truth. Their loss was fearful. A few days after the battle of "Malvern," we returned to Richmond and remained there some time Gen. Whiting was taken ill and went home. I also was very sick with camp fever. On my recovery I reported to Maj. Gen. Hood and was assigned to duty as Chief of Artillery of the 1st Division of Longstreets' corps. On the first of August we left Richmond and proceeded to Ceder Mountain to join Gen. Jackson. We found Pope and his robbers rapidly retreating towards the Rappanhannock, and commenced a hot chase after him. We did not overtake him until we got to "Freeman's Ford." It was during an awful thunder storm But we at once attacked him, cutting up two of his divisions, and driving the rest of them across the river. We followed the next day, encamping one night near Salem. I went to "Meadow Grove" to see our old friends, the Miss Carters. They were delighted to see me, and I staid and took supper with them. The next day we met the enemy at "Thorofare Gap," and had a warm engagement. Our troops crossed over the hill by Sam Bailey's house and formed line of battle across the gap, from the depot to the old mill. Sister will remember the situation- We then marched through the gap and along down the run. The yankees were in the village and the mill and Mrs Chapman's house. We drove them out of there, and many were killed in the yard. I slept that night on the ground in Mrs C-'s yard with plenty of dead yankees all around me.

The next day was Friday. We marched early, passing through Haymarket and down the turnpike. At 10 oclock we came up with the yankees near old Polly Clark's house- ask sister if she does not recollect a white house in the field just beyond there on the right of the road as you go towards Alex- Well, at that house I put my artillery. The yankees were occupying the woods in front and about 400 yards off Gen. Stewart ordered me to fire, and I blazed away—seeing some ladies in the porch of that house I rode up and advised them to go away, but they declined saying that they knew that I would not fire into the house, and there they stood looking at the fight Soon after the yankees broke and ran, and I was ordered to go over to the left to Gen. Jackson. I mounted a high hill on the left of the turnpike just above Groveton The yankee batteries were all around Groveton house. There we had a fearful battle. The ground was covered with tall dry grass, and during the fight a cassion exploded and set fire to it. It burned fiercely- the ground was covered with dead and wounded men, and O, it was the most awful sight, it made one sick to look at it, or to think of it. Many of the men had their heads, and hands burned off. I lost many of my men and horses there- The next day I did not go into battle until 3 oclock in the evening, at that time the fiercest of the battle was raging. Gen. Longstreet sent his aid and ordered me to come up. I started down the road at a gallop, all along the dead men were lying thick. I came up with the Gen. about half a mile above Groveton. He ordered me into battery and I moved into an orchard on the left of the [sic] and commenced firing Soon the enemy opned an awful fire. The cannon balls flew like hail, and soon they lay along the ground just as if they had been emptied out of a cart, Horses were killed and men shot down at their guns while others stepped into their places- and there they fought away as if they did not care at all about. Near by, in the road, sat dear old Generals Lee and Longstreet on their horses looking as càlm and quiet as if nothing was happning It was very warm work, but soon the enemy retired, and we started in pursuit, dashing across the fields in many places the dead and wounded lay so thick we could not avoid running over them. Masses of the enemy were flying in front of us, our troops firing on them from every direction. It was very exciting, unlike any thing I had ever seen before. At Dogans house, just below Groveton, and the old stone house—Sister will recollect—where we used to turn off the turnpike in going to "Willow Green" There the yankees made another stand. The artillery was brought up and opned fire, and at the same time Gen. Lon charged them. Part of them ran down the pike, while the rest ran along the road towards Sudley, hundreds were killed there. I started on the road towards Sudley firing all the time, the chase did not stop until it was so dark we could not tell friends from foes. I then went back and laid down near some hay stacks near Groveton The ground all around was covered with, dead wounded and dying. It rained heavily and O it was fearful to hear the cries of the poor wretches, begging for help, and the grouns of the dying men and horses was heartrending- all night you could see the glimmer of lanterns as parties wandered over the field looking anxiously for dead or wounded friends In one place 3000 wounded were collected togather, in another 1900 dead strewed the ground with their pale faces turned up to the passer by- The yankee loss was fearful more than 30,000 men- Our loss was not very great— Sunday we buried the dead and on Monday marched to

Germantown, and attacked the enemy again, driving him almost within sight of Washington City. I often wondered during the time if you all did not hear our guns, and if you had any idea who was there. On Wednesday we marched back to Leesburg and crossed the Potomac into Md. For several days we lay in camp But on Sunday 14th the enemy advanced on us at Boonsboro, and a fierce battle took place. We drove him back and then crossed the Antitam. In the mean time Harper's Ferry fell, with 11000 prisoners,- and all their guns, stores and arms- Our work was done and we commenced moving slowly towards the river- But the enemy followed so closely that we were obliged to fight him. On Tuesday morning the battle of Antitam began at day light, and lasted until dark without any decisive result. The next day the enemy crossed the river and advanced upon Sharpsburg. Then commenced one of the most furious battles of the war. The yankees outnumbered us four to one, but our men never faltered, they stood their ground and fought like devils, all day long the very earth seemed to tremble with the shock of contending hosts. Great black columns of smoke ascended up and hung around the mountains like a pall. Time after time the enemy hurled his masses upon us, but they reeled back scattered and broken- Our men had had nothing to eat since Sunday morning, and in the mean time, had marched and fought night and day. But they stood up to it like horses. Ambulances and wagons loaded with wounded, and limbless bodys, passed by, but not a groan escaped them. Men covered with gastly wounds sank down and died in every direction but they uttered no cry. Silently they met the foe, silently they drove him back, there was no shout, no yell of defiance, but a settled look of determination on the faces of all to conquer or to die- Near by stood a young Lieutenant of artillery bravely fighting his guns. He came up and asked if I would permit him to unfurl his flag and hoist it on his gun, I objected as it would make him more than a mark for the foe. He went back and a moment later after a cannon ball tore away his right leg. He fell, but attempted to rise again, and finding he was unable, he took off his cap and waving it above his head shouted to his men "fight on fight on, and never surrender"—He had fallen to rise no more. We laid him in his narrow bed, and he sleeps there far away upon the banks of the Potomac Poor fellow! he was a gallant youth, and loved by all for his amiable and gentle deportment His last thoughts were of home—his mother—and the one to whom he was shortly to have been married- "Tell them" he whispered with his dying breath, "that I did my duty-" Many of my best and warmest friends fell that day, but no tears bedewed the sod that covers them- With fierce and sullen faces friends laid them down to rest while the silent prayer went up, "Oh! God how long-" The next day the silence of death rested on the field which had been so fiercely contested. We waited but the foe did not come. 28000 of his best troops lay piled among the dead and wounded, and he could not resume the battle. On Friday we quietly crossed the Potomac in sight of him- On the 10th Nov. I was ordered by the Sec War to report to my old commander, Maj. Gen. Whiting for duty as Chief of Artillery in this department. The Gen. had asked for me. The post is a very pleasant one, I prefer it to any in the army. Some days ago I declined the appointment of Colonel because I did not wish to leave it. After the battle of "Gain's Mill" I was made Maj. in the army and will probably get the rank of Col before long with my present assignment, at any rate my command is much more important than that of Col of a regiment

We live very nicely, have every thing we want. I am living with the General. Do not believe any reports you see in the yankee papers about our suffering, there is no truth in it. This day the Confederacy is stronger and better provided with arms, amunition, etc etc, than ever, and they are united to a man. Our army is in splendid condition, and we are ready to fight the yankees again harder than ever. We are paid regularly every month. My pay is $251.50 pr month, and I am allowed three horses. When you write let me know if you have those stock certificates of mine for Alex. Corp. Stock, and also the orange Alex. R. R. bonds. I wish I had them. Can you draw the interest on the Corporation Stock, if so do it and use the money if you want it. Two years interest is due now. Get the bonds and certificates if you can. I left them in the Exchange Bank with Charles Hooff and take care of them for me. Should you have an opportunity you might send them to Richmond to Wells Lockwood. He is in the "Commerical Bank" at that place. But do not send them unless you have an opportunity by a reliable person. Write me all about the servants, what has become of them, and any thing, and every thing else you can think of, it will be most interesting to me. I am going to send this letter by Nassau. It is said the yankees read all letters sent that way. In answering can you not send your letter to N. Y. to a friend there, and get them to give it to a Cap. of one of the Nassau steamers, where it would come without being opned. Give a great deal of love to cousin M. and Mrs. W. and to sister. I will write again so soon as I hear from you

I am dear Lizzie ever your devoted brother B W

O this precious darling letter! it has given us so much comfort, and happiness, and we were so delighted to get it, and it is so interesting, doubly interesting to me, having traveled so many times over most of the ground on horse-back with the two dear boys. and then too the letter had not been Paul Pried into by the yankees. Mr Massie the post master, has been very good in letting us have our letters without being opned, and if one comes to the office and he finds a good opportunity he sends it out to us, and I know he knows B. hand-writing as well, almost, as I do. I do believe we have heard the guns of nearly all the battles Bushrod has been in, excepting those about Richmond and on the York and James rivers- Mr Reid tells us the alarm among the yanks is still very great, the men, and forts are kept in readiness, expecting momentarily an attack I think some thing has occured, more than we know of. Charles left home on Saturday 23rd the day before Whitsuntide, and we have not heard a word of him until to day he sent a note saying he has made several ineffectual attempts to get home but was stopped by the guards, of one thing I am very certain the guards would not prevent his getting to W*a* when he wishes to go, no doubt this time, "he has gone to look for freedom," as old mammy terms it

Wednesday 3rd The Rev. Mr Wall came from town to see us today. He seems to think our situation very lonely and unprotected, and wanted us to go to town with him. But we concluded we had better remain where we are, we have got nothing to pay board, and where would we go. Mr. W... says the yankees are seizing the negroes where ever they find them, and that yesterday five hundred were sent away from town, no one knows where Numbers are wondering about and hiding themselves in the country, and when they come out of their hiding holes are all armed with shovels and spades to make believe "da imployen de gobermen works" Two of them came to the door this morning dressed in U.S. blue and buttons, gave the military salute and asked if we wished to hire, they would do any kind of field work for twelve dollars a month. The spokesman used precisely the nasal yankee dialect, and stood up with the most self important air twirling his mustach all the time.

Thursday 4th More targets are being fixed up to day to our great terror, every now and then we [hear] of a man, or a woman, or child being killed. almost every practicing day a cow, or horse, or some animal is killed. Targets are now fixed up on every hill, and in every valley, and field as near to the houses as they can get- a day or two ago old Mr Burgen brought us a little money for house rent, which has enabled us to send for a barrel of flour, we thought we had better expend it in that way than any other, and get it while we could. and Mr Reid was so good as to buy it and bring it to us- We are dependant on our neighbours now for every thing of the kind we need. and Mr Reid is so good to us.

Friday 5th More barricading fixed up in the roads again to day I can not imagine their object. These great immense piles of brush and things are fixed up here and there and every where and the roads completely stopped, but still there are ways left to go round the barricades. For three or four hours to day the cannon balls, and bombs flew through the air frightfully. Milly picked up her lap full of pieces of shells that had exploded some where near the house. Two mounted officers came dashing into the garden, and through the grasse, round, and round the house, then stopped and dismounted at the kitchen door, and walked in with as home like an air as possible, and seated themselves, looked round, asked ever so many questions, sat and conversed with the servants as much as they chose, and then mounted and off again the way they came in. Lizzie was near the garden gate as they went out, and as soon as they saw her they both burst into the most boisterous insulting laugh, and then dashed off as hard as they could go, just like two drunken idiots.

Saturday 6th I wrote a long letter to Bushrod, and L. took it over to Mr McClurer to get him to mail it to England for her. Such, close prisoners as we are, we have no means of sending in the way he directed. But unfortunately Mr Mc was not at home and she had that long hot walk for nothing. Charles has been gone two weeks and to day sent a message beggin Col. Dulaney's assistance in getting him a pass But he declined having any thing to do with it, said he was afraid to interfere.

Monday 8th The weather for the past three or four weeks has been extremely dry and windy, every thing parched up. The grass as brown and crisp as it usually is in August, and O every thing so sad and dreary, the days come and go, come and go, I am afraid we will soon forget the day of the week, no employment to interest, and if we got a book to read (which is a rare chance) I can read a whole chapter, and then wake up to the recollection that I do not know a single word that I have read- Lizzie was at Mr Fairfax this evening and learned that Gen Cooper's house at "Cameron," has been torn down and a fort is to be made there. With a glass we could see an immense embankment of yellow earth. But every thing else gone We have been sending ever since strawberries were ripe to old Mrs Struder for them

Tuesday 9th and about two oclock to day we thought we would walk down there and get them ourselves. We had only been in the house a few moments when we were startled by a most violent thundering explosion, followed by another, in quick succession, the earth shook and trembled, and the old fabric we were in seemed to move, I was so frightened, I thought I saw the logs tumbling out and falling all about, every body sprang to their feet exclaiming "whats that, whats that" a shell burst very near, for a little stream of blue smoke came in at one door and passed out at the other, I cried run, run don't you see the house coming down, I shoved every one as I passed along, but I believe, I was the very first to get on the out side- I looked up at Ft Lyon which at that moment went up with a tremendous shock. It presented a splendid appearance, just my idea of a large volcano Indeed it looked very much like the pictures of Vesuvus during an eruption, in the old Woodbridge geographys I used to study at school, so many, many years ago- Every thing flew up into the air, an immense column of smoke and dust burst up from the center and seemed to stand still for a moment, and the sun reflected through it made it look like flames. The cloud then lifted and floated off towards the river, then the plants and heavy logs, timbers, pieces of steel, stones, and dirt, came rattling, and thundering down the sides of the fort, and embankments- then all was quiet—the stillness of death seemed there

We stood and looked, expecting every moment to see the soldiers rush out in a body and mount the parapet- but not a sign of life was there- after a time a few men, from the camp a short distance off appeared- they moved along very slowly, and cautiously, and after taking a survey of the outside ventured in. We were too far off to see or hear any thing more, and thinking old mammy might be alarmed, started for home. We found Mr McCluer and the children here when we got home. They did not seem to have felt the concussion way we did. In the evening Milly went over to the fort, so curious to see and know all that is going on there, she came back perfectly horrified at what she witnessed. She says a great number were killed, and many more wounded, she never beheld such a sight, the men were dragging out the crushed, mangled and disfigured bodies from the dirt and rubbish, some without heads, the dismembered bodies, and disevered limbs are scattered all round the fort and through the woods and fields in every direction- Every thing happned so quickly, I could not imagine so much mischief had been done

Wednesday 10th To-day President Lincoln, Sec Staunton, and Gen Hyntzleman and a number of others visited the ruins of Fort Lyon. The President manifested great displeasure, as carelessness was the cause of the catastrophy. Their stay was but short. The soldiers have been telling us for several weeks past that the fire was still smouldering in among the logs of the old bombproof and some day it would go *up with a rush*. But the President, and secretaries, need not have fretted much about it, for neither they, or the government they represent, have ever paid one cent for the logs it is made of, if it is the crag- fort in the

GEN S COOPER's RESIDENCE
CAMERON
1866

Washington defences. To-days papers mention the casualty, as a thing of very little moment not much mischief done Some eighteen or twenty men killed and as many wounded. Eighteen hundred pounds of powder burned and eighteen hundred shells exploded. But a single cannon injured and very little damage done to the fort.

"Cameron," residence of General Samuel S. Cooper— a sketch from memory made by his son in 1866*
Courtesy of Samuel Cooper Dawson

One of the soldiers from there was here this evening and he told me that the timbers under ground have been burning for the last three weeks, but the men would not trouble themselves to get water to put it out. He says the fort is a wreck perfectly shattered, two of the guns very much injured, twenty three of the bodies have been found a number of the wounded were sent to the hospitals in town, and others whose recovery was thought doubtful were compelled to take poison, and they died off in a moment. A barrel of whisky was sent out from town for the use of the wounded, and the surgeon got so drunk he could not stand. He says the Magazine that exploded had about four thousand pounds of powder

* General Cooper was Adjutant General of the U.S. Army until he resigned his commission on March 7, 1861, and was appointed to the same rank as the senior ranking officer in the Confederate Army. His home, "Cameron" was located on the west side of Quaker Lane just north of the Little River Turnpike. The house was demolished by the Union Army for the construction of Fort Williams.

in it. The officers estimate the loss at three hundred thousand dollars. Two officers a Capt. and Lt. killed. They were all so torn to pieces and disfigured it was almost impossible to recognize them, or to tell to which the scattered limbs belonged to. He was quite indignant at the newspaper figures, says it was absurd. I was at Mr Fairfax this evening and could see from the top of the hill the funeral procession as it moved from Ft Lyon slowly along to the soldiers grave yard near town. I watched it all the way. There were nine ambulances, each containing three or four coffins a piece, a small body of men followed and a band of music. Curiosity took a number of the people to the camp where they were getting the bodies ready for burial, and all said, what with decomposition and flies it was a disgusting scene, and the soldiers were in such a state of noisy tumult, cursing and blaspheming over the dead that it was shocking to hear. They could not find out the cause of the excitement I heard six cars loaded with wounded soldiers came down the rail road last night. But no one knows where they came from or any thing about a fight.

Thursday 11th Ft Lyon is now maned by the 3rd N. Y. Battalion, all Dutchmen and decidedly the best behaved, and more like human creatures than any we have ever seen among the yankees. Every thing about here is as quiet to day as possible. I spied at the camps near town and they all look deserted. The poor Dutchmen at Ft. Lyon thought as their numbers were so reduced they were going to be discharged and sent home, and then a report came that the President was so enraged with them for blowing up the fort that he had determined to have them all drumed out of the army- *They were delighted* But all their high hopes, and expectations of so honourable a release proved fallacious They are to remain where they are, at least for the present.

Friday 12 Two trains of cars filled with soldiers went up the O, A-rail road to day. But no one seems to know what is going on Heavy cannonaiding was heard in the direction of Fredricksburg. Milly, the *sensationalist*, brings daily *thrilling* accounts of scraps of the human form being picked up about ft Lyon. One day it is a foot and leg with a boot on, a tongue, hand—head

Saturday 13 Cars are still bringing the wounded down the rail road. The soldiers say the fire is still burning at Ft Lyon and they were very near having another explosion The man in charge of the government cattle came to day to ask if we had any objection to their being put here. L- told him the little grass we have here we want for our own stock It would not last his immense herd two hours. He said his directions were to put them where ever he could find grass, but he had never done so where people objected to it. The yankees seem some what to have lowered their tone, a year ago they would have put that head of cattle in our flower garden if they chose "without with your leave, or by your leave" But of course he saw there was nothing here for them to feed on.

Milly, our news carrier, brought word this morning that Friez is among the men who were injured by the explosion. He was once a guard here, and was always very civil and respectful, and Lizzie to show her appreciation of his good manners and behavior has been all the morning making him some nice things to tempt his appetite, and this evening Milly was dispatched with a basket full for him and for others among the sick. I believe Milly visits the hospital every day, and she reports the patients as very poorly provided for. L.'s little school is added to every few days. The people are perfectly delighted with the idea of having some one to teach their children, of course the war broke up all the schools in this vicinity, and for more than two years now the children all are entirely without instruction Some good kind lady friends in town hearing of the work L. is engaged in, went from house to house among their friends and collected up all the old school books they could find, and sent them out to her, a whole carriage load- and O such a treasure as it was to her, she was delighted, and so were the children, if only to rummage them all over. And as we are at this time pretty free from the annoyance of soldiers we are getting along more quietly and comfortably. The nearest camp is at Ft Lyon- But we are bounded by two roads, the telegraph road to Fredricksburg, and the old Backlick road to Manassas, and both roads are nearly all the time thoroughly picketed, and we have the *pleasure* of their company of the pickets from both sides. *Pies*, and water, are always the excuse, an old man in the neighbourhood said to a whole crowd who came to his door, and asked for water, "Water is free to *all*, there is plenty of water for *all*, and it is the only thing you ever ask for." One night I was aroused by a noise I did not understand and got up and went to the window, I stood and listened for some time, and then came a rustling along the hedge side and through the bushes, and out came a man on the walk. I asked who is that, and what do you want here at this time of night, "He said I came for a pie." I replied in no very pleasant tone, I've got no pie, I don't keep a pie shop, we are annoyed enough by you all in the day time, you might at least let us sleep in peace, and I wish you would stay away from here. His reply was "I'll come when I've a mind to," and off he pushed into the kitchen. The door was not fastned, and he walked in very much as if at home, and we found out after that they are in the habit of coming here at all seasons, night, and day, and the negroes keep a regular eat house for them, and every thing is in readiness for them whenever they call for it. Lizzie and I made a sleeping apartment of first one room and then another. If we get frightned up stairs, and if frightned down stairs we move up stairs again. One night while sleeping down stairs, L. had retired, and I was getting ready, I had put the light down to the lowest notch, and gone to the window as is my usual custom to reconnortie, and there I saw just behind a tree in front of the window the outline of a man's figure. I could not see very distinctly but I stood there until I was positive there was a man there. The tree was very large but it was crooked, and leaned over, and as the man would move or change his position I could see first his hat and face against the sky, then his knee, then the whole figure I was so frightned, I ran to the bed and put my mouth into L-'s ear, and said, a man here behind the tree. "O" she said, "no man there at all, only your imagination." But I persuaded her to come and look for herself, and she was convinced there was no imagination about it, off she flew into the kitchen, and from the window there she could see him distinctly enough, fortunately mammie's nephew, John Allen, was there, who hallowed at and ordered him off. But he did not seem at all inclined to go, but drew off as if pointing a gun. "Very well," she said, "you stay there until I get my pistol." When he heard of the pistol he took to his heels and away he went. She did not have the pistole at the time but seized it up as she flew through the house and opning the front door gave him two or three parting shots. She did not see him and had no idea of shooting him, but says if any of them do come here again molesting us in the night she is going to try and shoot them in the legs. She will not shoot to kill, but she will try and lame them. The commander at Ft Lyon is a dutchman named Shermer, and the next morning Milly went over there and gave him a full and graphic account of the nights adventure. He seemed much excited and in his dutch way of talking said, "Now you go back and tell your mistress if any of my men comes over there either night or day and interferes with her in any way, she has my full and free permission to shoot, and not to shoot to lame but to shoot to kill, and I will see her safely through it." A few days after this the gentleman himself made his appearance at our door, in a splendid carriage, with a fine dashing pair of horses, both carriages and horses resplendent with silver mountings, only a few moments before him Mrs Fairfax had come in, I was very glad she happned to be here. He descended from his carriage and walked in with a very stately mein and introduced himself, (as well as I could understand Col Shermer) But we guessed who he was for Milly had apprised us of his coming, but she did not know when. He was a tall fine looking man, and his broad-cloth, and beaver, black kids and furs were perfectly astounding. He sat and talked very pleasantly indeed, particularly so as he made us so many promises. He said he was very sorry we had been frightned by one of his men, if indeed it was one of his men, but he will send us a guard, a man we can rely upon, and he will come himself often to see how we are getting on, and as his men picket this road for some distance above us he will give them special orders to look after and take care of us, and we can call on them at any time to do any thing we want done. He also offered us the use of his elegant horses and carriage whenever we want them, and we shall have a pass to go when and where we please, as also a permit to bring from town any thing and every thing we want When he arose to make his congees before leaving, no doubt he thought he had made an indelible impression, and it would never do to leave us under fals impressions or to *awaken fals hopes*, and he turned to L. in rather a jocose manner and said "I know what your politics are, but it does not matter with me what they are, but if I was a single man I would come here every day until I made a good Union woman of you-" "O" she replied, "no doubt if you were a single man you would find that a very easy matter." Before he left he wrote a permit and handed it to her saying, "you can get a wagon load of provisions if you please." After he had gone we made out a list of our wants, and they were many and great, and gave it with the permit to Mrs. Fand told her to say to Mr Fairfax, it was best to strike while the iron was hot. The very next day he went to town and not only brought us a wagon load, but one for himself on the same permit. -After that we never wanted a friend at court as long as Gen Shermer lasted. He was ever ready to do any thing for us whenever we wanted him, and his men were as kind and attentive to us as they could be. But we never saw his face again, unfortunately for us, one day his accounts with the government fell short and the last thing we heard of him, they had seized him up and landed him in the penitentiary. I was sorry for him, and sorry for ourselves. The only difference between him and all the rest his peculations were on the yankees. The others divided their *favours* in that way with the people. That is they steal from the people, and sell to the government.

The yankees have incited the negroes every where to keep a constant watch on the white people- to listen, to peep and pry, and find out every thing and report it to them, and we discovered recently that Milly keeps a constant and vigilant espionage on all we say and doe. We are in the habit, late in the evening, when there is little danger of meeting soldiers, of taking a little walk, generally from the house to the public road, two or three times. We walk in the open road, and she hides herself by lying down flat on the ground and draging along through the high weeds to listen and watch. I think she has a suspition we walk out to meet some of the rebels and then she goes over to the fort and makes her reports to suit herselfe. on several occasions she has had a company of soldiers out scouring the whole neighbourhood. We did not know it at the time it was her doings but found it out afterwards- at one time she pretended to see a man in a tree at least a mile away and called my attention to it of course I saw no one, or she either, and I never thought of what she ment until I found out the game she was playing- One morning a little scholar of L.'s said to her, "Mother says you and Miss A- must come down there this evening, she has some thing she wants to tell you, and you must be sure to come for she knows you will be delighted to hear it," of course as soon after dinner as we possibly could we flew down there, and as soon as she could find an opportunity she whispered into our ears. What do you think of my having a visit from Col. Moseby last night, and he had a whole company of mounted men with him. They did not all come up to the house with him he was afraid of arousing the echos, but how they all got inside to picket lines, without being seen or heard is the marvel. For they were miles and miles inside the yankee lines. He asked a great many questions about people and things, roads and so on, and says he is coming again to night to take Slough the military governor of Alex. Has a man there to look out for him and tell him where Slough lives, when he leaves his office, and where he sleeps and all he can find out about him. He gave them the watch word and they gave it to us. They said they did not suppose we would have any use for it, but if any thing unforseen should occur and we should hear that word we would know who was about and to keep quiet. "But sleep did not visit our eyes that night, nor slumber our eye lids." We sat up all night and listened, and listened, but no watch word came to break the stillness, neither did Moseby come, and we never did learn why he failed to come. He is certainly the idol of this vicinity, and always has been since first we heard his name and of his many daring, dashing exploits. I do think he has been our safe guard, although this is the only time I have heard of his being any where near to us, yet the fear of his vicinage has, I am sure, kept the yankees some what in check, and saved us all from many a deed of violence. Mrs F- has a negro girl the very counterpart of our Milly, and the night they expected Col Moseby the second time Mrs F was very uneasy about Jane's finding it out. L. Suggested a few drops of laudanum, but she said she had never used it in any way, and was afraid of it. L. said "O there is not the slightest danger. I'll take the responsibility, and fix it for you." So she made a tumbler of nice sweet tody and put fifteen or twenty drops of Laudanum in it, and placed it on the side board. "Now," she said, when you are all about to retire for the night you can say to Jane, there is a tumbler of toddy on the side board, I don't want it and you may have it. Jane is fond of toddy, and that will quiet the *lady* for the night"

The next morning Jane slept until long after sunrise. She said "O Miss Margaret I never slept so soundly in all my life, and what can be the reason." -Milly knew the horse tracks, no one could tell how. She went to the fort and reported to the Col. that an immense body of rebel horsemen had been here, within the lines, she had tracked them all through the woods, and up and down the roads. Her report made quite a sensation, and all the soldiers were on the alert in a moment, and every one who could be spared was sent out to investigate, we saw bodies of them several times during the day noseing around, but had no idea what they were scenting out with their heads bent over and eyes fixed steadfastly on the ground. The search lasted all day long but without any results, and late in the evening they all returned to the fort, tired hungry, and foot-sore to make their reports. The Col. sent for Milly and told her if she came there again with any more of her lying tales he would have her taken up and put in the Sweat Box, and there she should be kept all day, and all night too-

I was too glad when I heard it. I could never think of it without laughing. I only wish he had carried out his threat. It is likely we never should have heard of it but Jane told it. There is a great intimacy, and still a great deal of rivalry between the two, as to the soldiers favour, and one is always delighted to have some thing to tell on the other

I was in town this morning, and found every one in a great state of excitement perfectly in armes at the violence and wrongs perpetuated on the poor defenseless people by the yankees. It appears that a short time since an official notification was sent to Alex. that such and such familles and persons were to be sent out side the yankee lines (of the old inhabitants). They were all ordered to hold themselves in readiness that on such a day a steamer would be at the wharf to take them. I think there was a list of about one hundred families. The poor unfortunates went to work to dispose of their effects as best they could, not being allowed to take any thing with them They packed and stowed away in other people's houses as much as they could, many sold off every thing they could getting little, or nothing for it, for the poor people, be the will so good had not the means to pay for things they did not actually need. They broke up their homes and scattered their goods, and when the day came, never was such scene witnessed as the whole town presented.

The streets were thronged and packed, with one dense mass, of weeping and wailing humanity. Fathers and mothers, little children and big children, the old, and the young, some young girls by themselves, all going they know not where, and with no means of making for themselves another home, and into a country too, where two years ago according to yankee accounts every thing like food and raiment was exhausted- and after this state of anxiety and suspence had lasted for hours and hours over the time, an order came revoking the edict, they are not to be sent at this time, but not by any means saying it was done away with altogather. And now, these poor creatures, after having disposed of all their goods and chattles, with not a house, or home to put their heads into, are as badly off, or worse than if they had been sent away. I do think of all the cruel, inhuman acts ever perpetrated by a *civilized* people, and on a community too, entirely in their power, and under their control, with no offense alleged against them. This certainly does stand near the head of the list of yankee barbarities. Every one I met on the street asked, "were you among those sent out side lines." No not this time- "O well, your turn will come with the next steamer, this is not the last of it."

Our resources are entirely exhausted, and when our good, kind, thoughtful friend Mrs Fairfax came in this morning, Lizzie said to her, "We have not a cent of money in the world, and there is scarcely a mouthful of provisions in the house, and I do not know what is to become of us. She reflected for a while, and then asked if we had not milk. L. said yes we have two right good cows, but we all can not live on milk alone," well, she said send me every day what cream you have, and I will see if I can not dispose of it for you." And so she did for weeks and months she sold cream enough to buy us such little things as are indispensable. But every thing is so high priced, and almost an impossibility to get any thing from town that L. and I live almost entirely on tea and bread. Now and then some kind neighbour will summon up enough temerity to smuggle us a pound of tea in his pocket, and L. little boys, if any of them can kill a bird, or a rabbit, they are so delighted to bring it to her-

The yankees seem to have been for months employing all their energies and skill in mining and burrowing about Petersburg. I do not understand, and can not imagine what they expect to effect by it, whether in that way to enter Richmond, or to blow up the whole Confederate army. The papers have been filled with it, and also of the success, and great discoveries made by balloon ascentions, But one day their great doing ended in great disaster to themselves. Instead of blowing up the

"rebel strong hold," they blew up and destroyed hundreds and hundreds
of their own men

They are so far away now that not many of the wounded are brought
this way. But droves and droves of disabled horses are driven past here
on both roads every day, and rafts and rafts of dead ones pass up the
river. We have seen a number of the poor creatures shot as they pass by
here. The men who have the care of them say, they are often sorry to
have to kill such fine splendid animals as they are, when only a few days
rest and care, they would be as good as ever. But their orders are positive
when one fails, is not able to travel, to shoot him down, not to leave a
live horse on the road for the rebel citizens to get. But notwithstanding
their peremptory orders, they do constantly sell them on the sly. A little
boy in this neighbourhood bought a mule for a pie- and after he was
fed, and rested, and resusitated a little he proved to be a valuable animal-
worth at least a hundred and fifty dollars. But he kept the little fellow all
the time on the *qui-vive* for fear he would be taken away from him—
hiding him first in one place and then another. There is an establishment
on the river between Alex. and Wa where all the sick and diseased horses
are doctored. Those that are passed cure are knocked in the head, and
they with the rafted ones are manufactured. I do not know whether it is
a government hospital and institute, or a private yankee enterprise for
making fertilizer for the canal, or Cox's sparkling Gelatine for the table.
But at any rate you can smell boiling horse flesh for miles up and down
the river. One morning Milly came in and said "Miss Lizzie do you want
a nice little riding horse, if you do, I can get one for you," and she pointed
out a horse in our field, you see that little bay horse, well, he does not
belong to any body, no one knows any thing about him, he has been
grazing about here for more than a week, and if you say so, I'll catch
him and bring him in to you." L. started off with her, Milly with a bridle
in her hand, and in a very short time they returned leading the pretty
little creature, he proved as gentle and as docile, and as well acquainted
and as much at home, as if *to the manor born*. We had no other inclosure,
so they put him in the flower garden and called him Moseby. L. made
the greatest pet of him, he soon learned his name, and when she would
call *"Mosby"* he came trotting up to the house, he knew which window
she sat by and would put his head in and eat bread, or any thing she
gave him out of her hand. Isler, the guard was delighted at having a
horse and said, Now Misch Lischie if you vill lot me ride that horse
schom time, I vill groom him, and take care of him for you, as if you
vants a schaddle or bridle I will go over to the fort and steal dem for
you. She could not help laughing. But she said, "O no indeed. I have a

side saddle but if I have not I could not think of giving you any such commission as that. I do not want all the soldiers from Ft Lyon to come over here and kill me and tear the house down for a saddle and bridle." Lizzie did not venture to mount the horse for some time after she had captured him. But she first made Isler mount him *lady fashion* and ride round and round the yard. This was practiced several days then she ventured, while Isler walked by her side, then she rode a short distance alone and every day the ride was lengthened until she became bold enough to ride any where alone. And every body she met, and every house she passed would run and congratulate her on having a horse to ride once more. But one day an old Irishman who had lately come into this neighbourhood, came with his boy and laid claim to Moseby. At first she refused to give him up, but she was very sick that day and it worried her, and here these creatures staid and staid for hours, and talked, and talked, and argued, and told ten thousand .... until she just gave him up to get rid of them, although she knew every word they uttered in regard to the horse was false for he had U.S. marked on his shoulder. O! I was so sorry to see beautiful little Moseby trotted away, for it was such a pleasure to Lizzie to ride him sometimes Afterwards we heard these irish people were perfect *Jay hawkers*, claiming every thing that the people had taken up in that way. Horses, cows, sheep, hogs, poultry

The winter of 63-64 was a terrible winter on us. And although we were some what exempt from the annoyance of soldiers, we were shut up here, almost as bad as if we were in the Penitentiary. Charles was gone and we had no one to do for us, or get for us what we needed. O it was a dreary, dreary, trying winter to our whole household- not enough to eat, and scarcely enough fire to keep us from perishing with the cold- I don't know how or where we got the little wood we did have. The orders were so stringent in regard to picketing the roads, that no market carts or wood carts passed here. Sometimes, as I had nothing else to employ, or interest me I could indulge in day dreams, sitting by the window looking out—suppose—O suppose—I should see a wagon drive up to the kitchen door, filled- loaded with all sorts of good things, so much of this, and so much that, and the other, things that I imagined would taste so delightfully- Suppose some person that could afford to do it—were to find out in some unaccountable manner how destitute and hungry we were, and were to send us a wagon load- But O, I could eat up a wagon load in a little less than no time- almost at a mouth full- suppose they were to send two- One day while I was indulging in these imaginary feastings Mr A. J. and his mother drove up- and O after being debarred the sight of the human face so long, I could not express the delight with which we welcomed once more the sight of the human face divine. And then when they got out of the carriage and brought in ever so many nice things- O I never—never can forget it. One thing was a great bushel basket of delicious fresh crackers, of all kinds just hot from the bakery, and how we did enjoy them- These good friends just brought us all these nice things in the kindness of their hearts, as they were coming they thought they must bring us some thing. But they had no idea how low our larder was or how very hungry we were, and what a blessing they were bringing to us. After that they came to see us a number of times, and never empty-handed. Some times a great can of oysters, packages of sugar, fruit, oranges, cake- I know it would have made their hearts glad had they known how much we enjoyed and appreciated their many kindnesses, but they never knew how desperate our needs were- In the night mammie was taken very sick, and we were up with her nearly all night rubbing and scrubbing her with every sort of thing. and giving her hot toddy, and hot drinks, and hot bricks to her feet. It was a very cold night. But towards morning she got easy and fell asleep, and we went to bed. But in the morning when we awoke the whole face of the earth was covered with snow, knee deep.—What were we to do- mammy sick- no wood.- We had a little wood but it was too long for the stoves. We were just consulting togather whether it would not be better to remain in bed all day, when a whole troop of Lizzie's little boys passed the windows, all with their little axes on their shoulders, and in the least time the wood boxes were filled up, the fires going, the kettle singing, and old mammy sufficiently recovered to make her appearance in the kitchin, and all this we owed to the thoughtful kindness of our good friend Mrs Fairfax.—In the summer and fall of 64—Moseby, Stringfellow, and Kinchelow made occasional raids into this neighbourhood. Some times they carried off obnoxious persons, sometimes they burned the rail road bridges, they fired into the cars, some times they captured a train or two and carried them off. Then the yankees would get furious and the poor citizens would have to pay the penalty. At one time they seized up all the gentlemen, all about the town, all the old men (for there was no other there)—the decrepit, the lame, the maimed, the halt, and the blind, and put them on the cars to protect them, and there these old men were kept night and day, in all kinds of weather, traveling up and down, up and down, for weeks and months. And then there was an order issued that every house within five miles of the Orange and Alex— rail road was to be burned, and every body we saw the first thing was you do, or do you, come within that order, and thus we were kept for months on tenter hooks- expecting every day to be burned out. But I suppose our being so many miles within the Federal lines saved us. But the atmosphere for weeks was thick with smoke, and the smell of burning feathers, and all sorts of burning smells. They burned all the mills, and destroyed all the corn, and all kinds of grain wherever they could find it.

A proclamation was issued by the government, and published in all the news papers to all the families, citizens, and non-combatants who had fled before the army, to return to their homes and take possession, all their property should be restored to them and they should be taken care of, and protected both in person and property But the people were too smart for that, they were not to be taken in by such fallacious promises as that. They knew too well how we poor creatures who had been left behind had been maltreated and abused to be caught in any such trap as that

One day in the early spring, when vegetation was somewhat advanced, the birds were singing and flowers and trees begining to bloom. Lizzie and I were up stairs reading or writing, or doing something else, and old mammie was knocking about in the kitchin, getting dinner, such as it was. We could hear her come in, and set the table and bring it in, and then come to the stairs and call us to come down, "dinner was ready." But we knew what dinner was, and were in no hurry for it, Then she came and called again. She called several times before she moved us, then she seemed to get very impatient and called loudly, "You better come along down stairs, and eat dis here little mouf full of vittles before some body come along and eat it all up from you." *Then we flew-* she was standing at the door looking very smiling when we got there, and when we opned the door, there was some thing very out of the common, the [blank] on the table, and when we lifted the cover O joy of joys, it was filled with the most delightful-delicious Asparagus soup.

To my dying day I never can forget the taste of that delightful soup, and it came so unexpectedly too. We did not know there was a stalk on the place, and never thought of it making its appearance as yet. But she had been around and scratched it out of the places where the fences and bridges had been, and possessed herself of a little piece of meat, the dear knows how or where. But she is very much delighted every now and then to give us these little surprises. Some times it is a bowl of hot hominy and cream for supper—fruit or any thing she can lay her hands upon and if she cooks for the soldiers she is certain to scrimp off a little for us, if it is nothing but baked pork and beans.

For several days past we have observed a number of horses at the end of the rifle-pit where there is a picket stationed, the pickets were mounted, it was some thing we had never seen before. Then we heard a rumor *from underground* that on a certain night the Southerners were coming in to capture the horses, But that very evening just before sunset the horses were all taken away. The yanks must have gotten wind of it some how, and of course the rebels did not come. At another time we heard they were coming to take all the horses out of the Burgundy stables. They wanted particularly the carriage horses, but learned the carriage horses were not kept there, and there were now in the stables but very indifferent horses and that night too they failed to come. One evening L- was invited to a neighbours to meet a party of Rangers who came in there every week to get letters papers, packages, or what ever there may be awaiting transportation. They always find a nice elegant supper prepared for them. They sit there for an hour or two enjoying themselve, talking and laughing, and hearing and telling all that is going on, and then late in the night they go as they came, dodging through brier and brake to avoid the pickets, and find their horses tied in the woods away out side. We have to contrive, and make use of strange devices to elude the yankees. I am afraid after this experience we will become as artful and crafty, and as much of Paul Pries as they are- and know all about the *Secret Service* business. But I do hope we may never be tempted into the picketing and stealing business that they have been practicing so extensively in these parts for years past. We have been sending letters in this way, by the Rangers for a long time. But the return letters do not come in the same way, have to go by way of England. and the yankees call it the underground rail road. But Lizzie was disappointed. The Confederate gentleman did not come in that time. The next time it was my turn to go, and I was more fortunate I met and spent the evening with Capt. Kinchelow and five or six of his men. There were several young ladies there and we all spent a very pleasant evening. We laughed and talked like old times although we were very near the road which was thoroughly picketed, and we were directly under the guns of Ft Lyon. And when we parted Capt Kinchelow cut a button off his coat and gave it to me. They were the first Confederate soldiers I had ever seen

One night a party of Moseby's boys came very unexpectedly to "Rose Hill" and took off Col. Dulaney- One of them was his own son, I was very much amused when I heard the story, and the whole scene narrated- This boy's first greeting to his father when he rushed into the room where the father was in bed, In his gruff boyish voice, "How do Pa- I'm very glad to see you," and the father's answer sitting up in bed, with *proper dignity* "Well Sir- I'm d- sorry to see you." But they took him down to Richmond nevertheless- I laughed although I always liked Col- Dulaney.

and think it was well for us to have such a person in the neighbourhood he is kind hearted and inoffensive, and could do, and did do, many things for the people around that they could not have gotten done otherwise. In a day or two after this Burgundy was deserted by its owner- and in a few weeks the Band family came to reside there, and in them we found most charming, good, kind neighbours and friends.- For some time past the negroes have been secreting here two soldiers who have deserted from their regiment. The first thing that aroused our suspitions was when an officer rode up to the door one day they both rushed into the house to hide and Milly shewed them where to hide. We are afraid to let them, or the negroes know we suspect them of desertion. We do not know what to do. If they stay here we run the risk any moment of their discovery, and then of course they will say we were secreting them, so we will be arrested and imprisoned, and our house and home and every thing destroyed. Then if we inform against them, and they find it out, there is no telling the very scare that will be wreaked on us.

We talked it over, and made plans what to do, and how to do all night-long, and came to the conclusion it would be best to tell Mr B. and although he is a stranger perhaps he will be kind enough to get us out of this difficulty- So the next day we went over to Burgundy and while I talked with Mrs B., L. took him aside, and very secretly, and in very low tones told him her troubles and asked his help. He very kindly promised to do any thing for her he could. They planed that we both should go from home the next day, and he would manage it so as not to appear in it himself or that we should either- So we did according to arrangement, and the Provost marshal of Alex- sent out a whole company of cavalry, and the first thing the soldiers and servants knew, the house was surrounded and the men ordered out, and marched off. And when we got back late in the evening two more furiously enraged people than Milly and mammy I never saw- they were so mad they could scarcely tell what had occured. They wondered and wondered who could have told upon them, and how any one knew the men were here, of course we *wondered*, and *marveled* as much as they did. But they never found out, or suspected, we were the guilty party

The day before Christmas we walked over to Burgundy for a short time and when we got back home found Milly gone, mammy was in tears. But we knew they were crocodile tears, she said, "a yankee man who keeps dat counterban hole in town come an took her away, He come in a wagon and took her, and every thing belonging to her," and then another violent *outburst* of *grief* "an now dar is no body here but me." No doubt we shall miss Milly very much, but He who gave her to us knows what is best. She is the last one to leave us of our old Maryland negroes, handed down to us by our forefathers through countless generations.

I heard a tale of horror yesterday that perfectly shocked and unnerved me- I had heard something of it before, but did not believe a word of it until I met with the brother and inquired of him.- There is a family of sisters living in this neighbourhood, and another family of the same sisters with their mother, a very old lady, blind and infirm, living in the vicinity of "Falls Church." When the invasion occured they were so entirely separated by the military that infested the whole country around that they never saw or heard one word of each other for more than two years although they did not live more than four miles apart. In that time one in each household died—a little boy down here whose funeral we attended, the remains were taken to town and intered in one of the Church Cemetarys- But such a time as we had getting there- a short time previously there had been a great scare, of a rebel attack, and all the roads, through the woods and every where were thoroughly barricaded and the military authorities would not allow the obstructions to be removed even for a funeral to pass- The day before some of the neighbours turned out and partially opned a way to pass around, But such a frightful road never did I travel, in some places the hills were so precipitous that the men had to get off their horses, and hold up the horse, and other vehicles to keep them from falling and the horses just slid down on their haunches. And the poor little remains had to find its way through corn fields, cow pens barn yard to its place of rest- The other family near the "Falls Church" were, like ourselves, shut up without a man on the place, and out of the reach of civilization or humanity, surrounded by Blanco's men, the vilest set of savages, jabbering and chattering in some unintelligable jargon. This family suffered every privation, insult, indignity and cruelty that the human mind could think of inventing and inflicting on a house full of suffering unoffending females. One of the ladies was in very delicate health, and under these terrible inflictions she languished, and daily grew worse, and worse until she died- And then, to get a coffin, and get her laid away in the grave- how was that to be done- I could not tell of the difficulties and delays- But at last they accomplished to get her placed in her narrow bed- She was a lovely Christian lady, lovely both in person and mind- She was an occupant of the grave one month when these savages dragged her out of it They placed the coffin on the ground, wrenched off the silver plate with her name on it, and all the silver clasps- They took the body out, stripped of its grave clothes- (I think she was dressed in her wedding dress), and just left it lying on the ground A

Colonel in the Federal army gave me this account who said he had helped to put her back into her coffin and rebury her. But I really did not credit it, that such enormities could be committed by a people calling themselves Christians, until months after I saw her brother and he told me the same story- He said they would not let him go to the grave yard for a long time, indeed would not allow him to go outside the house, not even to the barn without a guard walking on each side of him, but when he did get to the grave he found remnants of her clothes, and coffin lying about, and tresses of her long black hair hanging in the bushes and briars. The hair could not be mistaken, it was the longest, most beautiful, glossy, raven black hair I ever saw- Dear Julianna- she was one of my earliest best loved friends!- Why these people should thus disturb the dead I can not imagine. This was the forth body, they have dragged out of the grave, belonging to that one family

One of the deserters who we had arrested, was a Dutchman who had once been a guard here and was a very good, inoffensive kind of creature, and we would not have gotten him in trouble for the world if we could have helped it. But we felt bound to take care of ourselves as well as we could. One day a note came to Lizzie, the most curious looking, and in hieroglyphics almost undecipherable, and after spelling and guessing it out found it was from Isler telling her how uncomfortable, and miserable he was, shut up in Mr Greens old furniture factory, and begging her for the love of heaven and pity sake to send him some pipes and tobacco- Soon after he came back to us as a guard

Old mammie was always very much scandalized that Lizzie should teach the children of the neighbourhood, Seems to think it entirely beneath her dignity What would old *Mars* say to see her a settin up all day, and havin dese here little poor white children, an she a larnin dem, an havin dem here runnin ove his flowers Ah! I tell you what Miss Lizzie he'd never stand dat- L- went into the kitchen one day and found the stove covered with pots and pans, and skillets, she lifted a cover and found the vesel filled with water onely, and the next, and the next, every thing filled with water and nothing else! She said "Mammy what in the world are you going to do with so much hot water-" She sat for a long time looking very grim, but never answering a word, and after several repetitions of the question, she said in the madest gruffest tones "Den dar children kees a runnin in here, and you think I'm guine to let em think I got no dinner cokin, an nothin to eat, and den run home an tell it, No I aint aguine to do no such a thing-" and up she got and out of the door she went, no doubt to hide a flood of tears- She feels all this a great degradation, and thinks it is her province to keep up the honour and dignity of the family- She has a vast deal of family pride

One night in the cold winter weather, there came an unusually bitter bitter sharp cold wind that seemed to penetrate to the very bone, and in the middle of the night, after we had been for hours snugly ensconced in bed, there came a violent startling rap at the front door. We both started up and ran to the door, could see men indistinctly through the glass, we had no light and they could not see us. We asked who was there and the answer came, they were a party of Moseby's men who were out skouting, as soon as I heard the nasal sound, and *shout* I knew who they were and as Lizzie was the spokesman, I whispered, "yankees Lizzie yankees." I was so afraid she would commit herself, but she recognized them as soon as I did. They wanted to come in and warm themselves, and get something to eat, "had *nothing* to eat all day- Gen. Lee had broken out of Richmond and was at Fairfax Courthouse and would be down here in a day or two" Then they went on to ask a number of

questions the names of the people living around and their politics,how many pickets on the road the number of men at the forts etc etc. She told them, she never went to the forts and had no means of knowing the number of men there, They had come through the picket lines and must know more about them than she did, and as to letting them in the house, that we were only two ladies

Fairfax Courthouse—sketch taken from a war time photograph
Courtesy of Castle Books, A Division of Book Sales, Inc.

here, and would not let in friend or foe at that time of night, the fires had all gone down, she had nothing for herself to eat, the yankees had taken every thing she had away from her. One of them seemed to forget himself and snarled out "yankee." Then recovering his wits, he said in a more subdued tone, "Wal never mind we'll pay the yankees up in a few days" But they still persisted in coming in, and stood there parleying until we were almost frozen They held a whispered conference among themselves, then said they would go out to the road and talk to the Captain, and whatever he said, whether to force their way in or not they would abide by. They went off and we went back shivering to bed thinking confidently we had gotten rid of them- When at least a half hour after there came another thundering knock at the door- O mercy! I thought I should die- "The Captain said they must and should have what they wanted, and if we did not open the door they would break it down." They cursed, and swore, and raved, and stormed stamping their feet on the porch floor, and ordered the door to be opned that moment or they would beat it down. L. told them they could do it if they chose, it was not very strong but they would do it at their peril She had Gen. Wadsworth's *Safe Guard* and to violate that was death, she would certainly go, or send to W*a* and have them punished as they deserved- She did not know the penalty, but thought that in such straits she might venture on the death sentence. She was so resolute, they found she knew who they were and after another whispering among themselves they marched off. It was almost day light when they went away. There was no more sleep for us, we were almost frozen.

The next morning we learned it was a party of men that had stolen out of a camp near Ft Lyon and spent the whole night searching and plundering peoples houses. The men all went to the camp and complained. The Col sent a squad of men over to inquire into it and if they had been here and what mischief they had done. They told us the Col. was as mad as he could be, said he would find them all out and make them pay well for all they had taken, and he would punish them to the very extent of his authority.

I am so nervous, and ever on the alert, not knowing night, or day, what moment an attack may come, that the slightest unusual noise awakens me directly, and one night when Isler was away, I was aroused by a slight sound at the well like drawing water in the most careful quiet manner possible, I bounded up and flew to the window—and there— the whole yard and garden was bristling with bayonets, all glistening in the moon light- I crept back to the bed and whispered in Lizzie's ear, "The whole place is filled with soldiers." We both went back noiselessly and watched expecting every moment a furious onslaught, we could not imagine what had brought them out in such force- it could not be to capture or arrest us, for one or two would be all sufficient to do that. But they never made the slightest sound excepting the little creaking of the bucket in drawing the water which was unavoidable- they never even spoke a word to each other, and after refreshing themselves for a few minutes with copious drafts of cool water, all withdrew as noiselessly as they came- These were Col Shirmer's men from Ft Lyon, They have always been as respectful and considerate of us as possible, always ready to help us when an opportunity occured. Not one of them ever molested- or took any thing from us while they remained in this vicinity and we will always cherish a kindly remembrance of them. They had been out scouting and only stopped here for a drink of water. The water here has a wide spread reputation among the soldiers as being the coolest most delightful they ever drank and they avail themselves of every opportunity of refreshing themselves with it.

The winter of 64-65. This has been another miserable, wretched winter to us, of want and privation, we cannot help feeling too from all we know, and all the terrible accounts that come to us, through the news papers, and other sources that our cause is loosing ground. O wretched, wretched, people that we are- If we have always these low inhuman, selfish, tyrants to rule over us- and to think of that horrid Sherman with his thousands and millions of savages carrying devastation blood, and misery as he goes tramping tramping from end to end of our beautiful, flourishing Southern country. O how can we ever bear these horrible northern people in our sight again One of their own officers said to me, "he should indeed feel sorry to know they had succeeded in subduing the South, for he knew their domineering malevolent burning hatred of the South, and how they would glory in walking over them should they get them in their power." At one time we had Kilpatric and his hords of raiders just from about Richmond where they had committed all manner of brutal atrocities Dalgreen was killed and they were driven off with their pockets filled, with silver spoons knives, forks, juelry, pictures, every sort of beautiful, elegant thing they had stolen from the citizens, and had hawking about here for sale, and a more savage insulting swaggering set of wretches I never saw- and now we see from time to time little squads of confederate deserters coming in escorted by yankee pickets. One day I saw a party coming in, and ran down to the road and got very near them without being seen, a little piece of old scorched seder hedge screened me from their sight- They came on talking, and telling the yankees every thing they knew and perhaps more. O I felt it then in my heart's core what was coming, and threw myself on the ground, and cried, "Father have mercy—have mercy—deliver from the hands of these wicked horrid people. -And then the news that Gen. Lee had surrendered But we did not take any notice, did not put the slightest faith in the report, had learned of it so often in the past two or three years, until the morning of the 4 or 5th of April, when there was a simultaneous burst of cannon from all the forts around and in Wa, and every where, and they bellowed, and roared, roared all day long as if a battle was in progress, and the whole face of the earth was enveloped in a dense fog of smoke- O mercy! That was another day not to be forgotten, I neither ate nor drank, I threw myself down on my face and,- cried- O it was an exceeding bitter cry- But it is useless- I cannot depict the agony of that day- The next day soldiers were sent round to every house in the towns, and all about the towns, and ordered the people to throw open their houses at night and illuminate, on penalty if they failed to do it of being arrested- Many did it through fear, not by any means as a token of rejoicing, others refused, and their houses were stoned, and their windows broken by the soldiery, after that day after day reports would come in of first this army and that surrendering- until I thought my heart would brake- The Texian soldiers swore they would never surrender- and they just picked up each man his belongings and scattered to their homes, and they never did surrender. Huzza for the "Lone Star"! Every thing is as quiet as possible, as far as we are concerned, all the pickets have been withdrawn from the roads. But Isler, our guard still remains with us- On Saturday the 15th day of April, early in the morning some of L.'s little boys came in and said some thing was the matter, something had gone wrong, for there was such a noise, and confusion. So many soldiers and people in the road, and so many pickets, but said they could not learn or understand what it all ment. They would not let a thing pass "Cameron-run" and for about a mile this way the road was filled with wagons, carts and vehicles of all sorts- Isler said as soon as he got his breakfast he would go and find out what was the matter, and in about an hour he returned with the startling and incredible information that last night the President and all his cabinet was murdered, and I cannot tell how many others. But he could not learn how or by whom. Very little information could be obtained the wildest commotion reigned every where. Every avenue to the city was barred not a living thing was allowed to pass in or out, of either of the three places Washington, George town, or Alex- The military was out in force, and every thing is turned upside down to capture the murders. In a little while we saw squads of officers and soldiers, scouring the roads fields and woods, scattered all over the latest news, and what one party tells the next will contradict. But after a day or two we learned the name of the murderer was Boothe, John Wilks Boothe. I think with horror of his sufferings- traveling, and hiding about for days and days with a broken leg- Poor-poor creature- none but a mad man would ever would have dreamed of committing such an act. There was such an immense reward offered for killing, or capturning him that the yankees were as insane about it as he was about committing the deed. L. and myself remained in doors all the time afraid to shew ourselves outside for fear of encountering the horrid soldiers. Several days after a gentleman, a neighbour, called to see us, he was dressed in a full suit of gray clothes, and after sitting here about an hour he invited us to walk over to Burgundy with him, when there persuaded us to remain for supper, and we got back home about 9 oclock Mr F. came back with us. We had been seated in the dining room only a few minutes when there was the greatest noise of tramping feet, and the clatter of swords dragged down the gravel walk, then the stamping of heavy boots on the porch, and a thundering furious banging on the door as if with the loaded end of a heavy horse-whip. I never heard such a clanging I said well, what in the world does all this mean, and got up and opned the door.

There stood quite an array of officers all dragging their broadswords, I said good evening won't you walk in. They made some mumbling demur and then one asked for the man of the house, I said there was no man here- "O yes," another replied "a man dressed in gray was seen to come in here." O I said, I did not know you wanted to see Mr. F. he is here, walk in and see him. But they seemed very reluctant to accepting my invitation, they ought to have felt highly honoured, for they were the first of the yankee nation I ever asked into the house/ Mr F. hearing his name spoken came forward and was very urgent for them to come in, and after much hesitancy they slipped in five or six, one after the other with their backs to the wall, and so they sled along to the dining room door where there was a light and one of them recognized Mr. F- having been camped on his place some time before and there was quite a cordial greeting between them. They explained their business, the search for Boothe, and then went off- and after laughing and talking it all over for a few minutes Mr F. also took his leave- after a few days we met Mr F- again and he said you have no idea what a number of "*them devilish yankees,*" surrounded your house that night there were hundreds and hundreds of them, and they were very near taking him again for Boothe, and all this mischief was caused by a vile negro boy we had hired to cut up some wood. He saw the gentleman in gray clothes come into the house he dropped his axe and slipped over to Ft Lyon and reported it, and he and they were watching this house all the evening until away into the night, and if Mr F- had not happened to be here what would have become of us

Friday 28th April 1865 Every day we hear of fresh atrocities committed by the searchers after Boothe- An old woman was here to-day from the neighbourhood of "Pohick" who says the same party that were here on Saturday night, came to her house about one oclock that same night and roused up the whole family. They treated her most shamefully, cursed and abused her and threatened to shoot her for (as they avered) taking Boothe outside the lines, She said she *had* picked up an old man, on the way from market and helped him along by taking him in her wagon a few miles, but how they found it out she could not imagine. Then they took the little boy who drove her wagon, and knocked and cuffed him about greatly, and threatened him with torture and death if he did not say that was Boothe they had in the wagon on Saturday. But the little fellow, she said stood up to them like a man and said, they might kill him but he would not tell a lie for them And after hanging about for an hour or two and behaving as shamefully as they could while she prepared something for them to eat, they consented not to take her off that night, but enjoined her to keep herself in readiness to appear at the Provost's office whenever they thought proper to sumon her- Cousin M- and Miss M. J. came to see us this evening. They tell us a number of old friends and acquaintances have returned from Richmond- But they bring no tidings of our own poor boys. I am weary of asking myself—where, O where are they. The ladies gave us some fearful accounts of the scenes incident to the death of Lyncoln. Ladies, for days did not dare to appear in the streets, bands of soldiers, and negroes, lead by officers, went from house to house and ordered every one to drape their houses in mourning for the President and where any demur or objection was made, (which was pretty generally the case where the persons did not know what the consequences would be) they were assaulted and beaten, and all manner of violence was the immediate result- Brick-bats and stones were the order of the day and now every old negro hut in the town is hung in mourning at the expense of government Since Hancock's proclamation to the negroe's to be ever on the alert night and day, to watch, and listen, to search and spy out, and never to slacken in their vigilance to find out what the white people do and say, and all their movements and report it all to the nearest commanding officer. And they have been most obedient to the order, their espionage is untiring. They not only want to know all you do and say, but even try to dive into your very thoughts

Saturday 29 The whole country around seems filling up with soldiers again, their tents whiten the fields and hills and valleys everywhere- after breakfast two officers rode up and ordered a room for Col. Gregg of the 179 N Y regiment. But as we had no servant to prepare it for him, they soon found two soldiers who fixed up every thing to their satisfaction, One of the officers Maj Tyrell was here in 62 with Col- Ward's regiment, he claimed us as old acquaintances But I am sure I never saw him before, nevertheless I found his name on one of the old playbills of the Sedgwick theater He says his Col. met with an accident yesterday, in attempting to jump from the steam boat to the wharf he fell into the river and was considerably hurt. I know I smiled when I heard him tell it, for I felt sure his heart was made glad and his heels light, by *something*. However I wish he had prefered the kingdom of Neptune to the *Glorious* Old Republic, and concluded to remain there. But a very heavy thunderstorm came up after dinner and we did not have the pleasure of the Col's company at tea, as expected. We had yesterday's paper containing the account of the killing of poor miserable Boothe in a barn near Port-Royal V*a* and the capture of his accomplice (Harrold), and although the barn was fired and surrounded by thirty soldiers he could not be taken alive, they were obliged to kill him. I heard it predicted long before he was taken that he never would be brought to W*a* alive- Whenever the yankees feel like committing any violence or wrong on the people of Alex or vicinity they, send the soldiers round to inquire what is thought of old Lyncoln's assassination, and if (as is almost invariably the case) any pleasure is expressed, that is used as an excuse for all manner of robbery and abuse. One was here a day or two ago making that very inquiry, but having heard of the move we were ready with an answer

Sunday 30th Although the whole face of the earth is again filled with soldiers, we remained unmolested by them. Looking out of the window in the evening I saw an old white headed man with his *Spread eagles* on, and an old slouched hat, turned up behind, one shoe and one boot, hobbling up the avenue, leaning on the arm of another officer, a negro man walking after them with the other boot and slipper in his hand. They proved to be Col. Gregg and party of 179th N. Y. regiment. They came in and took possession we were introduced to a number of them. But we had very little to say to them, their manner was altogather too patronizing, and their conversation about their success so exultant, that I would like to have- but I will not say what I would like to have done with them.

The Rev. Mr Taft is a clergyman of the Baptist persuasion. He sat up and talked with the most unblushing face of his negro schoolmates in *Bosting*, many of them he said were much smarter than himself- But it really does seem strange how they keep them so humble and subservient to them when they require so much more of them than we ever did. The boy with the boot and slipper stood here behind Col. Greggs chair until it made me feel faint to look at him. I think he must have stood there two hours without speaking or moving, until the Col- thought proper to dismiss him I thought how much better disciplinarians the yankees are than we- and what splendid overseers they must make. I thought if those boots, and shoes, and that servant was mine, they would all have been thrown down at the door, and the boy not to be found.

Monday May 1st 1865 Col. Gregg's visitors are coming and going all day long, most of them to inquire after his health and we have to listen to the reports of first one army and then another surrendering. I try to school myself to it, and to appear as if I did not hear a word. One comes in and slaps a news paper down on the table I know very well it is for our benefit, but I take no notice, then another stalks in with *"Wal* Johnson has surrendered, but Gen. Grant was not satisfied with the terms made by Sherman and went down himself and has just returned with fresh *Laurels*, having received the surrender himself, the terms the same as made with Gen. Lee." and this is the way they go on from one days end to another until I think my heart will brake, or my sences will surrender- at dinner Col- G- asked me if I did not think his regiment ought to be a very superior one as he had a number of clergymen in it. I told him, yes it ought to be, but I had my doubts about the goodness of any of them. I knew them all too well, and their clergymen were not a bit better than any of the rest- after tea the door opned and Chap- Taft and Lt Marshall were announced and here they sat and sat and talked much in the same strain we had listened to all day The Col- took occasion during the evening to tell that the Lt. was a Reverend, gentleman a learned man, fine preacher, had an elegant church, and wealthy congregation, devoted to him, "But had left all to attend to his country's call." Lizzie says after she heard he was a preacher, she was meditating how she could give him a shot, but as it grew late she feared she was going to loose the chance. But when they arose to say, "goodnight," the Lieutenant lifted his tall commanding figure up to its full hight and turning to his Col said, with the most military and self important air said, "Col- I have now fulfilled my duty to my country- and- I- must- go home. My people are calling loudly for me, and their call I *must* attend to, and if you do not get me, (some thing I do not know what, perhaps) leave of absence I will have to resign my commission, for I must go back to my charge." The old Col looked at him with such an approving smile and said, "Yes, now your country no longer needs your valuable services, you are anxious to get back to preaching again, and Lizzie looking up at him, said in the most quiet manner possible, "You seem indeed, in a hurry to get on your *sheep's Cloathing* again" The poor Lieutenant! he opned his mouth and looked agast, but never a word spake he. The Chap looked as if about to faint. The Col was not well enough versed in Biblical lore to clearly appreciate or understand- and I—O whither shall I fly! my brain reeled, I expected to see her head dissevered from her body But she sat and looked as cool, and collected, and smiling as if she had said something she approved of very much herself. There was a dead silence for a few seconds and then the most prolonged shout of forced merriment, in which the poor Lieutenant took the lead Poor fellow! it was all he could do. He never spoke another word but both bowed themselves out, and that was the first and last we ever saw of Lt Marshall

Tuesday 2nd Col Greggs visitors to day were many, and their conversation took in various themes, and they boasted much of how cordially the Confederate officers and Soldiers shook hands with them after the surrender, and how delighted they all expressed themselves at being back again in the Union. And when they entered Richmond the windows were all thrown open and thronged with ladies all smiles and waving of handkerchiefs and on all sides there was every demonstration of pleasure and satisfaction. One of the officers sitting here said he was determined to have a Southern lady for a wife, and another, and then another were of the same mind. Then Col- Gregg was so good as to inform us he is a widower, and then said none but a Southern lady should ever preside over his house-hold. Lizzie said, "You gentlemen must remember it takes two to make a bargain. Then the conversation turned on prison life. The surgeon said he had been a prisoner in the "Libby," and of all the suffering from starvation, and cruel treatment that I ever did hear of he had the longest catalogue to unrol, not one word of which did I believe. But he said the treatment in the Libby was delightful to what was given to prisoners in "Castle Thunder," that took the lead in barbarity. The men were all kept in dungeons, and food given to them only once a week, and then thrown into them as if they were wild beasts. I just looked at the man in perfect amazement, how he could have the impudence to sit there and talk to us in that manner and imagine that we believed it. (I afterwards learned the prison the Confederates' called Castle Thunder the yankees never saw the inside of, it was only used for their own men who had misbehaved) But I did feel like executing vengeance on that man for his false tongue- Then they told of some of their own barbaritys, and the dreadful *raids* they had been on, and laughed and talked of it as something very war-like and brave, how they had burned and destroyed, and how they had turned out poor females and little children without food or shelter, They talked of the Weldon raid and its horrors, I had heard Col. Gregg speak of it before, and of its unheard of horrors, and always with a shudder, but he would not tell of how it was, and then they talked of the battles they had been in and of the terrible battlefields and how they had seen the dead rebels in piles on the hill sides with the blood streaming from them until all the little rivulets were swollen, and died red with their blood- Poor Lizzie! her feelings were so wrought upon that she burst into tears, and got up and left the room. I was very sorry she gave way so, I knew it would be a subject of exultation with them, and an incentive to them to harrow up our feelings in that way on all occasions- Indeed I sometimes wonder how we have retained our senses through all we have gone through- after tea another party came to make a visit, and their heads seemed filled with the ladies of *old Virginny*, a thousand questions were asked and always how many acres they possessed, a rich widow was mentioned, and a daughter of about seventeen, and a little insignificant youngster who was introduced as Ensign Wood actually started off his chair and said, "Well, this is the first time I have heard of a daughter. I shall certainly make my way over to that place. He seemed so excited, and in such raptures I expected he would fly off at once. I could but sit and listen to the impudence and presumption of the miserably low wretches- I understand Lt Marshall is terribly disconcerted, and says he will never put his foot in this house again, *at that, we were greatly distressed* and *mortified*.

Wednesday 3. Two of the officers came hurriedly in directly after breakfast, before the table had been cleared off. We knew at once their errand was to tell something they thought would be disagreeable and painful to us to hear. Col- G asked the news this morning, and in a careless way one of them said, "O nothing," and then catching his breath as if it was so unimportant he had forgotten it, "O yes," he said, "Curly Smith had offered to surrender, and a band of Gurillas had been captured," and this one, and the other had been captured or surrendered until he made out quite a long list- Col G- said, "Yes, the rebellion is now entirely crushed out, and before six months have rolled over, those rebels will be sending to us at the north for armed negroes to protect them from the Gurillas." I knew this grand speach was made to provoke a retort, but continued what I was engaged in as if I did not hear it- Some time after Lizzie and I were in the garden planting some flowers, when the surgeon of the regiment walked in and seated himself on the porch, and then a number of officers came, some seated themselves with the surgeon, while others sauntered about the garden, none of them said a word, but seemed to be observing us very closely- Then two soldiers came in, and asked if either of us was Miss Lizzie Frobel she said yes, then they said they had arrived from Richmond on Saturday night last, and had been making inquiries for us ever since, as they were about to leave there and trudging along the street to take passage for Alex- two Rebel officers on the opposite called out, "Halloo boys where are you bound." and when they found Alex- was the place of destination re-quested them as a great favour to find us out, and let us know they were both well had been paroled with Lee's army, and were on their way home. I asked them all the questions I could think of, how the boys looked, and if they were ragged, and if they looked starved etc etc- They replied, "No they look foine" I knew from the first there was not a word of truth in any thing they said, But was obliged to pretend to be very much indebted to them for the trouble they had taken in searching us up. In the first place I knew Bushrod was in Georgia, and had not been with Gen Lee's army for more than a year, then if the boys were on their way home why had they not arrived. I felt perfectly sure the whole story was made up by the officers, and they were sitting by listening to see what effect it would produce- They had talked in the same boastful way of the flattering reception they had received on entering Richmond as the officers had done, the bows and smiles and waving of handkerchiefs from the ladies, and the shaking of hands with all the men kind. But one of the men talked, and after a while when he thought we could not hear him, he gave the other one a push with his elbow, and said in a low tone, "You are making great head way, why don't you talk and tell some." If I had believed them at first this would have settled the matter. They followed us about and talked, and talked the same thing over and over until I was perfectly worn out and glad to get rid of them, and to my utter amazement, after they were gone I found Lizzie believed what they had told, and to comfort her we both went into the kitchen and told old mammy what we had heard. She was stooping down blowing the fire, and I said mammy Miss Lizzie believes that story- She turned her head to one side and looked up at her and said, "tell laws! Miss Lizzie you don't believe any sich a tale as dat, Now Mars David mout'er holloed after dem and sent you a message, Mars David he don't know But is to Mars Bushard he nuver had no use for poor-white people no how, and nuver put his self down to talk to none of dem, an is to his calling after dese here low-life yankee soldiers an er callin dem boys- Shaw! you mouter knowed dat wuz a lie!" This argument seemed to comfort Lizzie, and to convince her that mammie knowed all about it, at dinner Col-Gregg told us that a guerilla was taken this morning near Occoquan and brought in his wife crying and following after him. I wish they had brought him this way I would like to be introduced to one, and to know what sort of a thing he is

Thursday 4 Minute guns have been fired all day at Wa for Lincoln's interment and at sun set there was a tremendous burst about a hundred fired off at once, I do hope it is the last we are to hear of President Lincoln, The yanks have been dragging him about for exhibition for the last three or four week, in every state, town and village east, north and west. They did not take him South I suppose they feared the people would welcome him too heartily. They seem to know no bounds in the lavish expenditures of public money on that miserable old carcass thousands upon thousands have been spent on catifalque and in shewing him up in every way to the gaze of the adoring multitudes- I wonder if poor old Lincoln while splitting rails in the western wilds ever in his highest flights of ambitious fancy ever dreamed of a Catafalque to drag him to his grave in- I wonder if he ever heard of a catafalque- *I never* did before- But I really am glad he has reached Springfield at last and hope I shall never hear of him again- Chap Taft came in with the paper for Col- G- who seemed deeply absorbed in it for a time and then read aloud for our benefit Pres- Johnson's proclamation in which he accuses Jefferson Davis and five others of complicity in Lincolns assasination, a reward of one hundred thousand dollars is offered for the capture of Mr. Davis- Twenty five thousand for that of Clement Clay. The same for Jacob Thompson, Geo- M- Saunders and Beverly Tucker. Ten thousand for Wm. C. Clary I am afraid if they all are caught it will exhaust the United States Treasury

Saturday 6 We heard to day that we are again to be over-run with the army, and Col Gregg verifies the information, and said if we had no objection he would bring his regiment here before Sherman's came, and place them so as to protect us in some measure which of course we very readily assented to. There was a general review of troops to-day. They tell us that Sherman, Sheriden, and the army of the Potomac, are to lie around Wa from now until August before they can possibly be mustered out, and we are to have them all on us again, O mercy, mercy! I think of it with feelings of intense horror- We walked over to Burgundy after tea expecting to meet Mr R. H. Carter. But were disappointed We

learned from Mr B- that Winship would not allow him to come. Mr C-
was paroled with Gen. Lee, and obtained a permit to remain in Alex- ten
days. after staying there a day or so went to the Provost Marshal's office
for a pass to go to W*a* which so enraged Mr Winship that he ordered
him out of the office, and peremptorily to leave town tomorrow for his
own home I do not know what Mr Winship's authority is, but he seems
to be lording it over the people with a high hand. I do not know how
our gentlemen do to stand the insulting impudence of that man

Monday 8 Three regiments fixed their camps on our fields to-day.
We had one nice little field of grass which grew up early in the spring
while the army was away, and have been most anxious to save it for the
use of our cows next winter. But every night now the soldiers turn about
twenty horses in on it, and turn them off again early in the morning Col-
Gregg has tried his best to protect it for us, but in spite of him every
night it is the same thing, and every morning bright and early, we hear
mammie banging at Col- Gregg's door and calling to know- Can't you
come out here an stop dese here men furn turnin dem hoses on dis here
Timty lot, da dun cut up mos every mouf-full of it now, and whats our
cows a guine to do fur some thing to eat nex winter- Poor Col. Gregg!
he laughed at it at first but is begining to tire of being aroused up so
early every morning and advised us to go over Burgundy and see Gen-
Griffin, and ask him to protect both grass field, and garden. So accordingly
we went. The Gen- was very polite, and promised every thing, but all the
same, I know the horses will eat up every thing we have.

Wednesday 10 We have had many applications to take yankee
women again into our house But we do not want them, and the only
means we have of keeping them out is to ask them a big price for board-
At Burgundy they have Gen Griffin and staff, besides ten or twelve other
officers. and several women. I was over there this morning, and found
poor Mrs B- in the greatest state of excitement and perturbation at the
talk she had been forced to hear at the table. They said Gen Lee was the
meanest, vilest wretch that lived, and a great deal more in the same
strain, and then a Maj Smith related his experience in the way of cruelties
and barbaraties practiced on the people of Richmond, particularly on
the men who they said had kept the prisons. The women would laugh
and exult and show great pleasure at these accounts of the enormities,
and one a Mrs Snow was very boisterous in her mirth, she would throw
herself back in her chair and clap her hands exclaiming, "good-good-I
wish I had been there to see it-" I do think it was the most indecent
insulting conduct I ever heard of- But our boarder Gen- Gregg has been

as kind, and considerate of us as he possibly could be. To day he had the garden gate mended up by one of the soldiers and places a guard on each side of the garden to keep the men from going through the hedge. The camps are filled with impudent worthless negroes, and so is our kitchen. They all flock there to be fed and of course mammy will give them some thing to eat if she has it. The yankees tell us it will not be long before we have negro representatives in Congress and in a few years we will have a negro President. Col- Gregg says negroes have been already allowed to vote at the north, and Fred Douglass has been a candidate for the Presidency. I listen to their vile talk until I get so exasperated, I feel as if I would like to see the whole yankee nation annihilated. They make one as wicked as themselves

Friday 12 There are soldiers, soldiers every where Cameron valley is filled with tents and more coming. I had a letter from C. W. she says Phil- has returned and she hopes B and D- have. She says Phil- has had a trying time since he got back, but she seems afraid to tell me any thing by letter, only wishes we could meet that we could talk over our troubles- These are troublous times, she thinks, and O it does seem we are doubly tried. Miss M. I- sent her little nephew this morning with a letter written by Lt Beaumont to his wife, which she received on Saturday last, and sent to Alex- to be sent to us. Lt. B says that on 22nd April when near Macon Ga the 2nd regiment of Wilson's cavalry stumbled on a party of Confederates and captured them, and he never was more surprised and delighted than he was to find among them Lt Col. B. W. Frobel- He had a long talk with him, and told him all about the first winter of the war, and his sojourn at Wilton, and how fond himself and wife became of his sisters, and how kindly they had been treated by them, and that he intended making the Col's captivity as pleasant and comfortable to him as possible. O the idea of Bushrod being a captive makes my very heart sick, although I knew it must come sooner or later, and I feel thankful he met with Lt Beaumont, for I am sure he is a good friend of ours- One of the regiments was mustered out to-day, and at night a grand torch light procession, and any amount of yelling. We had not seen it but the Chaplain came in to call our attention to it, he did not know what it was, and neither did we, never having seen any thing of the kind before. It looked like an immense serpent of fire twisting and squirming about on the opposite hills. They all thought it very, but I was most delighted at the thought of saying farewell

Saturday 13 This morning two of Col. Gregg's officers Compton and Carpenter, called to engage board for their wives, and a more common looking, yankee set I never saw before, and Col Titus' regiment, and head quarters was removed from Burgundy and places in our field. The head quarters just at the garden gate- A number of men came with them they called Pioneers- and a viler looking set of wretches, or a more ill behaved I never did see. They ran all over the yard and garden, into the barn and every place and helped themselves to whatever they could find, it was some time before they could be stopped, but all they carried off was gone forever.

Sunday 14 This morning soon after Col. Gregg had gone out to the camp, a soldier came with the paper for him, he turned the great black letters up and placed it on the table, after he went out I glanced at the paper and found the conspicious letters were to announce the *great news*, "that Jeff- Davis was at last captured," on the 10th April, some where in Georgia Presently the Col- came hurrying in, and first thing asked for the paper, and then tried to read it first to Lizzie and then to me, but we would not listen to it- But ran off into the garden to comfort ourselves working among the flowers, after a while he came out there, L- had been crying- he laughted at and ridiculed her, and then another soldier stepped up and handed him another paper, and I said you all seem most anxious to desseminate your news- "O yes," he replied, "we are going to hang him, Jeff- has got to be hung." L- turned so quick upon him and said, in the most defient manner, "don't you dare to do it, if you dare to tutch one hair of his head, we will never forgive you, as long as we live." He seemed utterly astonished, but never said another word

Tuesday 16 Some one passing through Danville recently sent us word David was there- Poor boys! I know this surrender, and downfall has gone to the quick, and no doubt the reason they do not come home is they do not wish to encounter all the hords of yankees that are packed in and about Wa, particularly Bushrod "Poor Mars Dave, he don't keer so much."

We find Col- Titus and his head-quarters very unpleasant neighbours. They seem very much at home, have gone regularly to house keeping- have a cow haltered in the stable, and pastured about on the best spots of grass in the fields, have torn down all the racks and petitions left in the barn, to make fires of, and the yard, barn and every place is filled with their horses.

Thursday 18—Col- Gregg went with his regiment to Mt. Vernon this morning on a pleasure excursion. The ladies expected to go, but were disappointed in getting an army ambulance. They sent to town, to a livery stable for a carriage, but when they found they would have fifteen dollars to pay for it, they declined the trip and sent the carriage back to town. They were very urgent for us to be of the party, the Col- and all, but we found many excuses, nothing on earth would have induced either of us to have been seen with such a crowd as that. Col- Gregg who is always a kind and polite to us, offered us the use of his horses whenever we choose to call for them. He has a pair of elegant horses, which he had the hardi-hood to tell were captured from the rebels- stolen I said, I suppose, "Well," he said laughing, "if they were stolen I did not steal them." He also has a negro boy to wait on him, he confessed to have stolen him two years ago at Fredericksburg, him also we have the use of, every morning he is sent up and ordered to report himself to Miss Lizzie. The Col- returned from Mt Vernon highly pleased with the trip- of course decay, and dilapidation was discussed, and the comparison drawn between north and south particularly in old Virginia. They thought the burning and destruction that has been carried on for the past four years would-will be such an advantage to the state they all hated old houses so. But still the old man has his head filled with a second marriage, and insists that none but a Southern lady would suit him

Friday 19 Our barn, barn yard, and every place is filled with the most beautiful, elegant horses, and although I am a great admirer of fine horses I can not bear to look at them, I know they are all stolen from Southern people who are now suffering for the use of them. Some times when I see a very beautiful one as sleek and glossy as satin I can not help going up to him and patting and petting him, and saying to him beautiful creature where is your poor master, and I think he looks sad at the inquiry, and I know I feel so- To day we see tents and camps springing up in every quarter Sherman's army coming in. The roads filled with soldiers as far back as we can see through the woods, coming-coming, coming- thousands and tens of thousands I hardly thought the world contained so many men, and the wagons, O the wagons, long lines of white wagons coming by roads and cross roads- such a horrible sight. Col Gregg went over to "Clouds Mill" to meet some regiments that were coming that way and brought back with him Col- Crain and Lt Colonel some body else to take tea with him here. They had just arrived from a march through North and South Carolina and Virginia. They were all so filled with themselves and their recent, exploits, and what they had seen and done as they passed along, how much property they had destroyed, and how many families they had reduced to starvation- But the plantations- O the beautiful elegant plantations and the rich country they had passed through- one said he would like to have this place, and another he was determined to have such another place- and another said such a place particularly struck his fancy, but he did not want to own it, unless he owned the negroes too. We sat up and never said a word, only sat and listened until I thought my sences would leave me I hoped and almost believed I was in a terrible dream, there was no reality in it all.

After these *gentlemen* had left Col- Gregg called one into the dining room to see a splended, first rate likeness of Jefferson Davis- I was sure it was some thing the Shermanites had stolen from the South- But it proved to be a horrible caricature, a man dressed in woman's clothes. I did not understand it at first, but when I did, I made no remark whatever, just said Shaw! and threw it from me, and walked out of the room He said to L- he had no idea I had so much temper. The next time we met, he remarked to me, "I had no idea you would have exhibited so much temper at that little joke of mine and I replied I had no idea a man of sense like Col- Gregg would have exhibited such a thing as that to *me*. I never heard another word of Jeff- Davis in that garb.

Saturday 20 Immense throngs of negroes are pouring in to day, all packed and loaded with plunder piled upon their backs. They alternate, for perhaps an hour a stream of negroes will be passing, and then a stream of wagons, all covered with white canvas then of soldiers, and to day we see fixed up on the hill in front of us the bigest U.S flag I ever beheld, waving, and flapping, and dragging on the ground. To day Col. Titus introduced his sister Mrs Marble, to stay as he put it, "for an indefinate period." She looks like a person in feeble health, and of *feeble mind* likewise. Sergeant Sampson called to see his brother's wife who is boarding here, and here he sat and had the barefaced assurance to boast of the plunder they had all collected, on their way back after the surrender, said for one thing he had a silver ladle, he had gotten from Petersburg

Sunday 21 The army still continues to pour in, and every wagon is filled with plunder of all kinds, and every one has a horse or cow, carriages buggys, farm wagons, carts- every one some kind of stolen goods tied on behind. Col. Gregg went as far as Baileys x roads yesterday and then to Wa, and returned this evening very much *overcome* with the ride or some thing else much to the amusement of the other officers- He says the whole country as far as he went and as far around as he could see in every direction is one vast encampment.

Monday 22 Tomorrow there is to be a *grand review* of the *grand U. S* army at Washington and great has been the stir of preparation. Of course, there was no doubt we would go to witness such a magnificent sight, But when they found that was not our intention, they urged and insisted, and offered every inducement for us to go Such a grand military display was never seen or known in this country, or any other, since the world was made, and never would be seen again. They would send and get a carriage for us, the nicest that could be hired and they would ride on each side as a body guard, and Col- Gregg said he would buy one if we would promise to ride in it. But, no, our determination was fixed.

Mr F- called in the evening- He says "Rose Hill is literally covered with Sherman's army and such an immense, immense, number of splendid horses and mules he never saw, and such herds of beautiful little ponies as they have stolen from Georgia, North, and South Carolina, there can hardly be horse or mule left in any of the states they passed through A negro boy sold one for four pies, and one of the Generals sent to the house a large silver pitcher for some milk- Now all this robbery was done after the surrender. I asked Mr F- if he intended going tomorrow to see the grand review, he answered very brusquely indeed, "No-" What do you think I want to see all them devilish yankees for, I can see more than I want to see at home!" Mrs Carpenter and Compton, went off this evening, and O such a relief to be rid if only for a day

Tuesday 23 Mrs Marble- (Poor Crazy Jane as we call her) went off to the review this morning and we are rejoicing in a clear house to day. Every thing seems moving towards *Wa* even Sherman's rabble who are still coming in. I was obliged to go to Burgundy after breakfast, and had to stand on the road side for some time before there was a brake in the ranks so that I could cross the road. After I passed the stream divided and one half took the route through Burgundy, and it was 12 oclock before I could possibly pass in going home. We all stood in the yard to look at them

It was one unbroken mass of men, wagons, horses, mules, and negroes. The wagons as usual all filled with plunder, and all dragging something behind. There was one very large old fashioned carriage that particularly attracted my attention, with large oval windows, all round, and silk curtains, and fringes gently moved by the breeze. It was in good condition, but some what traveled stained- But it was something elegant and costly in its day. I looked after it, as far as I could see it and wondered what the history of that old carriage was. It looked like an old family coach. It was closely closed up and I could not see if there was any one in side, and driven by a soldier. Immense numbers of negro men marched behind each wagon all dressed in the hateful blue, But all armed with shovels, and spades, instead of guns and bayonets, Some few negro women, some on foot, and some on horsback, O all such sights! how it stirs the Southern blood, and arouses feelings indescribable

Col- Gregg's regiment returned this evening, but he did not, and we were congratulating ourselves on having our house to ourselves, when there was a knock at the door and Lt Compton introduced two clownish looking yankees "to stay the night-" They told us there never was such a concourse before in W*a*, that a front window on the avenue could not be rented for less than $75 just for an hour or so while the crowd passed.

Wednesday 24 Mrs B- was here this morning. She says her boarders returned very much disappointed, and out of sorts about the review, say there was no enthusiasm, no shouting, no applause, no flowers strewed on the paths of the returning conquerors as they expected. The troops passed quietly from one end of the city to the other and that was the end of it. They asserted also, that there was as much bitterness of feeling between Grant's and Sherman's armies, as both felt towards the South- One of the officers said he was going up to-morrow to see Sherman's rabble reviewed. He called them the robbers, and said Johnson had mobbed them out of North Carolina.

Thursday 25 The army seems now as if settled down on us for life, and women from the north are pouring in daily, and yankee pedlers by the thousands, running in and out and up and down, buying from the officers and men all the plunder they have brought from the South. I sit at the window and watch their movements until I am tired of seeing them Mrs Marble and Carpenter returned to-day Col- Titus came in after tea to read to the ladies the description of the "Grand review" He said it sounded very well, for the news paper, but was very different in reality, every one who witnessed it was disappointed.

Saturday 27 Lizzie has been quiet sick for two or three days, and it has rained all the time, making our house and every thing so uncomfortable, officers and then servants running in and out bringing in mud and wet. The officers make a great pretence of protecting us, and our belongings, only a very short time ago and had another new fence put up around the yard, and garden, and this morning find it torn down in places, and the meadow with about a hundred horses in it. We just determined to let it all go finding it useless trying to protect it. It seemes Col- Titus had made arrangements with the sutler in his regiment to have Mrs Marble's room here, for his daughters, when she left it and he came this evening with them to claim it. But Crazy Jane had changed her mind and positively refused to give it up, and they all got into a high dispute and quarrel and the Col. ordered the sutler, and daughters out of the house, and threatened to turn out all the officers and wives, and said he had the power to turn us out, also if he chose

Sunday 28 To day has been one constant succession of annoyances, officers and soldiers, women and negroes tramping in and out the whole time. The *ladys* are still at loggerheads about the room- but crazy June was determined to have her way, and she overmastered the sutler, and his party. We had shut ourselves up in our room, and were engaged reading. The morning service, when mammy came bustling in, for "Miss Lizzie jest to look out and see all dem dar people, trampin, and sailin all over the garden pullin all your flowers." We looked out, and sure enough there was a whole bevy of the company from Burgundy parading through the garden and slaying the flowers, right and left, Dr and Mrs Oaks, Dr and Mrs Snow, Capt Weeks, and many others whose names we did not know That was a little too much for L- She told her mammy to go out and tell them, her mistress said she had no objection to them walking through the grounds, but please be so good as not to brake the shrubbery. Presently she came back with the most triumphant air and said "Miss Lizzie I tol dem what you said, an dog my cats if I dident make dem mosy out of dat garden." But she did not tell what she added to the message.

To-day's paper contains an account of the treatment of President Davis at Fortress Monroe, confined in a dungeon and heavily ironed. We received a letter from poor David to day he is among the paroled in Richmond and in a state of great destitution. Poor boys! it grieves us greatly, and we so utterly powerless to help them. This is the first communication from either

Monday 29 As our Green house is empty Mrs Marble has taken a fancy to making her head quarters in it, and Col Titus has had a number of men preparing it for her reception He apologized to L- for his last nights exhibition of himself. Said he ment no disrespect to her, but has no idea of being ordered about by a sutler, particularly by one in his own regiment. And the sutler says they are all officers and men, nothing but poor low ill bred tradesmen, making use of their short lived, brief authority while they may, and in a month after being mustered out of service will not have a cent to buy themselves bread

Wednesday 31 I am in town to day, having walked in yesterday with Mrs Cloud- Have seen, and heard of a great many persons and families who have returned to Alex- and O such shocking accounts as they do bring of the brutal behavior of the yankees. They tell us we have not heard half of the enormities committed by the 8th Ill. cavalry. At one time they captured five or six of Moseby's men, they murdered them with the utmost cruelties, all but one, him they took to Front Royal where his mother lived, and in the street before her door, and in her sight they tied him between two horses and literally tore him limb from limb- at another time they overtook a Baptist minister in the road, they took his horse from him, stripped his clothes off and left him there in the road perfectly naked, another Baptist minister the Rev Mr Morris, a highly educated and Christian minister, they told him they intended to hang him, he begged for his life, saying he had done nothing to them or any one else worthy of death. They said it did not matter, one of their men had been killed, and they had sworn to hang the first man they met. He then asked time to sing a hymn, and offer up one prayer, which they permitted and then took him into the woods and hung him. The next day his friends found his body suspended from a tree- O Father in Heaven! can such deeds go unpunished? My feeling have been stirred to the veryest depths, almost of despair, hearing countless such stories, and seeing old friends and acquaintances returning homeless, and penniless, and looking so worn and forlorn, many finding their elegant mansions burned or destroyed, many claimed and occupied by these horrible detestible yankees What is to be done I cannot think. The wharves and streets have been thronged all the week with soldiers, and wagons, Sheriden's and Shermans armies have been acting so badly in Maryland they have determined to send them back to this side of the river. I got from the post office two letters today, one from Aunt B- in Indianna, and the other from Com. Forrest who writes begging me to find for himself and Mrs F a room, says he is entirely ruined by the war, and will have to content themselves with very humble quarters. The last he heard of Douglas he was in Havanna, and the last time he saw Bush he was in fine health and spirits. But it has been a long time since. I got back home late in the evening to find L- had received while I was away a letter from poor Bushrod, and had that to grieve over. It was dated 23rd- April, written from Macon Ga and post marked Port royal S C. Poor fellow! I can imagine how he feels, from the very looks of the letter. I never saw such a scrawl from his pen. He says he was sent into Sherman's lines with a flag of truce, and Macon was surrendered before his return without his knowing of it, and they took him and party prisoners. He protested against it, but they paroled him and allowed him to keep his horse. He makes but little mention of our friend Maj- Beaumont, only says he claimed to be an acquaintance of ours, and through him he expects to get this letter sent to us

Poor Bushrod! poor boy! he seems utterly in despair, says as soon as he possibly can he is coming home to see us once more and then to leave the country forever. He was not aware of the surrender, but says such is the report.

Thursday [June] 1st 1865 I have been sick all day, scarcely able to move or do any thing, the consequence of the walk and excitement of all the terrible things I heard and saw. The yankees still continue their drilling every day, I can not see the wit of it as they expect to be disbanded so soon, still it gives the soldiers plenty of leisure to poke about and search every hole and corner- Whenever two of them meet, one is almost sure to say to the other, "Wal, I should like to own this piece of property." I have never seen a yankee yet that did not want this place

Friday 2 Summer has come upon us all at once, and a terrible fatigueing time we have of it. Every thing we get to feed these horrible people upon, comes from the market, first by one neighbour and then another, and we have to go for it and lug it home. This morning we brought a basket full from Burgundy, and then one full from Mr Fairfax through the boiling hot sun, and before night I was sick, perfectly prostrated, and had to give up and go to bed- leaving poor Lizzie and mammy to battle it alone

Col Gregg came back perfectly delighted with the "Great Review." He says there never was such a Grand Military display seen in this country or any other, and there never will be again,-and we were very wrong to have missed it. It was worth the ride only to have seen Gen- Custer ride up Pen. Avenue. The grandest looking man that ever sat a horse, he could not find words large enough to express his admiration of such a noble mein, and such a magnificent horse, and the shouts and plaudits that greeted him was deafning a lady threw a bouquet which struck the horse which made him rear and plunge so violently they all feared the Gen.'s neck would be broken. I said it would have been only what he deserved, for I felt confident he had stolen that horse out of some Southern gentleman's stable, Ah! he sneered, that is the way you rebels talk of us poor yankees, we can not have a thing but immediately you say it is stolen. I said, you know it is your national proclivity. Poor old Col. Gregg! I used to give him back, as good as he sent. Some times he would walk up and down the floor and grit his teeth at me. But he was a real good old man and would soon get over it. Some times he would threaten to have me arrested, but I soon learned not to mind that (Soon after Col. Gregg left here there was a paragraph in the paper stating that some gentleman at the South hearing of that horse in Custers possession recognized it as his, came to W*a* and demanded it, and Custer was obliged to give it up to him I cut the paragraph out, and wrote on it, *"told you so"* and inclosed to Col. Gregg)

Saturday 3 One of Col. Gregg's men came to the kitchen this morning to beg mammy to try and get her mistress to employ him to work on the place for her after the regiment is mustered out. "No," she said, "I wont car her no sick a message, fur I knows she will be too glad to git rid-ur you all, to think er paying you to come back agin." Whenever the soldiers get into any sort of mischief she screams and bawls at them so as to be heard all over the place, and then bawls at us to let us know what they are doing, she treats officers and men just alike. Col- Gregg told me they hate her and call her that d- old secesh nigger and Capt Goodwin, the Provost first threatned to arrest her, and now he says we have put her up to being impudent to him, and the first provocation she gives him, he intends tying her up to a tree and giving her a hundred lashes, she was within hearing distance and marched into the room and said "Col. you tell dat man, please to member I is in my own home, an he had better go an find his own *dungle* to crow upon."

Monday 5 Mrs Marble and Mrs Oaks the surgeon's wife seem to have struck up a great intimacy, and Mrs Marble spends most of her time in Mrs Oaks' tent which is just at our garden gate. They spent this morning saundering about our garden, and just act as if the whole place belonged to them. Then they retired to the tent, and presently they broke out into the highest quarrel, threatening each other. "Ill' take no more of your sauce and Ill' throw these soap suds into your face." It got so furious at last that two of the officers went over to Burgundy to request Gen. Griffin to relieve Col Titus of his command and about one oclock an ambulance was driven up and Col. Titus and Mrs Marble got in pack and baggage, plunder and all, and were driven away. She sent Mrs Oaks not to dare to put her head out of that tent to look at her as she got in the ambulance. Poor old Crazy Jane! we were too glad to get rid of her- But her doings were very amusing Col. Titus pretended to have our flower garden worked and put in order for his sister's gratification. But they have destroyed more flowers and shrubs than their work is worth The head-gardner cuts and carries them off by the bushel, and to day we learned he is engaged retailing them at a dollar a bouquet.

Wednesday 7 More yankee women are constantly coming in. Last night about nine oclock, two officers with a woman and child came to beg quarters for the night. They introduced her as the wife of the surgeon 2nd Md regiment. Said they had no place of shelter for her, and as Col. Gregg was away we let her have his room for the night- To day the garden has been filled with women and officers, sailing about gathering the flowers and helping themselves to whatever they please

O how domineering these yankees can be, only give them a little power. There is a poor foolish negro boy wandering about among the tents constantly, about half witted, and how the soldiers do persecute that creature. This morning while I sat at my room window I observed a number of them drag that boy out of the officers kitchen by the hair, then they raced him into our back yard, one would give him a kick, and another a cuff, another man with an immense sword gave him three or four severe blows across the back with it, and while he was writhing and howling with pain, another ran out of the kitchen with a handful of pepper, or something else, and dashed it into his eyes. Then they all set up such a shouting and hurrah, as if it was something very witty. I thought if such cruelties had been seen by them, practiced by Southern people, what volumes would be written to the yankee papers about it. Last Saturday Chaplain Taft came into our garden, with a boy and basket and gathered a quantity of flowers We learned after it was to decorate the theatre, his chapel as he calls it, especially for our reception the next day, and Sunday morning Col. Gregg came and said to Lizzie, "Now, just put on your bonnet and go with me to church, Taft has decorated it beautifully with flowers certainly expecting you will be there" as soon as I was aware of what he was saying, I knew she would refuse to go, and then the invitation would be extended to me. I got up and tried to slip out of the back door without being observed, but he was too quick for me- he called after me saying, "O you vile rebil I see what you are doing you are trying to get away from an invitation to go to church. I laughed but kept on. I did not see him again until dinner, then with an air of great contrition he came up to me and said, "I owe you an apology-" An apology, I said- to me, for what, "O," he replied, "I called you such a dreadful name- the very vilest name that could be thought of." Why, I said you utterly astonish me. I certainly did not hear it, or have entirely forgotten it. You say so many vile things to me, do tell me what it is- "O," and he seemed as if he could not utter the shocking word, and he gasped out O—I—called you a rebel. I just threw myself back in my chair and laughed and laughed. Why I said you could not have called me any name that I prefered to that you know Gen Washington was a rebel,- I never [saw] such a blank look- it was an effectual quietus to his fun- he never said rebel to me after that.

This morning Col. Gregg said, "When he passed through Prince William County Va with the army, there was at the village of Brentsville a large house belonging to one of *your* Generals, his was a most singular name and I never have been able to recall." I don't know how it was, but the very first name I struck upon was Hunton Gen Eppa Hunton, "Well," he exclaimed, "that's the *very* name, I can not understand how it is that you Virginians seem to know every name, in the whole state, we, the soldiers went into that house and completely gutted it, and when I got here, nothing was left in it but the old bibles, and I took them and sent them home" I replied—well—the idea of your going all the way to Brentsville to steal Gen. Hunton's old family bibles. The *Bible of all things*, what did you want with the bible. You yankees have no *earthly* use for the bible, and what did you take it for. "O," he said he did not want them, they were curious looking old books, unlike any bibles he had ever seen before, and had some writing in them that appeared to be an old family record, which he thought might be valuable to the owner, and he might make capital on them some day by returning them, and if I could take charge of them and see they were returned to Gen. Hunton, he would send them to me. I told him I certainly would take charge of them with pleasure, and see that they were returned

Thursday 8 Mr F. F- was here this morning, and we took advantage of his escort to visit our barn. We found it in a most deplorable condition, doors all gone or off the hinges all the petitions torn out- and gone, all the farming tools and machinery gone, or smashed up the carriage a perfect wreck, the curtains and lining all torn out, and every part of it broken and destroyed. Mr F- says it is the same way at "Rose Hill," and now they are cutting down the cherry trees just to get the fruit, he asked one party if they had not better let the trees stand they might want some next year, the reply was, they would not be here next year, and they did not care a d- who wanted them next year, so they got what they wanted. He has been trying all day to get a guard, and they will wait and delay until all the trees are cut, and all the mischief done and then send him a guard to feed. I know too well what they are, and how they manage. Soon after dinner Capt. Carpenter came to take his wife away, he disputed the board bill- paid just what he thought proper, and no more, and then walked off without even saying good evening to you. About four o'clock Col. Gregg came in and took a very hurried leave, and in a little while we were glad to see 179 N.Y. regiment marched off.

Friday 9th Mrs Cloud brought us to day another letter from poor David, he complains of great destitution, has not yet received the letter with money in it, which we sent him a short time ago, Poor-poor boys! it makes my heart ache, how I wish I had money to send them both. There are robberies and outrages committed on all sides by Sherman's outlawes we hear of the Miller at Clouds Mill, seized while standing at the mill door and robbed of $60, and his pockets turned inside out. The same thing done at Watkins mill, and in the roads and every where- Citizens are afraid to travel the roads, and Gen. Griffin is besieged day and night for guards. Mrs Mason was so kind as to send her wagon for L- to go to town Every one is shocked at the appearance of things here, every thing utterly destroyed again

Saturday 10 There was another torch-light procession last night, every now and then we hear of them when a regiment is mustered out. There was also a tremendous fight in one of the camps on Burgundy. The men swearing they would kill the officers, several of them were severely beaten. But on our side they seem as quietly fixed down as if for life- ladies with all the requisites, and conveniences of house keeping, servants, in abundance, horses and dogs, cows driven up in the evening to be milked, and pastured on our fields. They have just taken possession of every thing belonging to us, and when they please. Every man seems to have a dog, and such yelping as there is with them all night long, the noise is enough to craze us. They cleaned up the field today where Col Gregg's regiment was camped and burned up all the litter and trash and we flattered ourselves it was done on our account, when this evening the regiment was drawn out there to drill

Wednesday 14 Col. Weld seems to have taken Col. Gregg's place and fixed his headquarters at our garden gate. He sent in this evening and ordered, sheets, pillow-cases, and towels, to be sent out to his tent. L- told the man who came for them, it was something she had never heard of before, of course we had to send them rather than encounter any more violence and robbery, than we can avoid- Every day—we hear more and more complaints from the people of how they are plundered and robbed by the soldiers, they take every thing worse than when the war first broak out. Every family is obliged to feed two or three guards, and then they are of no use. They are so troublesome to us that we have been obliged to call on Col Weld, we have sent to him three times, but he takes no notice of the messages whatever at one time they sent word the Col. was out gunning, guns, dogs, and field-sports seem now to be the order of the day with these grand military men, and they tell us there is no prospect of our being rid of them for months to come.

Friday 16 Mr and Mrs Cloud called to see us to day They say Mr R Fowle was at Burgundy this morning imploring Gen. Griffin to do something for his part of the country That more shocking things are done in his neighbourhood than he ever heard tell of, a poor woman with a little infant in her arms, came running into his house last night, to beg his protection from Sherman's savages. They get worse and worse every day. The citizens do not dare to travel the road, they are robbed, beaten and murdered all over the country. The whole army are nothing but highway men, murderers, and pickpockets, and to think of such horrid wretches being let loose on the people that they yankees have disarmed. a deputation of negroes called on President Johnson this week to offer their complaints of the terrible treatment they are receiving at the hands of the military in Richmond, they told him it was much worse than any they ever knew while in slavery- Mrs Dr Oaks who has been invisible ever since her friend Mrs Marble left, made her appearance again to day with a child three or four [years] old- She passes by our windows about a dozen times a day, about half dressed, with a blue vail thrown over her head, and always crains her neck to look in The Dr appeared at the kitchin window this morning and sent in to us a requisition for hair pins. I *do* think there never was on earth any thing equal to yankee impudence.

Our guard sent word in that the Col. said we must board him as it was inconvenient for him to board elsewhere. L. sent word back to tell the Col- she would have his rations cooked if he thought proper to have them sent to the kitchin. But as to furnish him board, that was entirely out of the question, they had taken every thing away *from* us, and we found it a hard matter to get enough for ourselves to eat. I did most sincerely hope he would take the guard away from us, as that would have given us a good opportunity of applying to Gen. Auger. But I find this morning the guard is still in status quo. Mr F. F. came to see us this evening, after having paid a visit to Gen. Griffin to complain of and ask protection from the depredations of the soldiers at "Rose Hill." He was greatly excited, said, "that scoundrel had treated him with the greatest insolence and contempt. Said all the people in the neighbourhood were rebels and deserved every thing they got," and that was all the satisfaction, or protection he got.

Wednesday 21 Mrs Dr Page came to-day to engage board for herself, aunt and two little sons. The youngest is extremely ill, not expected to live- We walked over to Burgundy this evening, and returning saw a long panel of fencing fixed up just below the garden, for these *gallants* to practice the racers they have stolen, in jumping. Col. Weld on his firey charger was coursing round the fields- He went *away* off, and then came back furiously, sweeping by us in a current of wind, the horse lifted himself high in the air—but—O horrors—his hind feet hung in the rail- and such a crash- and such a fall- the earth shook- I never heard any thing like it before. I was sure they both had crushed every bone in their skins. The rider went ever so far over the horse's head- they both lay stretched out for a few moments, and I thought both were dead, the soldiers flew to them from every direction, and after a time righted them on their feet again- But I believe they were both very much injured- certain it was the last jumping bout Col. Weld tried while here. The yankees are still inciting the negroes to keep a vigilant watch on the white people, and to report all they see and hear. I can not understand why that is, now the war is over, and they have made all the negroes free What more do they want, or what they expect to do next

Saturday 24 L- engaged Ben Risdon to take her to town twice a week, to get what we want from market, and this morning was her first trip with him, and going along he talked to her about and deplored the fate of poor Mrs Surratt. He said, "I was born in Maryland, and lived all my life on the adjoining place, and very near to her house, and knew her well, and a better woman never lived- She was a good Christian woman, and Miss Lizzie, she had no more to do with, or knowledge of that murder than you had, and if they hang her it will certainly be murder." He seemed so sad I believe he cried- L- received a letter from Maj Beaumont, inclosing one from poor dear Bushrod who is now in Milledgeville Ga, he says he is living with his friend Maj Mackintosh, but is entirely without means, has only some Confederate paper but it is utterly useless to him. He is hoping, and expecting an engineership on some rail road, and hopes it may not be very long before he has an opportunity of coming home to see us, but for the present thinks it advisable that he should remain quietly where he is. Maj Beaumont, who has recently been promoted, writes most kindly, and affectionately. He says we are never forgotten by him. He has had the pleasure of meeting and becoming acquainted with our brother, and is trying, and will be most happy if he can be of any service to him. I also had a letter from Westmoreland County V*a* telling of the wide spread desolation, and of destitution, and want, and of the deaths within the past four years of many of my old friends and relatives. about 10 oclock Mrs Page and party arrived. The little boy is extremely ill, I never saw any thing living so reduced and emaciated

Sunday 25 This morning, Cesar, one of our negro men who had behaved so badly, and insolently the first year of the war, as to cause L- to order him off the place, and never to put his feet on it again, made his appearance here on a miserable old horse, he dismounted and walked into the kitchin where she was. She asked what he wanted, and if she had not ordered him never to come here again. He broke out upon her in the most insufferably impudent manner. Said he had as much right here as she had, and would come when he pleased, and stay as long as he pleased, and he defied her to drive him away She called the guard, he said he did not care any more for the guard than he did for her, but she told him he was a negro of hers, who for his impudence she had been obliged to drive him away once before, and asked him to be so good as to make him leave at once- Then he pretended to be drunk, poured out a torrent of abusive insulting language called her "that woman." But the guard would not listen to any thing he had to say He took him by the shoulders and ran him out of the kitchin, and off the place, and told him if he dared to come back again he would shoot him. We live in a most miserable uncomfortable state, subject every day, and all day, to all manner of annoyance The two cows that have been our support for years are taken up first by one and then another and we not only have the impudence and insults of the people to encounter but the cows to pay for before we can get them back- Osgood, one of the yankee soldiers who has the management of Burgundy farm, is our constant pest, he is for ever drunk, and so insulting, to day he shut the cows up and refused several times to let them be driven home and at last we just paid him what he demanded, rather than have any words with him

July 1st 1865 I am so tired and wearied out with it all, I feel as if I had no home There is no annoyance conceivable that these dreadful people do not inflict on us- we are surrounded by them on all sides, and the weather is so hot we are obliged to have the doors and windows open, and their gaze is ever fixed upon us. They use the water so much that it is constantly so muddy as to be unfit for our use, and we suffer in that way.

Sunday 2 This morning Dr Page with all his belongings, servant, horse, and tent arrived Says his regiment at Baileys Crossroads have been disbanded, broken up camp and gone and he is going to pitch his tent here. He gave us the pleasing intelligence that the, Grand Army of the Potomac was no more. I wish the whole yankee nation would follow suit. I cannot under stand how it is that so many Confederate prisoners being sent home are lost, In every paper we see now there is some terrible account of disaster to Confederates at one place a boat was snagged and two, or three, hundred drowned. Then a train ran off the track, and a great number killed, The last account was of a boat load, between Ft Lookout and Savanna being scalded to death by the steams being turned on them (accidentally of course)

Monday 3 This evening Mrs J........ Mary, and one of the brothers-ex-Confederate came out to see us- He was with Gen. Johnsons army, and with Bushrod in all the battles about Nashville. But they did not meet, knew nothing of each other being there. I don't suppose they would have known each other never having met since they were little boys.

Tuesday 4 Great preparations have been making to celebrate this day, with grand sports, and hundreds and hundreds of soldiers have collected here from all quarters. They had an immense greased pole planted in one of our grass fields, with a bottle of whisky and ten dollars fixed on the top, who ever could succeed in climbing to the top the prize was to be his. Then they had a greased pig racing and squealing, and hundreds of hands grabbing at it Then a gander pulling- Then an omnibus with a little negro boy fixed up as a monkey—which suited him exactly, with an immense long tail I think it must have been a cows tail from the length of it, he seemed greatly pleased, drawing it through his hand all the time. Then they had sack races, and foot races, and a wheelbarrow race. We were shocked to see our old wheelbarrow make its appearance, and taking parts in the sports, but its course was but short- it soon broke down, and was banished from the field in disgrace. Gen Griffin was there with a carriage full of ladies, and any number of other vehicles filled with officers and *camp ladies*. We all sat in Dr Page's tent and looked at the foolishness until I got so warm, and tired I came away, and found the well surrounded and the yard swarming with soldiers, and the water entirely unfit for use. We called the guard but found it impossible to get them to go away. Then Dr P. stepped up and took the buckets off, then they went off cursing and swearing, but in an under tone they were afraid of him. They grumbled some thing about calling ourselves Christian people. I thought how exactly that was the yank, after drinking our well dry, and leaving us without a drop of water—selfish- miserable wretches are they all.

Wednesday 5 The poor little boy continues very ill and last night the cows and calves were very noisy, and annoying I felt so sorry, that the poor little fellow should be so disturbed, there was no such thing as sleep. I cannot imagine what the soldiers were doing to them. But they have pulled down all the fence around the barn yard again, and the water is in the well so muddy we cannot use it. I determined to go to Col- Weld and make complaint, but as usual he was not at home. I saw however his adjutant standing under the cherry tree, and made my way up to him and made requests. I told him I wanted all their horses taken out of our stables and barn and I wanted him to have the fence fixed up, that the soldiers have torn down. He said he would have the fence fixed up, but did not think the Col- would be willing to give up the stables. It does seem to me such a piece of impudence for them to come, now that the war is over, and take possession of every thing, and turn us out of our home. At the gate I met Dr Oaks who asked if we were not greatly inconvenienced by the soldiers constant visits to the well, and making the water so viley. It was the first time I ever heard that term for muddy water, but I guessed what he meant. He said it was very unhealthy to use such water and it would make us all sick, and he would have a talk with the Col. and see if he would have a guard placed there. In a little while the guard was placed, and six or eight men at work on the fence, and such a fence as they made of it, a rail stuck in here, and a plank and stick there, not enough done to it to be of any earthly use- just a perfect *"free nigger job* L- received a letter from Col. now Gen Gregg saying he had a very satisfactory trip and reception at home, and had shipped Gen. Huntons bibles to us and a large box of maple sugar, to be divided between us and our neighbours at Burgundy.

Thursday 6 We walk to Mr Fairfax's to-day to try and get some one to cut a little grass for hay, and was shocked to hear there was none to cut. Mr F. said, "the officers have stolen all the horses in the country, and now have to steal enough to support them, and all our grass that the *black cow* has not eaten, has been cut and fed away to them." O me! where will our losses end- What a prospect before us for next winter! where is our food to come from as we returned home we met Col Weld riding very leisurely through the woods, But as soon as he caught a glimpse of us he put spur to his horse and dashed furiously past us causing us to move pretty speedily out of the road, and out of the way of the sticks and stones that were flying from under his horses feet. I do not know what his object was in that movement. If he thought he was showing off to advantage his fine figure and superior horsemanship he was greatly mistaken. He certainly did show himself deficient in good manners

Friday 7 This has been an intensely hot day, and it has also been poor Mrs Surratt's dying day. She with three others (men) were hung at noon to-day in the yard of the Penitentiary at Washington. It makes my heart sick to think of it. O what an everlasting disgrace to the nation to hang an innocent woman. I do not think a white woman was ever hung in this country before.

Saturday 8 I went to town this morning to market. I found very little there, and so high priced I scarcely knew what to buy. It is my first, and I hope will be my last trip to market Every body I talked with are in high hope that next week will relieve us entirely of our yankee friends- I suppose I am to call them friends and brothers now, but I don't feel that way by a great deal. To day's papers give full accounts of the execution yesterday They say Mrs Surratt knew so well how perfectly innocent she was of the crime charged against her, that she never for a moment had a thought of being hung, up to the time that the information was brought to her that her death warrant was signed, that she and her daughter both were perfectly paralyzed- and in a state of frenzy, the daughter particularly She flew to the President's house and begged and implored admission to his presence, and then to other members of the family, and then that a note might be taken in, but not one would see or hear from her, and she threw herself down on the steps in utter despair her wails, and lamentations were pitiable- at last they dragged her away in almost an unconscious state Dr Adams, a friend of the Pages came out this evening with the two Miss Claggetts Mrs P. told me after they were gone that they did provoke her too much to hear them talk about the hanging of Mrs Surratt. Dr Adams said hanging was too good for her he wished that nine lives had been given her, that she might suffer death nine times, by hanging.

Sunday 9 Col. Titus came in very unexpectedly this morning dressed in citizens clothes. He came by order of Gen Griffin to pay up his arrears of board. Poor Mrs Marble, he says became violent insane before he got to Phil- so much so as to oblige him to put her in an asylum His lip trembled while he was talking of his sister, and L- says she forgot for the time he was one of our bitterest enemies, and she felt very sorry for him. We hear there has been great trouble with some of the regiments about W*a* Some of them were in a high state of revolt and tumult, and the Col. went in among the men with his drawn sword, and was shot down instantly and his body pined to the ground with bayonets, and three or four of the other officers were killed before the riot was quelled. The circumstance was mentioned to our guard. "O" he said, that was nothing, such scenes are of almost daily occurance. His regiment the 56th New Haven is to be mustered out to-morrow. Col. Weld was so good as to send Mrs Page an ambulance to go to town in and I accompanied her It was the first, and the last time I ever occupied a seat in an army ambulance, But I saw a great many nappy headed *ladies* riding in ambulances, and elegant carriages decked out in their mistresses old frippery, they had borne away from home when they escaped

Wednesday 12 Col. Weld's regiment was mustered out yesterday. He called this morning to take leave of us- and instead of coming to the front door, went round to the kitchin- Well- "Ruling passion strong in death." Col White 31st Maine is to take his place. They all tell us that a week or ten days will finish up the business, and we will get entirely rid of the military. I wish the whole nation could be mustered back to yankeedum

Thursday 13 Newspapers this week filled with descriptions and accounts of the hanging of the four conspirators (as they call them) Dr Page brought two pictorial papers- all four are represented in every stage of preparation for execution. Poor Mrs Surratt! a cap tied tightly over her head and neck, her clothes all tied at the knees, and feet, and her hands tied behind her. O, just the thought of that poor woman fills me with sickning horror, how do we know at what moment the same fate may overtake us

Friday 14 Adj Gen. Childs now seems to be our dictator. We saw him this evening, and he promises every thing, to have the barnyard fence fixed up, the barn repaired, and to see to our being paid the rent of it. But I know well how fallacious that promise will turn out, all the morning he has been collecting togather all the rubbish left in the camps and selling it off, all the plank the officers borrowed from us to make their tent floors, and then left

We had a terrible fright just after dinner, heard Mrs Page screaming and flying to her room found the little boy in convulsions- one flew for the Dr another for hot water, every one ran for some thing. We all were sure he was in the death struggle, but before night he revived enough to speak. But his father says his days now will be but few. Poor little boy! It will be a terrible strain on our nerves, after all we have gone through, to have him die here- I look forward to it with dread, but suppose it is inevitable.

Saturday 15 The soldiers now seem to rove about at will, They rob the people of every thing they can lay hands on, they are traveling all over the country trying to sell their plunder, peddling now seems to be the order of the day, they steal horses and cows in one place and sell them at another, even dogs. One was here this morning with a dog tied by the neck, the property of Capt Weeks who is now at Burgundy, he stole it on his way from Richmond and now offers it for sale- We were surprised and delighted this morning by a visit from our old friend and neighbour Dr R. C. Mason who lately returned from Richmond. He told us a great many things we had not heard before, and about many old friends—and so many,—so many have reached that home from which no traveler returns- We told him how disturbed we were at hearing with what delight they all received the yankees into Richmond welcoming them with every demonstration of joy, and with what favour the ladies received the attentions and addresses of the Federal officers and this General officer would bear off a wife to the North, from the sunny South, and that one "Pshaw! Pshaw! There is not a word of truth in it," he said, "It is altogather a fabrication, be assured of that. So far from receiving them with favour, the ladies would not even speak to them, or allow them to enter their houses.

Monday 17 All is excitement and anxiety. Regiments moving off daily, and all here expect to be off tomorrow- The fields where the camp have been are filled with both white and black, piling up, and carrying off all the rubbish left by the soldiers, and soldiers ladened with all kinds of trash walking from place, to place and from house, to house offering it for sale- Both officers and men are now on the alert to dispose of all the plunder they have collected Torch lights, and bonfires have been blazing every night for over a week. Most of the soldiers shelters are made of pine and ceder brush, and the officer's tents are covered with it to protect them from the hot sun, and as the regiments go away all that is set on fire at night, much to our annoyance and terror for every night we watch most of the time expecting every moment either the house or barn will be burned- We have been walking all over the neighbourhood trying to find some one to haul us some wood. and also to get milk for the sick boy, our cows are gone

August 1st 1865 After all the camps were removed and the officers all gone we thought we were entirely rid of the soldiers, but find we are greatly mistaken, numbers of them are now prowling all over the country- and they with the negroes are a constant nuicence and terror to the people- we were at "Rose Hill," and met a lady who lives in the mountains of Loudon Co and was subjected all through the war to the raiders who every now and then poured through the country- robbing and seizing every thing they could find, they were regularly organized bands of robers, plunder was their only business, and of all the thieves and villains that ever crossed her path Sheriden and his gang would bear off the palm. They would rush into the houses, and pack up the furniture, pianoes, mirrors, glass, china, silver, house, linen, the ladies watches, and juelry, every thing they could lay their hands upon and send them off- and then set fire to the barns, stables, and out houses, and mills. She had sat at her chamber window and counted twenty or thirty houses burning at one time, and the smell of burning grain would last for weeks- Dr Mason went to town a few days ago on horse back, a detective saw him and seized his horse and sent it to Provost Marshall Wells. The doctor followed and after much discussion, in which he gave Mr Wells pretty much his mind, the authorities at *head quarters* concluded to keep the horse, and the Dr a feeble old gentleman was obliged to walk back home. Before leaving the office he asked Wells if he might be permitted to walk the streets of Alex- with his umbrella. Dr Page has been here for nearly two months and obliged to keep his horse at a livery stable in town for fear of loosing him, and wherever he goes, to town or any where else has to walk, and although he and all of them, have been very kind and considerate of us, and I like them all very much, I cannot help feeling glad when any of these things come home to themselves-

August 26 1865 Dr Page and family left here this morning after a sojourn with us of nine weeks- The Dr was ordered to Richmond eight or ten days ago, but remained as long as possible on account of his little boy's extreme illness. He was taken out of the house this morning as he was brought in, on his bed Ever since he came we have expected every day would be his last, but he has weathered it out wonderfully, He has not moved or spoken a single word for the last four weeks, Poor little Charlie! I never expect to see you again And now we have a clear house again. But we do feel lonely and unprotected with so many marauders prowling around, and O, such a desolate, desolate home, with nothing but the naked land and the old dilapidated house left, and how we are to get through the coming winter- How to be warmed, feed, and clothed, God only knows. But he who tempers his winds to the shorn lambs, and observes the sparrows when they fall, will not forget us-

Monday Dec. 25th 1865 Christmas has come again, and we are as desolate and lonely and as badly off as at any time during the war, Cinderela has not yet visited us and Bushrod has not turned his face homeward yet. But every thing, and every body lives in a state of expectancy and excitement. All think the negroes intend *some thing* The yankees have all the time been promising them the whole country, and they think the land should be theirs, and the way to get it will be to exterminate the whites, and from their manner and talk and every thing it is believed some such attempt will be made about Christmas times- and every thing we see and hear makes us believe it too- and O what a dreadful—dreadful state we live in, night after night we sit up until almost daylight, watching and listning for every sound, and if a rat or a mouse moves, or a dog barks we are up and at the doors or windows in a moment There is no sleep, or rest for us, we start up at every little noise. We walked into town on Saturday last, and found the streets filled with negroes, all rushing along in gangs and looking at all white people in the most sullen and insolent manner. I am sure I was not run against less than six times by negro men while walking down King Street. They would take you with their baskets, and yell and whistle right in your ear Some times it was deafning, and push you off the side walks, or run you over the cellar doors- We could scarcely walk the streets for them.

Part II
January 1873

This is the first day of January eighteen hundred and seventy-three. I have for some time thought of writing down certain events as they occurr that are of interest to me, or that I may wish to remember. Not that I have anything especially interesting to record today for I am about too sick to hold up my head, severe cold taken in helping in the decoration of "Sharon" for Christmas. But I felt as it is New Year's day it is a good day to make a beginning. So I have dashed boldly into it with little or nothing to write. The weather is uncommonly cold, and has been all the month of December. The whole face of the county is one sheet of white, covered with snow for more than a week, and what a sad, sad month the first has been to many. The papers are filled with sickening accounts of floods- storms of snowfires, Ship wrecks- not only all over this county, North and South, East and West come these terrible accounts but also from Europe. Hundreds have lost their lives. Bushrod was in W*a* [Washington] most of the month with a committee of gentlemen from Georgia who are soliciting Congress for aid in making a canal to connect the waters of the Mississippi river with the Atlantic at Savanna. But he has not once visited home although we have expected him, and gone to town for him a number of times. We certainly expected him to spend the Christmas holidays with us, but he has disappeared from Washington without giving us the slightest notice of his intention of doing so. We have been expecting and expecting him and making all the little preparations we were able to do. I have not even seen him. Lizzie met him twice in town. He may have gone home, or he may have gone to New York. In last week's papers there is a most shocking account of a train of passenger cars being run into by a train of bricks and smashing up ever thing, braking the stoves and setting fire to the cars a great number of the passengers were burned in the most shocking manner, some were taken out without eyes or arms and so blackened and chared as not to be recognized Yesterday the thought occurred to me perhaps _____ but no- I cannot write it- Father of mercy spare us!

6th A messenger to town to day brought the good news that B- [Bushrod] was there on Saturday—all well—he has been so much occupied with his business he has not left the city even to enjoy the Christmas recess- He sent for our papers relative to our claim on the Government. O, I pray he may succeed in getting it, for never could it come in a time more acceptable. This winter we are almost destitute, having been defrauded and robbed by our tenants until there is nothing left on the place

1873

Nothing for food for men or beast, and so little to buy with, I cannot see how we can get through the winter. The last tenant B. P. who we considered our friend, and treated like a brother, has behaved to us worse than any of the rest. He sold off, and took off, every thing he could lay his hands on, and then ran away without giving us the slightest notice- first persuading off Richard, our hired boy, Lizzie and my self were on this place for three weeks with no living soul on it but ourselves. The thing we did was to nail up the cows in the pen as well as we could, lock up the house and run over to Sam Pullman's and beg them to take the cows and take care of them until we could get some one on the place. a family named May moved into the farm house about three or four weeks after- During the time we were alone we got entirely out of provisions, we were in such straits we did not know what to do, at last we concluded to stand on the public road until some one passed who we could ask to hitch up the carriage for us. Several people of whom we could not make the request, but at last we were fortunate enough to meet the right one- We both went to town, I drove but whenever we went out on such expeditions we felt anxious about home and hurried back as speedily as possible, fearing the people in the neighborhood finding out there was no one in the house might brake it open and rob it.

I could not pretend to tell the hardships and straits we were put to- no wood for the kitchen fire, we had to go about and pick up all the sticks we could brake short enough for the stove. Fortunately we did not require a great deal of cooking. But one felt desolate and lonely at night, particularly if the weather was cold and stormy. Some times, on such nights we would say suppose one or other of us were taken very ill to night- or suppose one should die suddenly, what on earth would become of the other-But God was very good, and took care of us. I mailed two letters today one to my poor sister in Alabama who is in constant trouble about her children. Now her second son is away off no one knows where, and she has been kept in a constant state of anxiety for ten months, hopeing, dreading every mail that arrives. The other to my aunt in Indiana

250

who is very aged, in her eighty sixth year- my dear Sainted Mother's only sister! I hope she may be alive I have shamefully neglected her not having written for a very long time. O, that I might go and see her once more before she dies!

22 I received a reply to my letter from my dear aunt Elizabeth D. Scott yesterday. I am thankful she is still living and well though so aged- She writes well though- as full of life and vigor as a young person She tells me of all her children, grand children, and great grand children and their where abouts. She sent me a draught for five dollars, which made me so sorry, I know she needs it as much as I do, and then I am afraid she thought I expected some thing from her. I wish she had not sent it but am afraid of offending her by sending it back. Bushrod still in Washington but has not yet been home. His canal bill he expected to have been brought up before congress on Saturday last, but I see no mention of it in the papers. This has been the most intensely cold winter that has been known for many years, and the papers contain terrible accounts of suffering, and the freezing to death of both men and animals.

February 1st Saturday The ground still continues covered with snow although the weather has moderated a little. But such accounts of the severe cold as comes from the far West I never saw, or heard of before. Hundreds of people and cattle frozen to death. Stages filled with people found standing in the road, the driver on his seat holding the reins all stiff and dead even the horses- Little children frozen to death on their way from School. The rivers all blockaded with ice- even on the Potomac in some places it is said to be piled up ten or twelve feet thick. There have been a number of sudden deaths in Alex. [Alexandria] this winter. One lady (Mrs Taylor) took a short walk late one evening and in returning home felt a little faint and sat for a few moments on a door step, and from there was assisted a short distance to a drug store, which she had scarcely entered before she fell and died in a few minutes, another, a friend of ours (Mrs Dude) a very old lady and very feble, but still as well as usual, went into Mrs Adam's room, her sisterinlaw who was sick in bed, and after a while laid down on a sofa in the room all supposing she had gone to sleep let her remain quiet for some time, when, I suppose, thinking she had slept an unusual time some one went to her and found her quite dead, and from appearance must have been dead for an hour or more- In a few days after Mrs Adam died. In our isolated condition all these sad things, and terrible accounts makes us feel more lonely and gloomy than I can tell.

Sunday 2. I went to town to church this morning, the first time I have been to town since Christmas day, Mr McKim preached and was assisted in the administration of the communion by Rev. George Smith-after church found Bushrod at cousin Mary's waiting for us. He has been weather bound, and ice bound, and business bound in W*a* this long time, but is looking well and in good spirits, and very sanguine in regard to his canal bill which is to come up before congress the 13th of this month.

1873

Wednesday March 5th It is now over a month since this old book and I had a friendly talk together- well old book I must tell you it has been a *hard, hard* time with us. For five weeks Lizzie has been a terrible sufferer from rheumatism or nuralgy- no rest night or day. But I am thankful to be able to say she is getting better now and today has gone to town on business, although I am afraid it is at a risk. It is still bitterly cold, and snow on the ground, not the least appearance of spring. It makes my head ache to think how long it may yet last, and our poor stock so much in want of food. a few nights ago our cows got out of their pen and in the morning we found one of the herd dreadfully cut and injured and after breakfast Peck one of our yankee neighbors came up to make his complaints, and charges us four dollars for the mischief she has done him. It is a hard neighborhood for two unprotected ladies to live in for themselves. We have tried and tried to sell the place, and to exchange it for city property but as yet without avail. I feel it will be like tearing my heart strings assunder to leave it- but I find it must come- Bushrod and David have both staid a few days with us within the last ten days, first one and then the other- It was a pleasure- but poor B- has gone back to his home in Atlanta Georgia sorely disappointed although he tries to persuade himself he is not. The day the canal bill was to have come before the House of representatives the whole day was taken up in the Credit Mobillia investigation (no doubt a trick to consume time) and it was postponed. But he is still very hopeful and says he knows it will all come right sooner or later. David, who has just returned from a tour through all the Southern States says the whole people are thoroughly awake to the importance of the work, and more than anxious to see its completion. Many little things have happened since I last wrote in this book which I am afraid I have forgotten. I wanted particularly to have written a little on the 20th of February as that was our father's one hundredith birthday. I wish I could write his whole history, it was a most remarkable and interesting one- and one that his latest posterity might be proud of. This much I do know, he was a man of the strictest integrity and truth- and never lived a man of purer moral, upright character from his earliest youth. "He was one of the noblest works of God a truly honest man." He was born in the city of Amsterdam capital of the Netherlands. But left there for America when he was twelve or thirteen years old. Of his father he seemed to know but little, having died before his recollection. He was a native of Germany, but removed to Amsterdam when quite young and of which place he was, after Burgamaster. Pa thought, I do not think he was positive about it he knew he held an office under government of some importance as a sentinel always _____ His mother was a native of Switzerland of the canton of Bean. Her name was Sophia Alleymon or Aleymond a daughter of Dr Alleymond a physician of great celebrity (I think in Zurich) Papa's mother was educated in a convent in France. This I think is pretty much all he recollected of her. I have often heard him say French was spoken altogether in his father's family excepting to the servants. To them they were obliged to speak Dutch. I have heard him say that after being in this country a few years he had almost entirely forgotten his own native tongue, and meeting with a lady from Holland (Mad—Readhazel) he could scarcely understand a word she said to him in Dutch for which she rated him, telling him what a shame it was to forget his native tongue. His sister married a Prussian named *Von Hagan* he was a titled man but I do not remember what his rank was but for some misadventure at court had to fly his country and soon after he married Pa's sister. He was a violent tempered and restless man- engaged again in politics- I have heard Pa describe temper scenes he witnessed during a rebellion or civil war, I do not know clearly about it, but believe it was about the time of the commencement of the French Revolution- There were two parties one was called "Patriots" and the other "the Orange party." Von Hagan's side was defeated, and he was banished for two years. They all came to America and brought Pa with them, he having neither father or mother. They intended traveling those two years, and then returning to Europe. But in the time his treatment to my father, and even to his own son, was so cruel that the both ran away and left him, and then this poor little boy had to make his way alone in the world But the dealings, and guiding hand of an ever watchful Providence was over him, and it is wonderful to have it through his whole life. How he was kept from evil, and the influence of bad company He never would associate with any but persons of the highest standing both as it regards morals and position in society, and a more upright, honest, honorable man than my father, the sun never shone upon. He never stooped to a meanness, not even so much as to receive a favour from any one, and although he lived at Mt Vernon with Judge Washington's family many years, and the Judge and Mrs Washington were like the most affectionate of friends he never was under the slightest pecuniary obligation even to them. He was in N Y. city the winter the first congress met there and Gen and Mrs Washington saw him there for the first time, he sang at a concert, it was such a pleasing sight to them, such a little boy with such exquisite taste, and such a thorough knowledge of music, that they were not satisfied until they had talked with him and learned who, and what he was, and then they persuaded him to go to Mt Vernon and live with them which he promised to do the next time they came to N. Y. to return with them to Mt Vernon, but they never went again, Gen Washington died and after some time I do not know how long, perhaps a year or two he met with Judge and Mrs Washington and they took the same fancy to him and made the same proposition (to live at Mt Vernon with them) and finally he did return, and live with them many years, and to the day of their death they were as kind and fond of him as they were of their own nephews, and after Pa was married and had a family, it was always, the same. I can remember when (I must have been a very small child) their coming here and dining and the Judge's saying to Pa "Frobel I shall require at least one visit as I do of my nephews of you a year" (he was only at Mt Vernon a part of the year, most of the time he lived on his farm in Jefferson Co), and O what a frolic it was to us children when the time came for us to spend the day at Mt Vernon, and every thing was done to make the day pleasant to us. O! it all seems like a faraway, almost forgotten dream The last time I was at, and seated in the old east room without carpet or furnituer, entirely empty, and thought of the grand old statley ladies, and lordly gentlemen that used to inhabit there, and traverse those old dim honored halls, and picture to myself Maria's wedding scene, how the brides-maids entered—that door—and circled round to the center of the room, with those blue and white favors on the left shoulder with the streamers floating so gracefully behind them all lighted candles in their hands, eight or twelve in number (I forgot; and the groom's men with their blue and white favors pined to their coats; and the beautiful young bride, and smiling happy groom, all so bright and joyous- but now all, or nearly all gone- I can remember but two or three of that large company that are now in the land of the living, and then another scene flouted before my mental vision that in which Ma—and myself with many, many others walked slowly from the wharf with the long funeral train attendant upon Mrs Jane Washington's obsequies. Rev McLippet the minister that I saw perform the marriage ceremony for the daughter I saw reading the solemn "earth to earth and ashes to ashes" for the mother- And then when I sat on the bank and looked down on the vault and thought of the highborn, the noble and the good all now crowded within that little narrow space. I was oblivious of all around me and carried away back into the almost forgotten past- It was a melancholy pleasure to visit that dear old place, it recalled so many scenes and images of the past- and so many dear ones now gone forever from this world of sin and sorrow-

Some time ago I was searching among my old hidden relicks under the stair-steps and found a package of old worn letters some dated as for back as 18 [blank] written on the coarsest, yellowest, almost brown paper. The most of them were Pa's, Some from Mrs Ann Washington. Some from Mrs David Mead Randolf, and some from Mrs Jas Wood, whose husband was governor of the State- all his most particular and dearest friends, and written in the kindest and most affectionate manner. I thought of transcribing some of them in this book- But I concluded *that* would not show what they were, and I have put them away as my most sacred treasures. One or two from dear Aunt Annie Scott to my own precious Mother All shew how pious and good she was, and Ma–loved and reverenced her as she would her own mother There is another little incident connected with Mt Vernon and our youthful days I do not want to forget. On one occasion when Pa–had taken us all down to spend the day, when Bushrod was about three years old- he stood by the piano and sang a little song called "Little Caprice" while Pa- plaid the accompaniment; and they were so delighted with the little fellow, the ladies all gathered round him and Miss Judeth Blackburn went down on her knees to listen to him, and the Judge took him on his knees and kissed him in his own jovial way and said "I know he'll be a smart man, for all the Bushrods are smart."

1874

May 6th 1874. More than a year *my old book* since you and I held any talk together, and what shall I say: What apoligy make for this long and seeming neglect! Every letter I write is commenced with excuses for long silence, and now I have to do the same even to you. Many ups and downs, many privations, and troubles and sorrows, have I had to encounter since this time last year- But in a few years who will know- It will all have passed away with us into the grave of forgetfulness- and who will ever remember that we have ever lived!- But many a wishful glance, my *old chum*, has been cast towards your hiding place, and many a wish for a little friendly converse, but all to no purpose. There are a number of things I would like to have kept a record of but they have passed away- as I soon shall-

This has been a most uncomfortable spring. March, April and thus far into May scarcely a day of sun-shine, nothing but rain, and cold blighting winds and frosts, all the fruit is supposed to be destroyed and O such disastrous floods in the western rivers Every thing has been so entirely swept away, that the government has been obliged to send out vessel loads of rations to the starving people- and every where money is being collected for their relief Bushrod is again in W*a* this winter, at work on his *canal* bill, and thinks he is going to succeed this time. He has also taken our claim in hand, and is very sanguine in regard to its success. O I do hope both may come to a successful issue this session, and that we may be able to sell out and move away. for this state that we are kept in, of uncertainty is perfectly wearing out to both body and mind.

Last summer we had our house filled with boarders, and hope to have again this, but the old house is so dilapidated, and last winter leaked in every part that I do not know how we shall manage. No one but Lizzie and myself has any idea how very poor we are We try to do as well as we can when any of our friends come to see us, and to make as respectable an appearance when we go out as possible, but O— poverty is ever pinching and grinding us down, it is- ever-ever- we can do without this, we must to do without that, "Poverty is the destruction of the poor."

July 3. Bushrod left us for his home in Georgia more than a month ago- nothing done with his canal bill- nothing done with our claim- The lawyer into whose hands it was entrusted wrote us, a short time since, he had lost the papers and requested us to make out more- I was truly provoked- I could no more do it than I could fly and we took not the slightest notice of his note. Bushrod has written us since that he had sent the papers, of which fortunately he had kept a copy. Said, they would be sent to us for our signature, and that we must make an exact and careful copy and keep it, but it is the last we have heard of either papers or lawyers. We did not receive the lawyer's note until the day after the claim was to have been brought before congress- Congress has now adjourned

1874

Saturday July 11 Received a letter from David to day. The first for several months. He informs us he is married again, to a girl he calls Agness but gives no other name, neither does he tell when or where he was married. It is the first we have heard of the affair, although Ned says his father told him before he left here last Feb., that he should be married the 20th of June to a Miss Agness, the only name Ned ever heard. David is a poor erratic, thoughtless being, never knows to day what he is to do tomorrow, or how he is to live. He has never been able to take care of one child, and how another family is to be provided for I cannot tell.

We have had Mr Charles Green's family boarding with us this summer for two weeks and two days, but only two or three boarders is only an expense and trouble for nothing. The weather has been intensely hot and dry, and we without a cook all the summer, no servant but two little negro boys- "Man is born to trouble as the sparks fly upward." This summer there is another long tailed comet—the wise ones say it portends war- It is not by any means as brilliant as the one we had the year before the last war. "The Rebellion," as the *Yanks* call it.

Sunday 25 Lizzie and Neddie gone to church today and I am left- (I was going to say entirely) alone, but we have two servants now, a negro boy to milk, attend to the horse and work in the garden, and a woman in the kitchin. It is a comfort to have a cook, although this one is not at all trustworthy, she had not been with us a week before we discovered several little thefts, so that we feel it unsafe to leave two on the place without one of the white family, and one or other is obliged to stay from church I wonder if it is right to stay from church to take care of, and attend to our worldy matters But the negroes are committing so many robberies, murders, and vile deeds of all kinds now that we scarcely know what to do- Every news paper is filled with their outrages. I received a letter yesterday from my poor sister, Mary in Tallassee Alabama. She says they are certainly going to move to Kansas as soon as Mr Mower can procure the means of removing his family there. He is at this time in Parsons Kansas and delighted with the place and all he has seen in that part of the country. Says Parsons is the most rapidly growing place he has ever been in- the town is only three years old has several R. R.- three public schools- two banks- three churches- three new papers- gas works and in short is a very desirable place to locate in on account of the children- his boys can find employment and still live with them. Mr. M- has found many kind friends, and among them a nephew of his old friend and groomsman the Rev. Mr Lockwood- a clerical brother writes Mr Mower "I feel delighted you have found so promising a field of labor as Parsons, I have heard of it occasionally that it is a flourishing well to do place. It has a rich future before it The West offers a finer field for church work than any other section of our land- The south- once so hospitable and generous is but a thing of the past, Whose record is in story, and song and the remembrance

Of his children "Mr Mower says he cannot remain at the South under negro rule and to have his children educated with negroes, and with the iron hand of the oppressor on their necks, how can the prostrated, down trodden people rise or do anything- The whole state is bankrupt- Some have their lands but of what avail are they with no means of cultivating them. Mary Marshall and family are also going to Kansas. Mr Mower has not yet come up with, or heard any thing of his wanderers, his two older sons. As I write this sitting before the picture of my dear Sainted Mother hanging in its old frame on the old weather stained wall, she looks so sorrowfully down upon me it makes my heart ache to think of her poor children and grand-children scattered to the four winds, and so powerless to assist one another. and now another family going still further- almost beyond the reach of civilization, as we have always thought of it- The land of *old John Browne*- The weather is still excessily hot and dry- The comet has disappeared several nights ago.

Saturday August 1st. This morning prevented from going to church (although it is communion day) partly by the threatening appearance of the clouds and partly from having to dismiss Richard, the negro boy who attends to the cows. We found this morning he had been stealing milk, and cream to a great extent.

When, O when shall we be able to live in any degree of comfort! We know the woman we have (Fanny) is a thief, and Neddie is a very bad boy, a constant source of trouble and vexation to us. Yet what can we do? There seems no way of extricating ourselves. Had a letter from Bushrod on Thursday, he is always hopeful and encouraging Thinks there is no doubt about getting our government claim, and next winter he is going to work hard for it and there he has a place already picked out for us in Atlanta, and there we will all live, and be so comfortable and happy. We have been expecting another boarder (Mrs. Popham) since Friday morning, but why she has not yet arrived we have not learned. She is very old and infirm, and we fear is sick-

Friday 21 Mrs Popham has been with us nearly three weeks, and such an everlasting trouble no one ever encountered before. There is no peace, or comfort in the house, night or day. We count the days, and hours until we will get rid of her If Mr Packwood (her son-in-law) would give me his house filled with silver and gold I would not board her for one year. Her whole studdy seems to be how to make herself as hateful as possible, and so disgusting in all her ways. I have always from my childhood loved old people, loved to be with them, and to talk to them, and to wait on them, such as I have always been accustomed to, such as my dear old aunt Betsy Scott. But *this no human being could love,* and O so excessively hot and dry! as the weather still is. The earth indeed seems iron and the heavens brass to us- No cook- no servant but a little negro boy. I do hope this is the last summer we will be compelled to take boarders. I think I would rather live on fish and corn bread, I feel it such a degradation to have people and inferior in every respect, but money, treating us with such indignity. I am afraid I have not an humble spirit.

1874

Tuesday November 3 Early in the spring I received a short letter from my cousin Molly Snyder telling me of her being called several weeks before from her home in Kansas by the severe illness of her Mother (my dear aunt Betsy Scott) who they all supposed was on her death bed, and that morning the family had collected about her expecting every breath would be the last, "but now" she said "late in the day she has rallied and is getting in and out of bed without assistance." But still she thought there was no hope of her living more than a few days, and when the event occurred she would write again. I wrote immediately but have not heard one word since until last Saturday Lizzie brought me from the office a letter directed in her own unmistakable hand. I cannot describe the feeling that thrilled through me at the sight of it, when for so many months I have mourned her as one numbered with the dead. She certainly is a wonderful old lady, she must be nearly ninety, but writes with as much vigor, and mental force as a young person. Says she waits on herself, and walks by herself wherever she wishes to go. Says her only son Admiral Scott is at this time in Paris. He has always been a very affectionate and dutiful son, and it seems to give her pleasure even to speak of him, she speaks of him, "My only son"

Dec. 30 Christmas has come and gone again, and we still at the old place,- no change excepting from bad to worse. The old house dropping to pieces, the green house we are afraid of every high wind- many of the bars in the sashes just pasted together with paper to keep out the frost- garden enclosure falling down- barn yard enclosure, and all the fencing in the same condition- barn- a perfect wreck- our cattle greatly reduced- only three cows left, and a week before Christmas our old horse was stolen, unhaltered and taken out of the stable, a bag and a rug taken out of the carriage I suppose to use in place of a saddle. We have not been able to get to town to church service, not even on Christmas day. Mrs Reid was kind enough to lend us a horse one day, but since then we have not been able to get one in the neighborhood for *love* or *money*.

the weather is so mild every farmer is using his horses to the plow. I do not know what on earth we shall do, as we are dependant entirely on market for our daily food. It is a terrible thing now in the depth of winter to be put afoot again. I feel that my health and strength will not admit of my walking much To-day Lizzie has determined to try her strength not with standing a terrible cold and cough which she has had for more than two months. She took Charlie a little negro boy, with a basket on his arm and truged away to town, hoping she may meet with some one who will be kind enough to give her a lift either going or coming back. I feel very anxious about her

We have not had a letter from Bushrod for several months- but see his name occasionally in the news paper. The last we heard of him was at a convention in Richmond- Since then we have heard he was not coming to W*a* this winter and then again we heard he was coming. We feel most anxious about his *canal* business, and also about our *claim* which he promised to persecute most vigorously this winter, but there are such complaints of *hard times*, scarcity of money and empty treasury that perhaps he will wait until better times, and some government changes. I am afraid if we do get our dues we will be too old to enjoy it.

David came about the middle of October and took Neddie away with him. They have all gone to Florida, the land of flowers, and they tell us it is indeed the land of flowers, a perfect Paradice, flowers all the year round. They are at Fernandina on the St. John's river. D- sent us a package of flower seed, and promises to send a box of plants in the spring. But Neddie and the *wife* both sick ever since they got there. I have not heard from Mary- do not know whether they have gone to Kansas or not, wrote a week ago and hope to have a letter soon. But my poor dear old auntie wrote again about three weeks ago- and O- such a letter! my heart dies within me to think of the situation as she describes it- can it be possible that such avarice—such inhuman unnatural covetousness can lurk within the heart of any human being! I am ashamed to record what she says of her daughters when I remember that they are of my kindred and blood- She writes at night, evidently with a very dim light, says several times she can scarcely see, and gives me every reason to think she is doing by stealth. Molly was called from Kansas to see her die. They induced her to believe her good affectionate son Hall was dead, telling her they did not know any thing of where he was but that she would never see him again, all the while they were corresponding with him and telling him (as they did me) that she was at the point of death—her mind entirely gone, she was incapable of sending a message, or even of knowing that they were writing. But still I can not understand it I thought her means were very small not even enough to make it worth while to travel all the way from Kansas to Indiana for. I suppose the little she has they were trying to defraud their brother out of his share. She complains of their taking every thing from her, and leaving her in want of common comforts, they never talk to her, leave her to wait on her self, walk by herself wherever she wants to go, and do for her self as best she can, which she says is no easy task at her time of life—eighty eight years old—poor dear old lady! I wish I could be with her the balance of her days, and she wishes it too, for she says she wishes E- was in Kansas with her sister and I was living with her- O my own dear mother, how different I am thankful to say were her last days! I so often think of her, and picture her to my self, as she sat in her arm chair, too feeble to talk much, her eyes would follow us from place to place, and she seemed unwilling for us to be a moment out of her sight, and as we would stand by her bed side night after night, and day after day, she would so often say "My children, my dear dear children, what would *I do* without my children" Dear precious mother! I sometimes think heaven would not be heaven without her I wonder if such thoughts are sinful- I try to banish them, and think of what a glorious hereafter, to be forever with the good, and those we love.

January 1875

Wednesday Jan 6th. Lizzie has borrowed a horse again from Mrs Reid and gone to town to attend to business matters and buy us a *little food*, as far as her money will go It is terrible to live in this way (as dear Ma used to say "from hand to mouth") We hear no tidings of our old horse But every one who dare to say anything about it thinks it has been made away with by three young men Harry Jarvis, Jim Simbs, and George Recker, who Mr Kerby arrested and fined about six weeks ago for outrageous disorderly conduct here. They have been in the habit of coming here time after time between ten and eleven o'clock at night blowing horns, and making all kinds of noises hooping and yelling like wild Indians. They would go into the farm house which was unoccupied and knock the plastering down, and do all manner of indecent-things, until it became perfectly unendurable Some nights when Lizzie and I were quietly seated by the fire, one at work and the other reading aloud, when we would be suddenly startled by a most unearthly yelling, and find a wagon load of these creatures passing near the house and tearing down the fences wherever they wished to go through. If we sent Neddie, or a servant to tell them not to do so they would curse and abuse them, and say they would go through where they pleased, and when they pleased. Lizzie tole Mr Kerby (the magistrate) about it, and asked if a little admonition from him would not prevent their behaving so again But he advised that they should be dealt with according to law, and now, the loss of our only old horse is the consequence

Saturday 23. So much has happened since I last wrote I scarcely know where to begin. In the first place then, we have heard at last from Bushrod who has Arthur Mower with him and they both have been for weeks surveying in the wilds of Georgia, all about the rivers and through the swamps and morasses until they feel almost like wild men themselves. B- has rented out his house in Atlanta and his family for the present are at Milledgeville, which makes me feel very uncertain about the wisdom of a move for us in that direction. He was so good as to send us $30 and when Lizzie came home with the receipt for our coal in her pocket and the carriage loaded with provisions I was *too too* glad. But I really am glad no body knows how destitute we are, and although I often say we are very poor no one seems to think it is so. We have had letters too from Mary Mower and Lilly, all out in that horrible place Kansas- and such accounts as they give the place and the people and all. It must be (as I have always believed it to be) the very fag end of the world. O why did not Mary stay where she was! as I begged her to do, But the hope of some day coming up with those unfortunate wandering boys urged her on. She gives me a horrible account of a family named Bender who lived about six miles from where they are. She says a number of persons were missed from time to time until at last it became so bad— so many would disappear at a time that suspicion fell on these Bender, and a number of people determined to collect a force and go out and search the place and see what they could. But unfortunately the Benders got wind of what was on foot and they all made their escape. But the house and premises were examined and no less than twelve bodies found burried in the yard, and all with marks of violence on them, some were females, and one a little girl. all were identified but one youth and nothing can persuade poor Mary that was not her lost boy George. In the front room in the house a curtain divided, and a bench place near it, and when a poor weary traveler placed himself on it if he was supposed to have any valuables about him, one of the family would step behind the curtain and deal him a heavy blow with an immence hammer they kept for the purpose, and then through a trap the body would be dropped into a deep cellar or pit beneath the house. and O, these are the horrid people my poor sister and family live among. But poor Lilly says if life lasts she is coming back to her dear southern home next summer- that she and the boys have fixed themselves up a box they call the *"Home Box"* and in it they put every cent they can make and scrape, to come home with. Mr Mower still has his house in Opelica, and fortunately Mary Marshall did not go to Kansas as they expected.- and then another letter a night or two ago in *deep deep black* telling us of the death of David's poor wife- she died at Fernandina 10th married only about seven months and sick all the time- Misfortunes never come alone, and it does seem as if our family certainly did have its share- But the bible tells us "Every heart knows its bitterness-'

March 6. More than a month ago I made my last entry in this old book, and as I am alone to-day Lizzie having gone to town I thought I would like to pour into the *ear* of *my quiet* old friend, something more about myself, something more of my trials and difficulties, and how impatiently I take them some times. and in the first place I must say this has been a winter to be remembered- cold—cold—bitterly cold ever since the first of the year. It is said to be the coldest for thirty years. The river frozen at all the time- ice from six to fourteen inches thick, and now I constantly forget it is *spring*, for the whole face of the earth is covered with snow and ice, and the clouds look as if more would come before night. Our old horse came back some time in Feb- L- had made a *severe* threat to one of the neighbors, that if it had been killed (as every one thought, and she could discover who did it, she would have them put in the penitentiary if money could put them there- It was talking *largely* but never the less the next day Billy Simbs came up and talked about the horse, and about every thing and every body until we were perfectly worn out with his visit. He told of this one stealing, and the other one stealing and how leniently they had been delt with when found out, and what a mistake it was in persons who were aggrieved to treat young people harshly, and at last he told of some drunken man who had gone to Bishop John's and committed some very flagrant outrages, and destroyed I don't know what. But after he came to his sober sences he went back and apologized, and asked ten thousand pardons, and repaired all the rongs he had done, and the Bishop freely forgave him, after sitting here about three or four hours he went off but in a short time came back with the news that George Struder's father in-law had come over from Maryland with the information of a horse having been sold in his neighborhood to a negro woman which undoubtedly was a stolen one But it seemed he could tell very little about it. Just at dark here they all three came (I really felt as if I was beset) We soon found the old man knew who had the horse, and where they lived, and all about it, and it

263

was soon arranged that George should start off the next day after it, but, that night it turned bitterly cold and the river froze over and he had to go by way of Washington. He returned with the horse in three days and charged us four dollars and a quarter $4½ a day almost as much as old Dolly was worth. She was all the time just on the opposite side of the river, nearly in sight of home. It appears a negro named Bob was the thief, he came originally from Md but has been living about in this neighborhood for years. He sold the horse first to an old negro woman for $17 the woman was busy in the house at the time, and as he was an old acquaintance she trusted him to put it in the stable for her. But some time after she thought she had better go and see if all was right, but *lo and behold* there was no horse there. Mr Bob was pursued and overtaken just as he had sold her again to another negro for $15 But after a parley the matter was compromised by his giving back the $15 to the man, and the old woman took the horse. Bob with several other negroes made horse stealing quite a business last winter, and sold them all within eight or ten miles of the places from where they were stolen. a number were arrested but proof positive could only be obtained against Bob and he was sent to the Penitentiary for 17 years

May 2 It has been a long time again since I have written a line in this book not for a want of time, but simply want of inclination—monotonous mode of life, and lack of any subject of interest. Since I last wrote I have had a letter from my poor sister Mary who does nothing but bewail the loss of her two boys until she has made herself wretched and ill, and that terrible place! They all seem to dislike it more and more. O that they had never gone there! Lizzie and I have pondered it all over and over. What can we do for them? how can we help them? May God in his goodness give us the power is our constant prayer. We have determined if we get our government claim (and B. is very sanguine of our success, he tells us so in every letter) to give Mary this place and every thing on it- and deed it to her and her children, and then help them from time to time as we can, to fix every thing up about it. O what an unexpressable happiness it would be to see them all established in the *Old House*, and for the balance of our days to live near each other. Mr Mower might have charge of all the little stations around and in addition Pohick church, Falls church and the church at Fairfax court house. We have never mentioned our plans to any one, nor do we intend to do so until the *happy moment* arrives, and then Mary Marshall's husband might find some employment in Washington- Bushrod wrote that the canal report, location and all about it are satisfactory to all concerned, but that himself, Arthur Mower and all the engineers on the survey were very ill after they left the marshes, and one died. The Doctor thought they were poisoned with the swamp water. But thanks to a kind Providence they are well now.- This has been a very cold and backward spring, about the middle of April it turned bitterly—bitterly cold, and remained so for more than a week. I do not think I felt the cold more any time during the winter. It was generally supposed the fruit was all killed, but I believe now the *nursearies* think not more than a forth is killed. We have never been able to dispense with fires a single day, the weather is cold and blustering like March- We have planted a good many vegetables, and are making a *desperate effort* to have a garden this summer- have a woman and boy at work in it, and L- and I spend most of our time looking after them.

Wednesday 5. Lizzie has gone to town to-day, and I am all alone, but have employed myself scratching about among the flowers- planting some out of the green house, and some seeds. I am so thankful to get rid of driving the carriage if only for a little while. That has been my business for the past two or three months, and it is so very disagreeable to me- Old Dolly is so dull and poky, it takes all my strength to get her along

1877

Wednesday March 28—1877. Only to think that very nearly two years ago I made the last date in this book, and now the first thing I must tell the melancholy fate of poor old Dolly after getting her back she served us for about a year, at that time we had George Struder for a tenant—a miserable drunkard—and one night she got into his corn, and he beat her to death with fence rails, and although his foot marks could be traced from his house and back, and the rails and sticks were all around her, and after her skin was taken off her back her back and sides were found beaten to a jelly, we could do nothing but bear the loss as well as we could and O- such a loss it was! I could not begin to recount the ups and downs, the toilsome walks, "through heat and cold, through mud and mire" to town and back and from place to place, to find some one to bring us out what we wanted from town that was too much for us to buy ourselves. Then we hired Buck Simbs and his horse to take us in our carriage to town once a week. Election day he got drunk and upset the carriage. as soon as he found it was going over he threw away the rains and jumped out, and saved himself, but left Lizzie and Lilly Mower (who was with her) to their fate without a single effort to stop the horse. The horse dashed off with the carriage lying flat on the side, Lilly managed to get out but poor Lizzie was dragged a long distance, until a Mr Martyes met them and extricated her from her perilous situation, Fortunately there were no bones broken, but she was one mass of bruises from her shoulders to her heels.

1878

Sunday July 14th 1878. I did not think when I made my last entry in this book it would be so long before another was made—but so it is, and I have had so much to say- so much to write about, and so many things that will never be written now, that have almost passed out of my mind- but mostly of trials, and vexations, and hardships to be borne. Times grow worse, and worse with us daily- less and less to live on- comforts drop off one by one, Our old house is so dilapidated it almost uninhabitable, it would be so to most people, It leaks in every part, and in every room, in a heavy rain it is almost impossible to get into the storeroom or kitchin, we have wet feet all the time In the back part of the house water comes through in torrents, and in the chambers we have to drag the beds and furniture from place to place to keep them from getting wet and ever thing else is in the same condition, in the house and out of doors. House linen and bedclothes all worn or gone entirely, not clothes enough to keep us comfortable, we suffer more for shoes than almost any thing else. In the kitchin the negroes we have hired have broken up, or carried off nearly all our cooking utensils, we are reduced to one pot and that is cracked nearly to the bottom, the cooking stove is so broken we can scarcely do any thing with it, and smokes terribly, when the fire is made we have to open the door, and window, and the smoke pours out as if the house was on fire. We can not afford a cook now, and poor Lizzie has the most of that to do. The heat overcomes me so, and the smoke affects my eyes and throat so, that I can help in the kitchin but little. I help by getting water, making the fire, washing up breakfast, dinner, tea and milk things and cleaning up the kitchin when the fire is nearly out. But my more particular business is cleaning up and taking care of every thing about the house, and doing the sewing, attending to the flowers, watering, planting, potting, sewing the seed, collecting the seed, and when the weather is not too hot- I do a great deal in the way of weeding and working in the flower garden. O how I do wish I could do something—any thing to bring in a little money, if it was only enough to clothe us both. But I can get nothing to do- Our garden is full of beautiful flowers, and the green house is full of exquisite flowers. But no body wants them excepting those who come to beg, and they are *legions*, from all around, persons we scarcely know. Whenever

266

there is a marriage or death there is a requisition on our garden and greenhouse No body seems to think of our wanting any thing but our good brother B- He gave us two years ago another horse and sends us from time to time a little money, but every cent he gives us goes for taxes. This spring he sent us twenty dollars- I said as soon as I saw it. I am so delighted, lets spend it all clothes- we are so much in need- But no there is so much that is due in town, and so much in the state, and if paid at a certain time will save so many dollars- and so all goes for what seems to do us no earthly good We try as much as possible to keep out of debt. This is the second year we have had a negro family But it does seem utterly useless for us to try to do any thing with our land for every tenant, white or black, our shair is always nothing, we never get enough to pay the taxes. O life, life! What have we to live for? It is only a struggle day after day to keep body and soul together. Some times I am afraid my murmurs are sinful, and when I see so many living in ease and plenty, O I wish, I wish, I could live so too. I don't think my feelings are envyous I know I would not take from the comforts of another to add to my own but O it is so hard to live from one year's end to another as we do, and now too that we are growing so old- no-body knows what we suffer- It has been so long since I wrote last that I scarcely know where to begin I do not believe I have written a line even to tell that our dear niece Lilly had been to see us. She staid a year with us, and it has been nearly two now since she left us. She came from Kansas, and went back to Uniontown, Kentucky, where her father and family had removed while she was here. My poor sister's troubles seem to have no end. Frank her oldest son they say is dead—murdered in Texas. Of George the second boy—they have never heard a word for years, and now she mourns him as dead- has given up all hope—and hopes soon to go back to Alabama Poor little Noddie David's only child died the 14th of last August in Thomasville in Georgia, very near the Florida line. D- is living there now with his third wife My dear old aunt Mrs Elizabeth D. Scott, died about three years ago at the advanced age of ninety. Leaving one daughter in Indiana with her family and the other in Kansas. Her only living son is handsomely established in Washington I received a letter a few weeks ago from Mrs Snyder the daughter in Kansas complaining bitterly of her brother's treatment to herself and sister, says she never knew until very recently her mother had left a will. The property she left was worth some fifteen or sixteen thousand dollars all of which was left to Admiral Scott The daughters are not even named. He reached his mother's house the day before her death, and as soon as she was laid in the ground he was off, leaving his sister Elizabeth who is in the most wretched state of health, in utter destitution without one cent to buy themselves bread. She and a blind daughter might have starved but for the kindness of neighbors. Poor Lizzie, she says has a tumer in her side which the Drs think would if removed weigh at least ten pounds, besides she has the dropsy, and in the tappings fifteen gallons of water was taken. Poor thing!- one half of the world knows not sufferings of the other half- and more than one half seem to live to prey on the others. Sometimes I think perhaps I am wrong in writing down all the things. I don't know why I write. no one will feel any interest in it but myself But there is a fascination about writing when no one knows of it. The weather is excessively hot. Last winter was very mild and delightful. But the spring was cold and wet, nearly all the fruit killed with frost and obliged to have fires late in June.

Wednesday July 24. Yesterday received a postal from Molly Snyder announcing the death of her sister Elizabeth Snyder, which occurred in Crawfordsville, Indiana on the 12th of this month. Poor thing! I trust she has gone to reep her reward of all her labour and toils, and the life of privation and suffering she had here! We think ours a hard lot, but when we hear of what so many others have to endure I feel humbled to think of my ingratitude to a kind Providence who has watched over, and taken care of my unworthy and useless life so long. Bushrod comes to Wa almost every winter, about two years ago he brought his wife and oldest child. We were very much pleased with his wife and the little daughter is a dear little thing, about five years old, and as smart as she can be. The weather all this month has been excessively hot But the 15, 16, 17 18th were the hotest days I ever felt. I see from the papers that on the 15th there were a great many deaths all over the country from the heat and sun strokes, in the city of St. Louis alone 54 persons died that day, and 100 horses- I had a long letter from Molly Snyder in which she tells me much of her poor mothers last days which makes me think all the terrible accounts she gave me in the last year of her life were the wild vagaries of a diseased imagination- She must certainly have been deranged- But certainly there was *method in her madness*.

Sunday 28. The weather continues very hot. But a shower on Friday was very refreshing. The papers are filled with the accounts of deaths from heat in the citys all over the country—1500 deaths in St. Louis in four days We had letters yesterday from Mary, Lilly, and David. Mr Mower and family have left Uniontown for Florence Alabama. Poor Mary's health continues very feeble, she has this summer had a violent attack of erysipelas, had to be carried to the boat in a chair, and taken from it in the same way. But since she has been in Florence seems to be getting better,

and is so desirous to see her old sisters, and her old home once more-
O that a kind providence would grant her wish! Poor Lilly too wants to
come back to us. I feel constantly as I grow older what a comfort it would
be to have all our dear ones gathered around us But those dearest and
nearest are scattered far and wide- and we are alone- in the old house.
Often in dark hours of night when the winds, and storms are raging, and
a brick comes thundering down one or two roofs, from the top of the
highest chimney, and we both start up in terror and then ensues a talk
how fearfully unsafe we are living, when the whole country is filled with
Tramps who are committing all manner of vile deeds, and our old house
could be so easily entered, the old doors and windows, any of them
could be shaken open by a child. But there is comfort in knowing there
is little or nothing to induce any one to rob us, and there is always a
revolver at hand, and the whole neighborhood knows we keep one, and
Lizzie has the credit of being more expert in the use of it than she really
is.

Saturday Aug. 17th The weather continues excessively hot although
we have had a great deal of thunder and lighting, and floods of rain on
Monday last. It was as wet in the house almost as out of doors. I was
the whole time wiping up the water, which gave me such a violent cold,
and pain in my limbs, that I could not turn in my bed for two days. Lizzie
has gone to town this morning, driving herself I was not well enough to
go. The yellow fever is said to be very bad in New Orleans this summer,
and last week two cases were reported in Fredericksburg.

Sunday August 18. I still feel the affects of the weather, constant
pain in the back and hip, but at my age infirmity is to be expected. Last
week was one of incessant storms and such floods of rain *I never did
see.* I suppose what makes us more alive to it is, that it is as wet in the
old house as out of doors, and still so hot—so sultry—and such wet
feet- O so uncomfortable! On Tuesday last as we were much in want of
some things from town I determined to drive in although I was far from
being well, and on the way back we picked up a dirty rugged little negro
boy who said "please lady will you hire a boy, I have no one to take
care of me, father and mother are both dead. I came from Culpepper
court-house on Saturday and don't know no body" He was a right innocent looking boy, and we thought if he knew no one, and had no body
to interfere with him we might perhaps be safe in taking him, so we
struck a bargain and brought him along home with us, and that evening
and the next morning he did very well indeed. Uncle Joe said he knew
the man he said he lives with in Culpepper and a number of others he
named, and I was so glad to think I should get some of the weeds taken

269

out of the garden. His promises were so fair, he would do every thing we told him to do- he did not tell stories- he did not steal- So I set him to work after breakfast cleaning the grass off the pavements, after a while he twisted about and said his knee hurt him, he had complained of it the evening before Said it had been hurt by his being thrown off the rail-road by the cow catcher and he had used several remedies for it- He said if I would let him he would go out in the back yard for a while but would soon come back, but he staid so long, went to look for him. Uncle Joe suspected something wrong directly and on looking around found he had stolen his tobacco, and matches, and vest, he tracked him as far as the railroad- and there was an end of my hopes of a *gardner*. Since then we have been so much afraid at night- perhaps he may be the spy for a gang of robbers- we lay our heads down at night in fear and trem-bling, but always see that the *Derenger* is at hand, and in order

1879

Saturday January 25th 1879. a new year has come in since I last wrote a word in my book. And so many changes to many but very little to us. Tommy Packard said in his discourse at "Sharon" last Sunday that all we found to do, our every day employment was serving God if it was done *in a right spirit*. I am afraid ours is not done in a right "spirit." We complain too much of our troubles and trials, and the burden of care, and labors we have to undergo, but I am going to try and receive it all in a more Christian spirit, without complaints- O if I could have strength given me to keep this resolution! This past has been a very severe winter. But I am thankful that we have been tolerably comfortable- back in the fall the roof partially renewed- Employed a negro man to do it. I think he is a good workman, but like all of the race he certainly wants a master, We paid him an exhorbitant price—just double what we would have to pay a white man, and then he came or not as he pleased- Sometimes he would work a day, and then we would not see him for weeks—commenced in September and now in Jan—it is not finished. The negro man and family we had living in the farm house for the last two years we discovered to be so openly dishonest and so intolerably insolent we were obliged to dismiss him, and the house is empty, but we hope after a while to find an occupant, and one who will work the land, and do us more justice than Wash Thomas did.

Bushrod has not come to Wa as yet, and the weather is so very cold I almost wish he may not until the spring. Our dear niece Lilly Mower was married on the 20th of Nov. last to a Mr David E. Gibson of Warsaw Ky. Dear child I hope her choice is a good one, and that she may be a happy christian woman is my constant prayer. Poor David has been sick, almost to death, but is better now.

Saturday April 5 The whole of the past winter has been terribly severe, and it still continues very, very cold, the last day of March, and the five first days of April have been fearfully blustering and stormy and this morning the ground was covered with a slight coating of snow We hired a negro boy the first of the year who staid until the 25th of Feb and one cold night without making any complaint, indeed without having any cause of complaint he ran off and left us entirely alone and so we have remained until the second of April when we found another boy who will no doubt go off some night in like manner. We have been on this place alone for five weeks, no human being but ourselves, and so low in purse we cannot hire any one to help us- every thing to do ourselves- House work- cooking washing and ironing, milking, feeding and attending to the horse and cows, pigs and poultry, and to make the fires and water the plants in the green house- Hard lessons to learn in old age- Sometimes when I am weary and worn almost to death, I go away off where Lizzie will not hear me, and throwing myself down on the floor indulge in a long and loud fit of tears and lamentations, and after being thus relieved I bathe my face, and come down to the parlor to find Lizzie sitting by a good warm fire looking comfortable and cheerful, some times her eyes look red, and I ask what is the matter she says smoke and wind, but I know she has been crying. We do up all our work as early in the morning as possible and as late in the evenings as possible, so as not to be seen by passers by or any one coming to the house, and at certain times, we brush up a little on our chess and sit in the parlor with our knitting, embroidery, or fancy work of some kind. I generally work while L. reads aloud. It is a bright comfortable room, and visitors coming in think and say, "We must be as happy as queens- nothing to do and plenty of every thing" Our table is always set with care and neatness and when we have company the very best we can possibly find is put before them, so that not even our own relations have an idea how very very hard it is for us to live at all. Bushrod was so good as to send us $20 to help pay for the roof, but it cost seventy five or eighty so there is a long score yet, and then the coal bill and the taxes- O it makes my heart sick to think of it all- we are so terribly in want of almost every thing, even our clothes are so worn and rusty and mended that they are scarcely fit to appear in. Besides the vast amount of hard labour we have been forced to do I have accomplished quite a quantity of sewing this winter. I took two matrasses and made three out of the material, one was of shucks, and the other English hair, imported sometime in the last century by Mrs. David Mead Randolph of Richmond, a very particular friend of my father's and sent

271

a present to him when he first went to housekeeping, some time early in the present century before he was married. The picking up of the hair was a task of tasks, it took me weeks to do it, the hair was in such hard knots I had to pick it open with an awl. I quilted and finished off a silk quilt, every stitch with my own hands. I finished pieceing two other quilts, knit four pair of stockings, made a cloth coat, one or two dresses, filled up all the beds, pillows, and bolsters with fresh feathers, besides darnings and patchings innumerable I am now finishing off an embroidered quilt for the next fair

Part III
1889

LETTERS

Letters written to one and another in regard to our claims to the government for damages during the War for property taken for army uses and destroyed. The first letter was written to Mr Rockwell of Junction City Kansas and pretty much the same letter was written to Mr David Gibson and Capt. Raoul.

Dear Sir   *Wilton Sep 10th 1889*

   No doubt you will be surprised at receiving this letter from me- but in consideration of the kindly feeling you have always manifested towards us and the relationship subsisting between us and learning from many sources that you a man extensively acquainted in your vicinity and also of popularity and influence I have presumed to address this letter to you asking a favour- a very great favour, and believing and hoping you can grant it without much trouble or inconvenience to yourself. It is that you will use your influence in our behalf in getting our war claim through Congress by stating our case to your Congressmen and Representatives and obtaining from them a promise to vote for it when it comes up and also doing any thing else in their power for its furtherance. The papers are all duly made out and certified by both officers of the army and citizens, officers who were camped during the war, and have been placed on file at the Capital since 1874. Every one who has seen the papers or knows any thing of the matter pronounced it a just claim and one that ought to have been paid long ago. We were two sisters living on our place "Wilton" when the war broke out, Our farm was well stocked and productive, and had every thing in abundance. We had nothing whatever to do with the war had neither husbands or sons to engage in it. We lived as it were under the very eves of the National Capital—in full view of it. We were comfortably quiet law abiding, tax paying citizens when the war came upon us like a thunder bolt. We did not know even the meaning of war. The army came and settled down upon us, and for the whole four years, and for six months after the surrender their white tents covered our fields, they camped over, and tramped over and drilled over our fields leaving them bear and hard as a brick yard.

   They cut down all our woods, not leaving a single tree. They made camp fires of it: they built soldier huts, forts—block-houses. They swept

273

off every thing on earth we had, leaving us poor and destitute- often and often time we suffered for the want of food- and thus it has been with us now, for over 25 years. We were never the whole four years of the War outside the Federal lines, but within numberless lines of Pickets. The officers were all friendly to us and many of them really kind and whenever a loss was reported to them, would give us every assurance that the governement would amply remunerate us for all, and many gave us certificates of losses and also for loyalty. During the war our property was confiscated belonging to our brothers, which we proved was not so, but exclusively our own. We were summoned to appear before a Magistrate and testify to the fact, and also to take the oath of allegiance, which we did, the news papers publishing the following day that the property had been released from confiscation on our taking the oath. We have Gen. Wadsworth's *Safe* Guard which guarantee's protection to both person and property which is with the other papers on file at the Capital in the *file room* and can be found there at any time with the claim all properly *made out by a lawyer*. Our claim has never appeared before Congress. I believe I have now told you as succinctly as possible all it is necessary for me to write, but if there is any thing else you would wish to know, or any other questions it necessary to be answered I will be only too glad to do so, and now believing that you can and will be so good as to help us in this matter, allow me to subscribe myself yours sincerely

A. S. Fröbel
Junction City Kansas
Oct 10th 1889

Mr Rockwell's reply

Dear Miss Frobel Your letter Sept 10th was duly recd I have delayed answering it hoping that I could get some information that would be of service to you before replying- I enclose a letter from Sen. Plumb which please return when you have read. It seems to me that to insure success this claim should be pushed by the Congressman from your District

A year or more ago I wrote to Gen. Lee regarding your claim- but he did not reply to my letter- Have you talked with the member from your District, and what encouragement has he given you regarding your claim? Is your claim in the hands of "Claim Agents"? It seems to me your claim is a just one and should be paid. Have you ever tried to interest Congressman Scott of Pensylvania? I shall certainly take great pleasure in doing all in my power to aid you. In order to accomplish any thing it will be necessary to know exactly what has been done. With best wishes and kind regards to your sister I am

Very truly yours,
B. Rockwell

Senator Plumb's reply

To B. Rockwell Esqr   *Emporia Kansas Oct 9th 1889*

My Dear Sir I have before me your favor of the 26th ult and return herewith the letter of Miss Frobel which you enclosed. It is impossible to tell what chance there may be for an appropriation to pay the claim mentioned. In 1864 I think Congress created a court known as the Southern War Claims Commission which had exclusive jurisdiction of every thing relating to property taken and used or destroyed in Southern States, whether by loyal or disloyal people. This Court sat continously in Wa until within about four or five years, when it was disolved, by reason of the fact that there was nothing further for it to do. It seems to me a little strange that during all this period of time, this claim was not brought to the attention of this court. It is true that Congress has allowed some claims that were of a kind that the court could not allow and it may be that the one you speak of is in that category as I hope it is. but it a little singular that during all this time it should have been presented to neither the Court or Congress. If you will [sic] to me after Congress meets I will take it up and see what the chances may be, and if the Claim is a proper one within the rules which have been established by Congress heretofore I shall gladly do whatever I can to promote its allowance

Truely yours
Wm Plumb

To Mr Rockwell in reply to his enclosing one from Sen. Plumb

My Dear friend I received yours of 10th Oct 1889 on Saturday 19th for which kindness please accept my warmest thanks. Our claim on the government was last year laid before The Congressional Claims Committee by the Representative of this District Gen. Lee but unfortunatley too late in the term to be acted upon and had to be laid over for the next session. In the first instance the damages were accepted and the papers

275

made out and certified to before a magistrate under the direction of Judge George R. Davis of Troy, N. Y. a friend of ours, he being here at the time and saw and knew all about the losses and saw and knew the claim was ecquitably made. Then he acquainted himself as to the proceedings of the *Southern War Claims Commission* but was not satisfied with it The Claims being so unmercifully cut down when they had been assessed by reliable men and at the very lowest figures.

Then he advised the Claim should be placed on file at the Capital until such time as Congress should pass an act to indemnify claiments, which act he said he knew would eventually pass. Of course we had to follow the directions of our legal adviser, he being learned in the law, and a man of high standing both in a legal and political point of view and we had the utmost confidence in his knowledge and judgment.

A year or two after the war closed Judge Davis died, and the next Agent into whose hands business was placed died also, in a short time, and so it has remained on file until now, we being two old and helpless ladies and disabled by sore and grievous family troubles from attending to things of any kind, and thus another have remained until the present year. When a friend a long way off wrote that Congress had passed such an act more than three years ago and that persons in his vicinity were receiving their pay and urging immediate attention to ours, we also saw a notice of the same kind in a news paper. I am greatly surprised that Gen Lee made no response to your letter if only a return of courtesy perhaps he did not receive it. He thinks very favourable of our claim and says he can see no reason why we should not get payed- I have no acquaintance with Sen. Scott, but as you kindly reminded me of him, and as he is a connection of the family it may be he will extend his kind offices to me. I think I shall try for it. Within the past few days, we had a visit from two of our old army friends who we had not seen since the first year of the war—Col- and Capt Owens, both were on Gen. Sedgewick's staff when his regiment was camped on our place. They were very friendly and delighted to meet with us again after so many years- They seemed interested in our affairs and asked us if we had ever received any remuneration from government for our losses, and were greatly surprised to learn we had not, and offered to do any thing in their power to help us get it. Col Beaumont had given a certificate several years ago, which is on file with the other papers, and Capt. Owens said he would call and see Gen. Lee when Congress meets and have a talk with him, and as he was quartermaster on Gen Sedgwicks Staff and knew of our losses and our property being taken and appropriated to the use of the army no doubt his testimony would be of service. He *said it was a just*

276

claim and *ought to be paid*. Capt. Owens lives in Wa is employed in the War Department and Col- Beaumont is with his regiment stationed at San Antonia Texas- My good kind friend I feel a reluctance in giving you all this trouble, but you must make allowances for age, infirmity, and dire necessity. We owe you a debt of gratitude for what you are doing for us that I fear can never be canceled, but we hope to see you some time at our house, and to talk it all over which will be a comfort. Till then please receive assurances or kindest regard and esteem in which my sister joins

Sincerely your friend
A. S. Fröbel

*Gen. Wm F Lee of Va (Fairfax County)
Col. Beaumont of Wilksbarre, Penn.

To Wm Scott—Senator from Erie Pa

Dr Sir I hope you will not consider it presumptuous in an utter stranger thus to encroach upon your time and patience, a dire necessity must be my apology- We have a claim on government for property seized and appropriated to army uses during the war and for which we are using every effort to get remuneration. The Claim was laid before the Congressional Claims Committee last year but unfortunately too late in the session to be acted upon It will be again be laid before the Congress this session by Hon. Wm F. Lee our representative from Fairfax Co. Va *The claim is all duly made out and certified to before a justice both by citizens* and *officers* of the army, and is now, and has been for a number of years on file in the *File* room at the Capital with all the certificates and papers connected with it It is a just claim and has been pronounced so by all who know any thing of the matter- and if I should be so fortunate as to obtain your influence and through you the influence of other members I feel and hope I may succeed in getting my just rights- I am in correspondence with my Scott relations in the West and also some of the Western members who have promised me their aid, and it is through their advice that I have made this application to you as a person of prominence and influence.

I am very sure my name will be a strange one to you, but never the less I am some what of a connection of yours, my aunt having married an uncle of yours, Mr Gustavus Hall Scott, and she was the mother of Admiral G. F. Scott, U. S. N. who no doubt you remember. We are two old sisters having lived here within sight of our National Capital all our lives. and have suffered more than I can express having had the army quartered on us the whole four years of the war, and all our property swept away from us

If there is any thing else you would wish to know or any questions, I will be too glad to answer them

Very respectfully yours
A. S. Fröbel

Appendix A

JOHN JACOB FROBEL FAMILY

1789   John Jacob Frobel's name appears on a recital program in New York, N. Y. Source: Oscar C. Sonneck, *Early Concert Life in America*, 1731-1800, New York, N.Y., Musurgia Publishers, 1949, p. 227.

1797   John Jacob Frobel's name appears in a recital in Richmond, Virginia. Source: Sonneck, *Early Concert Life*, p. 62.

1802   John Jacob Frobel gave music to Ann Washington, wife of Bushrod Washington. Source: James Heintze, "Music of the Washington Family: A Little-Known Collection," *The Musical Quarterly*, Vol. LVI, No. 2, p. 292.

1804   Ann Washington, wife of Bushrod Washington, wrote to John Jacob Frobel, asking him to come to Alexandria, Virginia, to teach music.

Sir: *February 11, 1804*

    I got your letter two days ago, and hasten to give you all the information in my power concerning your removal to Alexa. Since I wrote to you, I have been informed that Mrs. Campbell from Dumfries has advertised, and means if she can, to succeed Mr. Geib there. This however it is supposed she cannot do; having already at a former period attempted to teach musick there without success. I caused Doctor Dick to be informed of your intention to come if a certain number of scholars could be promised, he is a great amateur, and leads in all musical matters in Alexa. he says he will immediately enter his daughter and that it is his opinion that you may make up your number with ease if you will come up very shortly. Otherwise rather than lose time many may engage with Mrs. C. he says too, that alternately he is certain you may have as many pupils as you wish, and this I am certain will be the case. Miss Julia Manderville is also promised positively, and my niece Ann Craufurd. I have not the smallest doubt that in [illegible] you will have more offered than you chuse to take. The Alexandrians are however very anxious that you should come *very* soon among them, and wish to know your terms. Please sir let me know then as soon as possible and your determination. I will not repeat my good friend how anxious we are that you schold come up. You know it sufficiently. I wish also that you may come with all convenient dispatch. I have spoken to Mr. Washington about the schooner. 'he is about to use it but says that he will if possible send it and as soon as *possible* to Richmond. if that does not go, you will have an oppty. by Colo. Washingtons vessel which will perhaps go down sooner than ours. I wish with all my heart that it may be possible to accomodate you with ours because you would then have a third less freight to pay; for just so much of the vessel belongs to my husband. but as others are concerned he cannot decide upon her trips without their concurrence and the other owners seem bent upon selling her. I trust you will find Mount Vernon at least a more healthy residence than Richmond & we wish much [several illegible words] there. Meantime Mr. Washington joins me in evening. good wish for your welfare & in friendly regards, believe in haste but with much esteem your

Ann Washington

When you see my dear friend
Miss Chelsea give her my best love.

[In margin] I mentioned in my last I believe that you would have my three nieces at R. L. & a nephew of my husbands who now lives with us as pupils immediately.

Source: Original letter in the collection of the "Mount Vernon Ladies' Association," Mount Vernon, Virginia.

1804   Letter from John J. Frobel to Benjamin Crowninshield, a student at William and Mary.

Dear Sir   *Mount Vernon*
                                              May 24, 1804

I am extremely sorry that my leaving Richmond has disappointed my of being acquainted with you as it would have given me infinite pleasure to show particular attention to a friend of my dear nephew. I am much pleased to hear he is doing well and hope to see him and his little family this autumn if my health will permit. Accept my sincerest thanks for your polite offer.

John J. Frobel

Source: Virginia State Library, Archives, Richmond, Virginia; Personal papers, Acc. 20151, Benjamin Crowninshield.

1809   *January* 27 John J. Frobel married on Thursday evening at Bush Hill to Mary S. Marshall, daughter of Charles and Mary Marshall. Source: *Alexandria Gazette*, January 28, 1809.

FIVE DOLLARS REWARD Absconded from the subscriber, a negro woman called Letty, of a low statue and well made, she has lived some time in Alexandria with Mr. Thomas Janney, with whom her husband now lives. The above reward will be given if she is taken and secured in any jail or returned to me.

Wilton Hill, near Alexandria   *John I. [J.] Frobel*
Nov. 29, 1809

Source: *Alexandria Daily Gazette*, Nov. 30, 1809.

1810   John J. Frobel listed in *U. S. Census*, Fairfax County, Virginia.

1819   *May 25*, "My cousin Polly Frobel was delivered of a female child on the 11th early in the morning" Source: *Journal of Richard Marshall Scott, Sr., of "Bush Hill,"* Fairfax County, Va.

      June 8, "My beloved cousin E. D. Scott & her 3 younger children went home today with Mr. John & J. Frobel. My sister Ann came today with Mrs. Frobel in the hack that carried my cousin yesterday"—Source: *Journal Scott, Sr.*

1820   John J. Frobel listed in *U. S. Census*, Fairfax County, Va., as head of household consisting of 3 males, 4 females, 2 persons employed, and 4 slaves

1824   John Frobel Account

      January 1, tuition for two sons and one daughter $74.00

      Dec. 29, hogs, mutton $56.85

John Frobel, Fairfax Co., Va., Teacher of music credits

Lessons to Eliza & Margarette $162

Source: Ledger B of James H. Hooe of Burgandy, Fairfax County Court House Archives, Fairfax, Virginia

---

1826   *May* 30 Mr. and Mrs. Frobel & children Ann, Betsy, and Bushrod with Mr. & Mrs. McDonald dined with us. Source: *Journal Scott, Sr.*

June 1st "I have bought from Mr. Frobel the two lemon trees sent there to winter." Source: *Journal Scott, Sr.*

Sept. 12 "My beloved cousin Polly Frobel, I am just informed, delivered of a male child last night & is doing well, for which am thankful, as from her late illness I apprehended danger from the crisis." Source: *Journal Scott, Sr.*

Dec. 8 "Frobels with their 5 children dined with us." Source: *Journal Scott, Sr.*

1827   *April* 27 "This afternoon went over to Mr. Frobel and had my hair cut by my beloved cousin Polly, his spouse." Source: *Journal Scott, Sr.*

Aug. 22 "Frobels with 5 children spent the day John, _____, Ann, Elizabeth, & Mary." Source: *Journal Scott, Sr.*

1828   *May* 24 "E. D. Scott & Ann went to Washington in my carriage with J. Frobel to see the Congress in session & view the Capital." Source: *Journal Scott, Sr.*

1829   *Jan.* 1st "The new year, blessed be God, has found myself and family in good health. Polly Frobel at Mulberry Hill nursing Elizabeth D Scott, her sister, who is dangerously ill. Source: *Journal Scott, Sr.*

May 28 My relation Polly Frobel was delivered of a male child on Tuesday night the 26th Source: *Journal Scott, Sr.*

1831   *March* 12 Richard Scott Frobel died at Wilton Hill on the 12th in 9th year, 3rd son of John Jacob Frobel, Esq. Source: *Alexandria Gazette*, March 18, 1831.

1831 *Nov.* 9 Agreement between Ricd M Scott and John M Frobel, son of John Jacob Frobel

Memorandum of agreement between Ricd M Scott of Bush Hills and John M Frobel, eldest son of Jon J Frobel of Wilton Hills witness.

That the said John M Frobel, is forthwith to take charge of the land Scott hath called Farmington with the regular stocks therewith, to cultivate and manage the same, to the best advantage and with due care when working of the stocks thereon for the process of the Farm. All expenses of James Marshall, accounts, salary, accounts, clothing the negroes, and also other expenses in relation to the land Farm and its due cultivation, the said John Frobel is to pay, and then, as a full compensation for his trouble and extra work which he may personally do on the said Farm, he is to be entitled to one half of the profits. It being clearly the understanding of the parties aforesaid, that everything that is done toward the improvement of the land or the cultivation thereof, and the said Jno M Frobel is to make no use of the property or the Farm, by said agreement without the consent of the said Scott, and that this agreement is to continue to the 1st day of January 1833, and by mutual consent only longer- Witness the hands of both of the parties this 9th day of November in the year of our Lord 1831-

Land leases and witness in   Ricd M Scott
the possession of Mary Scott   John M Frobel

Back of document

The within agreement is by the mutual consent of the parties thereto for another year that is today the first day of January in the year of our Lord one thousand eight hundred and thirty-four given under our hands and hearts this 23 of February 1833

Ricd M Scott

No. 20

Richard M. Scott

Agreement

J. M. Frobel

9th Nov. 1831

Respecting Farmington Estate 2 A

Source: Fairfax County Court House, Fairfax, Virginia

1832   Thomas D. Frobel died on September 3 at Rock Island, son of John J. Frobel, Esq. of Wilton Hill, Fairfax Co. Source: *Alexandria Gazette*, October 22, 1832.

1838   John J. Frobel instructed Mary Marshall Scott Foote in music and was paid by Richard M. Scott. Source: Chancery Court Record, Fairfax County Court House, Fairfax, Virginia.

Sunday, July 15, confirmed by the Rt. Rev. Richard Channing Moore, presented by the Rector, C. B. Dana: Miss Ann Frobel, Miss Mary Frobel. Source: Christ *Church Parish Register*, Vol. I, Alexandria, Virginia.

1840   *Sunday, July 12*, confirmed in Christ Church by Bishop Moore, Miss Elizabeth Frobel. Source: *Christ Church Parish Register*, Vol. I.

John J. Frobel listed in *U. S. Census*, Fairfax County, Virginia.

1841   *January 19*, Baptized at Mr. Frobel's six coloured children— Winnifred, Matilda, Aaron, Eliza _____. Source: *Christ Church Parish Register*, Vol. I.

1845   *November 4* Married on Tuesday, the 4th inst. by the Rev C. B Dana, Rev. Benjamin F. Mower of Georgia to Mary Clagett; daughter of John J. Frobel of Wilton Hill, Fairfax Co., Virginia. Source: *Alexandria Gazette and Virginia Advertiser*, Nov 8, 1845.

1846   *Apr. 30* "Miss E. Frobel sent me a beautiful Beauquette (sic) which she brought down from Washington for me from a very sweet young lady" Source: *Journal of Richard Marshall Scott, Jr. of "Bush Hill,"* Fairfax Co., Virginia.

May 15 "Miss Virginia, Miss Carrie Clagett, Anna Frobel & Mary Clagett came over to see me yesterday to see what their sweet countenances' would have on my mumps" Source: *Journal Scott, Jr.*

July 24 "My aunt Polly Frobel & Bushrod came over & spent the day" Source: *Journal Scott, Jr.*

1849   *July 8* Died at Paducah, Kentucky on the 28th ult., Mr. John M Frobel, eldest son of John and Mary Frobel of Fairfax County Virginia. Also the same day and at the same place, Thomas D., infant son of John M. Frobel. Source: *Alexandria Gazette*, August 24, 1849.

1850   John J. Frobel, age 79, and Mary S. Frobel, age 69, listed in *U. S. Census*, Fairfax Co., Virginia.

1851   *August 7* Will of John Jacob Frobel

In the name of God Amen. I John J. Frobel of Wilton Hill in the County of Fairfax and State of Virginia do hereby make publish and order that my last Will and testament in manner and form following Viz:

I give devise and bequeath unto my beloved wife Mary Scott Frobel the use of all my personal property including slaves and dividends of stock for and during her natural life.

I give devise and bequeath unto my daughter Anna S. Frobel and Elizabeth Douglass Frobel (at the death of my wife) my farm called Wilton Hill in Fairfax County; all my household and kitchin furniture, books, farming utensils, carriage, horses, cows, and farm stock, with everything on the farm and in and about the house, together with thirty-one shares of stock of the Branch of the Exchange Bank of Virginia, in Alexandria, and eight of my slaves they to have the choice among all my slaves. And in case either of my daughters should marry she shall have only six shares of the above stock and four slaves until the other daughter marries when an equitable and equal division of said property shall be divided between them—And should either of my daughters die without having children, the surviving sister shall receive the whole of the property named in this bequest which shall be hers and her assigns forever.

I give and bequeath unto my son Bushrod fifteen hundred dollars which I have loaned to him and which he has received and a negro boy named Charles Parker son of Susan.

The remainder of my personal property and slaves together with a negro woman and girl I loaned to my daughter Mary C. Mower, I give and bequeath to my son David and my said daughter Mary to be equally divided between them, share and share alike.

I hereby nominate, constitute and appoint my wife Mary Scott Frobel and my daughter Elizabeth Douglass Frobel executrix of this my will and testament hereby revoking all former wills by me made. In witness whereof I have hereunto signed my name in the presence of witnesses. Done at Wilton Hill this 7th day of August 1851.

Executed by the testator in our   *John J. Frobel (Seal)*
presence who at his request and
in his presence hereunto subscribe
our names as witnesses

T. A. Stoutenburgh
William W. Smith

At a court held for the County of Fairfax this 15th day of september 1851

The last will and testament of John J. Frobel dec'd was this day presented to the Court and the same being proved by the oath of T. A. Stoutenburgh, a subscribing witness thereto is ordered to be certified. And at a Court held for said County the 20th day of October 1851, the same was again presented to the Court and being further proven by the oath of William W. Smith, another subscribing witness thereto is admitted to probate and ordered to be recorded.

Teste
SM. Ball C. C.

Source: *Will Book* W, 162, Fairfax County Court House, Fairfax, Virginia.

1851   *August 9* Death of John Jacob Frobel

At his residence at Wilton Hill, three miles from Alexandria on the morning of the 9th, John J. Frobel, esq., in the 80th year of his age.

Mr. F. has been long known, and where known respected. In all the relations of life he was most exemplary. Naturally amiable, this sweetness of temper had been elevated and purified by principle. Naturally regardful of the interests and feelings of others, he had learned by intercourse and communion with the Infinite Fountain of all real and moral excellence, to cultivate holiness in all the social relations. Mr. Frobel was a Christian and a member of the Protestant Episcopal Church; and while he highly valued the peculiarities of his own household of faith, he was tolerant of all those who differed from him. In his years of suffering, the communion and hopes, the varied exercises and holy ways" of our religion, constituted his chief comfort and joy. And when death approached and was contemplated by him eye to eye, he was still found perfectly composed and peaceful: "He knew in whom he had believed." In Mr. F. his family have lost a wise counsellor, a faithful guardian, a devoted friend, and a most pleasant companion; but though his society is thus lost to his mourning widow and children, on earth, they have the consolation of most sweet and pleasant and profitable memories.

Source: *Alexandria Gazette*, August 12, 1851.

1852   Bushrod W. Frobel was chairman of the Happy Valley Division, Sons of Temperance. Source: *Alexandria Gazette*, July 14, 1852.

Miss Frobel won a prize for the best counterpane at the Agricultural Exhibition's Annual Fair on the 15th and 16th. Source: *Fairfax News*, October 30, 1852.

1855   George Curtis, a slave belonging to Mr. Frobel of Fairfax County, was drowned. Source: *Alexandria Gazette*, April 23, 1855.

1857   *August 20*, 1857 Death of Mrs. Mary S. Frobel

Mrs. Mary S. Frobel died at her residence near Alexandria, August 20th in the 71st year of her age.

Her gentle and amiable disposition endured her to her circle of friends. She fulfilled the duties of the various relations of life, she is an exemplary manner, and her children rise up and call her blessed. She was ever ready to sympathize with the sorrows of others, and minister to their wants. For many years she had been a communicant of Christ Church, Alexandria, and manifested her Christian character by her interest in all good works and of the religious welfare of those around her. She died in a good old age. Her sun set as serene as the sun of the day, in which her body was consigned to the grave.

> "So fades a summer cloud away,
> So gently shuts the eye of day."

Source: *Alexandria Gazette*, August 25, 1857.

1857   Inventory of slaves belonging to estate of John J. Frobel

A true inventory and appraisement of the slaves belonging to the estate of John J. Frobel dec'd made 29th day of Dec. 1857 by Mary S. Frobel and Eliz. D. Frobel, Executrix of the last will and testament of John J. Frobel late of the county of Fairfax, Virginia, dec'd with the aid of John Ashford, James A. Stoutenbaugh and Frances P. Alford. Sworn appraisers according to law.

The following is an inventory of the slaves disposed of by the said will and their respective ages, sex, and value as near as we can judge of the same to wit:

Caesar	35	m	500	Rosetta	15		400
Agnes	45		150	Margaret	9		200
Rebecca	38		350	Emily	6		125
Chas. Curtis	31	m	600	Amelia	4		125
Susan	31		450	Moses	1	m	50
George	27	m	600	Chas Parker	18	m	300
Harriet	24		500	Eliza	18		300
Milly	30		350	Thomas	9	m	225
Frank	6	m	175	Antony	6	m	150
Edward	17	m	500			Total	6050

given under our hands this 29th day of Dec. 1857

John Ashford
J. A. Stoutenbaugh
Frances P. Alford
Appraisers

We Mary S. Frobel and Eliz. D. Frobel executrix of the last will and testament of John J. Frobel, dec. do hereby certify the foregoing to be the inventory of the negros belonging to the said deceased estate as taken by us with the aid of said appraisers.

December 26, 1857   *Mary S. Frobel*
                                                       Eliz. D. Frobel

At a court held for County of Fairfax this 15th day of March 1852. The inventory and appraisement of the slaves belonging to the estate of John J. Frobel dec'd was this day returned to the court and ordered to be recorded.

test
M. Ball C.C.

Source: *Will Book* W, No. 1, Page 211, Fairfax County, Virginia.

1859   List of Taxable Persons, Property and etc—within the District of J. B. Hunter, County of Fairfax, year 1859

Frobel, Bushrod W. and Eliz.

Free male persons above age 16 (1)
Slaves who have attained age 16 (4)
White males attained age 21, except those exempt in infirmity (1)
Slaves attained age 12 (4)
Horses, mules, asses and jennys (4)—value (300)
Cattle, sheep and hogs (10)—value (100)
Pleasure carriages (1)—value (50)
Watches (1)—value (50)
Value all household furniture 200
Aggregate of values 700
Amt tax on all persons and subjects 8.40
Amt tax for county purposes 2.39
15 slaves total tax 18

Source: Fairfax County Court House, Fairfax, Virginia.

1860   *U.S. Census*, Fairfax County, Virginia, lists Elizabeth Frobel, head of household, age 30, living with Ann S. Frobel, age 32

1868   *November 25* Married in this city on the 25th Ult, at the residence of P. M. Compton, Esq., by Rev. B. Franklin Mower, Col. B. W. Frobel to Miss Mary L. Compton. Source: *Federal Union*, Milledgeville, Georgia, December 1, 1868.

1869   *January 7* Death of Mrs. Anna C. Frobel

Died in Baltimore yesterday, after a long and painful illness, which she bore with Christian fortitude, Mrs. Anna C. Frobel, wife of David W Frobel, formerly of Fairfax Co. Source: *Alexander Gazette*, January 8, 1869.

1870   *U. S. Census*, Fairfax Co., Virginia, lists Elizabeth Frobel, 35 as head of household living with Anna Frobel, age 40; David Frobel, age 33, farmer; Edward Frobel, age 11, and Rena Gray, age 17, a black domestic servant. All persons listed born in Virginia except Edward Frobel who was born in Ky.

1880 *U. S. Census*, Fairfax County, Virginia, lists Ann S. Frobel, age 48, and Elizabeth, age 45, sisters keeping house with Joseph Gibson, black servant, age 69.

1882 *May 2* Death of E. Neufville Mower

Died of small-pox at the residence of his uncle Col. B. W. Frobel in Atlanta, Georgia, May the 2nd, 1882, E. Neufville Mower, youngest child of Rev. B. F. Mower and Mary C. Mower. Prayer, love, medical skill, nor the tender nursing of a devoted mother availed him anything. God love him best and took him from us to the shelter of his Everlasing arms.

> "Mother mourning, O'er the jewel
> Plucked from our the earthly crown
> It is well that God did tell thee
> Lay thy darling treasure down
> Safe from every earthly trial
> Safe from sin and earth's alarm
> He hath found eternal convert
> In the everlasting arms
> In this world he might have chosen
> Sin and evil for his fate
> Standing at the gate of Heaven
> Knocking when it was too late
> Now safe past Jordan's well
> With Christ in Heaven all is well

> - a friend -

Source: *The North Alabamian*, Florence, Alabama, May 26, 1882.

1888 *July 12* Death of Bushrod Washington Frobel

Colonel B. W. Frobel died yesterday morning at Monticello. The sad news came to Dr. A. J. Woodward, who received the following dispatch about noon yesterday.

> "Colonel Frobel died this morning. Make arrangements for interment in Oakland cemetery. Funeral tomorrow."

For four weeks Colonel Frobel had been sick with inflammation of the bowels. His condition was not considered dangerous until within the past week, when there was a sudden change for the worse.

Colonel Bushrod Washington Frobel was born on his father's plantation, near Alexandria, Va., fifty-eight years ago.

He was an exceptionally bright boy, and after receiving the usual training in the rudiments, he was prepared for the military school at West Point.

He made an excellent record there, and after graduating, entered the United States navy.

He was a member of the South Atlantic squadron which, before the war, made soundings for the gulf stream and went on an expedition to the equator.

At the beginning of the late war he resigned his position and entered the confederate states navy. He made such a fine record in the navy that he was complimented by General Robert E. Lee and transferred to the army of Virginia. He was made a lieutenant colonel of engineers, and served in the corps of engineers and the artillery through the war.

He won distinction as a most gallant soldier.

At the close of the war he became United States engineer for the northern district of Georgia.

He became very much interested in the effort to supply Atlanta with pure water, and to that end made an extensive survey of the Chattahoochee river above Gainesville. He established a grade from the upper waters of that river to this city.

His idea was to divert the waters of the Chattahoochee and open up a natural water course to this city, upon the banks of which manufacturies of various kinds might be built.

After completing the survey, he went to Washington city, where he worked with great earnestness for six months to secure an appropriation from congress to carry out his magnificent plan.

The recommendation for an appropriation which was at last obtained, was defeated by only one vote.

Shortly after this failure he left the engineer department and embarked in railroad building. He was made chief engineer of the Macon and Covington railroad, and more than one hundred miles were constructed under his direction.

At the time of his death Colonel Frobel was chief engineer, vice-president and general manager of the Macon and Covington railroad.

A short time after receiving his appointment as United States engineer, he married Miss Mamie Compton, of Milledgeville. He removed to

Marietta, and subsequently to Atlanta, where the family have resided for upwards of sixteen years.

His wife and two grown daughters [Ada and Lilly] survive him. The remains will reach the city this morning at 6:30, and will be met at the depot by the curators of St. Luke's church, of which the deceased was junior warden.

The funeral will take place at St. Luke's this afternoon at 5 o'clock. Source: *The Constitution*, Atlanta, Georgia, July 13,

Colonel Frobel was buried in Oakland Cemetery, Atlanta, Georgia, in Block 316, Lot 2. The grave is unmarked, however, the name Frobel is on the steps at the entrance to the block.

1891   *February 15* Rev. Frank [Benjamin Franklin] Mower, died in Florence, Alabama, on Saturday last, and his remains will be brought here on Wednesday and interred in Christ Church cemetery. Mr. Mower formerly lived in Fairfax county, and was well known in this city. He was a near relative of the Misses Frobel, of Fairfax. Source: *Alexandria Gazette*, February 16, 1891.

1898   Will of Elizabeth D. Frobel

In the name of God Amen. I, Elizabeth of Wilton Hill in the county of Fairfax and State of Virginia do hereby make publish and declare this my last will and testament in manner and form following viz -

I give devise and bequeath unto my dear sister Anne S. Frobel all my property personal and not which shall be hers her heirs and assigns forever

I hereby nominate constitute and appoint my sister Anne S. Frobel Executrix of this my last will and testament without bond or security

In witness whereof I have hereunto signed my name. Done at Wilton Hill this 19th day of January 1858.

Elizabeth D. Frobel

I also will and bequeath to my sister Anne S. Frobel all my interest in a claim which the said Anne S. Frobel and I Elizabeth D. Frobel have against United States Government for losses sustained by them during the war from 1861 to 1865.

In witness whereof I have hereunto signed my name. Done at Wilton Hill this 5th day of October 1891.

Elizabeth D. Frobel
M.E. Walsh

At a County Court continued and held for Fairfax County Va. on March 23rd 1898.

The last will and testament & codicil thereto annexed of the late Elizabeth D. Frobel were this day presented to the Court and the same being both proven to be wholly in the hand writing of the testatrix and her signature to each to be her genuine signature by the oaths of W. K. Mower & Mary E. Walsh witnesses sworn in open Court in the mode prescribed by law—the same is admitted to probate & ordered to be recorded as the true last will and testament & codicil annexed of the said Elizabeth D. Frobel.

Teste
F. W. Richardson

Clerk

Source: *Will Book*, G2, 654, Fairfax County Court House, Fairfax, Virginia.

1898   *March 19* Death of Elizabeth D. Frobel

Miss Elizabeth Frobel, an old and esteemed resident of Fairfax county and well known in this city, died at her home, "Wilton," about five miles southwest of this city, on Saturday night. Her funeral took place from Christ Church at 2:30 o'clock this evening. The services were conducted by Revs. Berryman Green and S. A. Wallis. Source: *Alexandria Gazette*, March 21, 1898.

1905   Will of Anne S. Frobel

Alexandria, Va.
Oct. 12th, 1905

I, Anne S. Frobel, being of sound and disposing mind and memory, do make and declare this to be my last will and testament, hereby expressly revoking all other will by me made.

First: I desire that my executor, hereinafter named, shall sell all the real estate of which I may die possessed as soon after my decease as he can advantageously do so, and the proceeds of such sale, after the payment to my said executor of a commission of five per cent, I will and bequeath to my grandnieces Elizabeth Douglas Gibson, of Kentucky, daughter of David Gibson, Mary Frobel Raoul, Lillie Raoul Wright, Grace Raoul and Theus Raoul, share and share alike. And if any one or more of my said five grand nieces should die before I do, then I will that the proceeds from the sale of said real estate shall be divided among the survivors of them.

If my claim now pending against the United States Government should be paid, or any part thereof, I will and bequeath one thousand dollars of the proceeds therefrom to each of my grand-nephews, Lewis Raoul, George Raoul, and Frank Raoul, and the remainder of the proceeds of said claim I will and bequeath to my said grandnieces, Elizabeth Douglas Gibson, Mary Frobel Raoul, Lillie Raoul Wright, Grace Raoul and Theus Raoul, share and share alike.

The rest and residue of my property real and personal of which I may die possessed, I desire and bequeath to my said grand-nephew, George Raoul.

I hereby appoint my said grand-nephew George Raoul executor of this my last will and testament.

Given under my hand this 12th day of October, 1905.

ANNE S. FROBEL.

PHILIPPA A. WATTLES.
C. W. WATTLES.
LEWIS H. MACHEN.

We the undersigned hereby certify that the foregoing paper was signed by the testatrix, ANNE S. FROBEL, and declared by her to be her last will and testament in our presence, present together at the same time, and at her request and in her presence and in the presence of each other and have hereunto set our hands as witnesses this 12th day of October, 1905.

PHILIPPA A. WATTLES.
C. W. WATTLES.
LEWIS H. MACHEN.

Source: *Will Book* 3, 497, Fairfax County Court House, Fairfax, Virginia.

1906 *May 2* Death of Mary Clagett Frobel Mower

Mrs. Mary C. Mower, the venerable mother of Mrs. D. E. Gibson, passed away to her heavenly reward at the home of her daughter near Warsaw early Wednesday morning after several weeks of painful suffering resulting from a fall in which she sustained a broken hip and caused her death, her advanced years hastening her demise, being in her 86th year. Mrs. Mower made her home with her daughter Mrs. Gibson for many years and was beloved by all who knew her for her kindly disposition and lady like bearing towards all. She was born at Alexandria, Virginia, but resided in Alabama before coming to Warsaw where her husband died, he having been a minister of the Episcopal church. Several grand children survive. The remains were taken to Alexandria, Virginia, for burial leaving Wednesday afternoon accompanied by Mr. and Mrs. Gibson.

Source: *Warsaw Independent*, Warsaw, Kentucky, May 5, 1906.

1907 *April 16* Death of Anne S. Frobel

Miss Ann Frobel, formerly of Fauquier [Fairfax] county, died in Alabama on Tuesday and was buried at Ivy Hill Cemetery this evening. Source: *Alexandria Gazette and Virginia Advertiser*, April 17, 1907.

April 19 Editorial—The Late Miss Frobel

The death of Miss Annie Frobel, formerly of Fairfax County, an aged lady well known by many Alexandrians, which recently occurred at the home of Mrs. Mary Marshall Raoul in Scotia, Ala., has been mentioned in the Gazette. The deceased had attained the age of 95 years. During a portion of her long life she resided in or near Alexandria, and when she removed to Alabama she carried with her the recollections of her residence among us, as well as the many friends and acquaintances with whom she mingled for so many years. Up to her death she was a regular reader of the Gazette, and kept in touch with Alexandria and the history the city is making. Source: *Alexandria Gazette and Virginia Advertiser*, April 19, 1907.

Appendix B

WILTON HILL

1807   John J. Frobel bought portion of Burgandy tract from James Hooe calling it "Wilton Hill." He received deed from James H. Hooe and wife, Eliza, on Feb. 16, 1808. Source: Fairfax County Court House, Fairfax, Virginia.

1847   Abstract of agreement between Bushrod W. Frobel and Daniel Crump to build a house.

An abstract of agreement entered into this fifth day of August in the year of our Lord one thousand eight hundred and forty seven. Bushrod W. Frobel and Daniel Crum that the said Crump does agree to build for the said Frobel a house the dimensions as follows. To be eighteen by twenty-six feet and two stories high the lower story to be nine feet the upper eight to be finished off with one room and a passage below and two rooms above with staircase in the passage front and back doors the front door to be finished with side and transome lights the house to have eight windows four in front and three back and also five doors two outside and three inside all to be panned the door and windows to be cased mouldings on the inside the hole building to be finished in a workman like manner for which the said Frobel does agree to pay the said Crump the sum of one hundred dollars. Also mouldboards and two mantle pieces the windows below to be fifteen lights ten by twelve those up stairs of twelve lights do-do—with neat stops to front door—stairs to be finished with hand bevils and railings.

1847   Frobel/Crump Agreement Account

Bracket	Cr
Sept 10 Fr 300 bricks run of the kiln	$ 1.50
Sept 13 Fr 300 bricks run of the kiln	1.50
Sept 16 Fr 300 bricks run of the kiln	1.50
Sept 17 Fr 300 red bricks	1.50
Oct 16 Fr 900 bricks	4.50
Nov 14 Fr 1800 bricks	9.00
	$19.50

Nov. 1   Feb. 11, 1848 *paid*

Source: This abstract of agreement and account are framed and hanging in Wilton Woods School, Fairfax County, Virginia.

1872   For Sale

"Wilton," the residence of the late John J. Frobel, in Fairfax County, 2½ miles from the city of Alexandria. The Farm contains 114 acres; is well watered; has on it a large barn, a comfortable dwelling, and an outhouse, suitable for a manager or tenant, and is well stocked with choice fruit trees.

Persons wishing to purchase will please apply to Green and Wise, Real Estate Agents, Alexandria, or to the subscriber on the premises.

E. D. Frobel

Source: *Alexandria Gazette*, June 25, 1872.

1910   "Wilton" to be sold at auction

R. F. Knox Auctioneer

PUBLIC SALE

of a

Valuable Tract of Land

In Mount Vernon District, Fairfax

County, Virginia

1910   Pursuant to a decree entered at the November term, 1910, of the Circuit Court of Fairfax County, Virginia, in the suit of Gibson et als vs. Raoul et als, the undersigned Commissioners of Sale will on Saturday, Dec. 10, 1910 at 12 noon, in front of the Royal Street entrance to the Market House in Alexandria, Virginia sell to the highest bidder at Public Auction that certain tract of land known as Wilton, located in Mount Vernon District, Fairfax County, Virginia, of which the late Anne S. Frobal died seized and possessed, and containing 112 acres more or less; bounded as follows, to-wit: on the north by the County Road, on the east by Sharon Chapel and the land of Peck and Ballenger, on the south by the County Road and the lands of Moore and Javins, and on the west by the lands of Javins, together with all improvements.

Terms of sale—one half cash and the residue in two equal payments at 6 and 12 months from date of sale, evidenced by the purchaser at time of sale. A cash deposit of $100 will be required at time of sale.

E. B. Taylor
Lewis H. Machen,
Commissioner of Sale
Alexandria, Va.

Source: Information from flyer publicizing the sale.

The property was purchased on the above date, December 10, 1910, by Frank L. Ballenger for $4100. The Report of Receipts and Disbursements of E. B. Taylor, bonded Commissioner of Sale, was filed in the Clerk's office, Fairfax County Civil Court, Fairfax, Virginia, August 5, 1911.

1915   Feature article on "Wilton Hall" by the Rambler

Wilton Hall, a venerable place, steeped in pleasant memories and changed by time and storm into a relic, lies or partially stands so close to Washington that from its decrept doorway and its lovely windows you can see the domes and spires of Washington. Alexandria's walls and steeples rise between the hall and the great city of the nation and the trees and monuments of Ivy Hill cemetery are in the picture and there sleep the good people whose feet in other years trod the gravel walks that wind among the rank and tangled box and ivy that over grow the garden of Wilton Hall.

It was a beautiful place and it is potentially beautiful today. Nobody lives there, and no body has lived there for a good many years, though it is easy to feel that ghosts, goodnatured and hospitable ghosts, stroll through the ruined garden and stalk across the creaking floors of the bare, cold rooms and the empty halls that are silent save for echoes.

The Rambler has mentioned Wilton Hall in connection with his story of his visits to Mount Eagle and Mount Pleasant, neighboring properties. The legend of Wilton Hall which the Rambler has heard from the lips from old-time folk whose minds are stored with neighborhood traditions is that when Gen. and Mrs. George Washington were residing in Philadelphia, when that city was the capital, they attended a theatrical performance and heard a boy singing. They liked the little chap and his parents or guardians, if he had any, being willing, the general and his wife finally brought him to Mount Vernon, where he developed into a landscape gardener of no small ability. It is said that that garden which is now known to everybody as Nellie Custis garden was in part his work. The name of the boy was Froebel. That is the story told in the Wilton Hall neighborhood and it has come down from Froebel and from his daughters Anne and Elizabeth, who were known and beloved by all the old dwellers in that neighborhood. Elizabeth Froebel died at Wilton Hall about a quarter of a century ago, and Anne, whom everybody roundabout today speaks of as "Miss Annie," lived there until the day of her death a few years ago at the age of ninety-two years. She was a remarkable woman in many ways. She retained a clear memory of all the people who had lived in the neighborhood and of all the events there during her long life, and she preserved a strong memory of all the stories which, when she was young, she had been told by gray and bent men and women. Another of the unusual things about this woman was her extraordinary stature. The Rambler had been told that she was nearly seven feet tall and that all her growth was not in the direction of height.

The person from whom the Rambler has learned these Wilton Hall stories speak of Froebel as "Bushrod Froebel" and his fame as a gardener survives him. In many of the historic places in that neighborhood old men and women are forever pointing out to you some flower or shrub which they prize exceedingly high and they tell you it came from the gardens at Wilton Hall, or that Bushrod Froebel gave it to their grandmother. The story of Froebel continues that when he had reached manhood the Washingtons at Mount Vernon bought for him the property which he called Wilton Hall, and if one could determine the origin of that name it might throw some light on the history of the man who lived there.

The garden is a wonderful place today, though it has grown wild. You can trace an intricate system of walks hedged with box, but this box has grown so that the design is nearly obliterated and the walks impassable. Ivy of several varieties abounds. For years it has been disputing with the box for possession of the place, and it may be that the contest has not been determined it, but to the Rambler it seems a draw, or that the box and ivy have agreed to a joint tenancy of the grounds. A number of old and large trees grow above the riot of box and ivy, and these will be pointed out to you as trees of an unknown species which Froebel brought from Europe. In the garden are several buckeye trees and two ancient holly trees. One of the hollies is thrifty and green, the other is ruinous and the story is that one bore scarlet berries and had been rifled and stripped and torn so often that it is nearly dead, while the other being barren so far as berries are concerned has been spared by vandals.

If you would go to Wilton Hall you should start out along the Little River turnpike from Alexandria, and at the site of the old toll gate turn to the left along the Telegraph road, cross Cameron run, pass the hamlet of Cameron at the junction of the Telegraph road and the original Mount Vernon road, and keep on along the Telegraph road until near a white chapel which sits on a hilltop surrounded with white tombstones. That is Sharon Episcopal Chapel. Before reaching this chapel a red clay road, deep, wet and, sticky at this season, strikes off to the right. It is called the Old Rolling road and would lead you over to Franconia on the WashingtonSouthern railroad. A few hundred yards along this road a tree-line lane calls to the left. Walk along that lane for a quarter of a mile and you come to box-bowered and ivy-wrapped Wilton Hall.

That is not the route the Rambler took. Leaving the Telegraph road at Cameron, he took the left-hand fork, which is the old Washington or original Mount Vernon road from Alexandria, and climbed up through the ruins and earth heaps of Fort Lyon. The weather was piercing even for walking and in a sheltered part of the road the Rambler and his friends built a comfortable fire and rested for an hour. Then the line of progress carried them to Mount Pleasant and from that homestead the path lay westward over fields and across the valley through which runs the Telegraph road and White branch, and which has the cheery name of Happy Valley. Climbing out of this muddy vale and passing Sharon Chapel on the right you come to the fencing which incloses the lands appurtenant to Wilton Hall. They are extensive and fruitful, but the Rambler's rain-soaked notes refuse to remind him of the number of acres in the tract.

It was one of the dismal afternoons of the winter that the Rambler and his friends stood shivering and foot-wet among the box and ivy and under the bare wind-swayed trees in the garden of Wilton Hall. It was the afternoon of Sunday, January 24, the day of the sleet storm which coated everything in the city with ice but did not make the clap roads and fields so hard that a man would not sink to his shoe-tops in the mud. The sky was dark and the light feeble, and on the whole it was a day many intelligent persons would rather woo a steam radiator than hunt history with a camera and notebook. But such is rambling.

The house of Wilton is in two parts. The north section is frame and the south part which is the main section is of brick. The frame section is the older, as often happens in the country around Washington. Froebel added the brick house to his domain as prosperity blessed him and as his property developed. The front porch has fallen, but the front door, of oak, is stout and sturdy and swings truly on its grating, monster iron hinges. In the rooms are stoned paved open fireplaces with a trace of ashes from cordial fires that burned out perhaps before many of the readers of these times were born. These fireless fireplaces seemed especially cheerless on the wet and icy afternoon. On the wall of the two front windows of the main room is the relic of what was once no doubt a handsome mirror. It is very heavy glass, but the reflective backing is nearly all gone. In the oaken window frames one sees still the curtain hooks, rusty and misshapen now, but suggestive that once that room was furnished and comfortable. The frame part of the hall is decrepit, but the main or brick portion is in an excellent state of preservation so far s the walls and chimneys are concerned.

Down deep in the garden is a ruin. A chimney stands, and around it are sections of broken brick walls, parts of the walls being tumbled into heaps. Over all this a mat of kindly ivy has spread itself, but whether the ivy has done this to screen the ruin from the eyes of men, or to make a right choice meal off bricks, the Rambler does not know. That ruin was Froebel's hothouse.

You will be told by people who live in the region that in the fair and pleasant seasons of the year many strange flowers bear their blossoms in the garden of Wilton Hall, and when genial, happy spring returns the Rambler means to ramble there again.

Source: *The Sunday Star*, Washington, D.C., February 7, 1915.

Appendix C

SHARON CHAPEL

1846   *May 5* "Rode over to Wilton Hill this afternoon to attend a meeting of the neighbors called for the purpose of organizing a Society to determine the best method of erecting a church in the neighborhood -" Source: *Journal of Richard Marshall Scott, Jr. of "Bush Hill,"* Fairfax County, Virginia

---

1849   *August 16* Gift Deed from John J. and Mary S. Frobel for Sharon Chapel

This Indenture, made the sixteenth day of August in the year of our Lord, one thousand eight hundred and forty nine, Between John J. Frobel, and Mary his wife, of the first part and Tobias Stoutenburgh, Richard M. Scott, Bushrod W. Frobel, and the Rector of Christ's Church, Trustees of Sharon Church in Fairfax County, Virginia, of the second part—Witnesseth, that, the said Parties of the first part, for and in consideration of the sum of one Dollar, to them in hand paid, the receipt whereof is hereby acknowledged, have granted bargained, sold, aliened released conveyed and confirmed and by these presents do grant bargain, sell, alien release convey and confirm, unto the said parties of the second part, in their actual possession now being and to their successors and assigns, forever,- all that certain lot piece or parcel of land, situate in said County of Fairfax, known and distinguished as being a part of the Tract of land called Wilton Hill and situated on the North Corner of said Tract, containing sixteen parcels of land to be in the form of an oblong square, and to be eight rods or poles on the East and West sides each, and four Rodes or poles on the North and South sides Each of said square, together with a Road or land leading to the same from the public Road, along said Frobel's North side, said lot hereby conveyed to said Trustees is to be held by them, their successors and assigns in Trust for the purposes of Burial and of erecting an Edifice to be used and occupied as a Protestant Episcopal Church, in Communion with the Protestant Episcopal Church of the United States of America, and for no other purposes, and when ever said lot shall cease to be used and occupied, for the purpose of five years then and in that case said lot shall revert back to the owner or owners of said Tract, called Wilton Hill together with all and singular the herediments and appurtenances to said lot belonging or in any wise appertaining, and the environ and environs remainder and remainders rents issues and profits, and all the Estate right title, Interest Claim or Demand whatsoever of the said Parties of the first part, either in law or in Equity of in and to the above bargained premises. To Have and to Hold the said lot to the sale and only proper use, benefit and behoof of the said party of the second part for themselves, their successors and assigns as above mentioned and the said Parties of the second part, their successors and assigns the above premises to warrant and defend—In witness whereof, the parties of the first part have hereunto affixed their hands and sealed the day & year first above written

sealed and delivered

John J. Frobel S.S.

in presence of

Elizabeth D. Frobel   Mary S. Frobel S.S.

State of Virginia

To wit-

County of Alexandria

We George Wise and Charles Koones Justices of the peace in and for the County aforesaid, do hereby testify that John J. Frobel a party to the annexed Deed, bearing date the sixteenth day of August 1849, personally appeared before us in our County aforesaid, the said John J. Frobel, being personally well known to us as the person who Executed the said deed, and acknowledged the same to be his act and deed, and desired us to certify the said acknowledgement to the Clerk of the County Court of Fairfax County, Virginia, in order that the same may be recorded- We further certify that Mary Frobel, the wife of the said John J. Frobel, also a party to the said deed, personally appeared before us in our County aforesaid, the said Mary Frobel being personally known to us as the person who Executed the said deed, and being by us examined privily and apart from her husband, and having the said deed fully Explained to her—the said Mary Frobel acknowledged the same to be her act and deed, and declared that she had willingly signed sealed and delivered the same, and that she wished not to retract it. Given under our hands and seals this 12th day of September 1849.

Geo. Wise S.S.
Charles Koones S.S.

Clerks Office, Fairfax County Court Jany, 15th A.D. 1850

This Deed from John J. Frobel and wife to Trustees of Sharon Church was this day received properly authenticated and admitted to record.

Teste

Examined   S. M. Ball, C C

Source: *Deed Book*, 03, 161-162, Fairfax County Court House, Fairfax, Virginia.

1974   History of All Saints—Sharon Chapel

All Saints-Sharon Chapel has a long significant, and proud history. One hundred thirty-five years ago, a small frame chapel was erected on

Sharon Chapel was built on land donated by the parents of Ann Frobel. It was served by students from the Virginia Episcopal Theological Seminary making it the Seminary's first mission church.

a parcel of land given by John Froebel, master of Wilton Hall and friend of the Washingtons of Mount Vernon. Miss Froebel established a Saturday school in this building to teach Christian morals and ethics to the young ladies of rural "Happy Valley," as this area was known many years ago. On Sundays, the Dean of the Virginia Theological Seminary graciously provided Seminary students to lead the worship services, which were attended by Christians of all denominations. Sharon Chapel thus has the distinction of being the first mission of the venerable Seminary.

For one hundred ten years, students from the Seminary cared for the needs of this rural mission. Many ministers-to-be received their early training in preaching and other ministries at Sharon Chapel. One such seminarian was Phillips Brooks, who preached his first sermon at Sharon Chapel in 1858. Brooks went on to become a preeminent preacher of the 19th century and has been described as one of the greatest preachers and most impressive personalities of the Episcopal Church. To most of us today, he is best remembered for the Christmas carol "O Little Town of Bethlehem."

We have maintained our historical association with the Virginia Theological Seminary, and we expect to continue to provide field work experience for seminarians each year. In addition, a number of people from our parish participate regularly in Homiletics at the Seminary.

During the Civil War, Sharon Chapel lost two of its youngest members. Samuel and Thomas Pulman, ages 9 and 13, were killed August 6, 1864, when a cannonball with which they were playing exploded. These boys were the first burials in the church cemetery.

That same year the chapel was accidentally burned to the ground by soldiers stationed at Fort Lyon, which was erected on the high ground to the east of Happy Valley to defend the capital city of Washington.

Another chapel was soon built. This building, a picture of which hangs in the office wing, was constructed from scrap lumber salvaged from the barracks of Fort Lyon. It stood until 1903 when it was replaced by a third frame chapel. Sharon Chapel was made an aided mission of the Diocese of Virginia and was assigned its first full-time minister in 1959. The congregation consisted of just twenty-five communicants. The potential for more existed as Happy Valley and its environs evolved from a rural area of small truck farms to suburban homes occupied largely by government workers.

As growth continued, other significant events occurred. In 1961, Sharon Chapel was admitted to the Diocese of Virginia as a Mission Church. Soon the small chapel was inadequate for the needs of its membership, and in 1963 the church in which we now worship was constructed.

In 1968, the congregation raised $2,000 to pave the parking lot. One year later, the Diocesan Missionary Society came to our aid with a loan to open a much-needed additional access road from Franconia Road. Our major improvement was the construction in 1971 of Gunnell Hall, a multipurpose brick building to meet our educational and social needs.

In April, 1974, Annual Council accepted our petition for parish status. Hereafter our church was known as All Saints Sharon Chapel.

A great strength of Sharon Chapel is its mixture of families some of who have spent generations on this land and some of who have just arrived. We cherish this diversity of people and consider it a major factor in the unity of our lives and the continuing corporate love and fellowship we share on this hilltop.

Source: *All Saints-Sharon Chapel, Parish Profile*, Alexandria, Virginia, 1974.

Appendix D
IVY HILL CEMETERY
ALEXANDRIA, VIRGINIA

1982   History of Ivy Hill Cemetery

Alexandria's history is closely associated with Ivy Hill Cemetery, for many of the prominent families who helped to shape the town's destiny, have been buried here. There are many other cemeteries around Alexandria, some older, but few are so well preserved as Ivy Hill.

Located on King Street extended, west of the Masonic Temple, Ivy Hill is on a series of gentle sloping hills, resembling a country churchyard. The graves are scattered beneath beautiful old trees and cover over twenty-four acres. It is a non-profit, non-denominational cemetery, still in use today, and in the process of expansion. For generations the Bryant family of Alexandria has directed, without compensation, the operation of the cemetery.

Internments date as far back as 1811, when Ivy Hill was a family burial ground. Some of the birth dates listed on the stones are mid-eighteenth century. As the result of the settlement of an estate, Ivy Hill was established as a community burial ground in 1856. According to the Alexandria Gazette, in May of 1866, subscriptions were solicited for the purpose of inclosing the grounds, and a committee was to ask remuneration from the Federal Government for damages sustained by the cemetery from Federal troops.

Source: Bruch, Virginia Irene Sullivan, and Sullivan, Josephine Elizabeth, *Beneath the Oaks of Ivy Hill*, Jennie's Book Nook, Alexandria, Virginia, 1982.

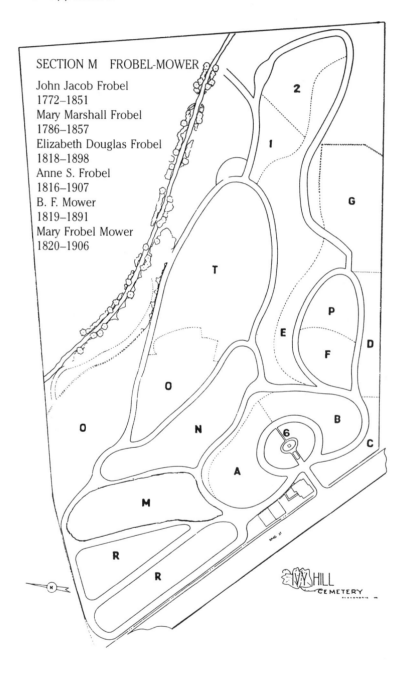

SECTION M   FROBEL-MOWER

John Jacob Frobel
1772–1851
Mary Marshall Frobel
1786–1857
Elizabeth Douglas Frobel
1818–1898
Anne S. Frobel
1816–1907
B. F. Mower
1819–1891
Mary Frobel Mower
1820–1906

Bibliography

Books-Journals-Periodicals

All Saints-Sharon Chapel: Parish Profile. Alexandria, Virginia, 1974.

Bruch, Virginia Irene Sullivan, and Sullivan, Josephine Elizabeth. *Beneath the Oaks of Ivy Hill*. Alexandria, Virginia: Jennie's Book Nook, 1982.

Christ Church Parish Register. Volume 1. Alexandria, Virginia.

Heintze, James. "Music of the Washington Family: A Little-Known Collection." *The Musical Quarterly*. Volume 65, No. 2.

Journal of Richard Marshall Scott Sr. and Richard Marshall Scott Jr., of "Bush Hill," Fairfax County, Virginia. Fairfax County Court House Archives, Fairfax, Virginia.

Sonneck, Oscar C. *Early Concert Life in America, 1731–1800*. New York: Musurgia Publishers, 1949.

Newspapers

Alexandria Daily Gazette, November 30, 1809.

Alexandria Gazette, June 25, 1832.

Alexandria Gazette and Virginia Advertiser, November 8, 1845.

Alexandria Gazette, August 24, 1849; July 14, 1852; April 23, 1855; August 25, 1857; January 8, 1869; February 16, 1891.

Alexandria Gazette and Virginia Advertiser, April 17, 1907; April 19, 1907.

Constitution (Atlanta, Georgia), July 13, 1888.

Fairfax News, October 30, 1852.

Federal Union (Milledgeville, Georgia), December 1, 1868.

North Alabamian (Florence, Alabama), May 26, 1882.

Sunday Star (Washington, D.C.), February 7, 1915.

Government Records

Fairfax County Court House, Fairfax, Virginia.

Agreement/Contract Ledgers, 1831 (Farmington Estate 2A), 1848 (Frobel-Crump).

Chancery Court Records, 1838 (Frobel-Scott).

Deed Books, 1807 (Frobel-Hooe), 1850 (Frobel-Sharon Church).

Estate Settlements, 1911 (Wright vs. Armistead).

Ledger B of James H. Hooe, 1824.

Tax List, 1859 (District of J. B. Hunter).

Will Books, 1851 (W1), 1857 (W1), 1898 (G2), 1905 (W3).

United States Census Records of 1810, 1840, 1850, 1860, 1870, and 1880 Fairfax County Virginia.

Index